Advisory, Conciliation ar

Industrial Relations Handbook

London: Her Majesty's Stationery Office

ISBN 0 11 700960 1

Contents

Note: The masculine pronoun is used throughout but applies equally to men and women.

Foreword

by the Chairman of ACAS

This Handbook is intended to provide, for practitioners and students of industrial relations, a basic factual guide to the institutions in Great Britain which are involved in the conduct of collective bargaining. The aim has not been to give a comprehensive account of industrial relations, but Part I begins with a brief history of collective bargaining and the different ways in which the State has intervened in this process over the years. Part I goes on to describe the main voluntary and statutory bodies that now exist and the recent changes, the present framework of collective and individual rights in employment. The second part is devoted to descriptions, industry by industry following the standard industrial classification of the Central Statistical Office, of actual arrangements for collective bargaining. These identify the employers' associations and trade unions involved, the main negotiating machinery, the balance between negotiations at different levels and the scope and coverage of agreements. The Handbook concludes with a series of appendices.

The Handbook has a valued and successful forerunner — the *Industrial Relations Handbook* originally published by the Ministry of Labour and National Service in 1944, and last revised in 1960. Its contents were, finally, overtaken by events and it was suggested that ACAS was the most appropriate institution to prepare a new Handbook. This Handbook follows very similar principles and owes a great deal to its predecessor and to the help given by the Department of Employment.

In preparing the text ACAS has also had extensive help from employers, employers' associations and trade unons in many different industries, and from staff in most of the institutions described. Without this assistance the task would have been impossible, and ACAS is deeply grateful.

In industrial relations the picture is constantly changing, and a book such as this can only give a snapshot at one particular point. Every effort has been made to ensure that the snapshot is accurate: if any errors remain, ACAS must take responsibility.

J E MORTIMER
August 1980

Part A

The background to collective bargaining

This first part of the Handbook sets out the historical, institutional and legislative context within which present-day industrial relations is conducted.

Chapter one describes the development of voluntary collective bargaining and indicates how the state has intervened at different points in this process to regulate the status in law of trade unions and employers' associations, of collective agreements and of aspects of negotiating behaviour. Chapter two complements this by describing how the role of the state in industrial relations has developed in a number of other ways:

— in underpinning collective bargaining with conciliation and arbitration facilities;
— in providing protection for employees not adequately covered by voluntary machinery;
— in limiting hours of work;
— in promoting health and safety at work;
— in establishing rights in employment for the individual employee; and
— in circumscribing the outcome of negotiations in the interests of incomes policy.

Chapters three and four are about institutions. Chapter three provides an up-to-date description of the main British industrial relations institutions — the major voluntary bodies, the responsible government department, the various statutory organisations, and research institutions. Chapter four describes the international institutions — the European Community, the International Labour Organisation, the Organisation for Economic Co-operation and Development, the Council of Europe, international trade unions and international employers' organisations, all of which, in different ways, have influenced and continue to influence the development of industrial relations in this country. The addresses of the main institutions mentioned in these chapters are given in Appendix 9.

Finally, chapter five summarises the body of employment law — both the rights enjoyed by collective bodies and the rights of the individual employee, incorporating and indicating the recent changes.

The superior [0] numbers in this part of the Handbook are references to the bibliography.

Chapter 1

The development of collective bargaining — the main landmarks

Early developments

The earliest effective organisations at the workplace grew up in the Middle Ages and were joint combinations of masters (small employers) and journeymen (skilled workers), known as gilds. The main function of a gild was to control entry into the craft concerned, though gilds also had a hand in regulating the pay of journeymen and the price of the service or finished product. Many journeymen aspired to become masters, and in time often did, and so there was a strong community of interest between the two groups.

In the 16th and 17th centuries, with the growth of paid employment, wages — usually paid as piece-rates — were commonly regulated by Act of Parliament and by local justices of the peace. At the same time, combinations of workers or of employers to alter wages and conditions were prohibited. Regulation of wages in this way, together with the gilds, declined in the 18th century with the increasing complexity and scale of operations in commerce and industry.

During the 18th century further legislation was passed prohibiting combinations in one trade after another, and the courts tended to hold that such combinations were in restraint of trade and therefore illegal at common law. Radical activity and unrest at home and abroad in the 1790s led to pressure for a further tightening of the law. The Combination Act of 1799 and an amending measure of 1800 provided for a general prohibition of combinations in all trades and permitted summary conviction of workers (and, nominally, of employers).

Despite these prohibitions on combination and the demise of statutory regulations skilled workers often continued to organise, although sometimes less overtly, in trade societies and were able to retain some influence over their pay and conditions by controlling entry into their trade. Amongst other workers, however, where organisation was difficult and there were no restrictions on labour supply — especially in handloom weaving — employers dominated the labour market, which occasionally led to violence by the workers. This came to a head with sporadic bouts of machine breaking, collectively known as Luddism, around the end of the Napoleonic Wars in 1815.

The repeal of the Combination Acts: 1824/25

In 1824 pressure within and outside the House of Commons for the reform of the laws restricting combinations led to the establishment of a Parliamentary

Committee. Its recommendations were incorporated in the Combination Laws Repeal Act of that year which removed the restrictions and provided combinations with immunity from prosecution under common law. This was followed by widespread industrial action in pursuit of improved pay and conditions of employment, and an Amending Act[1] was passed in 1825 which limited the purposes for which workmen could combine to influence matters of wages and hours of work. It also reinterpreted the criminal law on acts of violence and intimidation and outlawed, in particular, the 'molesting' and 'obstructing' of people at their place of work. Despite these legal pitfalls that surrounded industrial action, nothing appeared to stand in the way of workmen openly combining. For about 60 years, however, it was generally only skilled workers who took advantage of these changes in the law. In the second quarter of the 19th century many old craft unions came into the open and new ones were formed. Most were based in one town or district and only a handful of more widely organised craft unions — in some engineering, metal and building trades — survived beyond 1850.

Two attempts were made to organise 'general' unions on a national scale but both were short lived. The first was the National Association for the Protection of Labour which flourished alongside a general spinning operatives' union for two years at the end of the 1820s. The other was the Grand National Consolidated Trades Union (GNCTU) formed in 1834 on the inspiration of the social reformer Robert Owen. The GNCTU along with Owen's other schemes had broad political as well as industrial aims, and it fell apart after a year of confrontation with employers and the courts. The most notable court case resulted in the sentencing of seven agricultural workers from Tolpuddle in Dorset to seven years' transporation for administering unlawful oaths. In the remaining years before 1850, despite waves of political agitation connected with the Chartist Movement for Parliamentary Reform, there were few attempts at organising workers outside the local craft unions. An important exception was the Miners' Association of Great Britain and Ireland, established in 1842, which succeeded in organising men in most large coalfields. Its main industrial thrust was checked by the employers in 1844, and the union had virtually ceased to operate by 1848.

During this first half of the century employers in certain industries had been coming together for trade purposes, to hear deputations from their workers and to defeat industrial action. With very rare exceptions, however, they did not combine for collective bargaining.

The New Model Unions and the first Joint Boards

In 1851, most of the existing craft societies in engineering, with the notable exception of the unions of boilermakers and skilled foundry workers, joined together as the Amalgamated Society of Engineers (ASE). The ASE provided a 'new model' for craft unions with its national coverage and centralised control of finance (its headquarters was in London), its high subscriptions and its wide range of social security benefits to members. Like its forerunners, it sought to emphasise its members' craft status and to obtain for its members control over their work situation. It was cautious about sanctioning industrial action, although within a year it became involved in a three-month lockout imposed by an association of engineering employers formed in response to what they saw as the challenge of the ASE.

The first unions to adopt the engineers' model were in the building trades. The most important, the Amalgamated Society of Carpenters and Joiners (ASCJ), was formed in 1860 after a confrontation with building industry employers in London.

The craft unions were generally unwilling to recruit unskilled workers, and union organisation in other industries where workers did not have the craft status of the ASE and the ASCJ was more sporadic and less centralised. In cotton and coalmining, workers organised on a regional basis in the years between 1850 and the late 1880s, though the strength of the unions fluctuated with the state of trade and some unions disappeared altogether. This was also true of farm workers who were able to form a strong national union in the early 1870s only to see it wither in the depression that followed.

In most industries employers began to organise systematically for the first time in the years after 1850. Their associations were at first usually loosely constituted, district or regionally-based, and formed in response to initiatives on the part of their workmen. Once formed, however, many of the associations stayed in being to discuss movements of wages and changes in working conditions with trade union representatives on a regular basis.

These early collective bargaining activities began to be institutionalised in the 1860s with the creation of Boards of Conciliation. The best known early examples were in the Nottingham hosiery industry and in the North of England iron industry. The boards normally had equal numbers of representatives from both sides of an industry, and an independent chairman. Boards in some mining districts and in parts of the iron and steel industry regulated wages by a strict formula based on the price of the product.

Unions' status in law — the renewed debate

In the mid-1860s public attention became focused anew on the legal position of unions. In 1865 and 1866 there was a series of incidents in the Sheffield cutlery trades involving attacks on workers who were not members of the appropriate unions. Officials of some of the unions were implicated. There was a public outcry, and in 1867 a Royal Commission under Lord Erle was set up to inquire into the organisation and rules of unions generally as well as the events in Sheffield and similar incidents among brickmakers in the Manchester area. This was the first of what were to be five Royal Commissions appointed over the next hundred years to inquire into questions affecting industrial relations. In the same year a High Court decision in the case of *Hornby v Close*, where officials of the Boilermakers' Society attempted to recover funds from a defaulting local official, threw doubt on the legal status of unions, and the extent of protection afforded to their funds by the Friendly Societies Act of

1855 which enabled trade unions with welfare benefit functions to deposit their Rules with the Registrar of Friendly Societies. The decision in *Hornby v Close* was that despite the degree of immunity from criminal prosecution given to unions by the Act of 1825 they continued to be illegal at common law on the grounds that they were in restraint of trade and implied that they could be seen as a criminal conspiracy. This deprived them of the protection afforded by the Act of 1855 and indeed seemed to threaten their existence.

These developments led to increased involvement by the unions in conferences and political action. Through the Trades Councils in London, Glasgow and other major cities, union representatives had been able to influence a wide range of issues including extension of the franchise and reform of the 'master and servant' laws (see below). In 1867, a powerful London-based group of leaders known as the 'Junta' won an observer's seat at the Royal Commission while other groups held conferences to consider their tactics. One of these conferences — at Manchester in 1868 — founded the Trades Union Congress (TUC), although the annual congresses were not representative of all the major interests in the trade union movement until 1871. The 'Parliamentary Committee', formed at the 1871 London congress, was the only central and permanent organisation in the TUC for many years.

When the Royal Commission reported in 1869[2] it was not able to produce an agreed report. It recognised that many of the activities and purposes of unions extended beyond the narrow confines of the 1825 Act and were accepted as normal by workmen and many employers, and agreed that unions should be clearly legalised. However, the majority report argued that the protection of the law should not extend where unions sought to breach contracts, impose certain restrictive practices and engage in other activities not regarded as in the public interest, while the minority report wanted less restrictive legislation. The recommendation led to the passing of two important Acts in 1871, whose provisions are summarised below.

The Trade Union Act 1871 and other legislation 1871–76

The Trade Union Act of 1871 declared that the purposes of trade unions should not, merely by virtue of their being in restraint of trade, be deemed to be unlawful. It provided for protection of their funds by Registration, without most of the restrictive conditions recommended in the majority report of the Royal Commission. The Act debarred the courts from directly enforcing, or recovering damages for the breach of, any agreement between one trade union and another. This applied equally to agreements between unions and most employers' associations, which were regarded as 'trade unions' in this context.

Passed together with the Trade Union Act was the Criminal Law Amendment Act of 1871 which re-affirmed liability to criminal prosecution for molesting, obstructing, threatening and intimidating, as well as committing acts of violence, in the context of a trade dispute. A Lords' amendment went further by prohibiting elementary picketing in the form of 'watching and besetting', which had been explicitly legal since 1859.

For four years the TUC pressed for a change in the laws on picketing, conspiracy and breach of contract. The new Conservative government in 1874 set up a Royal Commission on Labour Laws, but its report in 1875[3] did not recommend significant changes. In the same year, however, the Conspiracy and Protection of Property Act was passed repealing the Criminal Law Amendment Act and legalising peaceful picketing. It also stated that no act done in combination and in furtherance of a trade dispute should be indictable as a conspiracy unless it would be criminal if perpetrated by an individual person acting alone.

Another piece of legislation, the Employers and Workmen Act of 1875, dealt with breach of contract by an individual person. Prior to this Act breaches of contract by an employee, including leaving work without due notice, were in certain cases criminal offences, although the Master and Servant Act of 1867 had considerably limited the power of magistrates to order summary arrest and impose penalties. The 1875 Act reduced the contract of employment to a purely civil engagement in which both parties were equal in law and the penalty for a breach was limited to the payment of damages. An exception to this rule was included in the Conspiracy and Protection of Property Act where a breach of contract, if calculated to endanger life or valuable property or cause serious bodily injury, could be a criminal offence. The same applied to breaches causing interruptions to gas and water supply (extended in 1919 to electricity under the Electricity (Supply) Act).

New Unionism and the 1891 Royal Commission on Labour

Economic recession in the years after 1870 hindered the growth of trade unionism, but there were further significant advances between 1888 and 1890.

In 1888 the majority of district miners' associations came together in the Miners' Federation of Great Britain (MFGB), the other districts joining over the following twenty years. Each association retained its autonomy, but the MFGB was empowered to raise a levy, where necessary, to finance industrial action. Unskilled workers began to form mass organisations and 'general unions' began to develop. Seamen and railway labourers joined newly formed unions, and in 1889 a Gasworkers' and General Labourers' Union was formed in London. It rapidly spread to the provinces, recruiting workers in other industries as it advanced. In the same year the London docks were brought to a standstill for a month by a strike of dock labourers who formed a union and forced major concessions. Similar unions were formed on Tyneside and Merseyside. Unlike the older craft unions, these 'New Unions' based their strategy not on restricting entry to a trade nor on providing comprehensive friendly society benefits but on directly pursuing demands for improved pay and conditions. Although on the whole these unions failed to consolidate their initial successes until shortly before the 1914–18 War, their emergence alarmed the government and a Royal Commission on Labour was appointed in 1891.

13

The Commission considered but rejected a proposal to make collective agreements legally enforceable. Its final report in 1894[4] supported the growth of strong voluntary organisations and industry-level collective bargaining though it argued that the government had a responsibility to minimise and help to settle industrial disputes (see chapter 2).

In the twenty-five years up to the First World War employers in several major industries tried to assert their 'right to manage'. In the engineering industry conflict came to a head in 1897 when the newly formed Employers' Federation of Engineering Associations imposed a partial lockout of its members' employees in an attempt to break resistance to the introduction of semi-skilled men to operate new machinery. The lockout broadened into a major stoppage which lasted into 1898.

Taff Vale and the Trade Disputes Act 1906

From 1871 onwards, government policy had aimed to minimise the role of the courts in industrial relations, but had not been wholly successful. In the 1890s there were conflicting judgments over third party injury in disputes; and in 1898 the Appeal Court in *Lyons v Wilkins* upheld an injunction against peaceful picketing.

The most important intervention of the courts occurred in 1901 during a strike of employees of the Taff Vale Railway Company supported by their union, the Amalgamated Society of Railway Servants. An injuction was obtained to prevent representatives of the union from interfering with the company's business by organising pickets and the Lords upheld an award of substantial damages. S4 of the 1871 Trade Union Act, in debarring the courts from jurisdiction over various types of agreement entered into by unions, had emphasised the non-corporate status of unions. However, the Lords held in the Taff Vale case that a union could be sued in its registered name in respect of injuries done with its authority. This ruling made almost any type of industrial action a basis for civil proceedings against the union involved.

The trade union movement pressed hard for legislation to reverse this decision, and despite the report of a Royal Commission in 1906[5] which did not recommend full reversal secured their objective in the Trade Disputes Act 1906. The Act re-affirmed that a union was not liable for any tortious act alleged to have been committed by or on behalf of the union, and also provided that inducement to break contracts of employment and interference with another person's right to dispose of his capital or labour at his will were not actionable, if done in contemplation or furtherance of a trade dispute. Similar immunity was granted to any act done in combination or by agreement if without such combination or agreement it would not have been actionable. Furthermore, the Act declared it to be lawful for a person, in contemplation or furtherance of a trade dispute, to attend at or near another person's residence, place of work or business or wherever that other happened to be, if he attended merely for the purpose of peacefully obtaining or communicating information, or peacefully persuading that other to work or not to work. In 1965 a further Trade Disputes Act was passed to nullify the decision of the House of Lords in *Rookes v Barnard* (1964). The Act gave immunity to persons threatening breaches of, or inducement to break, contracts of employment if done in contemplation or furtherance of a trade dispute. The 1906 and 1965 Acts remained the basis of statutory immunity in this area until 1971.

Trade unions and politics: 1874–1913

The immunities granted to trade unions in 1906 were in part a reflection of the growing political influence exerted by the movement. There had been trade union representatives in Parliament since 1874; and in 1899 the TUC instructed its Parliamentary Committee to call a conference of trade union, co-operative and socialist organisations to consider ways of increasing the 'Labour' representation. From this conference, in 1900, emerged the Labour Representation Committee, renamed the Labour Party in 1906.

In 1909, W V Osborne, a member of the Amalgamated Society of Railway Servants, secured a Lords' ruling against his union's expenditure on political activities. The Lords held that nothing in the Trade Union Act Amendment Act 1876, which defined the term 'trade union' in law, permitted a union to engage in political activity.

For four years most of the major trade unions were precluded by specific injunctions from contributing to the Labour Party. In 1913, however, a further Trade Union Act was passed which enabled a union to include in its constitution any lawful purpose so long as its principal objects were those outlined in the 1876 Act. The adoption of any political object, however, was governed by special rules including the holding of a ballot, and members had to be able to contract out of contributions to a political fund.

The 1914–18 War and the Whitley Committee

There was renewed growth in union membership in the years immediately before the First World War. Against a background of rapid price inflation there were national strikes in mining and on the railways and sporadic industrial action amongst dockers and seamen. This wave of industrial action was halted by the outbreak of war and the announcement of an industrial truce by the major trade unions. However, this did not prevent a major unofficial strike of engineers on Clydeside in 1915 which hastened the passage of the Munitions of War Act of that year, providing among other things for the prohibition of strikes and lockouts, and compulsory binding arbitration in any industry vital to the war effort (see chapter 2). However, there were no prosecutions under the Act despite major stoppages during the war in coal-mining and engineering.

During the course of the war the great expansion, re-organisation and flexibility demanded of, in particular, the engineering and shipbuilding indus-

15

tries led to a significant growth in the numbers and powers of local trade union representatives known as 'shop stewards'. The Shop Stewards' Movement of the war years reflected powerful rank and file aspirations for workers' control and many saw it as a challenge to the official trade union leadership, which since the 1890s had increasingly been concluding industry-wide agreements such as those in building, shipbuilding and engineering.

It was against this background that the government appointed in 1916 the Whitley Committee on the Relations between Employers and Employed. The reports of the Committee were published in 1917 and 1918[6] and met with broad approval from both sides of industry. The Committee advised that in industries with well developed voluntary organisation on both sides joint machinery should be established at national, district and establishment level — in the form of joint industrial councils, joint district councils, and works committees. This machinery should concern itself not only with the determination of wages and basic conditions of employment but also with a wide range of other matters with the aim of promoting efficiency, co-operation and job satisfaction. The councils and committees should have 'standing' status and at national and district level at least should consist of representatives of the appropriate employers' associations and trade unions.

To encourage the development of this machinery the Committee recommended the establishment of permanent but voluntary arbitration and inquiry machinery (see chapter 2). In industries where voluntary organisation was non-existent or deficient, statutory regulation of pay was recommended, by extending the Trade Boards system set up in 1909 (see chapter 2).

Post-War reconstruction and the General Strike

After the war voluntary pay determination returned, and with the help of the newly-formed Ministry of Labour 73 joint industrial councils were established between 1918 and the end of 1921. A model constitution and wide-ranging list of possible functions was drawn up by the Ministry, but although most of the councils followed the model constitution few extended their scope much beyond the negotiation of wages and basic conditions of employment. Most of the new councils differed little from the conciliation boards and similar machinery that had existed before the war. The main exceptions were in areas of government employment, notably the non-industrial Civil Service and the Post Office. In major industries like mining, engineering, cotton and iron and steel where collective bargaining was already established, the Whitley recommendations had virtually no impact.

Major advances were made in the extension of voluntary collective bargaining in the immediate post-war years, including developments among white-collar workers in the public services and engineering. Assisted by the provisions of the Trade Union (Amalgamation) Act 1917, important organisational changes took place among trade unions including the creation of the Amalgamated Engineering Union in 1921, the Transport and General Workers' Union in 1922 and the National Union of General and Municipal

Workers in 1924. In 1921 the TUC extended its co-ordinating role by replacing its Parliamentary Committee by a General Council with augmented powers. Meanwhile employers and employers' associations were beginning to recognise the need to organise centrally and the National Confederation of Employers' Organisations (NCEO) was formed in 1919.

However, in the depressed economic conditions of the 1920s trade unions and employers' associations failed to sustain the momentum that had led to the proliferation of joint industrial councils, and by 1926 the number had fallen to 47. The decade was also marked by the deep-rooted problems in the mining industry which at the time employed around a million workers. There were two Royal Commissions on the industry (in 1919 and 1925), a two-month lockout in 1921 and the six-month lockout of 1926. In the early stages of the 1926 dispute the miners were supported by a nine-day 'General Strike' of workers in many major industries, called by the General Council of the TUC.

The aftermath of the General Strike and The Depression

The defeat of the miners in 1926 left the trade union movement weak and divided. In 1927 the Trade Disputes and Trade Union Act was passed restricting the movement's scope and powers. 'Sympathetic strikes', that is, strikes outside the industry orginally involved in a dispute, and designed to influence government either directly or by inflicting hardship on the community were prohibited. Inviting others to take part in such strikes or supporting such strikers with funds became criminal acts. The law on picketing was tightened. Civil servants were prohibited from joining unions with political objects (those affiliated to the TUC, for example) and unions which did not consist wholly of State employees, though public authorities could not require their employees, or those of contractors to the authorities, to be or not be members of a trade union. Public servants could be prosecuted if, in breaching their contracts of service, they knowingly risked causing injury or serious inconvenience to the community. In addition, the 'contracting out' provisions of the 1913 Trade Union Act with respect to unions' political funds were replaced by 'contracting in' obligations.

In the same year a conciliatory move by a representative group of employers, on the initiative of Sir Alfred Mond, led to a series of talks with the General Council of the TUC led by its chairman Ben Turner. The 'Mond–Turner' talks resulted in proposals for a joint body made up of representatives of the TUC and the two central employers' organisations which would have tackled problems of collective bargaining and dispute resolution as well as industrial re-organisation and government economic policy. However, the employers' organisations were only willing to be involved in limited *ad hoc* consultative arrangements, and the proposals in the end were not implemented.

Trade union membership experienced a sharp decline during the depressed years up to the mid-1930s, partly because of high unemployment in the basic extractive and manufacturing industries. In the late 1930s, however, the level of organisation improved, boosted by recruitment in new centres of industry such as the light engineering establishments of the London suburbs.

The Second World War and the Post-War Labour Government

Early in the Second World War, as in the First, the government considerably extended its control over labour matters, mostly through Orders under Defence Regulation 58AA (see chapter 2). The most important of these made strikes and lockouts illegal and provided for binding arbitration. This was generally adhered to, although there were some unofficial strikes, particularly in coalmining towards the end of the war.

In 1939 a National Joint Advisory Council (NJAC) was established under the chairmanship of the Minister of Labour and National Service. It consisted of 15 representatives each of the TUC and the British Employers' Confederation (formerly the NCEO) and was intended to discuss matters of common interest and assist the Minister in formulating policy. It was largely superseded in wartime by a smaller constituent body known as the Joint Consultative Committee and this was important in getting co-operation for the many changes in working arrangements necessitated by the war. The NJAC was reconstituted in 1946, representatives of the newly nationalised industries were given seats on the Council in 1949, and it continued to function into the 1960s.

Despite the intervention of government, collective bargaining practice was not radically transformed in the war years. The number and influence of shop stewards was again greatly increased, but they were not seen to pose a threat to established procedures. In the Joint Production Committees of war production factories stewards participated in regular consultation with management.

With the encouragement of the Ministry of Labour and National Service, over 50 joint industrial councils or similar bodies were established or re-established and there was a marked overall rise in trade union membership. There were few major changes in trade union organisation in this period, the most notable being the formation of the first centrally organised national union in mining (the National Union of Mineworkers) in 1944.

In 1946, the government repealed the 1927 Trade Disputes and Trade Union Act, whereupon several Post Office and Civil Service unions joined the TUC. In addition, during the immediate post-war years there was a considerable extension of statutory regulation of pay in low-paid industries.

Collective bargaining in the years of full employment 1951–68

Strike action and lockouts were once again made legal in 1951 although either side to a dispute could invoke compulsory binding arbitration until 1958. The incidence of industrial disputes remained low in the early 1950s but a sharp increase in disputes from 1955 and controversy over union ballots and the closed shop in some areas led to renewed public debate about trade union power. One school of thought held that the 1906 Trade Disputes Act had gone too far in granting legal immunities to trade unions. The two most important expressions of this view were *A Giant's Strength*, published by the Inns of Court Conservative and Unionist Society in 1958,[7] and *Fair Deal at Work*, published by the Conservative Political Centre in 1968,[8] and these influenced the framing of the 1971 Industrial Relations Act.

During the 1960s white-collar unionism — particularly in the public sector — grew rapidly, though it was almost matched by a decline in membership of manual worker unions, as the industrial structure changed. Union amalgamations continued including those of the electricians' and plumbers' unions, the engineering and foundry workers and the combination of two white-collar unions to form the Association of Scientific, Technical and Managerial Staffs. A new Trade Union (Amalgamations, etc) Act of 1964 eased the process of merger.

Two further developments in the post-war years were the decline in influence of employers' associations, and the growth of plant bargaining with its increasing emphasis on the role of the shop steward. Both developments were highlighted by the Donovan Commission.

The Donovan Commission

In 1965 continuing concern over industrial relations led the Labour Government to set up a Royal Commission on Trade Unions and Employers' Associations under Lord Donovan

'to consider relations between managements and employees and the role of trade unions and employers' associations in promoting the interests of their members and in accelerating the social and economic advance of the nation, with particular reference to the law affecting the activities of these bodies'.

The Royal Commission issued its report[9] in June 1968 after taking evidence and sponsoring research for three years. Its principal conclusion was that Britain had two systems of industrial relations. One was the formal system embodied in the official institutions and sustained in general by the industry-wide collective agreements. The other was an informal system, most evident at the level of the plant and often at odds with the formal system. One symptom of the disparity between the two 'systems' was the gap between actual earnings and the rates of pay laid down in industry-wide agreements, and the widening of this gap in recent years indicated the increased importance of the 'work group' at plant level under conditions of full employment. This domestic bargaining had often led to fragmented pay structures. The transfer of authority to the level of the establishment had put industry-level disputes procedures under strain, yet relatively few well ordered or plant-level agreements had been developed. Although the Commission found that many of the parties to the informal system were content with its operation, there was evidence that it led to inefficiency and a high incidence of unofficial disputes.

19

The Commission had undertaken the most thorough review of industrial relations in this century, and its proposals were wide-ranging. Its central recommendation was that the informal system of industrial relations should be more effectively regulated through the conclusion of formal plant agreements (or company agreements in multi-plant companies) which, in companies above a certain size, should be registered with the Department of Employment and Productivity. An Industrial Relations Commission should be established to investigate issues arising from these agreements and to conduct inquiries into industrial relations issues including trade union recognition problems. Collective bargaining should be encouraged; no employee should be prevented from belonging to a trade union, and employers should rethink their attitudes towards unions for white-collar staff.

The Commission considered that this reform of collective bargaining machinery was the key to dealing with unconstitutional strikes. It took the view that the application of legal sanctions to individual persons for striking in breach of a procedure agreement or to unions for being a party to such strikes would be ineffective or counter-productive, though it did note that legal sanctions might have to be reconsidered if circumstances changed. It also recommended against the introduction of compulsory strike ballots and a compulsory 'cooling off period'.

The Commission also made a series of proposals on individual rights. Employees should be protected against unfair dismissal and statutory machinery to adjudicate in such cases should be created. The closed shop should not be prohibited, though workers dismissed because of a closed shop should be able to complain to an industrial tribunal, and an independent review body should be established to hear cases where people had been excluded from a union. This body should also deal with complaints about alleged irregularities in union elections, mergers or union rules.

The Commission's proposals also covered the structure of unions, their registration, and their legal immunities which, it thought, should be retained and slightly extended. Multi-unionism should be reduced, and unions should be encouraged to form joint union committees, or to conclude spheres of influence agreements. Union branch structures should be revised to focus on the plant and formally incorporate shop stewards.

'In Place of Strife' and the Industrial Relations Act 1971

In 1969, the government published the White Paper *In Place of Strife*[10] based in part on the Donovan recommendations. Contrary to Donovan, however, the White Paper proposed certain reserve powers for the Secretary of State: enforcement of a conciliation pause in unconstitutional strikes and other stoppages where adequate joint discussions had not taken place; compulsory ballots in certain serious strikes; and measures to deal with inter-union conflicts. These proposals met with strong opposition from the trade unions, who argued that these matters were best dealt with by voluntary means. The penal clauses were eventually dropped from the ensuing Bill, but this never reached the statute book because of the change of government in 1970.

In the meantime the Commission on Industrial Relations (CIR) was established by Royal Warrant. The Commission's duties were to conduct inquiries into 'the functioning and development of institutions and procedures for the conduct of industrial relations' and to act as a third party 'in improving and developing collective bargaining'. A summary of its work and a list of its reports are contained in its final report.[11]

The new Conservative government came to office in 1970 committed to a major reform of the law on industrial relations. Its Industrial Relations Act in 1971 markedly extended the influence of the law while seeking to promote the principle of 'collective bargaining freely conducted on behalf of workers and employers'. It replaced the Trade Union Act 1871 and its Amendment Act 1876, the Trade Disputes Acts 1906 and 1965 and several other pieces of legislation. The Act established a new industrial relations institution, the National Industrial Relations Court (NIRC), put the CIR on a statutory footing, and revised and extended the jurisdiction of other bodies such as industrial tribunals and the Industrial Court (renamed the Industrial Arbitration Board). The NIRC consisted of judges of the High Court and lay members with industrial relations expertise from both sides of industry. The Act removed from the jurisdiction of the ordinary courts most legal proceedings arising out of industrial disputes, and replaced traditional common law remedies in part by a new ground for legal proceedings — a complaint of 'unfair industrial practice'. These and other complaints — over union recognition, or the closed shop — could be brought before the NIRC or industrial tribunals. Moreover, the Act created a new presumption in law that written collective agreements were intended to be legally enforceable contracts unless they contained a disclaimer.

A Registrar of Trade Unions and Employers' Associations was appointed. Independent trade unions and employers' associations could be registered if their rules and procedures — notably over the rights of members and the holding of ballots — conformed to certain standards.

The traditional immunities were, in general, restricted to organisations which registered under the Act. In addition, registered organisations were given special facilities — notably over access to the NIRC — and one major new immunity, over breach of commercial contracts.

The CIR was given powers to deal with union recognition disputes. However, the Act made pre-entry 'closed-shop' agreements void, and aimed to make existing post-entry 'closed-shop' agreements unenforceable by giving workers the right to belong or not belong to any trade union, and by making it an 'unfair industrial practice' to prevent anyone from exercising this choice. As an alternative an 'agency shop' could be established under which employees would have to join the union, or pay the union the equivalent of its subscription in lieu of membership, or pay the equivalent sum to charity. The Act allowed in exceptional circumstances for an approved post-entry closed shop on application to the NIRC.

The Act contained a number of other provisions. The Secretary of State was given the power to order a 'cooling-off period' of up to 60 days where an industrial dispute threatened the economy or public health and safety, and to restrain industrial action in certain circumstances while a compulsory ballot was conducted. Picketing at a person's home (unless it was also his place of work) was excepted from statutory immunity for 'peaceful picketing'. A code of practice was issued giving guidance on promoting good industrial relations, and while failure to observe the code did not render anyone liable to legal proceedings, the code could be used in evidence before industrial tribunals or the NIRC. The Act extended individual employee rights to include a right not to be unfairly dismissed (generally adopting the Donovan recommendations) and also extended rights in relation to entitlement to notice and written contracts of employment.

Industrial relations 1970–74

The Industrial Relations Act was strongly opposed by the trade unions. In January 1971, a month after the Industrial Relations Bill was put before Parliament, the TUC set in motion a campaign of opposition. In March, at a special congress, member unions were recommended to boycott the Act when it became law. Unions were advised not to co-operate with the CIR and NIRC, not to enter into binding collective agreements, nor to serve on industrial tribunals. In particular, to frustrate some of the central principles of the Act, they were strongly advised to remove themselves from the provisional register of trade unions. This became an instruction, obeyed by all but about 30 unions, after the annual Congress in September. Engineering and ship-building workers expressed their opposition through two one-day strikes in March.

The most contentious early legal proceedings under the Act over 'unfair industrial practices' arose out of a series of disputes centred on container and cold storage terminals. These depots were being 'blacked' by dockers who resented the employment there of non-dockers. The Transport and General Workers' Union was heavily fined in 1972 after the House of Lords upheld a judgment by the NIRC in a case involving some of the union's officials and Heaton's Transport, a firm being blacked. In the same year, five dockers' shop stewards were imprisoned for ignoring an injunction against picketing the Midland Cold Storage Company depot in East London.

The dockers were released after the intervention of the Official Solicitor and no further proceedings of that nature were taken against individual persons. Unions, however, continued to be vulnerable to injunctions and the Amalgamated Union of Engineering Workers, which refused to co-operate in any way with the NIRC, was heavily fined on two occasions. The first of these involved the union's treatment of a person who, an industrial tribunal declared, was a member of the union and was denied his right to attend branch meetings. The second involved a strike over recognition at Con-Mech (Engineers) in Surrey.

All these events were accompanied by major protest strikes expressing widespread opposition to the operation of the Act. Some sections — such as the new laws on the closed shop — were largely circumvented or ignored by employers and workers. Collective agreements tended to include disclaimers rendering them not legally binding. The emergency procedures of the Act were used only once, during a dispute in 1972 in British Rail where the 'cooling-off' period' was observed but the compulsory ballot which followed produced an overwhelming majority in favour of strike action.

There was also a series of major disputes over the government's attempts to control the level of pay increases (see chapter 2). This began in 1971 and 1972 with disputes amongst public sector manual workers in local authorities, electricity supply, the Post Office, the mining industry and the railways, and culminated in an overtime ban by miners followed by a strike in early 1974 which led to emergency measures, including a three-day week in most industries, and was followed by a general election and a change of government. Statistics on numbers of stoppages and days lost through industrial disputes in different industries in the UK this decade are given in Appendix 2; international comparative figures for 1969–78 are given in Appendix 3.

The Labour Government 1974–79

While the Labour Party had been in opposition they had come to an understanding with the trade unions, known as the 'Social Contract'. This committed the government to a wide programme of measures, in industrial relations and other social and economic spheres, in return for co-operation from the TUC in tackling the country's economic problems.

The 'Social Contract' included a pledge to repeal the Industrial Relations Act and in July 1974 the Trade Union and Labour Relations Act (TULRA) was passed repealing the 1971 Act and abolishing the CIR, the NIRC and the Registrar of Trade Unions and Employers' Associations. The new Act retained the unfair dismissal provisions introduced in 1971 (amended to accommodate the removal of restrictions on the closed shop) and redefined the law on the status and regulation of trade unions, employers' associations and collective agreements, and on behaviour in disputes (see chapter 5). Certain amendments inititated in the House of Lords were carried in the Commons against the government. The principal one concerned the immunity for persons acting in contemplation or furtherance of a trade dispute to induce breaches of, or otherwise interfere with, commercial contracts which was restricted by amendment to 'employment contracts'. The Trade Union and Labour Relations (Amendment) Act 1976 extended the protection to cover inducement to break, and other interference with, commerical contracts. A number of judicial decisions between 1977 and 1979 narrowed the construction of the 'trade dispute' definition in section 29 of TULRA 1974, and gave a restrictive interpretation of the formulation 'in contemplation or furtherance' in section 13 of that Act. This trend was to some extent reversed by two decisions by the House of Lords in late 1979.

The government also introduced legislation in the field of individual and collective rights and health and safety (see chapter 2) including the Employment Protection Act 1975 the provisions of which, as subsequently amended, are described in some detail in chapter five. Two provisions of the Act, on

23

trade union recognition and the extension of terms and conditions of employment have, however, since been repealed by the Conservative Government under the Employment Act 1980. The procedure on trade union recognition required the Advisory, Conciliation and Arbitration Service (ACAS) — which had been established in 1974 but which the Act placed on a statutory footing (see chapters 2 and 3) — to attempt to conciliate in a dispute over recognition, but if an agreement was not forthcoming to make inquiries, ascertain the opinions of the workers concerned and report. If ACAS recommended recognition and the employer failed to comply the union involved could ask the Central Arbitration Committee to award specified improvements in terms and conditions of employment for the employees covered.

The government also set up a Committee of Inquiry on Industrial Democracy, under Lord Bullock, with a duty to report on how representation of trade unions on boards of directors of companies could best be achieved. In January 1977 the Committee issued its Report[12] from which the three employers' respresentatives dissented. Following widespread opposition to the Report's recommendations, particularly from employers and employers' organisations, the Government, in May 1978, issued a White Paper on Industrial Democracy[13] considerably modifying the Bullock proposals.

The Conservative Government 1979–

In May 1979 a Conservative Government took office. It was opposed to any statutory requirements on employee participation in companies but favoured a voluntary development of employee involvement within individual companies in whichever way was best suited to each company's particular circumstances, and also favoured an extension of employee share ownership. It was also committed to amend the law in certain respects.This has been effected in the Employment Act which, among other things, amends the law on immunities for industrial action and picketing, on unfair dismissal — notably in relation to union membership agreements — and on maternity rights; provides for funds for unions to conduct secret ballots; gives employees the right not to be unreasonably excluded or expelled from a trade union; and repeals the provisions of the Employment Protection Act on trade union recognition and on the extension of terms and conditions of employment. The whole body of employment law, as it now stands, including the provisions of the Employment Act 1980, is summarised in chapter five.

Chapter 2

The development of other areas of state intervention

ARBITRATION AND CONCILIATION

Early legislation and the Conciliation Act 1896

In chapter one it was shown that in the eighteenth century the state withdrew from involvement in determining workers' pay. Nevertheless there remained in 1800 the vestiges of a system of compulsory binding arbitration of various types of disputes, usually between individual workmen and employers, administered by justices of the peace. The system was modified under the Combination Act 1800, the Cotton Arbitration Act 1800 and the Arbitration Act 1824, to allow for nominated referees to arbitrate in disputes. However, with the exception of that set up under the Cotton Arbitration Act and its amending Acts, this type of machinery was rarely used.

Two further Acts, in 1867 and 1872, enabled boards of arbitration, set up in conjunction with voluntary bargaining arrangements, to make legally binding awards, but these Acts were also little used and were superseded in 1896 by a system where the State intervened only to assist and mediate in voluntary settlements.

The Conciliation Act of 1896 was the legislative outcome of the 1891 Royal Commission on Labour. It reflected the Commission's desire to foster the development of collective bargaining in a voluntary framework, and it repealed all the earlier provisions for compulsory and binding arbitration. The Board of Trade which, since 1886, had been collecting labour statistics and, since 1893, had been given the duty of conducting through a Labour Department special inquiries into industrial unrest, was charged with administering the Act. Wherever an industrial dispute occurred, the Board was given the power to inquire into the causes and to take steps to encourage the sides to meet together under an independent mediator, conciliator, or board of conciliation. The Board was empowered to conciliate and also to appoint an arbitrator or a mutually agreed chairman 'with a view to the amicable settlement' of a difference.

The Board of Trade also had to aid and encourage the new voluntary joint boards which were responsible for most conciliated settlements in the years that followed. The conciliation machinery set up under the 1896 Act was generally used — as had been intended — only in major disputes and when the parties had reached deadlock. The arbitration facilities tended to be used in smaller disputes which often had not involved a stoppage of work.

The powers under the Act were transferred to a new Ministry of Labour in

1916 and subsequently to that Ministry's successors. The Act was not repealed until 1975.

Wartime measures 1915–20 and the Industrial Courts Act 1919

This emphasis on settling disputes through conciliation and voluntary arbitration — undertaken only with the consent of both parties to a dispute — has been supported by successive governments throughout this century. However, during the First and Second World Wars powers were taken to provide for compulsory binding arbitration.

In 1915, against a background of inflation and a rising number of industrial disputes, and despite an agreement between the government and certain major trade unions to refer all disputes in munitions industries to arbitration, the Munitions of War Act was passed. This prohibited strikes and lockouts throughout a very wide range of industries and occupations, and provided for disputes to be reported by either party to the Board of Trade who could then refer them to arbitration. The awards were legally binding.

In 1916 an Amendment Act enabled the Minister of Munitions to fix rates of pay and conditions of employment for female, semi-skilled and unskilled labour in certain areas of munitions work, and set up special arbitration tribunals to deal with disputes over these provisions. A further Act in 1917[14] enabled the Minister to make terms and conditions which had been negotiated for the majority of workers in a given area of munitions work binding on all other employers in that area.

At the end of the war, most sections of the three Munitions Acts were repealed, but temporary legislation[15] was enacted to enable some State control of wages, and compulsory arbitration in certain key areas, to be continued for two years while working conditions returned to normal. One of the key recommendations of the Whitley Committee (see chapter 1) — the provision of 'a standing arbitration council for cases where the parties wish to refer any dispute to arbitration' — was put into effect by the Industrial Courts Act 1919. This established the Industrial Court as a permanent and independent tribunal composed of representatives of employers and workpeople, independent members, and including at least one woman. One of the independent members was to be appointed president; others could act as chairmen in proceedings, and a chairman had a deciding voice where the other members of the Court failed to agree. Its awards were not legally binding, but all were published.

Almost any actual or anticipated industrial dispute could be referred to the Court through the Minister of Labour, but only with the consent of both parties. Other conditions normally to be applied included a resumption of work pending arbitration and the exhausting of any 'in-house' conciliation and arbitration arrangements.

In addition, under the Act, single arbitrators and *ad hoc* boards of arbitration could still be appointed.

Part II of the Industrial Courts Act (whose provisions remain in force) enabled the Minister of Labour, on his own initiative, and not necessarily with the consent of the parties, to inquire into the circumstances and causes of any trade dispute by appointing an *ad hoc* Court of Inquiry of one or more persons, always with an independent Chairman, usually accompanied by persons with experience respectively as representatives of employers and workpeople. In practice, Courts of Inquiry have been primarily a means of informing Parliament and the public of the facts and underlying causes of a major dispute, although they have sometimes helped to solve disputes, especially where they have produced recommendations. Less prominent disputes continued after 1919 to be the subject of committees of investigation under the Conciliation Act 1896.

Certain further functions were given to the Industrial Court under subsequent legislation including Part II of the Road Haulage Wages Act 1938 and the Terms and Conditions of Employment Act 1959 (see below). The functions of the Court are now performed by the Central Arbitration Committee (see chapter 3).

Measures in the Second World War. The Industrial Disputes Order 1951

In the spring of 1940, when the war had reached a critical stage, the Consultative Committee of the National Joint Advisory Council (NJAC) (see page 18) unanimously recommended that although the normal machinery for the determination of pay and conditions of employment should continue to operate, matters in dispute that could not be resolved by that machinery should be referred to arbitration. Settlements both by negotiation and by arbitration should be binding and strikes and lockouts should not take place.

The Minister of Labour and National Service accepted the principle of these recommendations and made the Conditions of Employment and National Arbitration Order, commonly known as 'Order 1305'. This enabled him to refer disputes to compulsory arbitration by a National Arbitration Tribunal (NAT) composed, for the purposes of any particular case, of one representative each of employers and workers, chosen from panels, and up to three independents (including the chairman).

The order also prohibited strikes and lockouts unless the dispute had been reported to the Minister and he had not referred it to the NAT within 21 days. Employers were obliged to observe terms and conditions which had been determined by collective agreements or by arbitration for their trade or branch of industry in their particular district.

The order remained in force until 1951 when it was replaced by the Industrial Disputes Order of 1951, commonly known as 'Order 1376'. This removed the prohibition on strikes and lockouts, and the obligations on employers under Part III of Order 1305, but retained provision for compulsory binding arbitration through a new body, the Industrial Disputes Tribunal (IDT). Provision was also made for the reporting of 'issues' concerning the observance of recognised terms and conditions of employment by

27

individual employers. If not otherwise settled these 'issues' could be referred unilaterally to the Industrial Disputes Tribunal.

The Industrial Disputes Order was renewed year by year under the Defence Regulations procedures but was revoked in 1958. In tripartite discussions, employers' representatives did not support the continuance of compulsory arbitration on a permanent basis.

The Terms and Conditions of Employment Act 1959. Other recent measures

When the Industrial Disputes Order was revoked this ended compulsory arbitration in disputes where there had been a failure to agree improved terms and conditions of employment. Section 8 of the Terms and Conditions of Employment Act 1959, however, gave continued access to unilateral binding arbitration where an issue arose as to whether a particular employer was observing already established or recognised terms and conditions for his trade or branch of industry. 'Recognised terms and conditions' were those settled generally or, in a particular district, by an agreement or an award. Only representative organisations of employers or of workers, which were parties to the agreement or award in question, could make a claim under the 1959 Act. Claims were settled by the Industrial Court. Any award requiring the employer to observe the recognised terms and conditions for the workers covered by the claim had effect as an implied term of their contract.

S8 of the Terms and Conditions of Employment Act was repealed by the Employment Protection Act 1975 and replaced by Schedule 11 of that Act which extended the scope of this type of arbitration to include claims based on the 'general level of terms and conditions', that is, the general level observed for comparable workers by other employers in similar circumstances engaged in the same industry in the same district. Claims could only be made by a trade union which had at least one member covered by the claim (or if an employer recognised one or more independent trade unions only by these unions) or by an employers' association which had members engaged in the district or industry to which the claim related. Schedule 11 also enabled claims of this kind to be made in relation to wages councils and similar bodies. However, all these provisions on the extension of terms and conditions of employment came to an end with the repeal of Schedule 11 by the Employment Act 1980.

The conciliation and arbitration service

The voluntary conciliation and arbitration service begun by the government in 1896 was augmented during the Second World War by the provision of free advice to employers and unions on industrial relations and personnel matters. From 1960 these facilities were known collectively as the Industrial Relations Service. In 1969 this was renamed the Manpower and Productivity Service and given further responsibilities for the provision of a central consultancy and regional field advice service in management techniques and business efficiency. Its terms of reference were revised in 1971 to concentrate on industrial relations and personnel matters, and in 1972 it was renamed the Conciliation and Advisory Service (CAS). However, the constraints of the 1972–74 incomes policy made it difficult for the Service to operate effectively from within a government department, and in 1974 it was established on an independent basis as the Conciliation and Arbitration Service. It was renamed the *Advisory, Conciliation and Arbitration Service* in 1975 and was put on a statutory footing in 1976 under the Employment Protection Act 1975 (see chapter 3).

From 1919 voluntary arbitration was provided not only by individual arbitrators or *ad hoc* boards of arbitration but also by the Industrial Court. In 1971 the Industrial Court was renamed the Industrial Arbitration Board which was replaced in 1976 by the Central Arbitration Committee (see chapter three).

STATUTORY REGULATION OF PAY AND CONDITIONS

The regulation of pay by unilateral binding arbitration described above is a form of statutory regulation of pay, but apart from the wartime measures and those of the 1950s under the post-war Industrial Disputes Order it has been regulation on an *ad hoc* basis generally affecting small groups of workers for the limited duration of particular agreements. The State has also intervened more systematically to regulate pay and some conditions of employment of certain groups of workers — since 1891 through successive Fair Wages Resolutions of the House of Commons, and since 1909 by establishing Trade Boards and their successors, Wages Councils.

The Fair Wages Resolutions

The first Fair Wages Resolution was passed in 1891, in response to the reports of the Select Committee on the Sweating System,[16] in an attempt to counteract the widespread exploitation of labour employed on government contracts revealed by the Select Committee. The Resolution stated that it was the duty of the government in all government contracts to make every effort to secure the payment of such wages as were generally accepted as current for competent workmen.

This resolution was not applied uniformly nor was it universally enforced, and it was strengthened in 1909, requiring contractors to pay wages and observe hours of labour commonly recognised by employers and unions or prevailing amongst good employers, with provision for fines or other penalties.

In 1946, a further Resolution was passed. In principle it was the same as its predecessor but it covered all workers employed in establishments handling contracts, not just those employed directly on contracts. It extended its scope to include observance of 'fair' conditions of employment and to require assurances from prospective contractors that they were complying with the general conditions of the Resolution, and contractors had to allow their workers to belong to trade unions. If any question arose as to whether the requirements of the Resolution were being observed provision was made for it to be referred to an Independent Tribunal, if it could not otherwise be settled. The Resolution is still in force and is described in chapter five.

The principle of the Fair Wages Resolution has been extended to areas of employment other than those directly concerned with Government contracts. Nationalised industries and local authorities generally insert forms of fair wages clauses in their contracts. The principle has also been embodied in a number of Acts of Parliament providing for assistance to industries or public authorities through grants, loans, subsidies, guarantees or licences, where it was felt that collective bargaining arrangements were less than adequate. The normal requirement has been that the pay and conditions of the workers affected by the particular Act should not be less favourable than the pay and conditions which would have to be observed under a Government contract containing a Fair Wages Clause. The first Act containing a provison of this nature was the British Sugar (Subsidy) Act 1925 and several — including the Civil Aviation Act 1949 and the Films Act 1960 — remain in force today. The fair wages provisions in these Acts were intended to be temporary and some have been removed after the establishment of adequate negotiating machinery.

The Wages Council system

A more fundamental departure from the nineteenth century doctrine of non-interference by the State in pay determination was the system of Trade Boards, Wages Boards and Wages Councils which originated with the Trade Boards Act 1909.

The 1909 Act grew out of widespread concern and agitation about the low pay and very poor working and living conditions of large numbers of workers in 'sweated trades'. The machinery established under the Act differed little in composition from that now operating under the most recent Wages Council legislation. The Trade Boards, established in four industries at first, were tripartite bodies specific to each industry, with the power to fix minimum rates of pay which were legally enforceable throughout the industries covered. Additional Boards could be established on the initiative of the President of the Board of Trade and after ratification by the House of Commons. The grounds for creating a Board were that pay was considered exceptionally low relative to that in other industries. On this criterion, Boards were established in four more industries in 1914.

In 1917 the Whitley Committee[17] (see chapter 1) recommended that the Trade Board system should be extended, that industries with lack of organisation as well as low pay should be included and that the Boards should have the power to deal with hours of work and certain other conditions of employment as well as minimum pay rates. They were, however, to be seen as the precursors of voluntary joint machinery, to be superseded by such machinery when it became viable. These recommendations were embodied in the Trade Boards Act 1918.

By 1921, 37 new Trade Boards had been established, but in the depressed economic climate of the decade or so that followed it was alleged that the Boards delayed unreasonably in the industries they covered the general downward movement of wages that had taken place elsewhere, and no new Boards were established until 1933.

Most Trade Boards operated in the manufacturing sector and attempts to establish statutory minimum wage machinery in two major service areas — catering and retailing — were largely unsuccessful before the 1940s, partly through difficulties in applying the 1918 Act to these industries. The problem was overcome in catering in 1943 by new legislation. But before that, statutory protection had been extended by Parliament to workers in two other important non-manufacturing industries: agriculture and road haulage.

A system for determining statutory minimum wages in agriculture was established on a permanent basis in England and Wales under the Agricultural Wages (Regulation) Act 1924. Agricultural Wages Committees, constituted on Trade Board lines and with similar powers, operated on a local basis under the supervision of a Central Board, the machinery being administered by the Ministry of Agriculture and Fisheries. The committees were also empowered to set minimum rates for piecework and special rates and conditions for handicapped workers.

In 1940 and 1944, amending legislation enabled a national agricultural minimum wage to be fixed below which the local rates for adult males should not fall. In 1942, as a wartime measure, the power to fix local rates was transferred to the Central Board. The local Wages Committees remained in being as consultative bodies and retained the power to determine 'benefits and advantages' which might be allowed in part payment of minimum rates of wages and to deal with applications for permits exempting handicapped workers from the minimum rates. The transfer of authority was made permanent in the Agricultural Wages (Regulation) Act 1947 which further reduced the role of the local committees. The Agricultural Wages Act 1948 reproduced in consolidated form the legislation of 1924 and 1947 and relevant provisions of the Holidays with Pay Act 1938 (see below), and with amendments it remains the law today (see pages 101).

A similar system of district committees and central Wages Board was established in Scotland under the Agricultural Wages (Regulation) (Scotland) Act 1937. The Act gave the Department of Agriculture the power in Scotland to direct a district committee to reconsider a minimum rate. This power was transferred to the Wages Board in 1940, as was the power to fix district rates. The Agricultural Wages (Regulation) Act 1947 applied to Scotland and the Agricultural Wages (Scotland) Act 1949 consolidated the existing legislation.

In road haulage, Part I of the Road Haulage Wages Act 1938 established a Central Wages Board to replace a voluntary wage-fixing system which had

31

broken down. The Board covered workers employed in connection with vehicles operating under 'A' or 'B' licences, that is, in the 'hire or reward' section of the industry. Two-thirds of the workers' and employers' representatives on the Central Board were drawn from eleven bipartite area boards which had a consultative function. Unlike Trade Boards, the Road Haulage Central Board could fix minimum remuneration and holiday pay in addition to minimum wage rates. It also served as a liaison body between government and the industry. The Wages Councils Act 1948 converted the Board to the Road Haulage Wages Council, which was eventually abolished in 1978.

The Road Haulage Wages Act anticipated by a few months another piece of legislation by including paid holidays within the scope of its statutory machinery. The Holidays with Pay Act 1938 enabled Trade Boards and Agricultural Wages Committees to require the observance of one week's holiday per annum with pay. This measure was expected to set an example to employers generally. Its provisions were almost universally adopted within the statutory sector.

In catering, the 1943 Catering Wages Act set up a permanent Commission — the Catering Wages Commission — with powers to examine, on its own initiative or at the request of a Minister, matters affecting among other things the pay and conditions of employment and the health and welfare of workers in the industry. Where voluntary wage-fixing machinery was found not to exist, or not to be adequate or capable of sufficient improvement, the Commission could recommend the establishment of Wages Boards.

Catering Wages Boards were set up in five different areas of the industry although one never became effective. The establishment of these Boards anticipated certain major changes in the system of statutory wage-fixing which were embodied in the Wages Councils Act 1945. The catering Boards themselves were converted into wages councils under the Terms and Conditions of Employment Act 1959.

The Wages Councils Act 1945

Elsewhere in industry, the number of Trade Boards was increased in the second half of the 1930s, but this expansion of the system was not generally sustained during the war years. At the end of the war, a fear that the rather fragile voluntary negotiating machinery in some industries would be threatened by a possible return to high levels of unemployment and strong downward pressure on wages, led to the passing of the Wages Councils Act 1945. The provisions of this Act were amended several times from 1959 onwards: the original provisions, however, still largely remain in force and are consolidated, as amended, in the Wages Councils Act 1979. (The structure and operation of wages councils is described in chapter three.)

Under the 1945 Act new criteria for establishing and abolishing Wages Councils were laid down. Wages Councils were given the power to fix statutory minimum weekly remuneration rather than just minimum rates of pay. They were also given augmented powers to fix holidays with pay.

Another major change was that wages councils were able to cover any workers described in Wages Orders, and their employers, and were not restricted to specified trades. Finally the term 'Trade Boards' was dropped to remove association with the old concept of 'sweated trades'.

The immediate effect of the Act was the establishment, after inquiries, of wages councils in nine retailing sectors and in hairdressing. In 1947 the system reached its peak with 69 councils and boards (including those operating in agriculture, road haulage and catering) covering over four million workers. The number of councils stood at 34, plus two Agricultural Wages Boards, at the end of 1979. The councils are listed in Appendix 8. Amendments contained in the Industrial Relations Act 1971 and the Employment Protection Act 1975 eased the process of abolition.

The Employment Protection Act 1975 also enabled the Secretary of State for Employment to set up Statutory Joint Industrial Councils (see Chapter 3), designed to be a half-way house between the full statutory protection offered by a wages council and the entirely voluntary machinery of collective bargaining. None, however, has yet been created.

Hours of work

Since the early nineteenth century there has been statutory restriction of the hours of work of certain classes of workers in certain industries; the Factories and Mines Acts provided such protection for young people and women.

Today, the Factories Act 1961 limits the normal maximum working hours of young people and women in industrial employment to 48 a week and imposes other restrictions. Similar restrictions apply, under the Shops Act 1950, to young persons working in shops. A number of Acts have also restricted hours of work in specific industries. For example, the Baking Industry (Hours of Work) Act 1954 was designed to control the night work of male bakery workers and the Hours of Employment (Conventions) Act 1936 restricted the hours of everyone in automatic sheet-glass works. Both Acts are still in force. However, under the Sex Discrimination Act 1975 the Equal Opportunities Commission was given the job of reviewing sex-based health and safety legislation, including the various Acts on hours of work. Its report[18] to the Secretary of State has been passed to the Health and Safety Commission for that body's views.

Health and safety

Prior to 1974 health and safety legislation laid down detailed requirements designed to deal with particular hazards in particular types of workplace, new requirements being added as new needs became apparent. The resulting legislation, although complex, was not comprehensive, and parliamentary concern at this situation led to the appointment, in 1970, of a Royal Commission under Lord Robens, to review the provision made for the safety and health of persons at work and to consider the need for change. The recommendations of the Robens Committee[19] formed the basis of the Health and Safety at Work, etc Act 1974.

The 1974 Act placed a positive emphasis on the need for joint involvement of employers and employees in the development of health and safety policies and in efforts to reduce risks. It set up the Health and Safety Commission and the Health and Safety Executive (see page 63); extended the protection of the law to some 8 million workers who were not previously covered by health and safety legislation; brought protection to members of the public whose health and safety might be affected by the activities of people at work; and placed statutory general duties on all whose actions might create or aggravate risks at the workplace — employers, the self-employed, owners and occupiers of premises, manufacturers and suppliers of articles and substances for use at work, and employees themselves. In addition, it included enabling powers for regulations to be made providing for the appointment of safety representatives by trade unions, and for safety committees (see page 88); considerably increased the powers of the enforcing authorities to deal with dangerous situations and to secure compliance with the law; and provided the means for the progressive replacement of the existing legislation by a system of regulations, approved codes of practice and other guidance.

INDIVIDUAL RIGHTS IN EMPLOYMENT

With the exception of the Truck Acts and health and safety legislation, state intervention in the contractual relationship between the employer and individual employee to establish certain basic individual rights in employment is fairly recent. The main series of Truck Acts — designed to eliminate malpractices in the method of payment of workers, particularly the payment of inferior goods in lieu of money — began in 1831, but precursors of the legislation go back to the Middle Ages. Recent legislation in the field of individual rights began in 1963 with the Contracts of Employment Act which specified minimum periods of notice and required employers, in most circumstances, to issue employees with, or draw their attention to, written details of certain terms of their employment.

It was followed, two years later, by the Redundancy Payments Act 1965 which laid down certain minimum levels of compensation for employees made redundant. In 1968 the Race Relations Act prohibited discrimination in employment on racial grounds, and this was reaffirmed and strengthened by a subsequent Race Relations Act in 1976.

The Equal Pay Act 1970 (subsequently amended by the Sex Discrimination Act 1975) established the right of women to equal treatment in respect of all terms of their contracts of employment. The Sex Discrimination Act 1975 made unlawful both direct and indirect discrimination on grounds of sex or marital status.

The Industrial Relations Act 1971 incorporated a number of the recommendations on individual employee rights contained in the Donovan Report of 1968 (see chapter 1), notably those concerned with protection against unfair dismissal, and although the 1971 Act was repealed in 1974 the sections on individual rights were retained and extended in the Trade Union and Labour Relations Act 1974 and in the Employment Protection Act 1975.

In 1978 the Employment Protection (Consolidation) Act drew together the bulk of the existing law on individual employee rights. The Employment Act 1980 has amended several of these rights, and added new rights covering unreasonable exclusion from trade union membership and time off for ante-natal care.

INCOMES POLICY

Since the end of the Second World War recurrent periods of inflation have led successive governments to intervene in collective bargaining in an attempt to control the levels of wage increases. Since 1965 these efforts have been virtually continuous, and a number of different approaches have been tried, but none has been successful in restraining wage increases for more than relatively short periods.

The first attempt was made by the Labour Government in 1948, following an economic crisis during the summer of 1947, with a White Paper entitled *Personal Incomes, Costs and Prices*,[20] which argued that no general increase in money incomes was justified except in areas of labour shortage. The TUC was initially critical but eventually gave the policy its qualified approval. The next year the government secured from the TUC a commitment, with certain qualifications, to a year's wage freeze, but this was rejected by many individual unions and by the 1949 Congress, which voted for an end to wage restraint. The policy ceased to have effect during 1950.

There were occasional appeals for pay restraint during the 1950s but the next major initiative was in 1961, after a period of economic difficulty led the Conservative Government to announce a 'pause' in public sector pay increases. This was followed by a White Paper[21] in 1962 which set a 'guiding light' for average pay increases in the economy as a whole of $2-2\frac{1}{2}$ per cent. A National Incomes Commission was set up to interpret the policy and to review wage claims and settlements. However, the Commission had limited authority and the policy was not supported by the TUC even when the 'guiding light' was revised upwards to $3-3\frac{1}{2}$ per cent in 1963, following a report[22] of the newly formed National Economic Development Council, on which the TUC was represented.

The Labour administration which came to office in October 1964 abolished the National Incomes Commission. Instead, it secured a tripartite 'Declaration of Intent on Prices, Productivity and Incomes'[23] which sought to keep pay increases in line with increases in national output. This was followed in February and April 1965 by two White Papers[24,25] which, to meet the Decla-

35

ration's targets, proposed a 'norm' for pay increases — initially of between 3 and 3½ per cent — with scope for exceptions to reward increased productivity, to secure a necessary change in the distribution of manpower, to remedy low pay, or to correct pay anomalies. A National Board for Prices and Incomes (NBPI) was established to inquire into particular cases referred to it by the government. (A summary of its work, and a list of its reports, is given in its final report.[26]) Restrictions were also proposed for price increases.

Pay increases continued to be higher than the 'norm', and in September 1965 the government announced its intention of introducing compulsory notification of pay and price increases. Although this was not implemented for another year it led the TUC to set up its own voluntary 'early warning system' to monitor pay claims.

Further economic problems in the early months of 1966 led the government to impose in July, for the first time, statutory controls on incomes: a six-month freeze on prices and incomes (subject to certain exceptions) followed by another six months of 'severe restraint'. A Prices and Incomes Act of August 1966 gave legal force to the freeze, gave the NBPI statutory status and made the early warning system compulsory. A White Paper[27] in November outlined the policy for the period of severe restraint. The general standstill was maintained but exceptional pay increases were allowed on the same grounds as those specified in the 1965 White Papers. Over the next three years the policy was gradually relaxed through two more statutory phases introduced by White Papers in early 1967 and early 1968.[28,29]

The emphasis on justifying pay increases on the grounds already laid down remained, with increasing stress being laid on agreements to improve productivity and efficiency. During this period the TUC continued to operate its voluntary early warning system, though it was calling for the repeal of the Prices and Incomes Act from its September 1967 Congress onwards. In January 1970 the statutory controls were lifted though negotiators were urged to restrict settlements to between 2½ and 4½ per cent, subject to the, by now, well-established exceptions, or where a settlement incorporated moves towards equal pay.

In 1970 the incoming Conservative Government abolished the NBPI, and for a time it had no formal incomes policy. In 1971, however, it began to try to control public sector pay increases by a policy of progressive reduction of 1 per cent (the n–1 principle) in the size of successive pay settlements, an example which it was hoped would be followed by private sector employers. The policy led to a number of major disputes amongst manual workers in the public sector — the local authorities, electricity supply, the Post Office, the mining industry and the railways — most of which were settled by recourse to courts or committees of inquiry. The settlements, although reflecting those already reached in the private sector, were not at the levels intended by the policy.

In the second half of 1972 the government held a series of talks with the TUC and CBI in an attempt to produce an agreed policy. When these failed, the government introduced, in November, a statutory policy by the Counter-Inflation Act 1972. The policy came to consist of three stages, progressively less restrictive. Stage One was a five-month freeze on pay, prices, rents and dividends. Stage Two ran from April to November 1973 and permitted increases of £1 plus 4 per cent up to a maximum of £250 per annum for any individual worker. The only exceptions permitted were for moves towards equal pay for women, or where agreements had been reached before the freeze for subsequent application. Stage Three, which lasted from November 1973 until the machinery was dismantled in July 1974, permitted increases of 7 per cent on a total wage bill or, alternatively, £2.25 per worker per week, up to a maximum of £350 per annum. An extra 1 per cent was allowed for such measures as the adjustment of internal anomalies within a pay structure, and exceptional increases could be given on such grounds as moves towards equal pay, the implementation of proven 'efficiency' schemes, the working of unsocial hours, and to correct major anomalies which had occurred as a result of the freeze. There was provision for 'threshold' payments if the Retail Price Index increased by over 7 per cent.

The Counter-Inflation Act 1973 established machinery to operate the policy — a Pay Board and a Price Commission — and outlined detailed and precise codes for the regulation of pay and prices. Pay settlements and efficiency agreements covering over 1000 workers had to be approved by the Pay Board; settlements involving smaller numbers of workers had to be notified.

In November 1973 the National Union of Mineworkers imposed an overtime ban in support of a pay claim which, it appeared, could not be accommodated within Stage Three of the policy. The overtime ban became an all-out strike in February 1974, and led to emergency measures, a three-day working week in much of the economy, and a general election. The dispute was settled by the incoming Labour Government by treating the miners as a special case.

The Labour Government abolished the Pay Board in July 1974, but retained the Price Commission. For twelve months, to July 1975, no formal pay policy operated, but as part of the 'Social Contract' between the government and the trade unions (see chapter 1) the TUC issued guidelines to negotiators. These urged negotiators to concentrate on maintaining, rather than trying to increase, real incomes, to observe a twelve-month gap between settlements in general, and to give priority to helping the low paid, for whom a target minimum wage of £30 a week was set.

By the summer of 1975, accelerating pay and price inflation led the TUC to propose a revised policy, limiting pay increases to a flat-rate £6 a week, with no increases for the more highly paid, and maintaining the twelve-month gap between settlements. These proposals were endorsed almost completely by the government in a White Paper *The Attack on Inflation*[30] issued in July. The TUC undertook actively to oppose claims and settlements in breach of the policy and the government enforced the limits in public sector pay settlements, and applied pressure to the private sector through the power of the Price Commission to reject applications for price increases, and by making government grants and contracts dependent on observance of the pay limits.

The policy lasted for a year. From August 1976 it was followed by another, again based on TUC proposals endorsed by the government in a White Paper[31] maintaining the principle of a twelve-month gap between settlements, but modifying the flat rate principle by setting a general limit of 5 per cent, with a maximum of £4 a week and allowing the low paid increases of up to £2.50. However, in September 1976 the TUC Congress, while supporting this second year of pay policy, called for a return to 'free collective bargaining' from August 1977.

TUC support for a third year of formal pay policy was not forthcoming. The government, however, took the view that further restraint was necessary, and issued a further White Paper[32] in July 1977, urging negotiators to conclude settlements which would give a national earnings increase of no more than 10 per cent, though allowing higher increases where negotiators could devise self-financing productivity schemes. The September Congress reaffirmed TUC opposition to continuing restraint, though it did support a continuing twelve-month gap between settlements.

In July 1978, in a further White Paper[33] the government set out its policy for a fourth year, limiting increases to 5 per cent, though with exceptions for the lowest paid, self-financing productivity schemes, and a very few 'severe anomalies'. The policy was rejected at the September Congress. There was a series of major industrial disputes in both the public and private sectors, with a number of settlements well above the policy limits. In an attempt to resolve disputes involving manual workers employed by local authorities and in the Health Service, the government established in March 1979 a Standing Commission on Pay Comparability, to examine the possibility of establishing appropriate comparison with the pay of workers in the private sector. In February 1979 the government and the TUC published a Joint Statement — *The Economy, the Government, and Trade Union Responsibilities*[34] — which placed no limiting figure on pay increases but expressed a joint commitment to reducing the rate of inflation to the level of that of overseas competitors over the following three years. The policy came to an end with the General Election in May 1979 and the return of a Conservative Government.

Chapter 3
British institutions

3.1 VOLUNTARY BODIES

TRADE UNIONS

Trade unions are organisations of workers set up to improve the status, pay and conditions of employment of their members. The Trade Union and Labour Relations Act 1974 (TULRA) defines a trade union at law, and any organisation which fits this definition may apply to have its name included in the statutory list of trade unions which is maintained by the Certification Officer (see page 58). Entry on the list is an essential preliminary to applying for a certificate of independence, and also entitles trade unions to tax relief for expenditure on provident benefits.

At the end of 1979 there were 477 trade unions on the Certification Officer's list. In addition the Certification Officer knew of about 85 others which, though unlisted, probably satisfied the statutory definition of a trade union. Of the listed unions, 306 had applied for and been granted a Certificate of Independence.

Between 1975 and 1977 the number of listed trade unions increased, largely because of the decisions of already established organisations — including some professional bodies, staff associations and regionally based trade unions — to seek the advantages that listing confers, often as a preliminary to applying for a Certificate of Independence. The long-term trend has been in the direction of a reduction in the number of unions. In 1938 there were 1024, in 1958, 660 and in 1968, 586.

Any classification of British trade unions is difficult since the long and complex evolution of the present structure of organisation has led to a number of exceptions to every generalisation. The most commonly used classification, however, is into 'general', 'craft', 'industrial', and 'white-collar' unions.

(i) General unions do not restrict their membership to workers in any one industry or occupation or to those possessing specific skills. In practice this is true of the majority of major trade unions, although few set out to recruit on this basis. The largest general unions are the Transport and General Workers' Union (TGWU) and the National Union of General and Municipal Workers (GMWU).

(ii) Craft unions are based on the possession of specific skills, usually associated with the serving of an apprenticeship. Some medium-sized and small unions still restrict entry to skilled craftsmen and apprentices as was common practice in the nineteenth century. A number of the larger unions have a strong craft tradition, for instance the Amalgamated Union of Engineering Workers (AUEW), the Electrical, Electronic, Telecommunication and Plumbing Union (EETPU), and the Union of Construction, Allied Trades and Technicians (UCATT).

(iii) Industrial unions restrict their membership to a single industry and aim to recruit all or most grades of workers within it. The National Union of Mineworkers (NUM) comes nearest to the model of an industrial union; but even in mining, certain supervisory workers and management staff have their own (respective) unions. Other examples of industrial unions are the National Union of Railwaymen (NUR) and the National Union of Agricultural and Allied Workers (NUAAW).

(iv) White-collar unions restrict their membership to clerical, administrative or professional workers. Some, such as the Association of Scientific, Technical and Managerial Staffs (ASTMS) and the Association of Professional, Executive, Clerical and Computer Staff (APEX) recruit amongst employees in many occupations and in a wide range of manufacturing and service industries. Some — such as the National Union of Journalists (NUJ) and the National Union of Teachers (NUT) — organise on an occupational basis. Others — such as the National and Local Government Officers' Association (NALGO) or the Transport Salaried Staffs' Association (TSSA)—operate in specific industries or parts of the public sector. A number of the general, craft and industrial unions also have white-collar sections.

It is apparent that few trade unions conform easily to this typology. Some unions, such as the Union of Shop, Distributive and Allied Workers (USDAW), bear little relation to any of the stereotypes. Mergers and changes in recruitment boundaries keep the pattern constantly changing. A recent development has been the recruitment of managerial and senior staff in the private sector into trade unions.

Membership of trade unions at the end of 1978, according to the Certification Officer, was approximately 13·05 million. Membership has grown steadily during the 1970s while the total labour force has remained broadly constant. Figures showing the pattern of growth throughout this century are given in Appendix 4.

Of the listed unions in 1979, about 200 were affiliated directly or indirectly to the TUC. The list records separately the constituent sections of a number of the larger unions, and if this is taken into account the number of affiliated unions stood at 112 at the end of 1978. At the end of 1978, membership of the largest 20 unions numbered over 9·9 million, as is shown in Table 1.

The pattern of membership in 1956 was rather different and is shown in Table 2.

In the last twenty-five years the largest general union (TGWU) has grown substantially, and a large public sector union, the National Union of Public Employees (NUPE), has emerged; the two main craft-based unions (AUEW and EETPU) have grown, partly through mergers; two large white-collar

Table 1 The largest 20 trade unions and their membership in 1978

	Number of members
Transport and General Workers' Union	2 072 818
Amalgamated Union of Engineering Workers	1 494 382
National Union of General and Municipal Workers	964 836
National and Local Government Officers' Association	729 405
National Union of Public Employees	712 392
Association of Scientific, Technical and Managerial Staffs	471 000
Union of Shop, Distributive and Allied Workers	462 178
Electrical, Electronic, Telecommunication and Plumbing Union	438 269
National Union of Mineworkers	371 470
Union of Construction, Allied Trades and Technicians	325 245
National Union of Teachers	293 378
Civil and Public Services Association	224 780
Confederation of Health Service Employees	215 246
Society of Graphical and Allied Trades 1975	201 665
Union of Post Office Workers	197 157
National Union of Railwaymen	171 411
Association of Professional, Executive, Clerical and Computer Staff	152 543
National Association of Schoolmasters and the Union of Women Teachers	140 701
Royal College of Nursing	134 389
Amalgamated Society of Boilermakers, Shipwrights, Blacksmiths and Structural Workers	131 099
Total	9 904 364

[Source: *Annual Report of the Certification Officer 1979; Appendix 4*]

unions have emerged, one in the public sector (NALGO) and one mainly in the private sector (ASTMS); and the two largest industrial unions (NUM, NUR) have declined in membership as employment in those industries has fallen.

Since the war, union membership has grown in many traditional areas, particularly in manufacturing and extractive industries and transport, aided by a growing number of union membership agreements and *de facto* closed shops. In addition, white-collar workers such as teachers, civil servants, workers in local government and the utilities and office staff in manufacturing industry, have been joining unions in increasing numbers, compensating for the decline in numbers of employees in areas such as mining where trade unions traditionally thrived. A large proportion of these white-collar workers are female and, together with an increasing number of female members in retailing and in manual work in public services, this has raised female mem-

Table 2 The largest 10 trade unions and their membership in 1956

	1956 (000)
Transport and General Workers' Union	1263
Amalgamated Engineering Union	861
National Union of General and Municipal Workers	799
National Union of Mineworkers	674
National Union of Railwaymen	369
Union of Shop, Distributive and Allied Workers	349
Electrical Trade Union	228
Amalgamated Society of Woodworkers	198
Union of Post Office Workers	163
Civil Service Clerical Association	149

[Source: Department of Employment]

bership of trade unions to well over 3 million, almost twice as many as in 1945. A full list of trade unions, with membership figures, is given in Appendix 6.

Trade union government

Trade unions are autonomous associations of individuals. They are governed by a mixture of lay and full-time officials variously elected and appointed.

Policy is usually determined at a conference, normally held annually, attended by elected delegates. Policy is carried out between conferences by an executive body — usually called a committee or council — which may be elected at the conference by branches, on a regional or industrial basis, or occasionally by ballot of the membership. The executive body may consist entirely of lay members, of full-time officials or of a mixture of the two.

All but the smallest unions have a full-time 'chief officer' who is usually the general secretary. He may be appointed by the executive body, by the conference, or by ballot of the members, usually until retirement. In a few unions, the chief officer and other full-time officials are elected for a limited period. The president of a union may be a lay member elected periodically or may, like the general secretary, be a full-time official. Sometimes the president, not the general secretary, is the chief officer of the union.

Below the chief officer, the national full-time officers and the national executive body, is a network of divisional, regional, district and branch officials and committees. The number of officials and the complexity of the network depend mainly on the size of the union. Branches may — as in the mining industry — be based on the workplace. More typically a branch is based on a locality and may draw its members from more than one industry. Within an individual factory or office, members of trade unions commonly elect workplace representatives, known as shop stewards in most industries or, in white-collar areas, staff representatives. Their election to office must be approved by the union, and among their duties may be the recruitment of new members, the collection of union subscriptions (when check-off facilities, where subscriptions are automatically deducted by the employer, do not exist) and generally to look after the interests of 'constituents', including local negotiations on pay and conditions. There has been an increase in the importance of plant bargaining since the last war and this has meant a greater involvement of shop stewards in negotiations over pay as well as making representations over individual grievances.

A trade union is permitted after a ballot of its members to include the furtherance of political objects among its purposes and to maintain a political fund, though any member of a trade union which maintains a political fund may opt out of contributing to it. At the end of 1978, 75 trade unions maintained political funds.

Federations

Despite the long-term trend towards a reduction in the number of trade unions, largely through mergers, there remain problems of 'multi-unionism' in many areas. The TUC has developed machinery for handling these problems, but difficulties are also overcome to some extent by the formation of federations of trade unions, both for negotiating purposes and for the provision of common services. In 1977 there were 43 federations, of which by far the largest was the Confederation of Shipbuilding and Engineering Unions (CSEU) co-ordinating the activities of 23 constituent unions in those industries (see page 132).

A federation of a rather different character is the General Federation of Trade Unions. This was originally set up in 1899 by the TUC to act as a centralised holder of strike funds for its affiliates, but in recent times its main function has been to provide educational and other services for small trade unions. At the end of 1977 it had 43 affiliates, with a total membership of slightly under half a million.

There are, in addition, some federations of unions which are not affiliated to the TUC of which the main one is the Managerial, Professional and Staff Liaison Group, which covers approximately 500 000 members.

TRADES UNION CONGRESS

Any trade union with membership in England and Wales may apply for affiliation to the central co-ordinating body of the trade union movement — the Trades Union Congress (TUC), which has been in continuous existence since 1868. The TUC is an autonomous industrial body composed of affiliated trade unions paying annual fees based on memberships.

It has no single overriding criterion of acceptability for affiliation and is broadly representative of all trade unions in terms of numbers, types of unions and industrial and occupational sectors. Affiliated unions represent about half the workforce and over ninety per cent of all union members: few unions of any size are unaffiliated. In 1978 there were 112 affiliated unions, representing 11·9 million members who sent 1172 delegates to the 110th Congress. The TUC has become a key national institution exercising a powerful and continuous influence on governments, employers, trade unions and public opinion. It has become increasingly involved in the actual administration of the industrial system, nominating representatives of the trade union movement to a great variety of public committees, councils, boards and other organisations.

Aims

The objectives of the TUC as listed in its constitution are:

'To do anything to promote the interests of all or any of its affiliated organisations or anything beneficial to the interests of past and present individual members of such organisations.

Generally to improve the economic or social conditions of workers in all parts of the world and to render them assistance whether or not such workers are employed or have ceased to be employed.

To affiliate to or subscribe to or to assist any other organisation having objects similar to those of the Congress.

To assist in the complete organisation of all workers eligible for membership of its affiliated organisations and subject as hereinafter set forth in these Rules to assist in settling disputes between the members of such organisations and their employers or between such organisations and their members or between the organisations themselves.

In pursuance of these general objects, and in accordance with particular decisions that Congress may make from time to time, Congress may do or authorise to be done all such acts and things as it considers necessary for the furtherance of those objects.'

The Constitution formerly contained, in addition, a commitment to specific policy objectives. At the 1978 Congress the Rules were amended and now provide only the 'general principles', above. Policy on specific issues is decided from year to year at Congress.

The Annual Congress

Representation at the annual Congress in September is on the basis of one delegate for every 5000 trade union members or fraction thereof. The main functions of Congress are to consider the report of the work done by the

General Council (the TUC's executive) during the previous year, to discuss motions and to elect the General Council for the coming year.

The General Council

The General Council is the executive body of Congress, transacting business in the periods between each annual Congress. It is composed of 41 members who are nominated on a trade-group basis prior to Congress but elected by the vote of Congress as a whole. Most of its work is done in committees assisted by the permanent staff of the TUC. The duties of the General Council are to keep a watch on all industrial movements and to co-ordinate industrial action; to watch all legislation affecting labour and to initiate such legislation as Congress may direct; to adjust disputes and differences between affiliated organisations; to promote common action by the trade union movement on general questions; to assist trade unions in organisation; and to enter into relations with the labour movements in other countries.

Neither Congress nor General Council can override the autonomy of the affiliated unions, and in most areas of collective bargaining the TUC has a peripheral role. But if TUC policy decisions are not, strictly speaking, binding, the affiliated unions have recognised a strong obligation to follow lines taken by Congress and by General Council. Certain standing orders do give the General Council, and Congress, disciplinary sanctions and responsibilities. These relate in the main to three areas of disputes: industrial disputes, inter-union disputes and disputes concerning individual union membership.

The General Council and disputes

In 1976 Congress approved a revision of the TUC's Rules 11, 12 and 13 and the regulations governing procedure in regard to disputes.

Rule 11 (Industrial Disputes) obliges affiliated organisations to keep the TUC General Secretary informed with regard to matters arising between them and their employers and/or between one organisation and another, including unauthorised and unconsitutional stoppages of work, in particular where such matters may involve directly or indirectly large bodies of workers. While it is TUC policy that neither General Council nor General Secretary will intervene while there is prospect of settlement by the normal machinery of negotiation, advice and assistance can be offered in suitable circumstances and moral and material support appropriately organised.

Rule 12 (Disputes between Affiliated Organisations) as revised gives the TUC considerable powers in relation to inter-union disputes — the prevention or conciliation of which has long been a major preoccupation of the TUC. The TUC first developed formal principles for handling inter-union disputes in 1924, and these were greatly extended in 1939 by the Bridlington Congress which adopted a series of recommendations designed to minimise disputes between trade unions over membership questions and to establish procedures through which the TUC would handle, and rule on, complaints by one organisation against another. Broadly designed to prevent the 'poaching' of members, these *Bridlington Principles* play an important part in preventing the proliferation of unions in situations where more than one union is capable of representing a particular grade of worker. Their existence has substantially discouraged the formation of breakaway unions and the movement of groups of workers from one union to another.

The *Principles* were supplemented in 1969 by recommendations adopted by a Special Congress held at Croydon. Amendments to Rule 12 gave the TUC considerably greater powers in respect of official and unofficial inter-union disputes. In particular, no affiliated union was to authorise a stoppage of work in pursuance of an inter-union dispute until the matter had been considered by the TUC. As a result of Bridlington and Croydon the TUC has formal responsibilities in disputes and differences over membership, recognition, demarcation and wages and conditions of employment, between member unions. Further amendments were made in 1979.

Rule 13 (Conduct of Affiliated Organisations) empowers the General Council to investigate the conduct of any affiliated union on the ground that its activities may be detrimental to the interests of the trade union movement or contrary to the declared principles or declared policy of the Congress. The General Council has the (rarely invoked) ultimate sanction of suspension from membership of the Congress until the next Annual Conference.

TUC Disputes Committees

The TUC's Disputes Principles and Procedure constitute a code of good trade union practice on the handling of inter-union disputes accepted as morally binding by the affiliated organisations.[35] Upon application by affiliated unions the General Council investigates a dispute or disagreement between such unions and, if conciliation has been unsuccessful, may require them to submit evidence to enable a Disputes Committee of the Council to adjudicate. A TUC Disputes Committee is composed of not less than three persons appointed by the General Secretary from the General Council or from experienced union officials. The Disputes Committee exercises a triple function — as a fact-finding commission, as a conciliating body and as a tribunal. When an award is made the unions in dispute are expected to abide by it and if they fail to do so there is the sanction of suspension. An account of all inter-union disputes during the year is contained in the General Council's report to Congress.

Independent Review Committee

Since 1976 a small high-level Independent Review Committee has existed to consider appeals from individual persons who have been dismissed, or given notice of dismissal, from their jobs as a result of having been expelled from, or having been refused admission to, a trade union in a situation where trade

46

union membership is a condition of employment. Under its terms of reference the committee is enabled, after hearing both or all of the parties involved, to make such recommendations as seem to it equitable and reasonable. One criterion to which the committee is required to address itself is whether a union involved in a complaint has acted in accordance with its own rule book. The same question arises in respect of a member. Once satisfied that the rules have been observed, the committee inquires into the merits of the case presented by the union and by the complainant and reaches a finding on what it has heard. Post-hearing conciliation may be attempted. In the year ending 30 June 1978 twelve complaints were received and eight formal hearings were held, the decisions on which are quoted in an annex to the General Council's Report 1978.[36]

General Council committees

The detailed work of the General Council is carried out in committees: in standing committees made up of General Council members; in advisory committees composed of General Council members and other representatives of affiliated unions; and in industry committees, each chaired by a General Council member and including representatives of the trade unions involved in a particular industry.

Of the standing committees, the Finance and General Purposes Committee, made up of senior members of the General Council, operates as an inner cabinet and steering committee. The Economic Committee (senior General Council members) deals with general economic questions; six of its members are the TUC representatives on the National Economic Development Council. The Employment and Organisation Committee handles employment and trade union legislation, and manpower policy. There are also standing committees on education, equal rights, international affairs, social insurance and industrial welfare, the nationalised industries and the public services. Representatives from affiliated unions as well as General Council members sit on these last two committees.

The industry committees have largely grown up during the 1970s, and are each concerned with the specific problems of an industry and with the promotion of liaison between the industry's trade unions. They do become involved, on occasion, in the actual collective bargaining process.

Administration

The General Secretary of the TUC is responsible for the day-to-day work of the organisation. He is elected by Congress and normally remains in office until retirement. By virtue of office the General Secretary is a (non-voting) member of the General Council and sits on key committees. Assisted by a deputy general secretary and two assistant general secretaries he supervises and co-ordinates the work of departments and appoints the staff, who number about 120 at the Congress House headquarters in London and about 25 in Regions.

There are five main departments — economic, education, international, organisation and industrial relations, and social insurance and industrial welfare — which, in addition to servicing the various committees, are at the general service of the affiliated organisations. The Education Department provides a wide range of training courses and other educational services for trade union members, workplace representatives and full-time officials, and carried out a comprehensive review of trade union education in 1975.[37]

Regional and other machinery

The TUC Regional machinery consists of eight Regional Councils, the Wales Trade Union Council, 435 Trades Councils and 53 County Associations of Trades Councils. These bodies co-ordinate trade union activities, give effect to and disseminate policies adopted by the TUC and nominate representatives to serve on a variety of bodies. The Trades Councils are the TUC's local co-ordinating agencies and although registered with the TUC and functioning under its auspices and model rules they do not affiliate. It is a condition of TUC recognition that they affiliate to, and play an active part in the work of, the appropriate County Association of Trades Councils.

Scottish Trades Union Congress

The national central body of trade unionism in Scotland is the Scottish Trades Union Congress (STUC), in many respects similar in constitution and functions to the TUC. The STUC takes into affiliation not only unions with a membership confined to Scotland but also national (British) unions which affiliate in respect of their membership in Scotland. Unlike the TUC the STUC has Trades Councils in affiliation. In 1978 the 81st congress of the STUC announced 80 union affiliates, with 1 033 900 members in Scotland.

The annual congress elects a General Council and defines policy on economic and social issues, especially those affecting employment and welfare in Scotland.

EMPLOYERS' ASSOCIATIONS

Although the term employers' association is used colloquially to include bodies which are solely trade associations, in law the term is restricted to organisations of employers in individual industries who have as one of their main functions a direct concern with industrial relations, and the term is used in this sense throughout this Handbook. (For the full statutory definition see chapter 5.) Employers' associations commonly negotiate with trade unions at industry level — through joint industrial councils or wages councils, etc, — provide machinery for the resolution of disputes, and give advice and assistance to their members on a range of employment and manpower matters. A few associations offer financial support to members affected by industrial action. Most employers' associations are also trade associations and a large proportion of their members join for the technical and commercial benefits this provides.

An employers' association is usually governed by an elected committee or council, usually drawn mainly from the major firms in membership. Where member firms vary greatly in size it is often difficult to ensure the election of an executive body that is fully representative of the industry, and co-option of members is a common practice. In the large associations the various areas of activity are handled by sub-committees.

Most large and medium-sized associations appoint full-time officials. Smaller organisations sometimes employ the services of firms of chartered accountants or solicitors. National associations, as well as their federations, often have a network of regional, district or local associations, though this depends on the size and structure of the industry.

The Trade Union and Labour Relations Act 1974 (TULRA) defines an employers' association for the purposes of the legislation and any organisation which fits this definition may apply to have its name included in the statutory list of employers' associations which is maintained by the Certification Officer (see page 58). At the end of 1979 there were 191 listed employers' associations.

Listing confers no practical advantages on employers' associations, and there are thought to be about a further 260 unlisted associations. Many associations represent very small sectors of an industry and their numbers are tending to be reduced by merger and dissolution. In manufacturing industry, probably over 75 per cent of establishments employing over 50 workers are members of employers' associations. Appendix 7 contains both the listed and unlisted employers' associations known to the Certification Officer.

By far the largest organisation in terms of the number of workers employed by its members is in fact a confederation of local associations, the Engineering Employers' Federation, and so is the next largest, the National Federation of Building Trades Employers. Both function much as national associations in industry-level negotiations, but their local associations enjoy a greater degree of autonomy in other matters than do local branches of national associations.

CONFEDERATION OF BRITISH INDUSTRY

The Confederation of British Industry (CBI) is the major organisation of British employers. As their principal spokesman for industry and commerce it is the employer counterpart of the TUC. It is an independent body financed by its members in industry and commerce.

The CBI was formed in 1965 by an amalgamation of three existing organisation. The Federation of British Industries (FBI) represented predominantly larger private manufacturing companies and trade associations. The British Employers' Confederation (BEC), formerly the National Confederation of Employers' Organisations, was primarily concerned with labour questions, and had only employers' organisations in membership. The National Association of British Manufacturers (NABM), formerly the National Union of Manufacturers, represented manufacturing firms and trade associations in commercial matters, and although there was no restriction as to size, in practice the individual members tended to be small businesses. Thus the CBI inherited, and united into one national organisation, two different types of member structures and two different functions.

Aims

The fundamental aims of the CBI, as embodied in its Revised Supplemental Charter, are:

'To provide for British Industry the means of formulating, making known and influencing general policy in regard to industrial, economic, fiscal, commercial, labour, social, legal and technical questions, and to act as a national point of reference for those seeking industry's views.

To develop the contribution of British Industry to the national economy.

To encourage the efficiency and competitive power of British Industry, and to provide advice, information and services to British Industry to that end.'

In 1974 the CBI restated its objectives: they were to voice the collective views of its members; to promote and protect its members' collective interests and to help its members play their full part 'in the creation, in a free market setting, of the wealth on which national prosperity and social progress depend'.

In pursuance of these aims, the CBI seeks to represent the interests of its members at national and international levels and to assist them individually with any problems concerning the running of businesses and organisations. While maintaining political neutrality the CBI advises and consults with government on all aspects of policy affecting the interests of business. Like the TUC the CBI nominates representatives to various government and public bodies.

Membership

The CBI's membership, which is entirely corporate, includes individual firms; almost all the nationalised industries; trade associations; and employers' associations. In membership are over 4500 parent companies with between 11 000 and 12 000 subsidiaries, and well over 200 associations. The associations in membership represent some 300 000 companies. Some 12 million people are employed by companies associated with the CBI either directly, or indirectly through their trade associations. Of the associations, 110 are national employer associations and 90 trade associations; each type represents about 100 000 companies.

The membership coverage of the CBI is far greater than that of its founding components, in all three of which full membership extended only to manufacturing industries, transport and construction. In the industrial relations areas, the CBI can claim much greater coverage than the former BEC since CBI membership includes individual companies, many of which are not members of federations and where they are involved in collective bargaining conduct their own negotiations with trade unions. It also includes practically all the nationalised industries which cover at least a million-and-a-half workers. Even in the area of employers' associations the CBI has filled some of the gaps in the BEC coverage of manufacturing and includes food, clothing, footwear, timber and brewing.

Structure and organisation

The Council, which meets monthly, is the CBI's governing body and as such approves the proposals that become offical policy. It has over 400 members including representatives from employer, trade and commercial organisations, the public sector, the Regional Councils, and member companies. Council is chaired by the President — the head of CBI and its principal spokesman — and is steered by the President's Committee, an important group of leading CBI figures which advises the President on major policy issues and keeps the CBI's public position and overall strategy under review. The Council is served by some 30 Standing Committees and a wide range of working parties and study groups. Collectively the Standing Committees, serviced by Directorates, cover most aspects of CBI business and are responsible for the detailed work on policy-making. The Employment Policy Committee formulates the CBI's broad policy on industrial relations and employment and oversees the work of committees on safety, health, welfare, social security, industrial relations, international social affairs questions, and wages and conditions of employment. The Industrial Relations, Wages and Conditions Committee is composed of senior industry negotiators who use the committee to discuss common problems.

The Smaller Firms Council is a standing committee of the CBI. It co-ordinates the views of smaller firm members, defined as employers of 200 or under, who make up more than half the direct members. Although there are many more small firms outside the CBI than in direct membership many of the non-members belong to trade associations which are affiliated to the CBI. The Chairman of the Smaller Firms Council is a member of the President's Committee. At least 10% of the membership of a CBI standing committee must represent small firms — 25% in the case of the organisation's Regional Councils.

The Regional Councils are sounding boards for proposed CBI policy and a two-way channel of communication between members and CBI headquarters. There are 13, with CBI offices in the administrative regions of England and in Scotland, Wales and Northern Ireland. Members debate problems within a local context and contact is maintained with local authorities, government departments and constituency Members of Parliament.

In 1977 CBI staged its first National Conference, open to all its members. It was designed to provide a public platform for delegates from all sectors of British business to project thinking on major issues and recommend action to the Council. Further conferences were held in 1978 and 1979.

The CBI nominates employer representatives to a range of public organisations, including the National Economic Development Council and the Advisory, Conciliation and Arbitration Service. It also appoints employer representatives to industrial tribunals. It has extensive European and international affiliations and maintains an office in Brussels.

CBI Directorates

The CBI has a permanent staff of about 450 whose executive head is the Director-General, appointed by the President with the approval of Council. Ten Directorates cover the organisation's work and activities. Six are concerned with policy: Economic; Employment Affairs; Company Affairs; International; Education, Training and Technology; and Smaller Firms.

The Employment Affairs Directorate deals with all aspects of employment other than industrial training. It maintains contact with government departments and other important bodies, services the Employment Policy Committee and its related committees, disseminates information and advice through a fortnightly members' bulletin, undertakes research and handles a wide range of inquiries from member organisations.

BRITISH INSTITUTE OF MANAGEMENT

The British Institute of Management (BIM) was established in 1947 to form a central institute of professional management in the United Kingdom. In 1958 it absorbed the Institute of Industrial Administration and in 1978 received the Institution of Works Managers as an affiliate.

Until October 1976 BIM was registered as a charity. It then deregistered so that it could represent individual members — a function precluded by its former charitable status. At the same time a charitable trust — the British Institute of Management Foundation — was established to carry on BIM's professional and other activities. The two bodies together form a unified professional institute.

BIM is a company limited by guarantee. It is independent, non-political and non-profit distributing. Now the central professional institute for the practising manager, it maintains close liaison with other professional bodies and educational institutions in this country and abroad, and with government departments and agencies concerned with aspects of management.

The BIM Foundation is responsible for providing a central, comprehensive and up-to-date source of information and advice on management principles, practices and techniques. It has an important role in encouraging management education, training and development. It is managed by its own Board of Directors.

The central policy and executive authority of BIM is its Council, by which it is managed. There are 81 local branches. Staff number about 160, including advisers who are the Foundation's experts in a number of technical fields: notably management education and training, marketing, finance, personnel policies, industrial relations, physical distribution management and executive remuneration levels.

Organisations, including government departments, academic institutions and trade unions, together with individual persons associated in some way with management in industry and commerce, are eligible for membership. Total membership is about 11 200 organisations and over 64 000 individual members. It is estimated that collective subscribers cover a labour force of some $6\frac{1}{2}$ million people.

The organisation's activities include the provision of conferences and seminars, management development, in-company training and other advisory services, management education and consultancy information units and a separate advisory centre for physical distribution management. A variety of books, Management Check Lists, Information Sheets, Information Summaries, Information Notes and occasional papers has been published covering a very wide range of subjects including surveys of practices amongst companies. The subjects covered include labour turnover, employee handbooks, office efficiency, performance appraisals, management development and training, and company pension policies. The Institute also supplies members with a monthly publication — *Management Today* — and issues a quarterly Bulletin to members — *Management Review and Digest.*

THE INDUSTRIAL SOCIETY

The Society was founded by Robert Hyde as the Boys' Welfare Association. In 1918 the name was changed to the Industrial Welfare Society and in 1965 became The Industrial Society.

For over 50 years the Society concerned itself with human problems in industry, particularly those in the field of industrial welfare. Over the last 15 years, as the problems of industry have changed, the Society has concentrated on those subjects which it considers contribute most both to making working lives more worthwhile and increasing efficiency and profitability — that is, effective leadership, productive management-union relations and participation, practical communication and consultation, relevant conditions of employment and working environment and the development of young people.

53

The Society is an independent organisation whose 15 500 member organisations include industrial and commercial companies, trade unions, nationalised industries, central and local government departments and employers' associations. Membership provides companies with an information service which deals with all types of inquiries including legal and medical matters, numerous practical courses and conferences and a company advisory service on man-management and industrial relations. The Society has issued a range of booklets on its specialist fields including the Notes for Managers series, guides to employment legislation, and a number of surveys of company practice. It publishes a bi-monthly journal — *Industrial Society*.

The Society's Council is made up of 60 of the leaders of manufacturing industry, commerce, government and trade unions. The organisation is entirely self-financing, mainly from services to members.

INSTITUTE OF DIRECTORS

The Institute of Directors, founded in 1903 and incorporated by Royal Charter in 1906, is the representative body for some 23 000 business leaders in Britain and 7000 overseas. Full members hold directorships in bodies corporate: non-directors may be accepted into associate membership. Members sit on the boards of almost 90 per cent of the country's largest companies, including nationalised industries. There is no corporate membership.

The aims of the Institute are to provide general and personal services for directors, to promote their personal efficiency in the boardroom, to speak for them to government and the public and generally to represent their needs and their responsibilities in relation to those of the economy and the country. The principal spokesman is the Director-General, responsible also for national and international organisation and development. The work of the Institute is supported by 26 regional branches, seven overseas branches, and the Institute of Directors in Australia.

The Institute's Industrial Relations Advisory Service is used by small companies which do not have an industrial relations department. The service gives guidance on employment legislation and general industrial questions.

A wide range of courses, conferences and study groups provides coverage of all aspects of business practice and boardroom procedure including corporate and financial planning.

The Institute's monthly journal is the *Director*.

INSTITUTE OF PERSONNEL MANAGEMENT

The Institute of Personnel Management (IPM), founded in 1913, is the professional personnel management organisation in Great Britain. It is an independent non-political organisation which has, as its prime objective, the development of comprehensive professional knowledge and competence in personnel management.

In pursuit of its overall objective, the Institute aims:

to provide an association of professional standing for its members through which the widest possible exhange of knowledge and experience can take place;

to develop a continuously evolving professional body of knowledge in response to changing demands and conditions;

to develop and maintain professional standards of competence;

to encourage investigation and research in the field of personnel management and the subjects related to it;

to present a national viewpoint on personnel management and to establish and develop links with other bodies, both national and international, concerned with personnel.

The Institute keeps in touch, both centrally and through individual members, with government departments, employers' associations, trade unions and other national organisations for the purpose of obtaining and giving information and advice on matters related to personnel management. It organises conferences and courses, and operates an appointments service for both individual members and organisations.

The Institute is a registered charity, governed by an elected Council drawn from the membership. It has more than 20 000 individual members working in almost every kind of industrial, commercial and administrative private and public sector organisation in Great Britain. It is self-supporting, mainly from entrance fees and subscriptions, but also from fees for various activities. Membership, which is graded, is open to persons engaged or under training in the field of personnel management, subject to academic and/or practical qualifications and experience.

The Institute's library and information department offers guidance to members in all aspects of personnel management policy and practice and contains a wide range of books, pamphlets and company documents on the personnel function. The Institute initiates research and prepares and distributes a variety of reports and surveys covering topics within the field of personnel management.

The Institute publications include the magazines *Personnel Management* and *IPM Digest*, appearing monthly, and the quarterly *Personnel Review* as well as a wide range of books on management topics generally and personnel management in particular.

The Institute collaborates with educational establishments on education and training for personnel management. As the examining body of the profession it is responsible for maintaining standards of teaching and for setting and approving examinations.

3.2 GOVERNMENT AND STATUTORY ORGANISATIONS

DEPARTMENT OF EMPLOYMENT

The operations of the Department of Employment (DE) cover England, Wales and Scotland but not Northern Ireland. Overall responsibility for the wide range of matters covered by the DE is borne by the Secretary of State for Employment, a Cabinet Minister, who divides specific responsibilities among a Minister of State and two joint Parliamentary Under Secretaries of State. The Civil Service staff is headed by a Permanent Secretary responsible to the Secretary of State for the overall efficiency of the Department.

The present Department has had a number of forerunners, several of which are mentioned in the historical sections of this Handbook. The original Ministry of Labour was set up in 1916. It took over from the Board of Trade responsibility for the Labour Exchanges and renamed them Employment Exchanges. The functions of the Exchanges were to bring together employers and unemployed workers and to administer Unemployment Insurance. In 1939 it became Ministry of Labour and National Service, with the added responsibility of mobilising manpower for the war effort. In 1959 it was renamed the Ministry of Labour when National Service call-up ended, became the Department of Employment and Productivity in 1968 with additional responsibilities for productivity, prices and incomes, and in 1970 acquired its present title.

In 1973 and 1974 a number of parts of the Department were 'hived off' as separate organisations — the Advisory, Conciliation and Arbitration Service (ACAS), the Manpower Services Commission (MSC) and the Health and Safety Commission (HSC). Each is described elsewhere in this chapter.

The Department has a number of general responsibilities — for national and regional manpower policy, for the promotion of equal employment opportunity, and for the payment of unemployment benefit and supplementary benefit to people in the employment field. In the industrial relations area, it has specific responsibilities for Wages Councils (see page 64), industrial tribunals and the Employment Appeal Tribunal (see pages 60–1), Courts of Inquiry (see page 82) and the administration of most employment legislation.

These responsibilities are carried out by a staff of about 23 000, divided between a headquarters in London and a network of some 1000 regional and local offices. These offices are mainly concerned with the payment of unemployment benefit, though they also handle various payments to employers and employees under the Employment Protection (Consolidation) Act 1978, and carry out a number of other functions.

As part of its work the Department collects a variety of labour statistics. These include statistics on stoppages of work, earnings, unemployment and retail prices which are published monthly in the *Department of Employment*

Gazette,[38] a *New Earnings Survey*[39] and a *Census of Employment*[40] which are conducted and published annually, and the annual *Time Rates of Wages and Hours of Work*.[41] All the main statistics are brought together in an annual *Year Book of British Labour Statistics*.[42]

ADVISORY, CONCILIATION AND ARBITRATION SERVICE

This independent service was established on an administrative basis as the Conciliation and Arbitration Service in September 1974, became known as the Advisory, Conciliation and Arbitration Service (ACAS) in January 1975 and was established as a statutory body on 1 January 1976 under the Employment Protection Act 1975. It is charged by the Act with the general duty of promoting the improvement of industrial relations, and in particular of encouraging the extension of collective bargaining and the development and, where necessary, reform of collective bargaining machinery.

Although ACAS took over a number of industrial relations services previously provided by the Department of Employment, and for administrative purposes remains part of the DE Group, the essential break with the past was its independence from Government. With certain exceptions such as the appointment of members of its Council and presentation of its accounts, the Act lays down that 'the Service shall not be subject to directions of any kind from any Minister of the Crown as to the manner in which it is to exercise any of its functions under any enactment'.

ACAS is governed by a Council consisting of a full-time chairman and nine other members all appointed by the Secretary of State for Employment. All the members have extensive experience of industrial relations. Three members are appointed after consultation with the CBI and three after consultation with the TUC. Additional members may also be appointed by the Secretary of State.

The Service is empowered to undertake a range of activities. It may inquire into any industrial relations matter, provide advice on industrial relations and the development of effective personnel practices, and issue codes of practice containing practical guidance on the improvement of industrial relations. It may help to resolve industrial disputes through conciliation, or through providing facilities for arbitration, mediation or committees of investigation and offer conciliation in disputes over statutory employment rights between individual employees and their employers. It is required to carry out inquiries into wages councils if requested to do so by the Secretary of State for Employment (see below) and also had to examine applications for trade union recognition under the statutory recognition procedure described in chapter 1 until its repeal by the Employment Act 1980.

Advice on industrial relations and personnel practices is given in a number of ways: by answering queries on the operation of employment legislation, by short advisory visits, by in-depth assistance either to advise on a particular project or programme of work or to diagnose the causes of more deep-seated problems and make recommendations for action or to work with managements and unions jointly, and by helping to organise seminars and courses.

The services offered in the voluntary resolution of industrial disputes are described in chapter five. Conciliation can be offered either at the request of one or more of the parties or on ACAS initiative. Mediation can be undertaken either by an independent person appointed by ACAS or by an *ad hoc* board specially appointed to deal with the dispute, usually with a chairman and one representative each of workers and employers. Arbitration can also be undertaken by an independent person or *ad hoc* board, but the standing arbitration body is the Central Arbitration Committee, which is described below. Committees of investigation or inquiry are relatively rare; their reports are published.

Individual conciliation is provided in cases where individuals consider that their rights in employment legislation have been infringed. They are entitled to complain to an industrial tribunal, but ACAS conciliation officers are required to try to settle the complaint without the need for a tribunal hearing.

ACAS has about 730 staff, of whom about 130 work in the Head Office in London which, amongst other duties, provides conciliation in the major industrial disputes. The remainder are in nine regional offices carrying out the bulk of the day-to-day work — seven in England, one in Scotland and one in Wales. Although independent, ACAS is a Crown body and its staff have the status of civil servants. It publishes an annual report.[43]

CERTIFICATION OFFICE

The Certification Office was established in February 1976. Under the Trade Union and Labour Relations Act 1974 and the Employment Protection Act 1975, the Certification Officer is responsible for:

maintaining lists of trade unions and employers' associations;

determining the independence of trade unions;

seeing that trade unions and employers' associations keep accounting records, have their accounts properly audited and submit annual returns;

ensuring the periodical examination of members' superannuation schemes;

securing observance of the statutory procedures for transfer of engagements, amalgamations and changes of name;

supervising the statutory requirements as to the setting up and operation of political funds and dealing with complaints by members about breaches of political fund rules.

Under the Employment Act 1980 the Certification Officer is, in addition, responsible for:

administering payments towards expenditure incurred by trade unions in conducting secret ballots.

The Certification Officer's staff, accommodation and finance are provied by ACAS, but in exercising his functions the Certification Officer is not subject to any direction by the Service, or by any Minister of the Crown. He publishes an annual report.[44]

CENTRAL ARBITRATION COMMITTEE

The Central Arbitration Committee (CAC) was established by the Employment Protection Act 1975 and brought into operation in February 1976. It replaced the Industrial Arbitration Board which itself had replaced the Industrial Court in 1971. The provision of a standing national arbitration body in the field of industrial relations thus dates back to the Industrial Courts Act 1919.

The constitution and proceedings of the CAC are set out in Schedule 1 of the Employment Protection Act 1975. It provides for the Secretary of State for Employment to appoint a Chairman, Deputy Chairmen and Members, the last-named having experience as representatives of employers or workers. The Committee has wide discretion to determine its own procedure but, except at informal hearings, a Chairman, and a Member from each side of industry will normally hear a case. There is power to appoint assessors in addition to the normal Committee. The Chairman has powers of umpire. Decisions of the Committee in the exercise of its statutory functions are published in the form of an award which includes the considerations taken into account in reaching that decision.

The CAC provides both voluntary and unilateral arbitration. The power to provide voluntary arbitration derives initially from the Industrial Courts Act 1919 and is now contained in section 3 of the Employment Protection Act 1975 which enables references to be made to the CAC by ACAS. The CAC is also specified as the final stage in the industrial disputes procedure of a number of organisations.

The Committee provides statutory, unilateral arbitration under the Employment Protection Act 1975 on disclosure of information. It also provided such arbitration on the extension of terms and conditions under Schedule 11 and on trade union recognition until the repeal of these two provisions by the Employment Act 1980. The Committee also determines references made under the Equal Pay Act 1970 and several Acts, such as the Independent Broadcasting Act 1973, which contain a Fair Wages type clause. In its capacity as an independent tribunal it advises the Secretary of State for Employment on questions raised under the Fair Wages Resolution 1946.

CAC, whose headquarters is in London, is independent of government although staffed by civil servants. It submits an annual report of its activities[45] to the Chairman of ACAS for transmission to the Secretary of State for Employment.

INDUSTRIAL TRIBUNALS

Industrial tribunals are independent judicial bodies, each having a legally qualified chairman appointed by the Lord Chancellor in England and Wales, and in Scotland by the Lord President. Each tribunal has two other members drawn from two panels of members appointed by the Secretary of State for Employment after consultation with employees' and employers' organisations.

The administration of the industrial tribunals is carried out by two Secretariats, one for England and Wales and one for Scotland. They are based on a Central Office for England and Wales, a Central Office for Scotland, and a number of regional and other offices. They are responsible for the efficient administration of the tribunals to the President of Industrial Tribunals for England and Wales, and the President of Industrial Tribunals for Scotland, respectively.

Tribunals were originally established to hear appeals by employers against assessments of training levies under the Industrial Training Act 1964. They now have jurisdiction in a number of areas concerned with individual rights under the following legislation:

Equal Pay Act 1970

Sex Discrimination Act 1975

Employment Protection Act 1975

Race Relations Act 1976

Employment Protection (Consolidation) Act 1978

Employment Act 1980.

In most types of case coming before tribunals, copies of relevant documents are sent to an ACAS conciliation officer who is required to try to assist the parties to reach a settlement. If a conciliated settlement is not achieved, a hearing ensues at which employers and employees may present their own cases or be represented by persons of their choice. A tribunal decision may involve a monetary award which is payable by one party to the other. There is a right of appeal to the Employment Appeal Tribunal on points of law.

60

EMPLOYMENT APPEAL TRIBUNAL

The Employment Appeal Tribunal (EAT) was established under the Employment Protection Act 1975 in February 1976. It is a superior court of record, an appellate body on questions of law from industrial tribunals. Prior to its establishment, these appeals were dealt with by a Divisional Court of the Queen's Bench or, under the Industrial Relations Act 1971, by the National Industrial Relations Court. The EAT also hears appeals on questions of law or fact arising from certain proceedings before, or arising from certain decisions of, the Certification Officer, and, under the Employment Act 1980, on complaints of unreasonable exclusion from trade union membership.

The EAT consists of judges and other members. The judges are nominated both by the Lord Chancellor from among the judges of the High Court and the Lord President of the Court of Session from among the judges of that Court. The other members have experience of industrial relations, either as representatives of employers or of workers, and are appointed on the joint recommendation of the Lord Chancellor and the Secretary of State for Employment.

STANDING COMMISSION ON PAY COMPARABILITY

The Commission was appointed by the government in March 1979:

'to examine the terms and conditions of employment of particular groups of workers referred to it by the Government, in agreement with the employers and unions concerned, and to report in each case on the possibility of establishing acceptable bases of comparison, including comparisons with terms and conditions for other comparable work and of maintaining appropriate internal relativities'.

The Commission has a chairman and five other members.

In August 1980 the Conservative Government announced that the Commission would be abolished by the end of the year.

THE EQUAL OPPORTUNITIES COMMISSION

The Sex Discrimination Act 1975 established the Equal Opportunities Commission, giving it the following duties:

working towards the elimination of discrimination

promoting equality of opportunity between men and women generally

61

keeping under review the workings of the Equal Pay and Sex Discrimination Acts and putting forward proposals for change.

It is headed by a chairman, deputy chairman, and 13 part-time Commissioners appointed by the Home Secretary. The Commission operates through a series of committees and working parties set up to deal with different areas of discrimination, including an Employment Committee. Its staff number about 150 and are mostly based at its headquarters in Manchester, though there are small regional offices in London, Glasgow and Cardiff.

The Commission advises people of their rights under both Acts, and in certain circumstances can assist them to take cases to industrial tribunals, county courts, etc. The Commission can conduct formal investigations; issue non-discrimination notices enforceable in the courts; issue codes of practice in employment; and institute proceedings both in relation to advertising and in cases when there have been instructions or pressure to discriminate. It also publishes an annual report.[46]

THE COMMISSION FOR RACIAL EQUALITY

The Commission for Racial Equality was set up by the Race Relations Act 1976, replacing the Race Relations Board set up under the Race Relations Act 1965, and the Community Relations Commission created by the Race Relations Act 1968. It came into being in June 1977. It has fifteen members, including a chairman and a deputy chairman, appointed by the Home Secretary; about half are from ethnic minority communities. Its staff number some 230. Its headquarters is in London and there are regional offices in Birmingham, Manchester, Leicester and Leeds.

The task of the Commission is to work towards the elimination of discrimination and to promote equality of opportunity and good relations between different racial groups. It has similar powers and duties to the Equal Opportunities Commission (see above). Its position in relation to industrial relations is more fully described in chapter five. It provides advice to employers, trade unions and other bodies and also supports and co-ordinates the work of nearly 100 local community relations councils operating in areas with significant minority groups. The Commission publishes an annual report.[47]

MANPOWER SERVICES COMMISSION

The MSC was set up on 1 January 1974 under the Employment and Training Act 1973 to manage the public employment and training services and to take responsibility for the development and operation of a comprehensive manpower policy for Great Britain. The Commission's aims are:

to contribute to efforts to raise employment and reduce unemployment;

62

to assist manpower resources to be developed and contribute fully to economic well being

to help to secure for each worker the opportunities and services he or she needs in order to lead a satisfying working life

to improve the quality of decisions affecting manpower

to improve the effectiveness and efficiency of the Commission.

The Commission, which is separate from the government but accountable to the Secretary of State for Employment (and in respect of operations in Scotland and Wales, to the Secretaries of State for Scotland and Wales) has 10 members: a Chairman, three members appointed after consultation with the TUC, three after consultation with the CBI, two after consultation with local authority associations and one with professional educational interests. In Scotland and Wales the Commission has decentralised responsibility for the general oversight of the development and operation of manpower services to Scottish and Welsh Committees of the MSC.

The work of the Commission is carried out through three main operating divisions. The Employment Service Division operates a network of over 1000 local employment offices and Jobcentres, which provide a job information and placement service, employment advice, and a number of specialist services including occupational guidance. It also provides a professional and executive recruitment service. The Training Services Division provides support to Industrial Training Boards, encourages and helps to finance training in industry, and finances the training of individual persons in Colleges of Further Education and in Skillcentres. It also provides some training services direct to industry. The Special Programmes Division handles the government's special employment programmes, for adults and young people, which were first mounted in 1975 in response to continuing high levels of unemployment. The Commission has about 25 000 staff, and publishes an annual report.[48] The Commission is advised by nearly one hundred District Manpower Committees and thirty Special Programmes Area Boards.

HEALTH AND SAFETY COMMISSION

The Health and Safety Commission, appointed in October 1974 under the provisions of the Health and Safety at Work, etc Act 1974, is responsible to the Secretary of State for Employment for taking appropriate steps to secure the health, safety and welfare of people at work and to protect the public generally against dangers to health and safety arising from work activities. It is responsible for controlling explosive, highly flammable, radioactive or otherwise dangerous substances, and for the control of the emission into the atmosphere of noxious or offensive substances. The Commission has responsi-

63

bility for the progressive replacement of the existing legislation by a system of regulations and approved codes of practice (see page 86).

The Commission has nine members: a chairman, three members appointed after consulatation with the TUC, three after consultation with the CBI, and two after consultation with local authority associations. In formulating its policies the Commission organises widespread consultation on all aspects of health and safety, thereby providing a national forum for the discussion of health and safety. It is advised by a number of Industry Advisory Committees, as well as by experts within its own Executive. It publishes an annual report.[49]

The Health and Safety Executive is responsible for carrying out the Commission's programme of work and together with the other enforcing authorities, eg local authorities, harbour authorities, enforces the 1974 Act and other existing legislation. It brings together a number of different Inspectorates — the alkali inspectorate and inspectorates for factories, mines and quarries, explosives, agriculture and nuclear installations; has a staff of about 4000 operating through twenty-one area offices; undertakes research; provides information and advisory services; and, like the Commission, publishes an annual report.[50]

WAGES COUNCILS AND STATUTORY JOINT INDUSTRIAL COUNCILS

Wages councils are statutory bodies which operate under the terms of the Wages Councils Act 1979. The main function of a wages council is to fix statutory minimum remuneration and other terms and conditions of employment that must be observed by employers of workers covered by the council.

The legislation on wages councils is now contained in the Wages Councils Act 1979. The Act enables the Secretary of State for Employment to establish a wages council either on his own initiative or following an ACAS recommendation. He may establish a wages council on his own initiative if he considers that adequate machinery for the effective regulation of the remuneration of any group of workers does not exist and should be established, having regard to the remuneraton of the workers concerned. He is required to refer the question of establishing a wages council to ACAS if an application for a wages council is made by appropriate trade unions, employers' organisations or joint bodies, though he may also refer it to ACAS on his own initiative. ACAS can recommend that a wages council be established either when it considers that adequate machinery for the effective regulation of the remuneration of any workers does not exist, or that the existing machinery is likely to cease to exist or be adequate and a reasonable standard of remuneration will not be maintained.

A wages council may be abolished or its field of operation varied by the Secretary of State either on his own initiative or following an application by appropriate trade unions, employers' organisations or joint bodies. The application must be on the grounds that the existence of the wages council is no longer necessary to maintain a reasonable standard of remuneration for the workers concerned. Before deciding to abolish or vary the scope of a council, the Secretary of State may refer the question to ACAS for inquiry and report, after first consulting other interested bodies in the case of an application from an organisation of workers.

Wages councils are serviced by an Office of Wages Councils, located in the Department of Employment. At the end of 1979 the number of councils was 34. They are listed in Appendix 8.

The large majority of workers covered are in the retailing, hotel and catering and clothing industries.

Constitution and procedures

A wages council consists of equal numbers of members respresenting employers and members representing workers, together with a chairman and two other independent persons unconnected with either side of the industry concerned. The worker and employer representatives sit as representatives of their sides of the industry and not of particular organisations. The number of such representatives varies between councils according to the interests to be represented.

Appointments to the employers' and workers' sides of wages councils are made by organisations of employers and by trade unions nominated by the Secretary of State. The appointments are made to try to represent all major sections of the industry and workforce. If a sufficient number of suitable representatives cannot be found from these sources other members may be appointed by the Secretary of State.

A meeting of a wages council must be convened if either the workers' or the employers' side requests it. In practice, meetings are held invariably after a request from the workers' side indicating that they want to submit a motion for the improvement of wages and/or conditions laid down in the existing wages order. At the meeting the motion is formally tabled and replied to by the leader of the employers' side. The role of the independent members is to enable the sides, if possible, to produce an agreed motion; or if that is not possible, to vote with one side or the other. The majority vote then decides the proposals.

Once a motion has been passed the Secretary of State arranges that all employers covered by the council receive a note of the proposals. These must be displayed in each establishment for a stipulated period. Any objections to the proposals must be made in that time. After considering representations, the council makes an order giving legal effect to the proposals, amended if necessary. Once the order is made, notices are circulated to all the establishments in the trade where they must be posted for the workers to read throughout the life of the order.

An employer covered by a wages council is required to keep records of wages, hours and other relevant conditons of employment to show that he is complying with the appropriate wages order. The Secretary of State appoints Wages Inspectors who periodically visit employers covered by wages councils, and also act on complaints by workers that they are not receiving the minimum remuneration, holidays or other conditons due to them under the Act.

Statutory joint industrial councils

The Wages Councils Act 1979 makes provision for a wages council to be converted into a *statutory joint industrial council* (SJIC). An SJIC is similar to a wages council, but without independent members, and is intended to operate as a half-way stage between a wages council and a voluntary joint industrial council, for example, in an industry where the independent members on the wages council are not normally called upon to vote, but where organisation amongst workers and employers is not yet sufficiently developed to dispense with the enforcement services of the Wages Inspectorate. Disputes within an SJIC can be settled by compulsory arbitration at the request of either side. No SJICs have yet been formed.

3.3 RESEARCH INSTITUTIONS

In recent years there has been a substantial growth in the scale of teaching and research in industrial relations in universities, polytechnics and other institutions of higher and further education in Britain. Industrial relations (together with the related fields of industrial sociology, labour economics, labour history and industrial psychology) is not only included as a special subject in many management and business studies courses but is now increasingly studied as a separate field of inquiry. Several universities have established fully-fledged industrial relations departments with the aim of teaching the subject at postgraduate level and undertaking industrial relations research, often from an interdisciplinary viewpoint. The Social Science Research Council funds a considerable programme of postgraduate studentships at these and other institutions, including its own specially created Industrial Relations Research Unit based at the University of Warwick, and also finances a considerable programme of research.[51] Other major sources of research funding include a number of charitable and other Foundations and such bodies as the Department of Employment.[52] In recent years management and trade unions have also made a contribution to research funding, both through the endowment of teaching posts and the commissioning of particular projects.

Not only has the scale of these activities increased considerably over the past fifteen years but it is possible to see a change of emphasis in the kinds of issues explored. Increasingly researchers have sought to move away from the simple description and classification of industrial relations institutions, which marked earlier academic work, to more overtly theoretically based studies. Survey and case study methods have been extensively employed, looking particularly at issues connected with the development of industrial democracy and worker participation, aspects of trade union organisation and growth, the development and functions of workplace and industry bargaining with particular regard to their role in pay determination, and, more recently, growing interest has been expressed in monitoring the function and operation of law in employment and industrial relations processes.[53]

Results of much of this work are disseminated in book form and via learned journals such as the *British Journal of Industrial Relations* and the *Industrial Relations Journal*. A host of specialised publications more directly aimed at practitioners has also become available. The professional organisations, such as the Institute of Personnel Management, also publish journals and other material, much of which incorporates the results of academic research.

Chapter 4

International institutions

The context of collective bargaining in Britain is influenced in varying degrees by four international bodies — the European Community (EC), the International Labour Organisation (ILO), the Organisation for Economic Co-operation and Development (OECD) and the Council of Europe. The way each of these institutions operates and their different contributions to industrial relations in this country is discussed below. The chapter concludes with a discussion of international trade union groupings and international employers' organisations.

THE EUROPEAN COMMUNITY (EC)

The EC is primarily an economic organisation. Article 2 of the Treaty of Rome, which established the Community in 1957, states:

'The Community shall have as its task, by establishing a common market and progressively approximating the economic policies of Member States, to promote throughout the Community a harmonious development of economic activities, a continuous and balanced expansion, an increase in stability, an accelerated raising of the standard of living and closer relations between the States belonging to it'.

Consequently the Treaty sets out few objectives or guidelines for social policy, and apart from articles setting up the European Social Fund and relating to the free movement of workers there is virtually no provision for binding legislation in the social field. Of most relevance from an industrial relations viewpoint are Article 117, which expresses the belief that the proper functioning of the common market will led to the harmonisation of social systems; and Article 118, which stipulates that 'the Commission shall have the task of promoting close co-operation between Member States in the social field, particularly in matters relating to employment, labour law and working conditions, . . . the right of association and collective bargaining between employers and workers. . .'

By 1972 the lack of progress in the social field led the Heads of Governments of Member States to the conclusion that more needed to be done to present the 'human face' of the Community. A social action programme was conceived, for implementation between 1974 and 1976. It called for action to achieve full and better employment, improvement in living and working conditions, greater involvement of management and labour in Community decisions, and an extension of industrial democracy. Largely as a consequence of this programme several measures with a bearing on industrial relations have been adopted.

Community law-making

The normal procedure in Community law-making is for the European Commission to prepare proposals, often after consultation with expert groups including representatives of both sides of industry, and for these proposals to go forward for consideration and adoption by the Council of Ministers of Member States. Before they reach the Council there will have been discussion in working groups composed of national officials; where the proposals envisage legally binding instruments, the opinion of the European Assembly will have been sought and also that of the Economic and Social Committee, which brings together representatives of management, unions and a range of other interests. Once adopted by the Council the proposals become Community instruments of a legally binding or non-binding nature. The two most important types of legally binding instrument are:
(i) regulations, which have direct 'internal' effect, that is, they prevail over national laws, and
(ii) directives, which Member States are obliged to implement strictly and fully but with the method of their choice.
The non-binding category of instruments includes recommendations and resolutions which, although without legal force, are nonetheless regarded as moral and political commitments.

Industrial relations

It is part of the Commission's function to ensure that implementation of regulations and directives is carried out, which it usually does by calling for reports after a specified number of years. Enforcement of Community laws is a matter for the national courts of Member States, but failure to comply with binding instruments may result in a reference to the European Court of Justice.
The three main instruments bearing on industrial relations are:
(i) Council Directive of 17 February 1975 on the approximation of the laws of Member States relating to collective redundancies.[54] This is designed for the protection of workers and sets out the procedures to be followed. It has been implemented in the UK by the provisions of the Employment Protection Act 1975 relating to consultation on proposed redundancies.
(ii) Council Directive of 14 February 1977 on the approximation of laws relating to the safeguarding of employees' rights in the event of transfers of undertakings, businesses or parts of businesses: generally known as the acquired rights directive.[55] Implementation in the UK is expected to be through the Transfer of Undertakings (Protection of Employment) Regulations (1980).

69

(iii) Council Recommendation of 22 July 1975 on the principle of the 40 hour week and four weeks' annual paid holiday.[56] The UK Government has supported the recommendation on the basis that the progressive achievement of these conditions is a matter for collective bargaining, subject to the requirements of counter-inflation policy.

Agreement has also been reached in the Council on the substance of a Directive to protect employees in the event of the insolvency of their employer.[57] Formal adoption is expected at a future meeting of the Council once consultations with Greece, which joins the EC on 1 January 1981, have been completed.

There are in addition a number of legally binding instruments in the social field, covering aspects of social security, health and safety at work, and equal treatment for men and women in pay and employment,[58] which are reflected in UK legislation.

The Commission published in 1975 a paper on industrial democracy entitled *Employee participation and company structure*[59] which has influenced debate on this subject in the UK. There have been two proposed instruments touching on industrial democracy: a Fifth Directive on Company Law,[60] which preceded the Commission's 1975 paper, and a European Companies Statute.[61] The former is still under discussion in the European Parliament and it is unlikely that a decision on either will be taken in the near future.

Within its Directorate-General for Social Affairs, the Commission has a small directorate on industrial relations and labour law which has set up 'joint sectoral committees in a number of fields, eg road and rail transport, fishing, coal and steel. These committees consist of representatives from appropriate employer and trade union organisations (there is no Government representation), whose task it is to consider social problems of the sectors concerned. So far the subjects discussed have been mainly limited to aspects of safety and health and vocational training.

There have also been attempts to set up an index of collective agreements, to provide a computerised information bank on terms and conditions of employment in major industrial sectors as a basis for the development of Community policy.

There is an accelerating trend towards European-level discussion of a wide range of social policy issues by governments, Commission and the 'social partners' (that is, unions and employers). These discussions could influence the handling of issues in industrial relations in this country.

THE INTERNATIONAL LABOUR ORGANISATION (ILO)

The ILO, with headquarters in Geneva, is an association of states in which representatives not only of Governments but also of employers' and workers' organisations participate. It was set up in 1919 under Part XIII of the Treaty of Versailles and became a specialised agency of the United Nations in 1946. It operates under the general supervision of the UN Economic and Social Council. The UK Government played a prominent part in establishing the ILO and has consistently supported it.

It has in the region of 140 member states. The aims of the ILO are set out at length in its constitution. Its fundamental aim is to promote social justice throughout the world by establishing humane conditions of labour. This aim is pursued by the adoption of international standards in the form of Conventions and Recommendations, by the issue of codes of practice, by research, by the issue of publications, through meetings of various types and by field activities and fellowships. The permanent ILO machinery consists of the International Labour Conference, the Governing Body of the International Labour Office, and the International Labour Office (the Secretariat).

The International Labour Conference

The International Labour Conference normally meets once a year. Each member state is entitled to be represented by four voting delegates, two of them representing the Government and one each employers and workers. The employers' and workers' delegates must be chosen by the Government in agreement with the most representative organisations of employers or workers, where such exist (in the UK, the CBI and TUC). The agenda of the Conference is determined by the Governing Body.

Decisions taken by the Conference may take the form of Conventions, Recommendations or Resolutions. To be adopted, Conventions and Recommendations require a majority of two-thirds of the votes cast by the delegates present. Resolutions require a simple majority.

Conventions are in effect international treaties, to which Member States become parties by the act of ratification. This, however, is entirely voluntary: what Member Governments must do is to submit all Conventions within a year, or exceptionally within eighteen months, to the authority — usually the Parliament — within whose competence the matter lies, for a decision on ratification and the enactment of any necessary legislation.

Member states are under an obligation to ensure that their national law and practice comply with the provisions of the Conventions which they ratify. They must also report periodically on the measures which they have taken to give effect to the Conventions which they have ratified. Recommendations, like Conventions, must be submitted to the competent authority for the enactment of legislation or other action, but in their case the question of ratification does not arise. They often amplify the provisions of a Convention on the same subject adopted at the same time. Resolutions embody expressions of the collective opinion of the Conference but involve no binding obligations.

The Governing Body of the International Labour Office

The Goverining Body supervises the work of the International Labour Office and appoints its Director-General. It normally meets three times a year. It is composed of 56 members, 28 of whom represent Governments, and 14 each

71

employers and workers. The United Kingdom at present holds one of ten government seats reserved for major industrial States, and the employers and workers groups have always had members from the UK.

The International Labour Office

In addition to the Organisation's HQ, there is a network of field offices, branch offices (including a London office) and correspondents throughout the world. The International Labour Office provides the secretariat and makes arrangements for ILO conferences and meetings and carries on the day-to-day work of the Organisation. It collects information, undertakes research and issues periodicals and other publications on labour questions.

Other ILO activities

From time to time regional conferences are held with the object of examining problems of common interest to member states in a particular region of the world. These conferences may pass resolutions advocating action by the countries concerned or by the ILO, but do not adopt formal standards for their region. There are Advisory Committees for each region (except Europe) to advise the Governing Body on the needs and problems of the regions.

Tripartite Industrial Committees, both permanent and *ad hoc*, consider economic and social conditions within major industries, so that the special problems of those industries can be discussed at international level. There are also meetings of committees of experts, who discuss specific subjects such as night work, or women workers.

The ILO also gives practical assistance to (mainly developing) member countries by sending expert advisers, financing training, arranging special conferences or seminars, and issuing publications.

The ILO and industrial relations

The ILO is, of course, closely concerned with the question of relations between employers and workers and between them and Governments. It has devoted particular attention to freedom of association of employers and workers in the member states, and, in particular, freedom from Government interference. The two most important Conventions in this field are Convention No 87, concerning Freedom of Association and Protection of the Right to Organise, and Convention No 98, concerning Application of the Principles of the Right to Organise and to Bargain Collectively. The first of these provides that 'workers' and employers' organisations shall have the right to draw up their constitutions and rules, to elect their representatives in full freedom, to organise their administration and activities and to formulate their programmes' and that the 'public authorities shall refrain from any interference which would restrict this right or impede the lawful exercise thereof'. Convention No 98 provides that 'workers shall enjoy adequate protection against acts of anti-union discrimination in respect of their employment' and, more particularly, that this protection shall apply in respect of acts calculated to 'make the employment of a worker subject to the conditions that he shall not join a union or shall relinquish trade union membership' or to 'cause the dismissal of or otherwise prejudice a worker by reason of union membership or because of participation in union activities'. Both these Conventions have been ratified by the United Kingdom. The Governing Body has established special machinery, known as the Committee on Freedom of Association, for the impartial investigation of allegations of infringements of freedom of association so that it may, if necessary, make recommendations to the Governments concerned, or take other appropriate action.

More recently, Conventions have been adopted on such subjects as Rural Workers' Organisations, Workers' Representatives, Human Resources Development and Tripartite Consultation on International Labour Standards, all of which the United Kingdom has ratified.

However, a number of Conventions cover matters which in the United Kingdom are normally the subject of voluntary negotiation, including hours of work, equal pay, holidays with pay, and paid educational leave. Quite apart from the question of whether the prescribed standards exist in the United Kingdom, there is a general difficulty in the way of the United Kingdom's ratifying most of such Conventions. The UK Government normally abstains from intervention in the determination of terms and conditions of employment and therefore it cannot undertake international commitments as to what should or should not be provided for in collective agreements. This difficulty does not arise where the provisions of the Conventions apply only in a field covered by statutory wage-fixing machinery, and so it has been possible to ratify, for instance, Convention No 101 concerning Holidays with Pay in Agriculture.

Probably the most important recommendations on industrial relations have been two adopted in 1951 and two adopted in 1967. The first two concern Collective Agreements (No 91) and Voluntary Conciliation and Arbitration (No 92), and lay down general principles concerning voluntary negotiating machinery and voluntary machinery for the prevention or resolution of industrial disputes. The other two concern Communications within the Undertaking (No 129), and Examination of Grievances within the Undertaking with a view to their Settlement (No 130). The first stresses the importance of effective communication between management, workers and their representatives and gives useful guidance on how this may be achieved. The second seeks to establish the right of any worker to submit a grievance without suffering any prejudice as a result and to have it examined pursuant to an appropriate procedure; the Recommendation provides a framework for the promotion of such procedures.

The ILO has also issued, in 1977, a code of practice for multinational enterprises which lays down detailed requirements for employment and training policies, pay, fringe benefits, health and safety, and industrial relations.

This complements the code issued by the Organisation for Economic Co-operation and Development (OECD) in 1976 (see page 75).

The ILO's other main influence on industrial relations is through discussions at its conferences and in committees and through its publications. Its industrial committees devote much of their time to discussing problems of industrial relations and pass their conclusions to Governments and through them to employers' and workers' organisations.

Reports prepared for study by Conferences and committees are published, as are committee reports and the records of proceedings of Conferences and of the Governing Body. International standards adopted by the Conference, and other texts relating to standards of social policy formulated by the Conferences and meetings, have been codified and published with full explanatory notes in the International Labour Code. The ILO also publishes studies and reports, many of which concern aspects of labour-management relations, and workers' education manuals. Articles on labour questions are published in the *International Labour Review*, which appears every two months. The quarterly *Social and Labour Bulletin* contains information on developments in member countries. The most important laws and regulations on labour and related matters throughout the world are published in a collection called the Legislative Series. The Office publishes annually the *Year Book of Labour Statistics*, which includes statistics on industrial disputes, wages, consumer price indices and retail prices, employment and hours of work.[62]

THE ORGANISATION FOR ECONOMIC CO-OPERATION AND DEVELOPMENT (OECD)

The OECD came into existence in 1961 as the successor to the OEEC (the Organisation for European Economic Co-operation) which had administered the Marshall Plan Aid for European recovery after the Second World War. The increasing interdependence of industrialised countries called for new arrangements for economic co-operation at international level. Present membership is 24 countries.[63] The headquarters of the Organisation is in Paris.

The OECD's aims, as set out in its Convention, cover the promotion of policies designed:

(a) 'to achieve the highest sustainable economic growth and employment and a rising standard of living in Member countries while maintaining financial stability, and thus to contribute to the development of the world economy;

(b) to contribute to sound economic expansion in Member as well as non-member countries in the process of economic development; and

(c) to contribute to the expansion of world trade on a multi-lateral, non-discriminating basis in accordance with international obligations'.

Organisation

The Council, composed of representatives of all the member states, meets regularly at Permanent Representative (ambassadorial) level and from time to time at ministerial level. It approves the Organisation's work programme and budget and considers all questions of general policy. Chairmanship at ministerial level rotates between member countries.

The Executive Committee is composed of representatives from 12 member states designated annually by the Council; other countries are free to attend discussions on matters of interest to them. It normally meets twice a week to examine questions relating to the Organisation's policy or its work, prior to submission to the Council.

Various Permanent Committees, composed of senior officials of member states' governments, carry out the Organisation's work in the fields of economic affairs and statistics; environment; development assistance; manpower and social affairs; technical co-operation; trade and related activities; agriculture and fisheries; science, technology and industry; energy. The Manpower and Social Affairs Committee considers employment and social questions. It has studied such industrial relations issues as the development of wages policies, aspects of collective bargaining, unemployment, equal opportunities, labour disputes and job security. Its published studies provide useful comparisons of practices in industrialised countries.

The OECD has granted consultative status to a few international non-governmental organisations notably its Trade Union Advisory Committee (TUAC), to which the TUC belongs, and its Business and Industry Advisory Committee (BIAC) whose membership includes the CBI.

The OECD and industrial relations

The OECD can adopt a variety of instruments to promote its aims, ranging from decisions which are legally binding to recommendations and resolutions. However, none has been adopted solely dealing with industrial relations issues. Its main influence on industrial relations is through the discussions in its Manpower and Social Affairs Committee, and through its publications.[64] It has also issued, in 1976, a code of practice for multinational enterprises which covered a number of areas including employment, industrial relations and minimum standards for reporting data on companies' operations and policies.

THE COUNCIL OF EUROPE

The Council of Europe was established by a Statute signed in London in 1949 by representatives of the Governments of Belgium, France, Luxembourg, the Netherlands, Denmark, Ireland, Italy, Norway, Sweden and the United Kingdom. Most of the countries of Western Europe are now members.[65]

75

The Council's aim, as set out in its Statute, is to achieve a greater unity between its members for the purpose of safeguarding and realising the ideals and principles which are their common heritage and facilitating their economic and social progress. This aim is to be carried out by 'discussion of questions of common concern and by agreements and common action in economic, social, cultural, scientific, legal and administrative matters and in the maintenance of further realisation of human rights and fundamental freedoms'.

The Council's executive body is the Committee of Ministers, which consists of one representative of each member government, usually the Foreign Minister. The instruments which give expression to the Ministers' decisions take the form of binding Conventions (sometimes entitled Charters), Agreements and non-binding Resolutions which may take the form of recommendations to member governments.

There is also a deliberative body, the Consultative Assembly, which consists of parliamentary delegations from all member states. However, the Assembly has no legislative powers; it makes recommendations to the Committee of Ministers.

Industrial relations

The Council's main influence on industrial relations in member countries is the European Social Charter which was signed in 1961 and came into force in 1965. In the field of economic and social rights this is the counterpart of the Convention on Human Rights (which deals solely with political and civil rights) though unlike the Convention the Charter does not provide for the rights embodied in it to be enforced by a court. The Contracting Parties to the Charter accept, as the aim of a policy to be pursued by all appropriate national and international means, the attainment of conditions in which the following rights and principles may be effectively realised: the right to work, to just conditions of work, to safe and healthy working conditions, to a fair remuneration, to organise and to bargain collectively, of children and young persons to protection, of employed women to protection, to vocational guidance and training, to protection of health, to social security, to social and medical assistance, to benefit from social welfare services, of the family to social, legal and economic protection, to engage in a gainful occupation in a territory of other contracting parties and of migrant workers and their families to protection and assistance.

The United Kingdom has ratified the Charter, though it has not accepted all its provisions. Member states report every two years on the position in their countries in relation to the provisions which they have accepted. These reports are examined by a committee of independent experts, whose findings are considered by a Governmental Committee drawn from the contracting parties, usually with representatives of employers and unions present as observers. Both committees report to the Committee of Ministers which can make recommendations to contracting parties about their observance of the Charter.

INTERNATIONAL TRADE UNIONS

The TUC belongs to three international trade union groupings — the European Trade Union Confederation (ETUC), the International Confederation of Free Trade Unions (ICFTU), and the Trade Union Advisory Committee of the OECD (TUAC).

The ETUC was formed in 1973 to deal with questions of interest to European working people arising inside and outside the EC. The membership is about 40 million from eighteen countries; the TUC is the largest member. There is a small secretariat, based in Brussels. The ETUC co-ordinates approaches to the EC, the European Free Trade Association (EFTA) and the other Western European institutions, and has been active in developing policies — such as the 35 hour week — which cannot easily be introduced into an individual country and which can be internationally co-ordinated.

At European level there are also a number of industry committees, which bring together individual unions in the same industry from different countries. The committees are mainly involved in making representations to the EC Commission on their industries: they do not negotiate directly with employers. Some are 'recognised' by the ETUC if their composition reflects the ETUC's own composition and structure. Some of them are associated with international trade secretariats, each representing trade unions within particular industrial sectors on a broader international scale.

The ICFTU is one of three international groupings of trade union confederations; the others are the mainly communist World Federation of Trade Unions (WFTU), and the World Confederation of Labour (WCL) which brings together mainly Christian trade unions. The ICFTU is a world-wide organisation of mainly social-democratic national confederations which was formed in 1949. It meets as a Congress every four years and elects an Executive Board nominated on an area basis for the four year period. Its membership is about 60 million, the TUC again being the largest member. It has a headquarters in Brussels, and regional offices for the Americas, Asia and Africa. Its principal concern is with the promotion of free trade unionism, particularly in developing countries, and with the presentation of trade union views in the UN and other inter-governmental agencies.

INTERNATIONAL EMPLOYERS' ORGANISATIONS

The CBI belongs to three international employers' organisations — the Union des Industries de la Communauté Européene (Union of Industries of the European Community) (UNICE), the International Organisation of Employers (IOE), and the Business and Industry Advisory Committee of the OECD (BIAC). Nationalised industries and public enterprises concerned with the EC belong to the Centre Européen de l'Entreprise Publique (European Centre of Public Enterprise) (CEEP).

UNICE was founded in 1952 and has its Headquarters in Brussels. It brings together the national private-sector employers' confederations of the Member States of the European Community (EC) and, mainly in associate status, the private-sector employers' federations of other Western European nations.

CEEP was founded in 1963 to represent the interests of European public enterprises in the EC and also has its headquarters in Brussels. Its membership comprises over 150 public enterprises and 10 public employer associations in the EC Member States and applicant states, organized into national sections.

Both UNICE and CEEP hold regular meetings with the members of the EC Commission and also represent European employers' interests centrally and to individual Directorates of the Commission. Constitutionally neither has a direct collective bargaining role but they take part in discussions on employment matters with Social Affairs Ministers, the Commission and the European Trade Union Confederation.

The IOE was founded in 1919 and is an international non-governmental organisation based in Geneva, dedicated to the defence of free-enterprise at the international level. Its membership comprises 88 national employer organisations in 82 countries. Its primary function is to keep its members informed of developments in the economic and industrial field and to facilitate joint consideration of economic and social repercussions, particularly at the ILO and the UN Economic and Social Council, with which organisations it has a special status.

Chapter 5
Employment law

Employment law contains provisions relating both to collective bargaining and to the employment rights of individual employees. As the earlier sections of the Handbook have indicated, the legislation has developed considerably over time. This chapter summarises the position following the passage of the Employment Act 1980 but is not meant to be an authoritative guide to the law. Detailed explanatory leaflets are published by the Department of Employment.

The institutions named have already been described.

COLLECTIVE ACTIVITY

Despite the long tradition of voluntarism, the legislation relating to collective bargaining is now considerable, though it does not go as far as to make collective agreements legally enforceable contracts, as is the case in most other industrialised countries. The main statutes are the Trade Union and Labour Relations Act 1974 (TULRA), the Trade Union and Labour Relations (Amendment) Act 1976, the Employment Protection Act 1975 (EPA) and the Employment Act 1980 (EA)* though other legislation is involved, and is cited where relevant. Together these statutes make certain persumptions about collective bargaining; provide a legal basis for trade unions and employers' associations; establish procedures for determining the independence of trade unions; define for certain purposes union membership agreements; give rights to independent and recognised trade unions covering the disclosure of information by employers, consultation over proposed redundancies, time off for trade union officials, the appointment of safety representatives and the administration of pension funds; provide for conciliation and arbitration machinery; and give immunity for certain acts done in contemplation or furtherance of a trade dispute. The main provisions are covered in turn below.

COLLECTIVE BARGAINING

In the context of industrial relations, collective bargaining is the process whereby procedures are jointly agreed and wages and conditions of employ-

* EA received Royal Assent on 1 August 1980 and all its provisions will have been brought into operation by 1 October 1980 except that relating to the press charter (see page 82).

ment are settled by negotiations between employers, or associations of employers, and workers' organisations. Collective bargaining is defined in EPA as 'negotiations relating to or connected with one or more of the matters specified in section 29(1) of the 1974 Act' (TULRA) which can be the subject of a trade dispute. These matters are terms and conditions of employment, working conditions, engagements, termination or suspension of employment, allocation of work, discipline, membership of trade unions and facilities for their officials, and machinery for negotiation, consultation and other joint procedures.

Collective agreements reached through collective bargaining are presumed in law (s18 of TULRA) not to have been intended by the parties to be legally enforceable contracts unless they are written agreements containing a specific provision to that effect.

An agreement which prohibits or restricts workers' rights to engage in industrial action cannot form part of an employee's contract of employment unless the agreement is in writing, and each trade union party to it is an independent trade union. The agreement must also expressly provide for such a prohibition or restriction to be incorporated in the contract, which must expressly or impliedly incorporate those terms. The agreement must be accessible to the employee at the place of work.

TRADE UNIONS AND EMPLOYERS' ASSOCIATIONS

TULRA defines a trade union as an organisation of workers whose principal purposes include the regulation of relations between workers and employers or employers' associations, and an employers' association as an organisation of employers whose principal purposes include the regulation of relations between employers and workers or trade unions. Much of the Act is devoted to the status and regulation of trade unions and employers' associations and to restrictions on the legal liability of these organisations and their officials.

Trade unions may not normally be corporate bodies or be treated as such, but they are given some relevant attributes of corporate bodies, such as the power to make contracts and to sue and be sued. Under TULRA, unions included in a 'special register' maintained under the Industrial Relations Act 1971, which are registered companies or otherwise incorporated, may continue as such, and are known as special register bodies. Employers' associations may be either corporate bodies or unincorporated and, if the latter, are also given some attributes of corporate bodies. The purposes and rules of trade unions and employers' associations are not unlawful on account only of being in restraint of trade. This also applies to relevant purposes and rules of special register bodies and of employers' associations which are corporate bodies.

Under the provisions of TULRA the Certification Officer (see page 58) is required to maintain separate lists of trade unions and employers' associations. Entry in the lists is voluntary and means no more than that the body concerned satisfies the relevant definition in TULRA. Organisations refused inclusion in the list may appeal to the Employment Appeal Tribunal (EAT). Trade unions and employers' associations, whether listed or not, are required to keep proper accounting records and to submit a return relating to their affairs, including their audited accounts, annually to the Certification Officer. The returns are available for public inspection on request.

INDEPENDENCE OF TRADE UNIONS AND ASSOCIATED RIGHTS

EPA provides that a trade union whose name is entered on the list of trade unions maintained by the Certification Officer may apply to the Certification Officer for a certificate that it is an independent trade union as defined in section 30 of TULRA — that is to say, not under the domination or control of an employer or employer group and not liable to interference by an employer or employer group (arising out of the provision of financial or material support or by any other means whatsoever) tending towards such control. The Certification Officer must determine whether the applicant union is independent. He must enter his decision on the public record maintained for the purpose and if he determines that the union is independent he must issue a certificate accordingly; if not, he must give reasons for his decision. A union refused a certificate may appeal to the EAT. The granting or refusal of a certificate is conclusive evidence of the independence or otherwise of the union concerned.

Under EA the Secretary of State is empowered to make regulations containing a scheme for payments towards expenditure incurred by independent trade unions in conducting secret ballots on matters such as industrial action, union elections, amendments to union rules, and union mergers. An employer who, together with any associated employer (as defined in TULRA), has more than 20 employees must comply if reasonably practicable with a request from an independent recognised trade union to use the employer's premises to conduct a workplace ballot — provided this complies with a scheme laid down in regulations. An independent trade union that has secured recognition by an employer for the purpose of collective bargaining also has rights under EPA in relation to disclosure of information and consultation on redundancies; rights to paid time off for trade union officials under the Employment Protection (Consolidation) Act 1978 (EP(C)A) (see page 92); rights relating to the appointment of safety representatives and safety committees, set out in regulations made under the Health and Safety at Work, etc Act 1974; and rights contained in regulations made under the Social Security Pensions Act 1975 in relation to consultation about changes in occupational pension schemes.

UNION MEMBERSHIP AGREEMENTS

The law acknowledges that some agreements or arrangements exist between trade unions and employers which require employees to become members of a specified independent trade union although there is no statutory right to such agreements, termed union membership or 'closed shop' agreements. Under voluntary arrangements, in the case of a 'pre-entry' closed shop, membership of the trade union concerned is a prerequisite of engagement. In the 'post-entry' closed shop recruits are required to join the trade union concerned after engagement. The law safeguards employees who were not union members at the time the union membership agreement took effect (see also page 98). Safeguards were introduced by TULRA, amended in 1976 and extended under EA. As they now stand they are described on page 95. Another provision of the 1976 Act relevant to the closed shop provided, subject to parliamentary approval, for a charter on press freedom to be produced by either the parties concerned or the Secretary of State, on such matters as the application of a closed shop to journalists. The charter was not produced, and EA provides for the relevant section to be repealed in due course.

THE RESOLUTION OF INDUSTRIAL DISPUTES

(i) Voluntary conciliation and arbitration

A trade dispute is defined in TULRA as a dispute between employers and workers or between workers and workers connected with any of the matters listed in s29(1) of the 1974 Act (see page 80). EPA empowers ACAS to offer to assist in the resolution of a dispute by conciliation, or by other means. On exercising its functions in this way ACAS is enjoined by the Act to have regard to the desirability of encouraging employers and trade unions to use any appropriate agreed procedures for the settlement of disputes.

If a dispute cannot be resolved by conciliation, ACAS may, at the request of one or more parties to the dispute, but subject to the consent of all of them, refer it for settlement to an independent arbitrator or arbitrators or to the Central Arbitration Committee (CAC). There is no legal compulsion on the parties to accept an arbitrator's award but, in practice, arbitrators' decisions are almost invariably accepted.

(ii) Unilateral arbitration

Provision for unilateral arbitration exists in relation to the provisions on the disclosure of information to trade unions for collective bargaining purposes and under the House of Commons Fair Wages Resolution of 1946, both of which are described below. There is also provision for unilateral arbitration under the Equal Pay Act 1970, and under several Acts containing a Fair Wages type clause.

(iii) Courts of inquiry

A further statutory provision for the settlement of disputes is included in the

Industrial Courts Act 1919. Under this Act the Secretary of State for Employment may establish a Court of Inquiry to inquire into any trade dispute with a view to establishing the facts and making recommendations. Since the establishment of ACAS, which under EPA may itself set up an inquiry into a dispute, the power to set up Courts of Inquiry has been little used.

LEGAL IMMUNITIES AND RESTRICTIONS ON LEGAL PROCEEDINGS

There is no 'right to strike' in British labour law. Instead, the law in effect confers a freedom to strike by giving those who participate in or organise industrial action 'in contemplation or furtherance of a trade dispute' — the so-called 'golden formula' — immunity from civil liability for certain torts which are likely to be committed in the course of the action. The main provisions are to be found in sections 13–17 of TULRA, as amended in 1976 and, most recently, in sections 16–18 of EA.

TULRA, s13(1), as amended in 1976, protects the position of persons such as union officials and strike leaders by providing that an act done by a person in contemplation or furtherance of a trade dispute (as defined) is not actionable in tort solely on the ground that it induces another person to break a contract (whether a contract of employment or a commercial contract) or interferes with or induces another to interfere with its performance. The protection extends to threats to do such acts.

EA s17 (2) defines such action as 'secondary action' if the contract involved is a contract of employment and the employer under the contract is not a party to the trade dispute concerned. S17 removes the immunities under TULRA s13(1) in the case of acts or threats of acts to interfere with or induce a breach of a commercial contract arising from secondary action not designed to put direct pressure on the employer under dispute. The immunities remain if the secondary action satisfies any of the following requirements: (a) it is principally intended and likely directly to prevent or disrupt supplies under a contract during a dispute between an employer who is party to the dispute and a supplier or customer to whom the secondary action relates; (b) it is principally intended and likely directly to affect substituted supplies between an associated employer of the employer party to the dispute and a supplier or customer, the secondary action relating to one or the other; or (c) it is done in the course of lawful picketing (see page 84) by a worker employed by a party to the dispute or that worker's trade union official.

Under EA s17 a person is also liable to civil action in the courts if he induces or threatens to induce an employee to break his contract of employment with the intention of compelling workers to join a particular trade union or unions, unless those workers work for the same employer or at the same place as the employee concerned.

TULRA s13(2) (repeating the second 'limb' of s3 of the Trade Disputes Act 1906) declares that acts in contemplation or furtherance of a trade dispute are

83

not actionable solely on the ground that they interfere with another person's trade, business or employment or with a person's right to dispose freely of his capital or labour.

In s13(4) TULRA provides immunity against liability for civil conspiracy actions, where two or more people agree or combine to do an act not actionable in tort if done by an individual in contemplation or furtherance of a trade dispute. Immunity from criminal prosecution for conspiracy to commit certain offences in support of a trade dispute is now provided by the Criminal Law Act 1977.

TULRA s14 provides that no action in tort shall lie against a trade union or unincorporated employers' association in respect of any act alleged to have been done, threatened or intended by or on behalf of the trade union or association, except for acts not done in contemplation or furtherance of a trade dispute which result in personal injury or are connected with ownership or use of property. Relevant actions of special register body unions and employers' associations which are corporate bodies are also protected.

The statutory protection given to peaceful picketing in contemplation or furtherance of a trade dispute, previously set out in TULRA s15, is now to be found in EA s16. This redefines lawful picketing, for the purpose only of peaceful communication or peaceful persuasion, as:

a person picketing at or near his own place of work;

a trade union official accompanying a member of his union whom he represents when that member is picketing at or near his own place of work;

an unemployed person picketing at or near his last place of work in furtherance of a trade dispute connected with the termination of his employment;

a person who does not have one fixed place of work, or for whom it is not practicable to picket at his actual place of work, who may picket at any premises of his employer from which he works or from which his work is administered.

A picket not complying with these requirements who induces workers to break their contracts of employment or who interferes with commercial contracts does not have the immunity provided by TULRA s13 and thus can be sued in tort.

Picketing which causes offences such as obstruction, or occasions a breach of the peace, is subject to regulation by the police under their powers of enforcement of the criminal law.

Under TULRA s16 there is a statutory prohibition upon any court's attempting to compel an employee to work or attend at his workplace by requiring compliance with his contract of employment, although this safeguard does not mean that a breach of contract may not have occurred when an employee takes strike action. Finally, under TULRA s17, as amended by EPA, there are restrictions on the granting of orders restraining acts in trade dispute cases in the absence of the defendant, and provision ensuring that the legal protections for industrial action in such cases are not disregarded when such orders are sought.

STATUTORY CODES OF PRACTICE

In addition to establishing the legal basis for collective activity described above, the statutory framework provides trade unions with certain rights, related to collective bargaining or consultation. Before describing these it is appropriate to refer to the provision made in the legislation for statutory codes of practice.

Provision for statutory codes of practice, introduced into employment legislation by the Industrial Relations Act 1971, is now contained in EPA s6 and in EA s3. EPA s6 enables ACAS to prepare codes of practical guidance for the purpose of promoting the improvement of industrial relations. The codes are not legally binding but are admissible in evidence in proceedings before an industrial tribunal or the CAC which must take into account any provision considered relevant. In preparing or subsequently revising a code of this kind ACAS must first publish a draft and consider any representations made to it on the draft. If it wishes to proceed with the draft it must transmit it, modified as appropriate, to the Secretary of State for Employment. If the Secretary of State approves the draft it must then be laid before both Houses of Parliament. Once parliamentary authority has been obtained the code may be issued by ACAS in the form of the draft and is brought into effect by order of the Secretary of State. EA s3 gives the Secretary of State powers to issue or revise codes for the same purposes, and under similar procedures. The Secretary of State must consult ACAS before publishing the consultative draft of a code, and codes issued by the Secretary of State may be taken into account by the courts as well as by industrial tribunals or the CAC. Codes issued by both ACAS and the Secretary of State may supersede part or all of earlier codes issued by either.

The first code of this kind was the *Industrial Relations Code of Practice*[66] issued in 1972 by the Department of Employment under the Industrial Relations Act 1971 and continued in effect by TULRA. Under EPA, Schedule 17, and EA s3 the code remains in effect until superseded by one or more codes prepared by ACAS or the Secretary of State.

ACAS is required by EPA s6 to issue codes supplementing the Act's requirements on the disclosure of information to trade unions for collective bargaining purposes and time off for trade union duties and activities. These are described below. The codes were issued by ACAS and came into effect in August 1977[67] and April 1978[68] respectively. Another ACAS code issued, in June 1977,[69] under EPA s6 deals with disciplinary practice and procedures in employment. The three ACAS codes supersede parts of the 1972 Industrial Relations Code of Practice.

85

The Commission for Racial Equality and the Equal Opportunities Commission are also empowered to issue statutory codes of practice dealing with discrimination in the employment field. Such codes are of similar status to and subject to parliamentary consent in the same way as codes issued by ACAS under EPA s6.

Under the Health and Safety at Work, etc Act 1974 the Health and Safety Commission is empowered, with the consent of the Secretary of State, to issue 'approved' codes of practice to provide practical guidance on the general duties of the Act or on the requirements of any health and safety legislation. An approved code of practice enjoys a new and special legal status. Failure to observe any provision of an approved code does not of itself render a person liable to criminal or civil proceedings, but a court is required to admit in evidence any provisions of an approved code which appears to it to be relevant, and, unless the court is satisfied that the requirement has been complied with in some other way, failure to observe any provision of a code may be taken as proof of non-compliance with a requirement of the Act. Approved codes issued of direct relevance to industrial relations are referred to in the section on the appointment of safety representatives (see page 88).

THE EXTENSION OF TERMS AND CONDITIONS OF EMPLOYMENT: THE FAIR WAGES RESOLUTION

The Fair Wages Resolution adopted by the House of Commons in 1946 provides that government contractors must observe such terms and conditions as have been established for the trade or industry in the district by negotiations between employers and trade unions or by arbitration; or, in the absence of such terms and conditions, those not less favourable than the general level of terms and conditions observed by other employers whose general circumstances in the trade or industry in which the contractor is engaged are similar. A clause to this effect is included in all government contracts and the principle has been widely adopted in connection with local authority contracts and those placed by nationalised industries. The principle has also been embodied in a number of Acts which provide assistance to industries or public authorities by way of grant, loan, subsidy or licence. Any question arising as to whether the requirements of the Fair Wages Resolution are being observed is reported to the Secretary of State for Employment. A question may be raised by a trade union, by any individual, or by the contractor concerned.

If the Department of Employment is satisfied that a question arises under the provisions of the Resolution it refers the matter to ACAS for conciliation. If the complaint cannot be resolved by agreement the Department of Employment will refer it to an independent tribunal, in practice the CAC, which decides whether and to what extent the contractor is in breach of the Resolution. It is then the responsibility of the contracting Department to consider what action should be taken, by virtue of its contractual rights, to ensure that any breach found by the CAC is remedied.

DISCLOSURE OF INFORMATION TO TRADE UNIONS FOR COLLECTIVE BARGAINING PURPOSES

Sections 17–21 of EPA deal with the obligation of employers to disclose to recognised independent trade unions, on request, any information without which they would be materially impeded in collective bargaining and which it would be good industrial relations practice to disclose, having regard to the ACAS code of practice on the subject.

Certain information is protected from disclosure on the grounds that its release might be harmful to the employer's undertaking or national security, would be in breach of an enactment or confidence or was collected in connection with legal proceedings. Moreover, an employer is not required to disclose information relating to an individual without his consent, produce a specific document for inspection or compile information which would involve a disproportionate amount of time or cost.

A trade union may present a complaint to CAC that an employer has failed to disclose information in accordance with the requirements of the Act. CAC will then assess whether the matter is likely to be resolved by conciliation, normally by inviting both sides to an informal meeting under a CAC Chairman with an ACAS conciliation officer present. If there is no resolution, a full Committee will proceed to hear and determine the complaint and make a declaration stating whether it is well founded, giving reasons for this decision. In finding in favour of the union, CAC must specify what information is to be disclosed and the date by which disclosure should take place.

If an employer fails to disclose all or part of the information specified in a CAC declaration, the union may make a further complaint to this effect, accompanied or followed by a claim for improved terms and conditions of employment. If CAC upholds this further complaint, it may award that the terms and conditions specified in the claim, or any other terms and conditions which it considers appropriate, shall have effect as part of the contract of employment of the employees concerned.

CONSULTATION ON PROPOSED REDUNDANCIES

An employer proposing to make redundant one or more employees of a description for which he has recognised an independent trade union is required under s99 of EPA to consult the union about the dismissal. Consultation must begin at the earliest opportunity, and in any event at least 90 days in advance of the dismissals if the employer is proposing that 100 or more employees are to be made redundant within a period of 90 days at one establishment, and at least 30 days in advance if 10–99 employees are to be dismissed at one establishment within a period of 30 days. The employer must give similar notice to the Secretary of State for Employment, who has power to vary the notice periods by order, subject to the limits specified in the EEC Directive on collective redundancies. The present notice period of 30 days came into effect on 1 October 1979; prior to this it was 60 days.

The employer must disclose to the trade union, in writing, the reasons for the proposals, the number and descriptions of employees involved, the total number of such employees at the establishment in question, the proposed method of selection for redundancy and the proposed method and timing of the dismissals. He must consider any representations made by the union and reply, stating reasons if rejecting them.

If through special circumstances it is not reasonably practicable for the employer to comply with the requirements, the employer must comply so far as is reasonably practicable. If a trade union considers that an employer has failed to comply it may complain to an industrial tribunal, which may require the employer to pay remuneration for up to 30 days or 90 days, depending on the number of employees concerned and the circumstances of the case. If the employer fails to pay this remuneration the employees may complain to an industrial tribunal, which can order the employer to pay. An employer who fails to give notice of redundancies as required to the Secretary of State may have the redundancy payments rebate due to him under EP(C)A reduced up to the extent of one tenth, or be fined on summary conviction. The employer can appeal to an industrial tribunal against reduction of the rebate.

CONSULTATION ON PENSIONS

Regulations made under the Social Security Pensions Act 1975 require an employer wishing to contract out of the earnings-related State pension scheme in favour of a company pension scheme, or to reverse this process, to consult any independent trade union recognised by him for collective bargaining purposes. This requirement may, for example, arise when a company is acquired by a group which has a contracted-out scheme or when it leaves such a group and can no longer participate in the group scheme. The unions also have the right to be consulted if an employer introduces pension benefits without contracting out of the State scheme, or if he wishes to replace a contracted-out scheme by a new one or amend it in certain ways.

APPOINTMENT OF SAFETY REPRESENTATIVES

Under the Safety Representatives and Safety Committees Regulations 1977 (made under the Health and Safety at Work, etc Act 1974) an independent trade union recognised by an employer may appoint from among the employees safety representatives who must, so far as is reasonably practicable, have been in the employer's employ throughout the preceding two years or have had two years' experience in similar employment. Their functions include investigating dangerous occurrences and potential hazards at the workplace, and workers' complaints about health and safety matters; examining the causes of accidents at the workplace; making representations to the employer on health and safety matters; and carrying out routine and special inspections of the workplace or parts of it.

The employer is under a duty to consult safety representatives in developing and checking the effectiveness of measures to ensure health and safety at work, and on written request by at least two safety representatives he must, after certain specified consultations, establish a safety committee within three months. He must permit safety representatives such time off with pay as is specified in the Regulations to carry out their functions and to attend training courses and must give them reasonable facilities and assistance for making inspections. He must also make available, with certain important exceptions, any information within his knowledge necessary to enable safety representatives to fulfil their functions. Safety representatives also have the right to inspect and copy certain documents, but only those specified in the Regulations.

The Health and Safety Commission has issued a composite booklet containing the Regulations, an approved code of practice and guidance notes on safety representatives and safety committees;[70] and a separate approved code of practice on time off for training of safety representatives.[71]

INDIVIDUAL RIGHTS

Individual rights are conferred in most employments by the following Acts of Parliament:

The Employment Protection (Consolidation) Act 1978 (EP(C)A)

The Equal Pay Act 1970

The Sex Discrimination Act 1975

The Race Relations Act 1976

The Employment Act 1980 (EA).

The great majority of the individual rights are conferred by EP(C)A which brought together in a single Act individual employment rights previously contained in the Redundancy Payments Act 1965, Contracts of Employment Act 1972, TULRA and EPA. These rights are set out below, those starred (*) having been amended by EA, together with two new provisions introduced by EA as indicated.

the right to a written statement of the main terms and conditions of the employment

the right to a minimum period of notice

89

the right to an itemised pay statement

the right to a guarantee payment*

the right to time off work
    for trade union duties and activities
    for public duties
    prior to redundancy, to look for work or
    to arrange training

the rights of an expectant mother
    not to be unfairly dismissed because of pregnancy
    to time off work to receive ante-natal care [right introduced by EA]
    to return to work after the confinement*
    to receive maternity pay*

the right to payment while suspended from work on medical grounds

the right not to be unfairly dismissed*

the right to be provided with a written statement of the reasons for dismissal

the right to receive a lump sum payment if dismissed for redundancy

the right not to have action short of dismissal taken against an employee because of trade union membership or activities*

the right to certain payments which the employer cannot make because of insolvency.

The provisions identified above are explained in the sections which follow, as are the rights conferred by the other Acts:

the right to equal pay

the right not to be discriminated against on grounds of sex or marriage or race

the right not to be unreasonably excluded or expelled from a trade union [introduced by EA; described on page 98].

Many individual rights are subject to exclusions, qualifying conditions and time limits for complaints. These are not described in detail below. The conditions generally include the requirement that the employee should have completed a specified period of continuous employment with his present employer, with a certain minimum number of working hours each week. Rules are laid down in Schedule 13 of EP(C)A for deciding what counts towards continuous service, and on the calculation of working hours when the employee's contract does not provide for normal working hours. Rules are also laid down in Schedule 14 of the Act for calculating a week's pay for the purposes of the individual rights.

The employee has a right to complain to an industrial tribunal if he feels his rights have been infringed. There is provision in most cases for conciliation by ACAS to try to settle the complaint on a voluntary basis without determination by a tribunal: the exceptions are minimum period of notice; written statement of the main terms and conditions of the employment; redundancy payment; and payments when the employer is insolvent.

THE EMPLOYMENT PROTECTION (CONSOLIDATION) ACT 1978 (EP(C)A)*

The right to a written statement of the main terms and conditions of the employment

All employees have a contract of employment which may be oral, written or implied (except apprentices and merchant seamen whose contracts must be in writing). Within thirteen weeks of starting work employees are entitled to be given a written statement of the main terms and conditions of their employment including details of the job title, pay, hours, holidays and holiday pay, sickness and sick pay, pension and pension schemes, periods of notice, period of continuous employment, and details of disciplinary and grievance procedures. The employees may be referred to a reasonably accessible document containing the information on certain of these particulars.

The right to a minimum period of notice

An employee who has been employed at least four weeks is required to give the employer a minimum of one week's notice of termination of the contract of employment. Employers are required to give their employees at least one week's notice after four weeks' employment, increasing to two weeks after two years' service and then by one week for each completed year of service, subject to a maximum of twelve weeks. These requirements do not prevent an employer from offering nor an employee from accepting a payment in lieu of notice, nor do they preclude summary termination of the contracts of employment where appropriate. An employer or employee who considers that these rights have been infringed can take action through the county court for breach of contract.

* Provisions amended by EA are indicated in the text.

The right to an itemised pay statement

Whenever wages or salary are paid to an employee, an employer is required to supply an itemised pay statement which shows the gross pay, net pay and the amounts and reasons for all variable deductions. The statement must also show the amounts and reasons for all fixed deductions, unless this information is given to the employee separately in a statement supplied at least annually.

The right to a guarantee payment

Under EP(C)A as amended by EA, employees, after four weeks' continuous employment, are entitled to receive payment, subject to certain conditions, for up to five days in any three month period for each day on which they would normally work under the contract of employment but do not because the employer is not able to provide work. On 1 February 1980 the payment became £8 per day. The amount of payment, the number of days for which it is made and the length of the reference period are reviewed annually by the Secretary of State for Employment, who may vary them by order following the review.

The parties to a private agreement which provides a guarantee payment for employees on terms not less favourable than the statutory provisions may be exempted from the Act's provisions. A number of such exemptions have been granted.

The right to payment while on suspension from work on medical grounds

If an employee with at least four weeks' continuous employment is suspended on medical grounds under the provisions of certain health and safety at work legislation (for example, because of the levels of exposure to ionizing radiation, or chemicals such as lead) he is entitled to receive a week's pay for each week's suspension up to 26 weeks. To qualify for such payments employees must be fit for work but the payments do not have to be made if the employee unreasonably refuses suitable alternative work, or unreasonably withholds his services.

The right to time off work

(i) for trade union duties and activities

An employee who is an official of a recognised independent trade union is entitled to reasonable time off, with pay, during working hours to receive training and carry out trade union duties. The duties must be concerned with industrial relations between the employer and an associated employer and their employees.

An employee who is a member of a recognised independent trade union is entitled to reasonable time off (which need not be with pay) for certain trade union activities.

Practical guidance on these requirements is given in the ACAS code of practice *Time Off for Trade Union Duties and Activities.*[68]

(ii) for public duties

Employees who hold certain public positions are entitled to reasonable time off to enable them to perform the duties associated with those posts. The employer is not obliged to pay for the time off.

(iii) prior to redundancy, to look for work or to arrange training

An employee who has worked continuously for his employer for at least two years and who is being made redundant is entitled to reasonable time off with pay during the period of notice to look for another job or to make arrangements for training for future employment.

The rights of an expectant mother

(i) not to be dismissed because of pregnancy

A woman who has worked for her employer for the minimum period required for claims of unfair dismissal (see page 94) has the right to complain of unfair dismissal if she is dismissed because of pregnancy or for a reason connected with the pregnancy unless her condition makes it impossible for her to do her job adequately or her continued employment would contravene a duty or restriction imposed by or under an enactment. In the latter two circumstances she should be offered a suitable alternative job if one is available.

(ii) to time off work to receive ante-natal care

Under EA, a woman who is pregnant and who on medical advice has made an appointment to receive ante-natal care is entitled not to be unreasonably refused time off to receive such care, and to receive payment for the time off.

(iii) to return to work after the confinement

A woman who is absent from work to have a baby is entitled to return to her job at any time up to 29 weeks calculated from the beginning of the week in which the confinement took place. If her job no longer exists because of redundancy, her dismissal would be unfair if her employer (or his successor) or an associated employer does not offer a suitable alternative job if one exists. Under EA, dismissal is deemed not to have taken place if (a) it is not reasonably practicable for an employer to offer the original job for a reason other than redundancy and the employer offers a suitable alternative which the employee accepts or unreasonably refuses or (b) if the employer together with any associated employer did not have more than five employees immediately before her absence began, and it is not reasonably practicable to offer her old job or a suitable alternative. The entitlement is also subject to certain conditions (qualified in most cases by what is reasonably practicable), chiefly that the employee must be in employment until the eleventh week before the baby is due, have at that time at least two years' continuous employment, and must notify, in writing, her employer at least 21 days before her absence begins of her expected date of confinement, of her maternity absence, and of her intention of returning to work. Under EA if requested in writing by her employer not earlier than 49 days after the beginning of her expected week of confinement she must also give written confirmation within 14 days of her intention to return to work. Twenty-one days' written notice of her proposed date of return must also be given.

(iv) to receive maternity pay

A woman who has worked for her employer for two years and who is absent from work to have a baby is entitled to receive a specified minimum amount of maternity pay from her employer for the first six weeks of absence. This is payable whether or not she proposes to return to work after the birth of the baby but the employee must be in employment until the eleventh week before the expected date of confinement, have at that time at least two years' continuous employment and must give at least 21 days' notice of her maternity absence, in writing if requested. Employers can claim a refund of the specified minimum amount from a fund to which all employers contribute known as the Maternity Pay Fund.

The right not to be unfairly dismissed

The dismissal of an employee may be fair in certain circumstances if it is related to redundancy or the employee's conduct, capability or qualifications for the job; if continued employment would contravene a statutory duty or restriction; or if dismissal is for some other substantial reason. Employees are entitled to complain to an industrial tribunal if they feel they have been unfairly dismissed, normally provided they have a certain minimum period of continuous employment. When this right was first introduced under the 1971 Industrial Relations Act the minimum period in most cases was 104 weeks; it was reduced to 52 weeks by TULRA in 1974, and then to 26 weeks in March 1975. It reverted to 52 weeks from 1 October 1979. Under EA it is extended to two years for employees whose employer, together with any associated employer, does not have more than 20 employees throughout that two years. Employees also cannot complain of unfair dismissal if they have reached the normal retiring age for the position held or, if there is no normal retiring age, the age of 65 for men or 60 for women. Under EP(C)A as amended by EA, when a complaint is heard by an industrial tribunal the tribunal has to decide whether or not the employer acted reasonably in all the circumstances, and take into account such factors as the employer's size and administrative resources. The ACAS Code of Practice on Disciplinary Practice and Procedures in Employment[69] gives practical guidance.

If the tribunal upholds a complaint of unfair dismissal it can order reinstatement, re-engagement or a monetary payment. This payment may be reduced where any action of the employee contributed to the dismissal or the employee fails to mitigate any loss suffered.

Dismissal will always be unfair if it is for being a member of or taking part at any appropriate time in the activities of an independent trade union, or for refusing to become a member of a trade union which is not independent. Under EA the dismissal of an employee of a class covered by a union membership agreement for not belonging to a union specified under the agreement is unfair in the following circumstances: the employee genuinely objects on grounds of conscience or other deeply held personal conviction to joining any union or a particular union; the employee has been an employee of the class covered by the union membership agreement since before it took effect but not a member of a union specified in it at any time while it was in effect; the agreement came into force after implementation of the relevant section of the Act* and was not supported in a secret ballot by at least 80% of those to be covered, or was so supported but the employee has not been a member of a specified union at any time since the ballot was held. The length-of-service qualification does not apply to a complaint regarding dismissal for trade union membership or activities.

Under EA an employer may before the hearing of the complaint join in unfair dismissal proceedings a person or trade union who he claims induced him by actual or threatened industrial action to dismiss the employee for not being a member of a trade union. If the employer's claim is upheld the person or trade union may have to pay part or all of any compensation awarded. Similarly an employer may in certain circumstances join another employer in unfair dismissal proceedings if these arise from insistence on a union only labour term in a contract. The employer thus joined may in turn join a union in the proceedings.

The right to be provided with a written statement of the reasons for dismissal

An employee who has completed 26 weeks' employment is on dismissal entitled to receive from the employer, on request, a written statement of the reasons for the dismissal.

The right to receive a lump sum payment if dismissed as redundant

Employees who have had at least 104 weeks' continuous service with their employer after reaching 18 years of age are entitled to a lump sum payment from their employer if they lose their jobs because the employer can no longer employ them in suitable work. The amount of payment depends on the employee's age, weekly pay and length of service with the employer.

* 15 August 1980.

Employers can claim a refund of a proportion of the redundancy payments they have made, up to the limit which the law requires them to pay, from a fund to which all employers contribute known as the Redundancy Fund.

The right of employees not to have action short of dismissal taken against them because of trade union membership or activities

Employees are safeguarded against their employers' taking any form of action against them short of dismissal for being members of or taking part at an appropriate time in the activities of an independent trade union. Under EP(C)A as amended by EA, nor are employers allowed to take action against their employees to compel them to join a trade union (whether or not independent) or, where there is a union membership agreement, in circumstances where dismissal would be unfair (see page 95). Under EA a right of joinder is provided for the employer to use in proceedings involving such action, similar to that described for unfair dismissal (page 95).

The right to payments which an employer cannot make because of insolvency

If the employer cannot pay certain debts to his employees because of insolvency, employees may apply for payment subject to certain limits from the Redundancy Fund, which is controlled by the Secretary of State for Employment. The debts include arrears of pay for a period not exceeding eight weeks, holiday pay for a period not exceeding six weeks, payment in lieu of notice up to the statutory minimum entitlement and any basic award made by an industrial tribunal for unfair dismissal.

OTHER ACTS

The right to equal pay

The Equal Pay Act 1970 (as amended by the Sex Discrimination Act 1975) establishes the right of a woman to equal treatment in respect not just of pay, but all the terms of her contract of employment when she is employed on work of the same nature as, or which is broadly similar to, that of a man, or work established as equivalent under a job evaluation study, and there is no material difference other than the difference of sex between her case and his. A woman may only draw a comparison with the job of a man employed by the same employer or an associated employer. The Act gives the same right to a man vis-à-vis work done by a woman. Complaints under these provisions may

96

be made to an industrial tribunal which can award arrears of pay for up to two years before the date of application.

Provision is also made under the Act for the CAC to remove discrimination in collective agreements, employers' pay structures and statutory wages orders which contain any provisions applying specifically to men only or to women only.

The right not to be discriminated against on grounds of sex or marriage or race

The Sex Discrimination Act 1975 makes it unlawful for employers, trade unions, employers' organisations, partnerships, qualifying bodies, the Manpower Services Commission and its divisions, and other vocational training bodies and employment agencies to discriminate either directly or indirectly on the grounds of sex or marital status.

The Race Relations Act 1976 makes it unlawful for these bodies to discriminate on grounds of race, colour, nationality (including citizenship) or ethnic or national origins.

For the purposes of both Acts, discrimination means either the less favourable treatment of persons on the grounds referred to above or the application of a condition or requirement which, though applied equally to all, has a disproportionately adverse effect on a particular sex or racial group and which cannot be justified.

Both Acts cover discrimination in recruitment and advertising and, in relation to existing employees, in training, promotion, transfer, access to any other benefits or facilities, or in dismissal, or in subjecting a person to any other detriment. There are limited exceptions. For example, where an employer can show that a particular job has to be done by a person of a particular sex, or from a particular racial group, for reasons such as authenticity in dramatic performances, discrimination in selection may be permitted. The Sex Discrimination Act does not cover discrimination in employment, except for victimisation, in private households and by employers who, together with any associated employers, do not have more than five employees. Both Acts permit employers, under certain conditions, to train people of a particular sex or of a particular racial group to help fit them for work in which there are none or very few of that sex or group, or to encourage them to take advantage of opportunities for doing that work.

Individual complaints under the employment provisions of these Acts are heard by industrial tribunals. The Equal Opportunities Commission (EOC) (see page 61) established by the Sex Discrimination Act, and the Commission for Racial Equality (CRE) (see page 62) established by the Race Relations Act, both have discretion in certain circumstances to advise and assist actual or prospective complainants and to arrange representation at tribunal hearings. The Commissions may conduct formal investigations and issue non-discrimination notices enforceable in the courts. They may also issue codes of practice (see page 86).

The right not to be unreasonably excluded or expelled from a trade union

EA gives a person who is, or seeks to be, in employment where there is a union membership agreement the right not to be unreasonably excluded or expelled from a trade union. Individual complaints under the Act are heard by industrial tribunals, and there is a right of appeal, either on the facts or on points of law, to the EAT.

Where complaints are upheld, and complainants are admitted or re-admitted to membership of the union, they can apply to the industrial tribunal for compensation. If they are not admitted or re-admitted to membership, they can apply for compensation to the EAT.

Part B

Collective bargaining arrangements

This part of the Handbook is given over to descriptions, by industry, of the major arrangements which now exist for the negotiation of collective agreements covering pay and other conditions of employment and matters of procedure.

Collective bargaining is not universal throughout industry. The 1978 New Earnings Survey found that about thirty per cent of full-time employees in Great Britain were not affected directly or indirectly by any collective agreements; detailed figures for the coverage of collective agreements are given in Appendix 1. However, collective bargaining is widespread and negotiations can take place at a number of different levels. In many industries there is machinery at national or industry level which brings together representatives of employers' associations and full-time officers of trade unions. Sometimes this machinery is a permanent ('standing') body, with its own secretariat. These bodies can go under one or other of about a dozen different titles, of which the most common are probably — national joint industrial council (NJIC), joint industrial council (JIC), and national joint committee or council (NJC). These bodies are largely based upon the model constitution drawn up by the Ministry of Labour following the report of the Whitley Committee in 1917 (see page 16) but vary widely in their coverage of an industry, and in the nature and extent of their activities. In other industries, engineering for example, there is no separate machinery, but established arrangements for regular negotiation at national level.

In private industry, the substantive agreements at national or industry level tend to set minimum terms and conditions of employment. The items covered vary widely from industry to industry, but usually include minimum rates of pay, premia for calculating payments for overtime and shiftwork, normal hours of work, and holiday entitlements. Employers in an industry who are not 'federated' — do not belong to the employers' association — are not obliged to implement these agreements, although in practice those who employ a workforce of any magnitude tend to offer terms and conditions which are no less favourable. In some industries minimum terms and conditions are determined by a wages council or other statutory machinery (see chapter 3) and have statutory force. In the public services and nationalised industries where there is a single employer actual pay and conditions of employment are normally set by agreements at national level.

In industries where there is national negotiating machinery, there is sometimes accompanying machinery at regional or district level, also bringing together representatives of the employers' association and full-time officials of the trade unions. This will commonly deal with problems of applying the national agreement to the particular circumstances of an individual district, and often also operate as a stage in the procedure for resolving disputes. In some cases particular regional or district rates of pay or conditions of employment are agreed.

Bargaining at company level, covering all the establishments of a multi-plant company, or at plant or establishment level covering a single site within a company, is widespread. In a large company a company-wide agreement can involve the national full-time officials of a union, while bargaining in a small company or covering an individual plant may be conducted entirely by shop stewards. Where there is no industry-wide agreement, or where an employer is not federated, negotiations at these levels may be the sole determinant of pay and other conditions of employment. In federated companies the agreements may build on the minimum rates of pay set nationally—sometimes by establishing higher actual rates, sometimes by adding a productivity scheme or other bonus arrangements—or may cover matters outside the scope of the national agreement.

Finally, at workshop level, within an individual plant, it is common for shop stewards and foremen or other management staff to bargain over detailed conditions of employment — such as the allocation of work, allowances for specific jobs, arrangements for overtime, etc. These arrangements are rarely written, but become reinforced in time through habit and custom, and are known as 'custom and practice'.

Two other terms are also used to identify levels at which agreements are concluded. Local level is used, as in the 1978 New Earnings Survey, to describe all agreements concluded below district or company level — at, for example, an individual operating unit within a nationalised industry, in a division of a company covering several plants, or at plant or establishment level. Domestic level is used to denote all agreements at or within individual companies.

In many industries in addition to negotiations there are also arrangements for consultation between managements and employees about matters of common concern which fall outside the scope of the negotiating machinery. Consultation is highly developed in the nationalised industries; in some cases the same committees are used both for negotiation and consultation. In private industry there is no industry-wide machinery; companies have their own arrangements, often a works council at each establishment and sometimes a co-ordinating committee at company level.

Each of the descriptions which follow contains information on the composition of the industry, the employers' associations, the unions involved, the main negotiating machinery, the balance between negotiations at different levels, and the categories of employees and principal matters covered by agreements. The terms *manual* and *white-collar* are used throughout to denote the two main categories of employee, though where, within an industry, agreements cover more specific categories of employee — for example, *process workers*, *maintenance craftsmen* — terms such as these are employed. Within each industry Order the title of a union, employers' association or negotiating body is given in full when first used, and abbreviations are normally used thereafter. A list of the trade union abbreviations thus employed in Part B is given in Appendix 5.

100

Order I AGRICULTURE, FORESTRY, FISHING

The three industries within this Order have completely separate arrangements for determining pay and terms and conditions of employment, and are therefore described separately below.

Agriculture and horticulture

For industrial relations purposes there is no significant distinction between agriculture — farming, stock rearing and agricultural contracting — and horticulture: market gardening and fruit, flower and seed growing. In this text, both are covered by the term *agriculture*.

The industry employs about 350 000 people, but is highly fragmented; four employees on a farm is a relatively large workforce. Minimum rates of pay and some conditons of employment for ordinary manual workers and premium rates for craftsmen and employees with supervisory and managerial responsibilities are statutorily regulated by the Agricultural Wages Board (England and Wales), established in its present form under the Agricultural Wages Act 1948, or the Scottish Agricultural Wages Board, established in its present form under the Agricultural Wages Act (Scotland) 1949. The Boards are made up of equal numbers of employer and worker representatives, together with independent members appointed, for England and Wales, jointly by the Minister of Agriculture, Fisheries and Food and the Secretary of State for Wales, and for Scotland by the Secretary of State for Scotland.

Employers are represented by the National Farmers' Union (NFU) of England and Wales and the NFU of Scotland which together have some 150 000 members and represent the great majority of employing farmers. The NFU is primarily a trade association acting as the industry's spokesman on agricultural policy but it does provide an advisory service to members on employment matters.

Manual workers are represented by the National Union of Agricultural and Allied Workers (NUAAW) and the Transport and General Workers' Union (TGWU). The NUAAW, which represents about three-quarters of total hired farmworkers, including full-time and part-time or casual workers, in England and Wales, provides the majority of employee representatives on the Wages Board. In Scotland all the employee representatives on the Wages Board come from the TGWU.

The Agricultural Wages Boards operate very much on the lines of Wages Councils (see page 64), regulating minimum pay and conditions by means of

101

Wages Orders which are enforced by officials appointed by the relevant Minister. Below the Board for England and Wales, at local level, there are Agricultural Wages Committees, made up of equal numbers of employer and worker representatives and some independent members. Committee duties include issuing craft certificates to enable workers to qualify for craftsmen's rates; granting permits allowing employers of disabled workers to pay below the statutory minimum; revaluing cottages for the purposes of the AWB Order; and approving premium agreements between workers in training and their employers. Local committees no longer exist in Scotland. There is widespread collective bargaining in a number of sectors of the food industry (see page 109) which are closely connected with agriculture. Within the agriculture industry itself there are formal arrangements for negotiation in some of the larger establishments and the agricultural divisions of food companies. There is company-level and local bargaining in a range of activities such as glasshouse crop growing, mushroom growing, poultry rearing and egg production.

Forestry

The industry is divided between state forests, managed by the Forestry Commission, and privately-owned forests and woodlands. In total about 16 000 people are employed, about equally divided between the state and private sectors and with approximately 6000 manual workers in each.

Within the Forestry Commission, terms and conditions of employment for manual workers are set by the Forestry Commission Industrial and Trade Council which brings together representatives of the Commission and three unions, the NUAAW, TGWU and the National Union of General and Municipal Workers (GMWU). The agreement provides for piecework rates to be jointly determined at local level. Terms and conditions for the different groups of craftsmen are set by their respective industry agreements. For non-industrial staff, terms and conditions are set by the Forestry Commission Whitley Council on which the main unions are the Civil Service Union, the Institution of Professional Civil Servants, the Civil and Public Services Association, and the Society of Civil and Public Servants (Executive, Directing and Analagous Grades).

There is no significant collective bargaining in private forestry.

Fishing

The fishing industry can be divided into deep sea fishing, using trawlers, and 'in-shore' fishing. The workforce of upwards of 20 000 is mainly employed on a casual or 'trip' basis; the number of berths available at any one time is somewhat less than this.

In the trawl fishing sector, which is the major part of the industry, there are few large nationally-based employers. Most employers operate from a single port, and in most major fishing ports there are Fishing Vessel Owners' Associations or Fishing Industry Associations to which almost all employers belong.

Collective bargaining is widespread in the industry. Union membership is almost 100% for skippers and mates most of whom belong to their port's Trawl(er) Officers' Guild (TOG) which is normally affiliated to the British Trawler Officers' Association. The Merchant Navy and Airline Officers' Association (MNAOA) and the TGWU also have some membership. Engineers and deck crews are represented by TGWU; membership is high amongst engineers but relatively low amongst deck crews except in Scotland, where union members have priority of employment. Wireless operators are usually members of the Radio and Electronic Officers' Union (REOU).

Pay and conditions of employment for skippers, mates, engineers and deck crews are normally negotiated separately for each port between the port Association and the TOG and TGWU. There are different pay scales for each of these groups of employee and pay is usually related both to the number of days spent at sea and to the tonnage or cash value of the catch; payment is normally made separately for each trip undertaken. In addition, agreements usually cover holiday entitlements, manning levels, welfare schemes, discipline and disputes procedures, and registration and training of fishermen. For wireless officers, terms and conditions of employment are neogotiated nationally between a Marine Wireless Employers Negotiating Committee and the REOU.

Most in-shore fishing is operated on a 'share-fishing' basis, without collective bargaining.

Order II MINING AND QUARRYING

There are separate collective bargaining arrangements for the different industries in this Order, and they are treated separately below, with the exception of the extraction of petroleum and natural gas, which is covered under GAS (see page 191). The arrangements in coal mining cover also most employees in the coke ovens and manufactured fuel industry, which is formally part of Order IV. Together these industries employ about 350 000 people, over three-quarters of whom are in coal mining.

Coal mining

The National Coal Board (NCB) was set up by the Coal Industry Nationalisation Act 1946 and took over the control of coal mining and certain ancillary industries and activities from about 800 companies. It employs about 300 000 people and operates over 200 collieries in 12 Areas throughout Great Britain. It also operates, through contractors, a number of opencast mining sites and licenses private undertakings to work a number of small mines. Contractors' employees in opencast mining are covered by collective bargaining machinery in the civil engineering construction industry (see page 186).

The non-mining activities of the Board are carried on by a number of wholly-owned subsidiaries, associated companies and partnerships. These are organised into two groups. NCB (Coal Products) Ltd covers about 7000 people and manufactures and sells coke, smokeless fuel and certain by-products. NCB (Ancillaries) Ltd covers about 5000 employees and provides certain engineering, computer and other services.

Four principal unions operate in the coal, coke and by-products industries. The National Union of Mineworkers (NUM) is by far the largest. It represents employees in both the coal mining and coke and by-products industries. It is divided into Areas, some geographically and some occcupationally based, which have a high degree of autonomy. They elect their own full-time officials and conduct their own conferences. The Colliery Officials and Staffs Area (COSA) conducts its own negotiations for particular grades of staff.

The other principal unions are the National Association of Colliery Overmen, Deputies and Shotfirers (NACODS), the British Association of Colliery Management (BACM) and the Association of Professional, Executive, Clerical and Computer Staff (APEX). BACM and APEX represent staff in both the coal mining and the coke and by-products industries. Other unions with smaller membership, mainly in the subsidiary undertakings, include the National Union of General and Municipal Workers (GMWU) (whose members are mostly coke workers); the Transport and General Workers' Union (TGWU), the Amalgamated Union of Engineering Workers (AUEW), the Electrical, Electronic, Telecommunication and Plumbing Union (EETPU), and the Union of Construction, Allied Trades and Technicians (UCATT). Union membership in the industries is virtually 100%.

NEGOTIATING MACHINERY

Collective bargaining machinery covers all grades of staff employed by the NCB, with separate machinery for each of the groups set out in the table on page 105.

The collective bargaining machinery — or 'Conciliation Scheme' — for industrial grade mineworkers covers about three-quarters of the industry's employees. It provides the means of dealing with all questions which concern pay and conditions of employment. It is the basic model for similar schemes which exist for other negotiating groups in the industry. It has three levels — national, district and pit.

From 1972 virtually all aspects of pay and conditions of employment of industrial grade mineworkers have been dealt with at national level, within the National Conciliation Scheme, by the Joint National Negotiating Committee (JNNC) which consists of representatives from the NCB and the NUM.

The district and pit level machinery exists mainly to deal with questions arising from the implementation of the national agreements, and to resolve local questions. Although the NCB is organised administratively into 12 Areas, there are 13 District Conciliation Boards corresponding to the

Employee groups	Union(s)
1 Industrial grade mineworkers. (These are divided into underground workers, surface workers, underground craftsmen and surface craftsmen.)	NUM*
2 Weekly paid industrial staff (coal) (certain supervisory staff and mining specialists including safety and training officers)	NUM*
3 Colliery officials (deputies and overmen)	NACODS*
4 Coke workers (all daily paid workers)	NUM (some represented by GMWU)
5 Weekly paid industrial staff (coke and by-products) (Foremen)	NUM*
6 Clerical and junior administrative staff (both coal mining and coke and by-products)	NUM (COSA), APEX
7 Management and junior technical staff	BACM*
8 Other groups. (These tend to follow the terms and conditions of the main settlements in the industry or settlements in other appropriate industries. There are separate negotiations with the British Medical Association (BMA) for Area Medical Officers.)	

Unions which are starred (*) have sole negotiating rights for these employees.

territories covered by the pre-nationalisation district unions' and employers' associations.

The district Scheme provides for the appointment of independent district referees, acceptable to both sides, to act as arbitrators. Where questions arise which have significance beyond the district level they are transferred to the national level for resolution.

At pit level there is a six-stage grievance and disputes procedure culminating in a joint disputes committee appointed by the District Conciliation Board, and, failing resolution, reference to a pit umpire chosen from a panel appointed by the District Conciliation Board. Matters considered to be more than purely pit questions can be referred to the district machinery.

Use of the district-level machinery declined with the development of a national day wage job structure, until the introduction of an incentive scheme in 1977/78. Incentive scheme questions are dealt with through the normal district-level conciliation machinery except for questions relating to the settlement of standards for which separate procedures apply.

For both the clerical and junior administrative staff and for the management grades, a two-tier scheme — at NCB Area and National levels — exists. In addition, there is provision throughout the industry for voluntary arbitration at national level in the form of the National Reference Tribunal. This consists of three standing members from outside the industry appointed by the Master of the Rolls after consultation with the NCB, NUM, NACODS, BACM and APEX.

A comprehensive system of consultative machinery was set up in 1947 and has changed little in form in recent years. Consultative committees and councils at workplace, area (or regional in the coke and by-products industry) and national level discuss questions relating to safety, health, welfare, the organisation and conduct of the industries (such as absenteeism or the introduction of new machinery), research and any other matters of interest to employees and the NCB except questions relating to pay and conditions of employment — which are reserved for the conciliation procedure.

At national level there is a council for each industry — the Coal Industry National Consultative Council (CINCC) and the Coke Industry National Consultative Council (CONCC). CINCC has an important sub-committee — the Joint Policy Advisory Committee (JPAC) — which discusses major policy issues affecting the coal industry as a whole.

Stone and slate quarrying and mining

These industries can be divided into two sectors:
1. Roadstone quarrying
2. Other quarrying.

ROADSTONE QUARRYING

This is by far the largest of the quarrying industries and employs about 15 000 people. It is widespread geographically but dominated by a few large companies. Two unions, the GMWU and TGWU, are recognised for all types of manual workers. One or other of the unions, mainly the GMWU, tends to have sole representation facilities at plant level. Membership levels are high, especially in the larger companies.

Minimum rates of pay for youths and unskilled adult manual workers, and most other conditions of employment, are set by the National Joint Industrial Council for the Roadstone Quarrying Industry (NJIC). This consists of representatives (one from each side) from each of 17 Area Councils based on districts in Great Britain where quarrying is undertaken. The Area Councils, which are composed of representatives of the GMWU and TGWU and of local groups of employers, interpret national agreements and set differentials for most other groups of workers. The pay of some manual workers — notably maintenance workers — is negotiated at company and quarry level as are bonus and similar components of the pay of other groups. There is also an agreed disputes procedure, with stages at quarry, area, and national level.

There is no collective bargaining for white-collar staff.

OTHER QUARRYING

This covers the quarrying of other stone and slate. There is no national machinery, but in North Wales there is negotiation on basic pay and conditions for manual workers between the North Wales Slate Quarries Association and the TGWU, and bargaining over bonus payments at company level. Elsewhere there is some collective bargaining for manual workers at company or quarry level involving the TGWU and GMWU.

Chalk, clay, sand and gravel extraction

There is national negotiating machinery for manual workers employed in the extraction of four different materials — china clay, ball clay, brick clay and fire clay, and silica and moulding sands. In some of these industries there is supplementary local bargaining, and in sand and gravel extraction and in the chalk industry there is some bargaining for manual workers at company, quarry or plant level. There is, however, little collective bargaining for white-collar employees except in the china clay and brick and fire clay industries.

1 CHINA CLAY

This industry is centred on St Austell in Cornwall where the largest company, English Clays Lovering Pochin & Co Ltd (ECLP), has extensive operations and employs the majority of the industry's 7000 workers. Terms and conditions of employment for manual workers are set by the National Joint Industrial Council for the China Clay Industry (NJIC). This brings together the China Clay Association (St Austell) (CCA), which represents the six employers in the industry, and four unions, the TGWU, AUEW, EETPU and UCATT. The unions, however, do not negotiate all together: there are separate agreements for production workers (negotiated by the TGWU), engineering workers (AUEW and EETPU), drivers (TGWU), dockers (TGWU), and building and construction workers (UCATT). There is full trade union membership and employees are required to join as a condition of employment. The TGWU's Association of Clerical, Technical and Supervisory Staffs (ACTS) negotiates for some white-collar workers at ECLP.

107

2 BALL CLAY

The extraction of ball clay by opencast working or underground mining is undertaken in Devon, Cornwall and Dorset by ECLP and one other firm. The British Ball Clay Producers' Federation (BBCPF) represents the two employers. Terms and conditions for the 800 or so manual workers in the industry are set by the National Joint Industrial Council for the British Ball Clay Industry (NJIC), on which the BBCPF and the GMWU and TGWU are represented.

3 BRICK CLAY AND FIRE CLAY (MARL)

This industry is widespread geographically. Brick making is an integral part of the industry in which there are over 100 companies employing some 20 000 workers. Terms and conditions for manual workers are set by the National Joint Industrial Council for the Building Brick and Allied Industries (NJIC) (see page 163) where employers are represented by the employers' side of the National Federation of Clay Industries and employees by the GMWU and TGWU. There is some company-level bargaining for white-collar employees.

4 SILICA AND MOULDING SANDS

This industry employs about 1000 people. The Silica and Moulding Sands National Joint Council (NJC) is composed of representatives of the Silica and Moulding Sands Association (SAMSA) and of the GMWU and TGWU. The NJC sets a single basic rate of pay for adult operatives, rates for juveniles, and overtime premia and most conditions of employment for all hourly paid workers. There is some supplementary bargaining at company and plant level.

SAND AND GRAVEL

The sand and gravel industry employs about 15 000 people. The six largest companies and most of the 200 or so other firms are members of the Sand and Gravel Association (SAGA). Minimum terms and conditions for hourly paid employees were negotiated on the National Joint Industrial Council for the Sand and Gravel Industry (NJIC) between SAGA and TGWU and GMWU until 1979. Following the winding up of the NJIC, negotiations with recognised unions devolved to company and plant levels. A few firms are engaged in extracting sand and gravel from marine sources. These belong to SAGA's Marine Section. They were not covered by the national agreement and most negotiate at plant level with TGWU and the National Union of Seamen (NUS).

Other mining and quarrying

With the exception of tin mining, most employees in the various metalliferous

108

mining industries are covered by the collective bargaining arrangements in metal manufacturing (see pages 126).

In tin mining there are two companies operating three mines and employing some 1000 workers in South Cornwall. Both companies negotiate with the TGWU for production miners and general workers, and the AUEW, EETPU and UCATT for craftsmen. In the mining of salt and other non-metalliferous materials such as gypsum and graphite there is some company and plant level negotiation for manual workers involving the TGWU and GMWU.

Order III FOOD, DRINK AND TOBACCO

Food, drink and tobacco manufacturing together employ about 700 000 workers in firms of all sizes ranging from specialist firms employing a handful of workers to some of the largest enterprises in Britain employing many thousands and engaged in many product areas. For collective bargaining purposes food manufacturing can be divided into ten sectors, drink manufacturing into three, while tobacco manufacturing is a single sector. The sectors are:

General food manufacture

Grain milling

Bread and flour confectionery

Biscuits

Bacon curing and meat products

Milk and milk products

Sugar

Cocoa, chocolate and sugar confectionery

Animal and poultry foods

Vegetable and animal oils and fats

Brewing and malting

Soft drinks

Whisky and other alcoholic drink industries

Tobacco.

109

In many of the sectors minimum terms and conditions of employment for process workers are set by national agreements, and these are frequently supplemented by bargaining at company and plant level. Maintenance and craft workers are normally highly unionised and bargain at company and plant level. White-collar workers are, in general, not extensively unionised, but where they are covered by collective bargaining this is usually at company level.

Each sector is described separately below. The descriptions concentrate on the collective bargaining arrangements for process workers; the arrangements for maintenance and craft workers, or white-collar workers, are only indicated where these differ from the general pattern.

General food manufacture

The foods not covered by other specialised collective bargaining machinery include the canning of fruit and vegetables; the quick freezing of fruit, vegetables, poultry and fish; and the production and processing of preserves, mincemeat, honey, desserts, ice-cream, snack foods, vinegar, pickles and sauces, soups, infant and dietetic foods, vegetable protein, yeast, flavourings and essence, mustard, spices, tea and coffee blending, and corn and starch products. Some 120 000 workers are employed in these areas of the food industry.

The employers' association for the industry is the Food Manufacturers' Industrial Group (FMIG), to which firms employing about half the workforce in these product areas belong. This has close links with the largest trade association in the industry, the Food Manufacturers' Federation.

The main trade unions for process and general workers are the National Union of General and Municipal Workers (GMWU), the Transport and General Workers' Union (TGWU) and the Union of Shop, Distributive and Allied Workers (USDAW) although the National Union of Agricultural and Allied Workers (NUAAW) has some membership, particularly in some of the poultry processing companies. Usually one of these unions occupies an exclusive position in each plant but sometimes a different union predominates on each shift. Overall, union membership is fairly high and this is especially so in the larger firms, where union membership agreements are not unusual.

Craftsmen and maintenance workers are usually represented by the Amalgamated Union of Engineering Workers (AUEW), the Electrical, Electronic, Telecommunication and Plumbing Union (EETPU), or the Union of Construction, Allied Trades and Technicians (UCATT) and are particularly highly unionised in the manufacture of frozen foods which employs a substantial number of these workers in connection with the freezer plants.

White-collar workers have become increasingly unionised in recent years but even so union membership amongst these workers is still comparatively low. Where a union is recognised to negotiate for these workers it is usually the Association of Scientific, Technical and Managerial Staffs (ASTMS),

110

the Association of Professional, Executive, Clerical and Computer Staff (APEX), the TGWU's Association of Clerical, Technical and Supervisory Staffs (ACTS), the GMWU's Managerial, Administrative, Technical and Supervisory Section (MATSA) or USDAW's Supervisory, Administrative and Technical Association (SATA).

Minimum rates of pay, holidays, overtime and shift premia, a disputes procedure, and other terms and conditions for process and general workers are set by the Joint Industrial Council (JIC) for the Food Manufacturers' Industrial Group which brings together the FMIG, GMWU, TGWU and USDAW. These rates are often supplemented, particularly in the larger companies, by bargaining at company and plant level.

Grain milling

About 20 000 people are employed in this sector, about half in flour milling, and the remainder in the milling of grain for other purposes. The arrangements for flour milling are set out below. Firms involved in the milling of grain for other purposes tend to be primarily concerned with either flour milling, animal feed manufacture (see page 117), or agricultural merchanting (see page 229), and there is no separate machinery for this part of the sector.

FLOUR MILLING

Flour milling is dominated by three companies which together produce 80% of the total output of flour. The rest of the industry is made up of about 40 small independent millers. The companies are represented by the Incorporated National Association of British and Irish Millers which provides the employers' side of the National Joint Industrial Council (NJIC) for the Flour Milling Industry.

Process workers, of whom over 90% are unionised, are represented mainly by TGWU, GMWU and USDAW. These three unions provide the employees' side of the NJIC. Maintenance workers form a significant part of the workforce and are highly unionised. The main unions are AUEW, EETPU, UCATT and the National Union of Sheet Metal Workers, Coppersmiths and Heating and Domestic Engineers (NUSMW). Union membership among white-collar workers is low; the main unions are ACTS, APEX and ASTMS.

Minimum rates of pay and conditions of employment for process and transport workers are determined by the NJIC. Its agreements cover basic rates, hours of work, overtime and shift working premia, holidays and holiday pay, sickness benefit, and pre-retirement training and also provide a disputes procedure. NJIC rates are usually supplemented by bargaining at company level, which sets specific rates for individual mills, and often covers redundancy arrangements, sickness benefit and pensions.

Maintenance workers are covered by an informal agreement between the NJIC employers' side and AUEW, EETPU and UCATT which sets minimum

111

rates and conditions of employment. These are frequently improved by negotiations at local level.

Bread and flour confectionery

This industry, which employs about 100 000 people, manufactures a wide range of bread, cakes, pastries and pies. It can be divided into two sectors — master bakers, and plant or multiple bakers.

1 MASTER BAKERS

In general, master bakers are those who produce bread and flour confectionery on a relatively small scale, using traditional baking methods, and sell it in their own shops.

In England and Wales, most employers belong to the National Association of Master Bakers, Confectioners and Caterers (NAMB). Production and ancillary workers are represented by the Bakers', Food and Allied Workers' Union (BFAWU), and drivers, van salesmen and assistants by the TGWU, GMWU, or the United Road Transport Union (URTU). Clerical, supervisory and management staffs, where unionised, are represented by ASTMS, ACTS or MATSA. In general, unionisation in this sector is not particularly high.

The grading, pay, overtime and shift premia, and holidays of production and ancillary workers are set by a National Joint Committee of the NAMB and BFAWU. There is little supplementary bargaining at company or plant level.

In Scotland, there are two employers' associations: the Scottish Association of Master Bakers (SAMB), which represents most of the small bakers, and the Co-operative Employers' Association (CEA) which represents a small number of Co-operative bakeries.

The main union for production and ancillary workers is USDAW, but union membership is not high except in the Co-operative bakeries. Drivers, van salesmen and assistants, where unionised, usually belong to TGWU but membership amongst these workers is fairly low. Maintenance craftsmen are found almost solely in a few larger firms and are represented by AUEW and EETPU. White-collar employees are not usually unionised.

Until August 1978, pay and conditions of employment for production and ancillary workers in both master bakers and plant bakers in Scotland were set by the National Joint Council (NJC) for the Scottish Baking Industry. However, the employers' association for the plant bakers then withdrew from the NJC, and separate negotiating machinery is being set up for the two sectors of the industry. At present, SAMB and CEA negotiate directly with USDAW to set national minimum rates of pay, and have agreed to continue to observe the other terms and conditions of employment, including the disputes procedure, agreed by the NJC until a new comprehensive agreement is concluded. No other unions are recognised nationally and there is little collective bargaining at company level.

Statutory minimum wages, overtime rates and holiday allowances for drivers, van salesmen and assistants are established by the Retail Bread and Flour Confectionery Trade Wages Council (Scotland).

2 PLANT BAKERS

The chief product of the plant bakers is the standard loaf, which is produced in large scale operations by automated mechanical processes. The sector is dominated by two large firms — Ranks Hovis McDougall (RHM) and Associated British Foods (ABF).

In England and Wales most employers belong to the Federation of Bakers. In general, the same unions operate as in the master bakers sector, though in RHM and ABF, BFAWU's Salaried Staff Section also represents some white-collar staff, particularly bakery supervisors. Union membership in this sector is much higher than in the Master Bakers sector.

Rates of pay, hours, holidays, job grading, and overtime and shift premia, for production and ancillary workers are set by the National Joint Committee (NJC) of the Bakery Industry in England and Wales, which brings together the Federation and BFAWU. Assenting members to the agreement are not allowed to improve on these terms and conditions.

The NJC also has a National Joint Staff Committee, composed of assenting members of the Federation and BFAWU's Salaried Staff Section, which deals with matters of mutual concern and establishes a disputes procedure, for a number of staff grades including supervisory, clerical and junior management staff. This agreement now relates mainly to RHM and ABF and does not set substantive conditions, which are negotiated by member companies individually.

Rates of pay, holidays, sick pay and a disputes procedure for drivers, van salesmen and assistants are set on an area basis by Joint Standing Committees which bring together assenting members of the Federation and URTU, TGWU, GMWU, USDAW and BFAWU. The union side varies according to the area covered. There is little difference between the area rates. The only condition which can be negotiated at plant level is the rate of commission for van salesmen.

In Scotland, most employers belong to the Scottish area of the Federation of Bakers. Employees belong to the same unions as in the master bakers sector, though unionisation is generally higher, and there are a number of union membership agreements for production and ancillary workers.

Pay for production and ancillary workers is set by direct negotiation between the Federation and USDAW, and both have agreed to follow the other terms and conditions agreed by the NJC for the Scottish Baking Industry until a new agreement taking account of the changed circumstances has been developed.

Rates of pay and other conditions of employment for drivers, van salesmen and assistants are set by the Joint Councils for the Transport and Van Salesmen's Sections of the Baking Trade of Glasgow and West of Scotland which brings together the Federation and TGWU. Although the agreements nominally cover only Glasgow and West of Scotland they are applied throughout Scotland in most federated firms.

Biscuits

The biscuit industry manufactures many varieties of biscuits, rusks, short-breads, crispbread, etc, and is closely assoicated with the manufacture of bread and flour confectionery, chocolate, and with flour milling. It employs about 40 000 people.

Two firms, United Biscuits Ltd and Associated Biscuits Ltd, dominate the industry. Almost every firm in the industry is a member of the Cake and Biscuit Alliance, which nominates the majority of the employers' side representatives on the Joint Industrial Council (JIC) for the Biscuit Industry. The other employers' representatives on the JIC come from the Co-operative Wholesale Society (CWS) and the Scottish Co-operative Societies.

Production and ancillary workers in the larger companies are represented by the GMWU, TGWU, USDAW or BFAWU whose representatives together form the employees' side of the JIC. Union membership is at a high level and there are several union membership agreements in operation. Usually one of the four unions occupies an exclusive position at any one plant. Craftsmen are represented by AUEW or EETPU and membership is high. Drivers belong to URTU, TGWU or GMWU and some companies conclude joint national agreements with these unions. White-collar workers are not unionised to any great extent but there is some membership of ASTMS, MATSA and SATA. Senior staff in the CWS belong to the National Association of Co-operative Officials.

Minimum rates of pay, hours, holidays, overtime and shift premia, and other terms and conditions of employment for production and ancillary workers are negotiated by the JIC, which maintains close links with the JIC for Cocoa, Chocolate and Confectionery, and the National Joint Industrial Councils for Flour Milling and Baking. The agreement encourages supplementary bargaining on pay and productivity at local level, and this is widespread.

Bacon curing and meat products

This sector of the food industry employs some 45 000 workers in the curing of bacon and ham, the canning and preserving of meats, and the making of sausages, meat pies, pasties and puddings. Most of the firms are small but a few large firms account for the greater part of production, particularly so in the case of bacon products.

The principal employers' association in the industry is the Bacon and Meat Manufacturers' Industrial Group (BMMIG) which has about 40 member firms with a workforce of some 15 000. Some meat canning firms belong to the Food Manufacturers' Industrial Group (FMIG).

114

The level of union membership varies throughout the industry but usually manual employees in the larger companies are very highly unionised while in some of the smaller companies union membership is low or non-existent. Process workers are represented by USDAW, TGWU or GMWU with one union normally predominating at a particular plant. A number of union membership agreements exists in the larger companies. Maintenance craftsmen are mainly represented by AUEW, EETPU or, in some smaller factories, by the process workers' unions. There are union membership agreements in some larger companies but it is more usual for *de facto* closed shops to exist. White-collar workers, where unionised, are represented by ACTS, SATA, ASTMS or the National Union of Co-operative Officials.

Minimum rates of pay, hours, holidays, disputes procedures and other terms and conditions for about 15 000 process and related workers are set by the Bacon Curing Industry National Joint Industrial Council (NJIC) which brings together the BMMIG and USDAW, TGWU and GMWU. Terms and conditions in some meat canning firms are set by the FMIGJIC (see page 111). In the larger companies JIC conditions are supplemented by bargaining at both company and factory level.

Milk and milk products

Collective bargaining arrangements in the milk industry cover also milk distribution, which is formally part of Order XXIII, but not ice-cream manufacture which is covered by the JIC for the Food Manufacturers' Industrial Group (see page 111). In total the industry employs over 100 000 people, mostly in large organisations though there are also many small employers.

There are several specialised employers' associations: the National Association of Creamery Proprietors and Wholesale Dairymen, Amalgamated Master Dairymen, National Dairymen's Association, and the Co-operative Employers' Association. These, in turn, are federated to the Dairy Trades Federation (DTF). In Scotland, almost all employers belong to the Scottish Milk Trade Federation (SMTF).

Manual workers are, in general, highly unionised and there are some union membership agreements. Production workers generally belong to USDAW, TGWU or GMWU and some transport drivers are represented by URTU. Maintenance craftsmen generally belong to the TGWU, AUEW or EETPU. White-collar employees, where unionised, are usually represented by ACTS, APEX, ASTMS or SATA.

In England and Wales, basic terms and conditions for manual workers are set partly by the National Joint Council (NJC) for the Dairy Industry, and partly by its separate National Joint Negotiating Committees (NJNCs) for milk processing and distribution, and for milk product manufacture. On the NJC and the NJNCs the employers' representatives come from the DTF, the five major firms, the main federated employers' associations, and the Milk Marketing Board. The union representatives come from TGWU, USDAW, GMWU and URTU.

The agreements set minimum rates, holidays, overtime, weekend and night premia and provide a disputes procedure. These terms and conditions are supplemented at company and plant level by bargaining over conditions of employment such as sick pay schemes, payment by results schemes and efficiency bonuses.

In Scotland, terms and conditions of employment for most of the industry's manual employees are set by the Joint Industrial Council (JIC) for the Scottish Milk Trade, which brings together the SMTF, USDAW and the TGWU. The agreements set minimum rates of pay, hours of work, overtime, holidays and holiday pay, protective clothing, sickness pay, length of the normal working week, and the employment of school children. In some cases these may be supplemented at local level by bargaining over individual bonuses and commission rates.

Sugar

There are two principal companies in the sugar industry: the British Sugar Corporation Ltd, which processes only sugar beet, and Tate and Lyle Ltd which processes mainly sugar cane. The industry employs about 11 500 workers increasing to about 13 000 during the beet processing season.

Most process workers belong to the GMWU or TGWU although NUAAW has some membership in the British Sugar Corporation. Craftsmen, who are also highly unionised, are members of the AUEW or EETPU. Where white-collar workers are unionised they are represented, depending upon company and location, by ASTMS, ACTS or MATSA.

There is no collective bargaining machinery covering the whole industry. In the British Sugar Corporation bargaining is highly centralised; at Tate and Lyle there is significant bargaining at both company and plant level.

Cocoa, chocolate and sugar confectionery

This industry employs about 70 000 workers. It is dominated by three large companies — Rowntree Mackintosh, Cadbury Schweppes, and Mars — but there are many medium and small employers. Virtually all employers belong to the Cocoa, Chocolate and Confectionery Alliance but only a minority belong to the Cocoa, Chocolate and Confectionery Manufacturers' Industrial Group which appoints the employers' side of the Cocoa, Chocolate and Confectionery Joint Industrial Council (CCCJIC).

Unionisation amongst manual workers is relatively high in the larger companies but not extensive in the smaller companies. Process workers are represented mainly by TGWU, GMWU or USDAW. All three unions are represented on the CCCJIC. Maintenance craftsmen are generally members of AUEW, EETPU or UCATT. Where white-collar workers are unionised they are usually members of APEX, ASTMS or the white-collar sections of the manual unions.

116

The CCCJIC sets minimum rates of pay, hours, holidays, sick pay, shift and overtime premia and has a disputes procedure for about 20 000 process workers. However, none of the major employers is covered by the CCCJIC, and these negotiate separately at both company and plant level.

Animal and poultry foods

The industry employs about 25 000 people in the manufacturing or compounding of animal and poultry food, bird and pet foods. It has a complex structure in that, for historical reasons, process workers producing oil-seed cakes and meals are covered by the JIC for Soap, Candle and Edible Fats Trades (see page 124); process workers in the smaller mills producing grain animal feedstuffs are covered by the NJIC for the Corn Trade (see page 229); and some process workers in pet foods are covered by the NJIC for the Flour Milling Industry (see page 111), some by the Food Manufacturers' Industrial Group JIC (see page 111) while other process workers in pet foods are covered solely by company-level bargaining. Only about 8000 process workers in the larger mills producing grain and seed animal feeds are covered by the collective bargaining arrangements described below.

Four companies known as the National Compounders dominate this sector. There are also several regional employers' associations and one major national association — the Seed Crushers' and Oil Processors' Association.

Process workers are highly unionised and belong to the TGWU, GMWU or USDAW. Generally only one of these unions is recognised in any given mill. Union membership is also high amongst maintenance workers, who belong to the AUEW or EETPU. White-collar workers, where unionised, belong mainly to ASTMS though ACTS, MATSA and APEX have some members.

Minimum wage rates, hours of work, shift and overtime premia, holidays and holiday pay, and sickness benefits, for process workers are set by the NJIC for the Seed Crushing, Compound and Provender Manufacturing Industries. The employers' side is nominated by the four National Compounders, the Seed Crushers' and Oil Processors' Association and six regional employers' associations. The majority of employee representatives come from the TGWU with the remainder from the GMWU and USDAW. The national agreement is generally supplemented by negotiations at company and mill level over such matters as productivity and bonus schemes, shift allowances and flexibility.

Vegetable and animal oils and fats

This sector of the food industry is concerned with the production of margarine, cooking fats, dripping, suet, oil-seed, cakes and meals, olive oil, fish oils and other animal and vegetable oils. Most firms belong to the Soap, Candle and Edible Fat Trades Employers' Federation, which also represents firms in the chemicals industry and is dealt with on page 124.

117

Brewing and malting

These industries employ about 70 000 people. In brewing there are seven main companies and a large number of smaller brewers. In malting there are two principal companies and several smaller ones, though some of the larger brewers also have their own malting operations. There are no employers' associations in the industry. The Brewers' Society and the Maltsters' Association of Great Britain are essentially trade associations and are not involved in collective bargaining.

Union membership amongst manual workers is generally high, and there are union membership agreements in most large companies. Production workers generally belong to the TGWU or GMWU. Maintenance craftsmen usually belong to the AUEW or EETPU, though UCATT has members in some companies. White-collar employees are not highly unionised, though membership is expanding and there are some union membership agreements. The main unions involved are ACTS, ASTMS and MATSA, and some staff associations are also recognised.

Terms and conditions of employment for production workers are settled entirely at domestic level except in Yorkshire where one of the Brewers' Society regional associations, the Yorkshire Brewers' Association, has an agreement with the TGWU and GMWU covering overtime and shift premia, holiday pay and entitlement, paternity leave and a disputes procedure.

Soft drinks

This industry is concerned with the manufacture of aerated waters, fruit squashes, cordials, fruit and vegetable juices, ginger beer and other soft drinks. It employs some 25 000 workers in about 350 firms.

In England and Wales all the major manufacturers and many of the smaller ones belong to the National Association of Soft Drinks Manufacturers (NASDM) while in Scotland most are members of the Scottish Association of Soft Drinks Manufacturers (SASDM).

Levels of unionisation amongst manual workers are generally quite low, except in some of the larger companies. The main unions for process workers are USDAW, TGWU and GMWU. AUEW normally represents maintenance workers, and drivers often belong to URTU. White-collar workers are not usually unionised.

Statutory minimum wages, overtime rates and holiday allowances for process workers (and drivers in England and Wales) are established by the Aerated Waters Wages Council (England and Wales) and the Aerated Waters Wages Council (Scotland). NASDM nominates employers' representatives to the Council for England and Wales and the employees' representatives are nominated by TGWU, USDAW, GMWU and URTU. SASDM nominates employers' representatives to the Council for Scotland and employees' representatives are nominated by USDAW and TGWU.

There is some supplementary collective bargaining, particularly in the larger companies, often over job evaluation and pensions at company level, and over productivity, disciplinary procedures and redundancy at plant level.

Whisky and other alcoholic drink industries

This sector employs over 30 000 workers mainly in the distilling, blending and bottling of whisky, but also included is the production of gin and other potable spirits and the fermentation and bottling of British wines, cider and perry. Most parts of this sector are dominated by a few major companies, through their associated and subsidiary firms.

Process and general workers mainly belong to the GMWU or TGWU with only one union normally recognised at a particular location. Maintenance craftsmen are normally members of their appropriate union, principally AUEW, EETPU and UCATT. Coopers are found almost solely in the whisky industry and are represented by GMWU. Union membership amongst supervisors is often high, but membership among other white-collar grades is fairly low. Where a union is recognised for these workers it is usually ASTMS, ACTS, MATSA or APEX.

Terms and conditions for most process and general workers are normally settled by collective bargaining at company and plant level.

Only in respect of two small groups of workers — coopers, and general workers in the malt whisky distilleries — is there any form of industry-level collective bargaining. Minimum terms and conditions of employment for coopers are agreed by the National Joint Industrial Council for the Cooperage Industry (see page 172). The agreement in malt distilling between the Malt Distillers' Association of Scotland, TGWU and GMWU sets basic pay, hours, shift and overtime premia, holiday and holiday pay, guarantee pay, and provides a disputes procedure.

Tobacco

The tobacco industry employs about 35 000 people in Great Britain in the manufacture and distribution of tobacco, cigars, cigarettes and snuff. The main manufacturing centres are Bristol, Glasgow, Liverpool, Manchester, Newcastle, Nottingham and South Wales.

The industry is dominated by four large firms — Imperial Tobacco Ltd, Gallaher Ltd, BAT (UK and Export) Ltd, and Carreras Rothmans Ltd — who together employ over 95% of the industry's workforce. The rest of the industry is made up of less than a dozen small firms, some of them specialising in only one product, such as snuff. All the major companies and the majority of the small firms belong to the Tobacco Industry Employers' Association which provides all the employers' representatives on the National Joint Negotiating Committee (NJNC) for the Tobacco Industry.

Manual workers are highly unionised; there are several *de facto* closed shops and a few union membership agreements. Most process workers belong

119

to the Tobacco Workers' Union (TWU), though the TGWU, GMWU and the Tobacco Mechanics' Association (TMA) also have some members, and there are a number of small staff associations. All four unions represent employees on the NJNC, though the TWU has the majority of the seats. Usually only one union is recognised on any particular site. Maintenance workers form a significant part of the workforce as the industry is highly mechanised, and are represented mainly by the AUEW or EETPU. White-collar workers are represented by ASTMS, APEX or the clerical section of the TWU; generally membership is not as high as in the manual unions but there are some union membership agreements.

The NJNC sets minimum rates and conditions of employment for process workers, and there is widespread supplementary bargaining over job evaluation, productivity, sick pay, hours and holidays, mainly at company level. The NJNC provisions on the guaranteed week and overtime are applied as standard in all the companies covered by the agreement.

Order IV   COAL AND PETROLEUM PRODUCTS

This Order employs about 35 000 people, in two sectors:
1 Coke ovens and manufactured fuel
2 Mineral oil refining and the blending of lubricating oils and greases.

Collective bargaining arrangements in the first sector are included under Coal Mining (see page 104). The arrangements in the other sector, together with those in oil distribution which is formally part of Order XXIII, are described below.

The oil industry

The oil industry in Great Britain is composed of companies whose operations include the refining of oil, the blending of lubricating oils and greases, and the wholesale and retail distribution of petroleum products. There are no employers' associations concerned with collective bargaining and there is no industry-wide collective bargaining machinery. However, collective bargaining is well developed with different arrangements for oil refining, and blending and distribution, each of which is described separately below. The level of unionisation is in general high.

1 OIL REFINING

There are 21 refineries in Great Britain producing a wide range of products including some lubricating oils and greases. Three of the largest companies with oil refining operations are Shell, Esso and British Petroleum (BP). Refineries are situated mainly around the Thames Estuary, in West Wales and in North West England. There is one major refinery in Scotland. Oil refining is capital intensive and employs approximately 15 000 people.

Maintenance craftsmen are represented by the Amalgamated Union of Engineering Workers (AUEW), the Electrical, Electronic, Telecommunication and Plumbing Union (EETPU), the Amalgamated Society of Boilermakers, Shipwrights, Blacksmiths and Structural Workers (ASB), the National Union of Sheet Metal Workers, Coppersmiths and Heating and Domestic Engineers (NUSMW) and the Union of Construction, Allied Trades and Technicians (UCATT), although not all unions may be recognised at any given refinery. The Transport and General Workers' Union (TGWU) is recognised for general operatives in most refineries. Union membership is very high amongst craftsmen and general operatives though union membership agreements are rare.

Plant bargaining in respect of manual workers is well developed in the refineries, with the craft workers normally forming a joint negotiating committee and the general workers bargaining separately. Agreements tend to cover the main terms and conditions of employment, and disputes and grievance procedures, the final stages of which usually involve full-time union officials. One particular feature is productivity agreements which cover job flexibility between different crafts and between craftsmen and general workers, and include comprehensive job specifications listing specific tasks that are to be undertaken by operatives with given job titles.

White-collar staff, where unionised, are mainly represented by the Association of Scientific, Technical and Managerial Staffs (ASTMS) and the TGWU's Association of Clerical, Technical and Supervisory Staffs (ACTS).

2 BLENDING AND DISTRIBUTION

Some lubricating oils and greases are produced in refineries, others in separate blending plants. These blending plants are grouped together for collective bargaining purposes with oil distribution terminals, pipeline terminals, airport operations, and the oil companies' motor repair centres. Distribution is carried out both by the oil companies themselves and their authorised distributors.

In the oil companies the TGWU is recognised for all manual staff, which includes drivers, plant operators and mechanics, and has virtually 100% membership in this area. The general pattern is for company-wide agreements to cover hours of work, rates of pay and other allowances, holidays, discipline and disputes procedures, restrictions on the use of outside contractors, and productivity, with detailed job descriptions and clauses on job flexibility. Company-wide negotiations play a bigger part in this area of the oil companies' operations than they do in refining. At plant level there tend to be negotiations over such matters as overtime arrangements, work measurement and safety and welfare. ACTS and ASTMS represent white-collar staff in some companies.

The oil companies authorise other companies to distribute fuel oil to houses, offices, factories, etc. There are about 500 authorised distributors, for the most part small companies. In the oil companies' arrangements with the TGWU there is usually a clause whereby the company concerned undertakes

121

to advise its authorised distributors that it is expected that the distributors' pay rates should be not less than a certain level which is related to the pay of the oil company's own employees. Collective bargaining in the authorised distributors themselves tends to be concentrated in the larger companies. The TGWU is recognised for skilled, semi-skilled and unskilled manual employees. ACTS has some white-collar membership and is recognised in some of the larger companies in respect of staff grades up to a certain level.

Order V CHEMICALS AND ALLIED INDUSTRIES

In these industries there are about 3000 companies, employing over 400 000 people. The companies vary widely in size. ICI is by far the largest, employing about 20% of the industries' workforce. The industries make a wide variety of products, including inorganic and organic chemicals, gases, pharmaceuticals, toilet preparations, paints, soap and detergents, synthetic resins, plastics, synthetic rubber, dyestuffs and fertilisers. The industries are capital intensive, with rapidly changing technology, and there has been a steady trend towards concentration of production in the larger companies.

Collective bargaining arrangements within these industries differ for manual and white-collar workers, and so the two groups are treated separately below.

Manual workers

For manual workers there exists both national and company bargaining, with a growing trend in recent years for national agreements to set minimum rates, but for company bargaining to determine actual earnings. For process and general workers there are eight national negotiating bodies. One covers several main sectors of the industries, and the others cover individual sectors — drugs and fine chemicals; gelatine and glue; paint, varnish and lacquer; soap, candle and edible fat; surgical dressings; match manufacture; and printing ink and roller making. This last sector is covered in the entry for paper, printing and publishing (see page 179). There are also national negotiating arrangements for craftsmen. Government establishments involved in the production of nuclear fuels and isotopes have bargaining arrangements which are similar to those of the civil service.

EMPLOYERS' ASSOCIATIONS AND UNIONS

The principal employers' association is the Chemical Industries Association (CIA) which has about 300 member companies employing about half of the industries' workforce. For national collective bargaining purposes, CIA members fall into two categories: 'conforming members', who formally undertake to adopt terms and conditions agreed nationally, and 'non-conforming members' who do not. ICI and some other large companies are non-conforming members.

The other employers' associations in the industries are the Federation of Gelatine and Glue Manufacturers, the Paintmakers' Association of Great Britain, the Soap, Candle and Edible Fat Trades Employers' Federation, the Surgical Textiles Conference, and the Society of British Match Manufacturers.

For process and general workers the Transport and General Workers' Union (TGWU) and the National Union of General and Municipal Workers (GMWU) are the unions with the highest membership; the Union of Shop, Distributive and Allied Workers (USDAW) also has a significant membership. One of these unions normally occupies an exclusive position on a particular site. For craftsmen, apprentices and some semi-skilled engineering workers the main unions are the Amalgamated Union of Engineering Workers (AUEW) and the Electrical, Electronic, Telecommunication and Plumbing Union (EETPU) though the TGWU and the GMWU also have some membership in these categories. Other unions with membership are the Union of Construction, Allied Trades and Technicians (UCATT), the National Union of Sheet Metal Workers, Coppersmiths and Heating and Domestic Engineers (NUSMW) and the Amalgamated Society of Boilermakers, Shipwrights, Blacksmiths and Structural Workers (ASB).

On most sites the unions have a high level of membership. It is often 100% and there are some union membership agreements.

NATIONAL NEGOTIATING MACHINERY

For process and general workers, there are seven national negotiating bodies, each covering different sectors.

1 The Chemical and Allied Industries' Joint Industrial Council (CAIJIC)

This body brings together representatives of the CIA, and the TGWU, GMWU and USDAW. It sets minimum rates of pay, hours of work, overtime rates and conditions, shift premia and conditions, a guaranteed wage, call-in pay, holidays, and conditions for transfer to other jobs. There is a four-stage disputes procedure with provision for arbitration. The JIC does not, however, cover the whole industry. Its agreements are restricted to the sectors of general chemicals, synthetic resins, plastics materials and synthetic rubber, dyestuffs and pigments, and fertilisers, and directly affect about half the workers in these sectors.

2 The Drug and Fine Chemical Joint Conference

This body sets minimum terms and conditions for the pharmaceutical industry. Its members are also drawn from the CIA, TGWU, GMWU and USDAW, the three unions forming a Joint Trade Union Committee for the Drug and Fine Chemical Trade. Its agreements are similar to those of the CAIJIC, and directly affect about half the workers in this sector.

123

3 The Gelatine and Glue Joint Industrial Council (JIC)

This JIC brings together the Federation of Gelatine and Glue Manufacturers, which has seven member companies, and four unions — the TGWU, GMWU, USDAW and the National Union of Footwear, Leather and Allied Trades (NUFLAT). Although the Federation is an independent body, an arrangement exists whereby the CIA provides services for it in the collective bargaining field at national level, including the employers' secretaryship of the JIC. The JIC's agreements cover main terms and conditions of employment and contain a disputes procedure. Its agreements affect virtually all the process and general workers in this sector.

4 The National Joint Industrial Council (NJIC) for the Paint, Varnish and Lacquer Industry

The NJIC covers process and general workers in this sector who are not covered by ICI agreements. It consists of representatives of the Paintmakers' Association of Great Britain, the TGWU and the GMWU. The Association has 108 member companies, including all the large companies in this sector. The NJIC sets minimum rates of wages, holidays, hours of work, overtime conditions and rates and shift differentials, and the agreement contains a clause on equal opportunities. There is also an NJIC disputes procedure.

5 The Joint Industrial Council (JIC) for the Soap, Candle and Edible Fat Trades

This JIC which covers only process and general workers brings together representatives from the Soap, Candle and Edible Fat Trades Employers' Federation, which has about 40 member companies employing about 12 000 people, and from USDAW, TGWU and GMWU. It sets minimum wages, hours, holidays, overtime rates and conditions, shift differentials and conditions, and a number of other terms and conditions of employment. There is also an informal disputes procedure. The agreements affect most of the process and general workers in this sector. Craftsmen generally belong to the AUEW and the EETPU. White-collar workers, where unionised, are usually represented by ASTMS. There is widespread collective bargaining at company and plant level.

6 The National Joint Council (NJC) for the Surgical Dressings Industry

Representatives to the NJC come from the Surgical Textiles Conference, and the TGWU, GMWU, USDAW, and the National Union of Dyers, Bleachers and Textile Workers (NUDBTW). NJC ageements cover about 7000 employees and set minimum weekly rates, hours, shift allowances, and other terms and conditions.

7 The Joint Industrial Council (JIC) of the Match Manufacturing Industry

The Society of British Match Manufacturers and the GMWU nominate representatives to sit on the JIC. The dominant company in the industry, Bryant and May Ltd, is the only company at present represented on the JIC which covers about 600 employees and sets minimum wage rates, hours, holidays, overtime, job grading and other terms and conditions.

Craftsmen make up about 20% of the manual workers in the industries. Those employed by CIA conforming companies are covered by a CIA/Craft Unions Agreement, between CIA and AUEW, EETPU, NUSMW, ASB and UCATT. This agreement is similar to that of the CAIJIC, though there are additional clauses on the training of craft apprentices, and allowances for unpleasant working conditions.

COMPANY AND PLANT BARGAINING

Bargaining at company and plant level is widespread and increasingly determines actual earnings. This is formally acknowledged by the three national agreements involving the CIA. Company-level bargaining tends to include terms and conditions such as pensions, sick pay and redundancy, while bargaining at plant level tends to concentrate on local pay rates and differentials, disciplinary and grievance procedures, demarcation issues and local working conditions.

ICI negotiates centrally with eight 'signatory unions' — TGWU, GMWU, AUEW, EETPU, UCATT, ASB, NUSMW, and the Association of Pattern-makers and Allied Craftsmen (APAC). It has a weekly staff agreement under which manual workers receive an annual salary paid weekly, a company-wide job evaluation system, and a post-entry union membership agreement. At plant level, negotiations concentrate on the interpretation and application of company agreements.

White-collar workers

White-collar workers make up over 40% of the industries' workforce, more than in any other major manufacturing industry. In recent years there has been considerable growth in white-collar unionisation, mostly below management and professional staff level. There is no national negotiating machinery, but the CIA has issued a statement of policy to guide its members on the recognition of trade unions. The predominant union is the Association of Scientific, Technical and Managerial Staffs (ASTMS), which represents staff in many different occupations. The Association of Management and Professional Staffs (AMPS) has some membership amongst management, scientists and other professional staff. The white-collar sections of the manual unions also have some membership — mainly amongst supervisors and clerical and administrative staff. Union membership agreements are uncommon.

Particularly in the larger companies, white-collar employees tend to be organised, for the purposes of union representation, into company-wide 'common interest' groups, each frequently represented by a single union and normally bargaining separately.

Within ICI, there are six 'common interest' groups, five of which, covering over 90% of white-collar staff, are covered by the company-wide collective bargaining arrangements tabulated below.

Common interest group	Approximate number of employees	Unions
Works supervisors	4000	TGWU, GMWU, AUEW, EETPU, UCATT, ASB, NUSM, ICI Foremen's and Supervisors' Association
Commercial, clerical and administrative	9000	ASTMS, TGWU's Association of Clerical, Technical and Supervisory Staffs (ACTS), GMWU's Managerial, Administrative, Technical and Supervisory Section (MATSA)
Scientific and technical	6000	ASTMS
Engineering	2000	ASTMS, AUEW's Technical, Administrative and Supervisory Section (TASS)
Management and professional	9000	AMPS

Order VI METAL MANUFACTURE

Metal manufacture, in which some 450 000 people are employed, covers smelting, refining and alloying; rolling and drawing; and the production of castings, forgings and other basic forms of ferrous and non-ferrous metals. It can be divided for collective bargaining purposes into the British Steel Corporation and the private sector.

British Steel Corporation

The British Steel Corporation (BSC) was formed by the Iron and Steel Act 1967. BSC's main activities are the production of iron and steel, the manufacture of forgings and castings, and steel rolling. Unionisation is high, and collective bargaining is well developed. BSC is required by the Act both to negotiate terms and conditons of employment with the appropriate trade unions and to disclose information to the unions to enable them to negotiate on an informed basis. BSC recognises a number of different unions for industrial, staff and management grades.

For Industrial grades (manual employees) the following are the main unions recognised:

Iron and Steel Trades Confederation (ISTC)

National Union of Blastfurnacemen, Ore Miners, Coke Workers and Kindred Trades (NUB)

Amalgamated Union of Engineering Workers (AUEW)

Amalgamated Society of Boilermakers, Shipwrights, Blacksmiths and Structural Workers (ASB)

Electrical, Electronic, Telecommunication and Plumbing Union (EETPU)

Union of Construction, Allied Trades and Technicians (UCATT)

National Union of General and Municipal Workers (GMWU)

Transport and General Workers' Union (TGWU)

British Roll Turners' Trade Society (BRTTS)

National Union of Sheet Metal Workers, Coppersmiths and Heating and Domestic Engineers (NUSMW)

Association of Patternmakers and Allied Craftsmen (APAC).

All these unions are represented on the Trades Union Congress Steel Committee. The craft unions — ASB, EETPU, AUEW (Technical, Administrative and Supervisory Section (TASS) and Engineering and Foundry Sections), UCATT, BRTTS, NUSMW, and APAC — co-ordinate much of their policy through the National Craftsmen's Co-ordinating Committee for the Iron and Steel Industry (NCCC).

For Staff grades (clerical, laboratory and other technical staff up to and including foremen and other first line supervisors) all the Steel Committee unions are recognised though ISTC has the largest membership. The Association of Professional, Executive, Clerical and Computer Staff (APEX) and the Association of Scientific, Technical and Managerial Staffs (ASTMS) have local recognition in certain areas.

For Management grades the Steel Industry Management Association (SIMA) is nationally recognised for 'middle managers', who are staff above first line supervisors up to and including assistant departmental heads; and for 'managers', who are staff senior to assistant departmental heads up to but excluding those who report directly to a director. ISTC also has national recognition for middle management.

COLLECTIVE BARGAINING

For most of the industrial grades, all employment matters of common interest apart from wages — such as holidays, employment and income security, pensions, and sickness payments — are negotiated nationally with the Steel Committee unions. The TGWU however bargains at local level. General wage awards and frameworks for local productivity bargaining are negotiated nationally, and disputes procedures are agreed, by ISTC, NUB and GMWU separately for their respective memberships, and, for craftsmen and apprentices, by the NCCC. Negotiations may embrace all the members of a union or they may be on a sectional basis, covering for example shift workers, workers on maintenance conditons, lower paid workers, workers in particular departments, fully skilled craftsmen, semi-skilled maintenance workers or apprentices. For process and general workers wage rates are negotiated at works level. For most craftsmen time rates are negotiated at national level. For all industrial grades, manning and rating of plants, tonnage bonuses, and incentive and productivity schemes are negotiated at local level.

For industrial grades in two specialised sectors of the steel industry, strip mill production throughout the Corporation and tinplate production in Wales, pay and disputes procedures are agreed by three Boards which BSC inherited at nationalisation and on which it is the sole employer represented. The Sheet Trade Board has employee representatives from the ISTC; the Galvanizing Conciliation Board and the Welsh Tinplate Board have representatives from the TGWU. All the Boards adopt the appropriate national agreements between BSC and the individual unions and/or the Steel Committee on employment matters of common interest.

For staff grades there are national agreements between BSC and the Steel Committee covering conditions of employment and between BSC and the individual unions covering general increases. However, salary structures are negotiated at works level.

For both managers and middle managers terms and conditions of employment except pay are determined at national level. The salary structure for middle managers is also determined at national level but for managers salaries are determined locally within a national framework.

INDUSTRIAL DEMOCRACY

BSC was the first nationalised industry to experiment with employee directors; 12 were appointed to the then four regional group boards of the newly nationalised steel industry in 1968. At present employee directors sit on the five manufacturing divisional boards. The Iron and Steel Act of 1975 extended the principle of employee directors to the main BSC Board which at present consists of 6 union-nominated members, 6 senior management members including the Chairman, 7 independent members and 2 civil servants. Talks concerning a 'Steel Contract' — a new partnership to cover consultation, participation and negotiation at all levels in the corporation — have taken place.

The private sector

The private sector produces both ferrous and non-ferrous metals. Unionisation is generally high, particularly amongst manual workers, and most of the same unions that are recognised in BSC operate here, though not all are necessarily recognised in any one company or plant. Collective bargaining at company level is widespread, and there is also some national and regional bargaining, mainly involving firms manufacturing ferrous metals. There are two employers' associations with national coverage, the Independent Steel Employers' Association and the National Metal Trades Federation; and two regional organisations based in the Midlands, the Midlands Iron and Steel Wages Board and the South Staffordshire Iron and Steel Association. Some companies are members of the Engineering Employers' Federation or the Welsh Engineers' and Founders' Association and therefore are covered by collective bargaining in the engineering industry. In particular, some companies involved in the manufacture of special steels are members of the Engineering Employers' Sheffield Association which is a party to local collective bargaining machinery. Also covered under 'engineering' is the manufacture of wire and wire rope. In addition, some companies in brass-working and founding are members of the National Building and Allied Hardware Manufacturers' Federation and are covered by its agreement with the National Society of Metal Mechanics.

The Independent Steel Employers' Association (ISEA) represents the 15 major iron and steel manufacturing companies remaining in the private sector. These employ approximately 17 000 people, predominantly in producing heavy steel. There is a *de facto* closed shop for all manual workers. The ISEA negotiates with the members of the NCCC (see BSC above) for skilled and semi-skilled employees, with ISTC for production workers, and with both ISTC and NCCC for supervisory, clerical and technical staff. These agreements set general pay increases, hours, shifts and overtime premia, holidays and sick pay, and all except the ISTC agreement for production workers contain disputes procedures. Pay structures, however, are negotiated at company level.

The National Metal Trades Federation (NMTF) has about 100 member companies engaged mainly in the production of castings for the building industry and domestic appliances. Some member companies are engaged in the pressing and fabrication of metals, the extrusion and fabrication of plastic materials and the treatment of metals. The Federation negotiates at national level with the Joint Committee of Light Metal Trades Unions which has nine affiliated unions: AUEW (Foundry Section), GMWU, ASB, TGWU, TASS, APEX, NUSMW, APAC and the National Union of Domestic Appliance and General Metal Workers (NUDAGMW). The agreements cover over

20 000 employees. For manual employees the agreements set minimum time rates, hours, shift and overtime premia, holidays, and procedures for settling disputes and for fixing piecework moulding prices; for white-collar employees they provide a means of resolving disputes. Pay and other matters are determined at company level.

The Midland Iron and Steel Wages Board (MISWB) and the South Staffordshire Iron and Steel Association (SSISA) are closely linked. The MISWB has employer representatives from about twenty companies engaged in hot or cold rolling, and employee representatives from ISTC. Its agreements cover approximately 4500 manual operatives and set a minimum wage, basic working week, shift premia, guaranteed employment payments, holidays with pay, and a disputes procedure. The SSISA's members are the fifteen hot rolling companies in membership of the MISWB. The Association negotiates with BRTTS in respect of skilled employees and apprentices in membership of the Society, on a similar range of matters to those covered by MISWB agreements.

Orders VII, VIII, IX, XI and XII ENGINEERING

The engineering industry covers five orders of the Standard Industrial Classification — Mechanical, Instrument and Electrical Engineering; Vehicles; and Metal Goods not elsewhere specified — a complex group of activities concerned with the manufacture, installation, maintenance and repair of goods made mainly of metal, and the fabrication of articles of plastic material. It employs over three million people. About thirty per cent of the industry's employees work in mechanical engineering which includes the manufacture of metal-working and wood-working machine tools, pumps, valves and compressors, industrial engines, textile machinery, construction and earth moving equipment, office machinery, industrial plant and steelwork. About half of the employees in the industry are engaged in almost equal proportions in vehicle manufacturing and electrical engineering. Vehicle manufacturing covers the manufacture of cars, tractors and lorries, and the manufacture and repair of aircraft and aerospace equipment and railway rolling stock and track. Electrical engineering covers the manufacture of electrical machinery, insulated wires and cables, telephone equipment, radio and television receivers, computers, radar equipment and domestic electrical appliances. The remainder of the employees in the industry are employed in instrument engineering and the manufacture of a diverse range of other metal goods including cutlery, nuts and bolts, cans and wire. Shipbuilding, shiprepairing and marine engineering are dealt with elsewhere (see page 143) as are British Rail workshops (see page 200).

About three-quarters of the manual workers in the industry and about half the white-collar workers are covered by collective agreements at either national or domestic level. For manual workers collective bargaining is well developed at national and company level, and at plant level in most of the larger undertakings. For white-collar staff there are some nationally negotiated agreements, but pay and most terms and conditions of employment are determined at company and plant level. The majority of the industry's manual workforce is covered by national-level collective bargaining between the Engineering Employers' Federation (EEF) and the Confederation of Shipbuilding and Engineering Unions (CSEU). Outside these arrangements are a number of areas of the industry covered by small specialist employers' associations which have separate negotiating arrangements.

Engineering Employers' Federation (EEF)

The EEF is the largest employers' association in the country. It has sixteen local engineering employers' associations in Great Britain with about 6500 establishments in membership employing some 2 million manual and staff workers. The associations are the:

Central Lancashire Engineering Employers' Association

Coventry and District Engineering Employers' Association

East Anglian Engineering Employers' Association

East Midlands Engineering Employers' Association

Engineering Employers' London Association

Mid-Anglian Engineering Employers' Association

North of England Engineering Employers' Association

North West Lancashire Engineering Employers' Association

Rochdale Engineering Employers' Association

Scottish Engineering Employers' Association

Engineering Employers' Association of South Lancashire, Cheshire and North Wales

Engineering Employers' Association of South Wales

Engineering Employers' South Yorkshire and North Midland Association

Engineering Employers' West of England Association

West Midlands Engineering Employers' Association

Engineering and Shipbuilding Employers' Association — Yorkshire and Humberside.

The associations have a high degree of autonomy in the running of their affairs. There is a wide variety in the size of associations. For instance, the West Midlands Association covers nearly 375 000 employees while the member firms of the South Wales Association employ about 45 000. The associations provide their members with industrial relations information and advice, training, representation in tribunals and assistance in negotiations. The associations are thus concerned with the day-to-day problems of their members while the Federation is concerned with representing its members' interests at national and international level.

The governing body of the Federation is its General Council which deals principally with formal matters such as the election of the President and other office bearers, the annual accounts, and constitutional issues. The associations elect members to the Council in proportion to their relative size. Policy determination and executive action are handled through the Management Board.

A number of standing committees report to the Management Board to assist it in formulating policy. These are the Policy Committee, which is a Management Board sub-committee; the Director-General's Advisory Committee, made up of the Chief Executives of the associations; the Chief Personnel Executives Consultative Group containing Personnel Directors of the larger federated companies; the Commercial and Economic Committee which is composed of the Chief Executives and Chairmen of some federated companies, and the Manpower, Training and Representation committees. In dealing with major industrial relations issues the views of member firms are obtained through the associations as well as through these committees. National negotiations with the CSEU are undertaken through a small committee of the Management Board supported by the Federation's own staff.

Confederation of Shipbuilding and Engineering Unions (CSEU)

The CSEU is the largest grouping of unions for collective bargaining purposes in Great Britain and has a combined affiliated membership of over 2·4 million, of which manual employees account for about 2 million and white-collar employees the rest. The CSEU is organised both at national and district level. The unions representing manual employees are:

The Amalgamated Union of Engineering Workers (AUEW) (Engineering, Foundry and Construction Sections)

Transport and General Workers' Union (TGWU)

Electrical, Electronic, Telecommunication and Plumbing Union (EETPU)

National Union of General and Municipal Workers (GMWU)

Amalgamated Society of Boilermakers, Shipwrights, Blacksmiths and Structural Workers (ASB)

National Union of Sheet Metal Workers, Coppersmiths and Heating and Domestic Engineers (NUSMW)

National Society of Metal Mechanics (NSMM)

Union of Construction, Allied Trades and Technicians (UCATT)

Association of Patternmakers and Allied Craftsmen (APAC)

Furniture, Timber and Allied Trades Union (FTAT)

Associated Metalworkers' Union (AMU)

National Union of Scalemakers (NUS)

Screw, Nut, Bolt and Rivet Trade Union (SNBRTU)

National Union of Domestic Appliance and General Metal Workers (NUDAGMW).

Unions and sections of unions representing white-collar employees are:

Association of Scientific, Technical and Managerial Staffs (ASTMS)

Association of Professional, Executive, Clerical and Computer Staff (APEX)

AUEW's Technical, Administrative and Supervisory Section (TASS)

TGWU's Association of Clerical, Technical and Supervisory Staffs (ACTS)

GMWU's Managerial, Administrative, Technical and Supervisory Association (MATSA)

EETPU's Electrical and Engineering Staff Association (EESA).

Of the manual unions the AUEW has by far the largest affiliated membership. The TGWU, EETPU, GMWU and the ASB together account for the large majority of the remaining membership. Among the white-collar unions ASTMS and TASS have the highest affiliated memberships.

The overall governing body of the CSEU is its General Council whose

133

members come from affiliated trade unions and who are elected according to the rules of their own unions.

The CSEU has an annual conference which is the formal policy-making body. Each affiliated union is represented in proportion to its affiliated membership. The annual conference elects an Executive Council which has the authority to conclude agreements on behalf of the CSEU. The main standing sub-committees of the Executive Council are concerned with engineering, shipyards and railways. There are also sub-committees concerned with aircraft manufacture, and craftsmen in the gas and water industries, hospitals and local authorities. The CSEU acts at local level through District Committees (DCs).

National agreements between the EEF and CSEU

At national level the EEF and the CSEU negotiate agreements covering procedural and substantive issues on behalf of manual and white-collar employees although most substantive issues in respect of white-collar employees are left to be determined at company and plant level.

1 PROCEDURAL MATTERS

Agreements give a framework for union recognition for manual and white-collar employees in federated companies and also lay down disputes procedures. The recognition agreements, which cover the manual unions affiliated to the CSEU and ASTMS, TASS, APEX, ACTS and MATSA, give these unions the right to represent their members in any federated establishment in respect of all manual employees and certain specified classes or grades of white-collar employee. For 'non-procedural' categories of white-collar employee the arrangement between the EEF and the recognised white-collar unions is that the Federation will generally advise that recognition should not be withheld from one of those unions if it has a significant presence and is a major influence in a grade which is agreed to be an appropriate level for collective recognition.

The disputes procedure for manual employees provides for two levels, domestic and external. The form of the domestic stages is left for agreement in the establishment concerned, although the national agreement recommends that they should be in writing and jointly agreed, and cover such matters as the number of stages, the stage at which shop stewards become involved, the level of management involved at each stage, the level at which individual, sectional and general matters should be raised and time limits within which different types of questions should be discussed. Failing settlement at the final domestic stage the disputed matter may go to an external conference which will involve representatives from the local engineering employers' association and local officials of the union(s) concerned as well as management representative(s) and the shop steward(s) concerned. The agreement also mentions the possibility of informal discussions within the works with local officials of the employers' association and trade unions prior to an external conference in order to clarify and resolve an outstanding issue. There is no automatic provision for a national-level conference except on matters involving interpretation of national agreements. However, a meeting involving national representatives of the EEF and of the union(s) concerned can be held to discuss other matters where specially agreed by the parties.

For the white-collar employees covered by the national procedure agreements there are three separate disputes procedures agreed between the EEF and ASTMS: the EEF and APEX/ACTS/MATSA jointly; and the EEF and TASS. The three are virtually identical. If the issue cannot be resolved at domestic level a works conference will be held involving full-time union official(s) and representative(s) of the local engineering employers' association. The next stage is a final local meeting held away from the works. There is a provision for national-level conferences but not as a part of the procedure except in cases involving the interpretation of a national agreement.

2 PAYMENTS AND CONDITIONS

National-level agreements on rates of pay affect only manual employees. National minimum rates are set for skilled, unskilled and junior employees and apprentices, and guidance is given for the calculation of intermediate adult rates. Other terms and conditions of employment covered by national agreements with the manual unions are: the length of the working week, notice periods, guaranteed week, overtime, Sunday allowances, shiftwork and holidays and certain principles relating to the operation of systems of payment by results. The EEF has agreements with all the recognised white-collar unions covering the length of the working week. In addition there are agreements with TASS covering overtime, holidays of draughtsmen changing their employment, and the training of apprentices, and with APEX covering night shift allowances. All these manual and white-collar agreements cover the engineering industry as a whole.

There are also six specialised national agreements negotiated between the EEF and individual unions covering special classes of employee:

Employees covered	Union(s)
Foundry workers	AUEW (Foundry Section), AMU, APAC, GMWU, NSMM, TGWU
Skilled toolroom operatives	AUEW (Engineering Section)
Patternmakers	APAC
Plastics workers	GMWU, TGWU
Packing case makers	UCATT, GMWU, TGWU
Woodworkers	TGWU, FTAT.

135

These agreements are limited in scope. They tend to include job definitions and relate those jobs to the nationally agreed minimum rates. These categories of employee are also covered by the provisions in the more general national agreements described above.

In four specialised areas of the industry more comprehensive substantive sector agreements have been reached between the EEF and individual unions. All these agreements cover wage rates, supplementary allowances, grading structures, job definitions and disputes procedures. In these sectors bargaining is centralised to a far greater degree at national level than in the engineering industry generally where the emphasis is on highly developed plant bargaining.

Agreement	Number of firms party to agreement	Union(s)
Lift Manufacture	18	EETPU
Telephone Exchange Equipment Installation	3	EETPU
Patent Glazing	2	EETPU
Scale Beam & Weighing Machine Service & Installation	12	NUS
Mechanical Construction Engineering	350	AUEW (Construction and Engineering Sections), ASB, EETPU, NUSMW, TGWU, GMWU.

The last-named agreement is negotiated nationally by the Federation on behalf of the Sites Group Organisation, which consists of member firms engaged in erection and installation work on outside construction sites. There are Sites Group staff based in 9 of the 16 local associations. In oil and chemical plant construction there is also collective bargaining machinery independent of that set up by the EEF and the CSEU and this is dealt with below (see page 141).

3 PAYMENT BY RESULTS, DILUTION AND TRAINING

National agreements establish principles for the operation of payment by results schemes at domestic level. They also contain provisions for the training of craftsmen and for the relaxation of existing customs regarding the employment of skilled employees.

Local agreements between the Engineering Employers' Associations and various unions

At local level there are still a number of agreements between individual engineering employers' associations and various unions although the trend in recent years has been for local agreements with CSEU unions to be absorbed into the national agreement. The agreements tend to be limited to relatively small geographical areas and often to specialised occupations and to be limited in subject matter. Except for the Sheffield agreements employees are covered by the national agreement between the EEF and the CSEU for other substantive and procedural matters.

The main remaining local agreements are as follows:

Association	Union(s)	Subject
South Lancashire, Cheshire and North Wales	AUEW	Allowances for temporary outworkers, and local holiday rates
Sheffield	Iron and Steel Trades Confederation (ISTC), TGWU, GMWU, ASB	Earnings, district minimum time rates and other terms and conditions of employees engaged in the manufacture of special steels
Sheffield	British Roll Turners' Trade Society	Pay rates for roll turners
West Midlands	CSEU	A number of agreements on minimum time rates for specialist workers in such trades (and districts) as sheet metal working (Wolverhampton and Birmingham), malleable iron foundry (Walsall) and spring manufacturing

[cont. overleaf]

Association	Union(s)	Subject
East Midlands	CSEU	Minimum time rates in Lincoln district
Scottish	CSEU	Three agreements on outworkers' allowances in the Clyde District, Forth District and Falkirk District.

Company and plant bargaining

In general, company and plant bargaining is well developed and establishes actual levels of pay in both federated and non-federated firms in the industry. In federated firms the rates set at national level are only minimum rates for manual employees, and any further supplement to basic rates, together with productivity and payment by results schemes, is left for negotiation at domestic level. For white-collar employees most terms and conditions are determined at domestic level.

There is a wide variety of practice as regards company and plant bargaining in federated firms. Some bargain centrally; others prefer to bargain at subsidiary company and plant level. Collective bargaining for white-collar and manual employees normally takes place separately. Amongst manual employees maintenance and production workers sometimes negotiate separately.

The principal companies outside the EEF include three of the vehicle manufacturers: the Ford Motor Company, Talbot UK Limited and Vauxhall Motors. The TGWU and the AUEW have the highest number of manual employees in membership in motor vehicle manufacturing, and there are generally union membership agreements covering these employees. White-collar staff are represented by ACTS, APEX, ASTMS and TASS and unionisation in grades below management is high. Terms and conditions are usually negotiated at company level by joint negotiating committees, one for manual employees and one for white-collar employees. These committees comprise representatives of management and both full-time and lay officials of the trade unions. The committees also agree disputes procedures which have as their final stages meetings between central management and national union officials or local management and district union officials.

Other areas of the engineering industry with large companies which are not members of the EEF include the manufacturing of cans and metal containers (Metal Box), electrical engineering (Decca) and the manufacture of insulated wires and cables (BICC). Metal Box recognises a number of unions including TGWU, GMWU, AUEW, EETPU, the National Graphical Association (NGA), ASTMS and ACTS. Unionisation is high and there are some union membership agreements. Collective bargaining covers most employees except executive staff. Decca recognises TGWU, AUEW, NUSMW, GMWU, EETPU, ASTMS, TASS, APEX, MATSA and the Association of Cinemato-

138

graph, Television and Allied Technicians and negotiates terms and conditions mainly at group rather than plant level. BICC is the principal member of the Electrical Cable Makers' Confederation and is a party to the Joint Industrial Council for the Electrical Cable Making Industry (see below).

Other machinery in the engineering industry

Within the engineering industry there are a number of areas that have collective bargaining machinery independent of that set up by the EEF and the CSEU. The machinery in these areas with one exception covers manual employees only and sets minimum terms and conditions which are often supplemented by bargaining at company or plant level. Where collective bargaining in respect of white-collar employees takes place, it is at company or plant level only except for some of the terms and conditions within the lock, latch and key industry. Most of these areas contain a relatively small number of employees. However, in the manufacture of electrical cables, cutlery and flatware, hand tools, jewellery, silverware and allied trades, locks, latches and keys and wire and wire rope, and in engineering and foundry work in South West Wales, oil and chemical plant construction and specialist vehicle building, there is machinery covering more substantial numbers of people.

1 CABLE MAKING

The Electric Cable Makers' Confederation negotiates with the TGWU, GMWU and EETPU in the Joint Industrial Council (JIC) for the Electrical Cable Making Industry, in respect of about 20 000 cable making process workers.

Agreements reached in the JIC cover hours, overtime, shift working, holidays, a guaranteed week, minimum earnings levels and basic time rates related to the grades of an industry-wide job evaluation scheme. Also included in the national agreement is a stipulation that payment by results bonus schemes which are negotiated at company and plant level should provide the facility for earning a certain minimum amount for a specified effort. There is in addition a national disputes procedure.

The above parties also negotiate in the Telephone Cable Jointers Negotiating Committee which covers about 300 employees. The committee's agreements have broadly the same scope as those of the JIC.

2 CUTLERY, FLATWARE AND TABLE HOLLOW-WARE

The cutlery industry produces knives, hafted forks, scissors, steels and blanks for any of these articles. The employers' association in the industry, the Cutlery and Silverware Association of the United Kingdom (CSAUK), negotiates with the Sheffield Cutlery Council of the GMWU to determine hours, overtime and shift premia, holiday entitlements, minimum fall back rates, a grading structure and a sickness and accident scheme. CSAUK also negotiates with the National Union of Gold, Silver and Allied Trades (NUGSAT) as does the Manufacturing Silversmiths' Association, on behalf of workers engaged in the manufacture of spoons, forks and table hollow-ware. These agreements cover a range of matters similar to that of the CSAUK/GMWU agreement. About 4000 employees are covered by these agreements.

3 ENGINEERING AND FOUNDRY WORKS IN WEST WALES

The Welsh Engineers' and Founders' Association (WEFA) which is not federated to the EEF has some forty member firms mainly in South West Wales including the Port Talbot, Neath, Swansea and Llanelli areas. These firms are engaged in general engineering, sheet metal work, toymaking, steelwork fabrication, wire drawing, casting and foundry work. WEFA negotiates with the West Wales Allied Engineering Trades Committee in the Welsh Engineers' and Founders' Conciliation Board. The unions which are members of the Committee and are thus represented on the Conciliation Board are the AUEW (Engineering and Foundry Sections), EETPU, ASB, TGWU and the GMWU. The Board's agreements deal with a wide range of matters including basic pay, holidays, shift and overtime premia, outwork allowances and a disputes procedure and cover some 5500 manual employees.

4 HAND TOOLS

Collective bargaining machinery covering process workers engaged in the manufacture of hand tools has been set up by the Sheffield Lighter Trades Industrial Section, which is an amalgamation of specialist employers' associations covering some 70 companies employing about 5000 people, and the GMWU, TGWU, ASB, the Sheffield Sawmakers' Protection Society and the Sheffield Wool Shear Workers' Trade Union. Agreements reached cover time rates, piecework hourly supplements, piecework standards, hours of work, shift and overtime premia and holidays. The AUEW, EETPU, and UCATT are frequently recognised at company level for maintenance craftsmen. ASTMS and, to a lesser extent, APEX are recognised for white-collar staff up to middle management level in some of the larger companies.

5 JEWELLERY, SILVERWARE AND ALLIED TRADES

The majority of companies in this industry employ fewer than 50 workers and are either manufacturing jewellers, goldsmiths, silversmiths or electro-plated hollow-ware manufacturers. (The Royal Mint is covered by national government collective bargaining machinery.) London, Birmingham and Sheffield are the main centres of the industry which employs some 22 000 people. NUGSAT is the principal union for manual workers. The TGWU and the GMWU are recognised also by a limited number of companies. There are three principal employers' associations: the British Jewellers' Association (BJA) and CSAUK, which operate on a nationwide basis, and the Manufacturing Silversmiths' Association (MSA) which operates in the Sheffield area.

Minimum rates of pay and conditions of employment are set by a number of regional agreements. NUGSAT has separate agreements with the Southern and Northern areas of the BJA, with CSAUK for the Sheffield district, and with the MSA. Within this regional structure of the BJA/NUGSAT agreements there are separate agreements for those employers engaged in the jewellery/goldsmiths sector and for the silversmiths and electroplate manufacturers. There is no negotiated trade agreement for the Fashion Jewellery industry (which includes silver and base metals), nor is there industry-wide collective bargaining in respect of white-collar workers which is an area of relatively low union membership.

6 LOCKS, LATCHES AND KEYS

There are about 50 companies engaged in the manufacture of locks, latches and keys. The industry, largely centred in the West Midlands, employs about 8000 people. The British Lock Manufacturers' Association (BLMA) and the National Union of Lock, Latch and Metal Workers are the only parties to the Joint Industrial Council (JIC) for the Lock, Latch and Key Industry. JIC agreements for manual employees cover minimum rates of pay, overtime, shift working, holidays, sick pay, redundancy and redeployment procedures, facilities for trade union officials, and a disputes procedure. Also included in these agreements is an industry-wide job grading classification which has its own appeals procedure. A JIC agreement for white-collar employees below departmental manager level covers holidays, hours, sick pay and overtime payments.

7 OIL AND CHEMICAL PLANT CONSTRUCTION

Some of the firms engaged in oil and chemical plant construction are members of the EEF and are parties to the Mechanical Construction Engineering Agreement (see page 136). Some 50 other firms are members of the Oil and Chemical Plant Constructors' Association (OCPCA). OCPCA members negotiate with the AUEW, ASB, EETPU, NUSMW and TGWU and on some sites formal site agreements have been established which cover all terms and conditions of employment, including productivity and incentive schemes. The OCPCA also negotiates a separate agreement for offshore construction work.

8 SPECIALIST VEHICLE BUILDING

The Vehicle Builders' and Repairers' Association has in membership about 2400 companies who manufacture specialist vehicles and/or are engaged as specialist commercial or car body repairers. The Association's representatives sit on the United Kingdom Joint Wages Board for the Vehicle Building Industry. The employees' representatives come from the TGWU, the NUSMW, the EETPU and FTAT. The Board's agreement covers approximately 25 000 employees and deals with basic rates, holidays, hours, shift premia,

141

ratio of apprentices to craftsmen, guaranteed week and a disputes procedure the final stage of which is a National Conference between representatives of the Board and national officials of the union(s) concerned. These agreements cover only manual employees.

9 WIRE, WIRE ROPE AND OTHER WIRE PRODUCTS

About 37 000 are employed in wire and wire rope manufacture in Great Britain. About half of the industry's workforce is employed by the 82 member companies of the Wire and Wire Rope Manufacturers' Association (WWRMA) which negotiates with the Amalgamated Society of Wire Drawers and Kindred Workers (ASWDKW), the GMWU and the TGWU in the Joint Industrial Council (JIC) for the Wire and Wire Rope Industries. JIC agreements cover guaranteed pay, hours, overtime and shift premia, holidays, principles of productivity schemes, and a disputes procedure.

There are also two smaller employers' associations in the industry concerned with the manufacture of wire products: the Scottish Wirework Manufacturers' Association (SWMA) and the Wire Goods Manufacturers' Association (WGMA). The SWMA negotiates with the TGWU in the Scottish Joint Association for the Wireworking Industry. The WGMA negotiates directly with the ASWDKW.

10 OTHER AREAS

The remaining areas of the engineering industry with separate collective bargaining are shown in the table below.

Employers' Association(s)	Union(s)	Approximate numbers covered by the machinery	
		Firms	Employees
Scottish Association of Master Blacksmiths	ASB	52	800
National Master Farriers', Blacksmiths' & Agricultural Engineers' Association	AUEW	1200	2500
Metal Packaging Manufacturers' Association	NGA	28	2000
National Building & Allied Hardware Manufacturers' Federation	NSMM TGWU GMWU	130	Not known

142

British Surgical Trades' Association	AUEW NUSMW FTAT	220	2700
Scottish Master Patternmakers' Association	APAC	4	70
British Association of Lithographic Plate Manufacturers	NGA	3	150
British Dental Association; Dental Laboratories Association	NUGSAT Union of Shop, Distributive and Allied Workers (USDAW)	75	2900
Employers' Federation of Card Clothing Manufacturers	Society of Card Setting Tenters; Card Dressers' Society; ASWDKW	3	200

All of the employers' associations and unions above negotiate directly with each other except for the British Dental Association and the Dental Laboratories Association which with NUGSAT and USDAW have seats on the National Joint Council for the Craft of Dental Technicians. Most of the agreements negotiated between the employers' associations and trade unions above cover basic pay, overtime, holidays, arrangements for apprentices, and disputes procedures.

Two small areas of the engineering industry, each with only a few hundred workers, are covered by wages councils. The Pin, Hook and Eye, and Snap Fastener Wages Council has employers' representatives from the Pin and Allied Trades Association and workers' representatives from the TGWU. The Coffin Furniture and Cerement Making Wages Council has employers' representatives from the Funeral Furnishing Manufacturers' Association (FFMA) and employee representatives from the NSMM and the National Union of Tailors and Garment Workers (NUTGW).

Order X SHIPBUILDING AND MARINE ENGINEERING

For collective bargaining purposes the industry may be divided into the public sector, consisting of British Shipbuilders, which contains all the larger establishments, and the private sector. The industry employs over 150 000 people.

1 British Shipbuilders

British Shipbuilders (BS) was set up by the Aircraft and Shipbuilding Indus-

143

tries Act 1977. It employs some 80 000 people building tugs, container ships, cargo liners, passenger ships, tankers, naval vessels and other specialised vessels. Its establishments — a mixture of shipbuilding yards which build new ships and may carry out major conversions, composite yards where shipbuilding and shiprepairing are carried out, shiprepairing establishments which concentrate on maintenance, repairs and conversions, and establishments undertaking marine engine building and marine and general engineering — are largely concentrated on the Clyde and on the Rivers Tyne, Wear and Tees on the North East Coast, with other centres on the East Coast of Scotland, Merseyside, and at Barrow and Southampton.

The Act requires BS to negotiate terms and conditions of employment with the relevant trade unions, and under a procedure agreement with the Confederation of Shipbuilding and Engineering Unions (CSEU) (see page 132) the following unions are recognised for collective bargaining purposes:

Amalgamated Society of Boilermakers, Shipwrights, Blacksmiths and Structural Workers (ASB)

Amalgamated Union of Engineering Workers (AUEW) (Engineering and Foundry Sections)

Union of Construction, Allied Trades and Technicians (UCATT)

Electrical, Electronic, Telecommunication and Plumbing Union (EETPU)

Furniture, Timber and Allied Trades Union (FTAT)

National Union of General and Municipal Workers (GMWU)

Association of Patternmakers and Allied Craftsmen (APAC)

Transport and General Workers' Union (TGWU)

National Union of Sheet Metal Workers, Coppersmiths and Heating and Domestic Engineers (NUSMW)

National Society of Metal Mechanics (NSMM)

Association of Professional, Executive, Clerical and Computer Staff (APEX)

Association of Scientific, Technical and Managerial Staffs (ASTMS)

AUEW's Technical, Administrative and Supervisory Section (TASS)

EETPU's Electrical and Engineering Staff Association (EESA)

UCATT's Supervisory, Technical, Administrative, Managerial and Professional Section (STAMP).

The Shipbuilding and Allied Industries Management Association (SAIMA) is recognised for managers within its membership.

In March 1979 BS and CSEU reached agreement on a single nationally negotiated wage round covering both manual and staff employees. Corporate bargaining with the CSEU on wages and working conditions has therefore replaced individual company negotiations with separate trade unions, and there is now one annual review date from which settlements covering all employees take effect.

CONSULTATION MACHINERY

Consultation machinery is also required by the Act, in particular to promote industrial democracy. There are regular consultative meetings between the Corporation and the Shipbuilding Negotiating Committee of the CSEU, three of whose members are also part-time members of the Corporation's Board. There is a National Joint Steering Committee which is promoting the development of industrial democracy at establishment level.

2 The private sector

Boats built in the private sector range from small pleasure craft, usually of fibreglass, to fishing boats and other small ships. The pleasure boat industry is largely concentrated on the South coast; fishing boats are mainly built in Scotland. Shiprepairing is also undertaken. In addition there are a number of small and medium-sized marine engineering firms, some of which are members of the Engineering Employers' Federation (EEF) and are covered by the collective bargaining arrangements in the engineering industry (see pages 130–143).

There are several employers' associations in the private sector. The firms which were not nationalised established the Shipbuilders' and Shiprepairers' Independent Association (SSIA). The members of the SSIA are mainly the larger companies and together they employ about 6000 workers. The Fishing Boat Builders' Association (FBBA) has 13 member firms in Scotland covering around 1000 employees, and is affiliated to the Ship and Boat Builders' National Federation (SBBNF), though the SBBNF is not itself involved in collective bargaining. The East of Scotland Association of Shiprepairers and Shipbuilders (ESASS) has 5 member firms. In England and Wales there are also some small local employers' associations.

The manual unions which operate in BS are also recognised in the private sector. The degree of unionisation is affected by the size of the company. There is little white-collar unionisation.

Before the creation of BS many of the firms who are now members of SSIA were formerly members of the Shipbuilders' and Repairers' National Association (SRNA) and followed nationally-agreed minimum rates and conditions of employment for manual workers, with additional bargaining at plant level. This arrangement still exists, since the SSIA has negotiated a continuation agreement which provides for all previous agreements to go on operating until superseded. The SSIA and the CSEU are currently discussing new substantive and procedural proposals which will maintain the present pattern of bargaining. Manual workers employed by FBBA members have their pay, holiday pay and allowances set by an agreement with UCATT, AUEW and ASB. Those employed by ESASS members are covered by agreements with ASB, AUEW, UCATT, EETPU, GMWU, NUSMW, FTAT and APAC which set minimum pay rates, differentials, hours, shift premia, holidays, sick pay and other terms and conditions of employment, and include an agreed disputes procedure. There is supplementary bargaining over pay at domestic level, and throughout the sector many firms follow the substantive minimum terms and conditions operating in BS.

Order XIII TEXTILES

These industries together employ over 450 000 people. Firms vary widely in size, though there are a great number of small firms and relatively few large ones. For collective bargaining purposes the Order can be divided into thirteen separate industries, defined either by the raw material processed or the product and often highly concentrated geographically. These are:

Man-made fibre production

Cotton spinning, and cotton and man-made fibre weaving and finishing

Silk

Soft flax and hemp

Wool textiles

Jute

Rope, twine and net

Hosiery and other knitted goods

Lace

Carpets

Narrow fabrics

146

Made-up textiles

Asbestos textiles.

The industries vary greatly in size from hosiery, wool textiles and cotton which together provide about two-thirds of the Order's employment, to jute, or flax and hemp, employing only a few thousand people. Each industry is treated separately below, except for asbestos textiles, which is part of the asbestos manufacturing industry (see page 168). There are a few other small industries in the Order, but these do not have significant collective bargaining arrangements.

Collective bargaining for manual workers is generally highly developed, with industry-wide, company and plant bargaining. Most white-collar workers, however, are not covered by collective bargaining, though some are indirectly affected by industry-wide agreements and there is some company bargaining. Where white-collar collective bargaining in an industry is significant this is mentioned below.

Man-made fibre production

The industry employs about 30 000 people, producing fibres used in clothing, carpets, household textiles and industrial cords and fabrics. There are two companies in the industry, Courtaulds and ICI, with respectively about 20 000 and 10 000 employees engaged in man-made fibre production. There is no employers' association and no industry-wide negotiating machinery. Employees in ICI Fibres Division are covered by the company-wide negotiations described under Chemicals (see page 125). Courtaulds negotiates with the Transport and General Workers' Union (TGWU) for general and process workers; with the Amalgamated Union of Engineering Workers (AUEW), the Electrical, Electronic, Telecommunication and Plumbing Union (EETPU), the Union of Construction, Allied Trades and Technicians (UCATT), and the National Union of Sheet Metal Workers, Coppersmiths and Heating and Domestic Engineers (NUSMW) for craftsmen; with the Association of Scientific, Technical and Managerial Staffs (ASTMS), the TGWU's Association of Clerical, Technical and Supervisory Staffs (ACTS), and some of the craft unions for more junior grades of white-collar staff and COSESA, a union operating only in Courtaulds, for more senior grades of white-collar staff. Bargaining for manual and more junior grades of white-collar staff operates at plant level for most pay matters and at company level for other terms and conditons of employment; for more senior grades of white-collar staff bargaining is solely at company level.

Cotton spinning and cotton and man-made fibre weaving and finishing

In this industry, which employs over 75 000 people, there are separate national

147

agreements between the employers' associations and unions representing different groups of manual workers. The British Textiles Employers' Association (BTEA) represents the great majority of the industry's companies. The BTEA's Industrial Committee has negotiating sub-committees for spinning and weaving, finishing, road transport and maintenance.

The industry is still largely concentrated in the North West of England, and here a single Central Committee negotiates for employees in spinning and weaving. Its representatives are drawn from the constituent groups of the Amalgamated Textile Workers' Union (ATWU) and the member associations of the Northern Counties Textile Federation (NCTF) except the General Union of Associations of Loom Overlookers (GULO) which negotiates separately.

In the finishing sector, the National Union of Dyers, Bleachers and Textile Workers (NUDBTW) covers approximately 18 000 general workers and boilerfiremen; the TGWU and the United Road Transport Union (URTU) represent road transport staff; the Society of Lithographic Artists, Designers, Engravers and Process Workers (SLADE) represents engravers, painters and copyists; and the Trade Society of Machine Calico Printers represents printers. Outside North West England, the TGWU is recognised for some general workers in spinning, weaving and finishing.

Building and engineering maintenance workers are mainly represented by the AUEW, EETPU and UCATT. Foremen in the finishing sector are represented by the Guild of Textile Supervisors. There is some white-collar unionisation, mainly by the staff sections of ATWU and NUDBTW, ACTS, ASTMS, and the Association of Professional, Executive, Clerical and Computer Staff (APEX).

Rates of pay, hours, holidays and other terms and conditions for the different groups of manual workers are agreed centrally between BTEA and

(i) the Central Committee
(ii) GULO
(iii) NUDBTW
(iv) TGWU, URTU
(v) AUEW, UCATT, EETPU
(vi) The Trade Society of Machine Calico Printers, SLADE.

There is no central agreement for supervisory or white-collar staff, apart from one which recognises the Guild of Textile Supervisors (GTS).

At company and plant level, negotiations, in the case of BTEA-associated companies, are normally restricted to such matters as productivity, work measurement and redundancy. In the case of companies outside BTEA, plant negotiating follows central pay settlements and is generally in line with them. There is some collective bargaining for white-collar staff.

Silk

This is a relatively small industry employing about 16 000 people and concentrated in Staffordshire around Leek, and in Cheshire around Macclesfield.

148

Four employers' associations represent almost all of the silk industry companies. They are the Leek and District Manufacturers' and Dyers' Association; the Macclesfield Textile Manufacturers' Association; the British Throwsters' Association; and the East Anglian Textile Manufacturers' Association.

The Amalgamated Society of Textile Workers and Kindred Trades (ASTWKT) represents employees (up to first grade foremen) in the spinning and weaving sectors; the NUDBTW those in the finishing sector; and the TGWU and the National Union of General and Municipal Workers (GMWU) employees in all three areas.

Minimum rates of pay and conditions of employment for process workers were determined by the Joint Industrial Council for the Silk Industry, on which all four employers' associations and all four unions were represented. There was an agreed disputes procedure. The JIC was disbanded in 1980 and it was expected that employers and unions might try to use the former machinery as a guide for settling disputes.

In both Cheshire and Staffordshire, district rates are determined and there is a district stage in the disputes procedure. There is some company-level bargaining, mainly over productivity.

There is some membership of ASTMS and APEX amongst white-collar staff. In the Staffordshire area there are district-level negotiations for clerical staff, and in both areas there is some bargaining at company level.

Soft flax and hemp

This industry is historically based in Scotland and there has been no development in other areas. It is covered by the Flax and Hemp Wages Council (Great Britain), which sets general minimum time rates, piecework basic time rates, overtime and waiting time rates, holidays and holiday pay. The Flax Spinners' and Manufacturers' Association of Great Britain provides the employer representation on the wages council. The employee representation is shared by the Scottish Council of Textile Trade Unions, the NUDBTW, and the TGWU.

Wool textiles

The wool textile industry employs about 61 000 people and is mainly concentrated in West Yorkshire and neighbouring areas, with the remainder in Scotland and the West of England. Collective bargaining arrangements for manual workers are well developed, with about three-quarters directly covered by national agreement. There is separate machinery for each of the three main areas, with that for West Yorkshire regarded as national machinery, covering firms who are outside Scotland or the West of England. The arrangements are complex because the industry comprises both numerous companies which carry out only one of the wool textile processes and larger companies undertaking all stages of production. The arrangements in each of the three areas are described separately below.

1 WEST YORKSHIRE

The Industrial Relations Council of the Confederation of British Wool Textiles Ltd (IRC) represents the interests of employers in West Yorkshire and adjacent areas; and is also the central employers' organisation in the wool textile industry. The IRC represents the following sectors of the industry:

Raw materials, wool scouring and combing
Worsted and woollen yarn production
Manufacturing
Dyeing and finishing.

There are approximately 500 companies in membership of the Confederation, covering about 40 000 employees.

Amalgamation of local employers' associations has not yet been parallaled on the trade union side. In West Yorkshire seventeen trade unions are concerned with collective bargaining in the wool textile industry. The National Association of Unions in the Textile Trade (NAUTT) represents wool textile workers excluding the woolcombing and certain other preparatory sections. By far the largest union in the Association is the NUDBTW. The Association also includes the Cloth Pressers' Society, the Huddersfield and District Healders' and Twisters' Trade and Friendly Society, the Pattern Weavers' Society, the Scottish Council of Textile Trade Unions, and APEX. The NUDBTW includes a Craftsmen Staff Branch, previously the independent Yorkshire Society of Textile Craftsmen, and, similarly, a transfer of engagements to APEX has been effected in respect of the National Woolsorters' Society. Both the textile craftsmen and the woolsorters retain separate representation on the NAUTT. Process and clerical workers in woolcombing are represented by the GMWU; skilled maintenance workers mainly by the AUEW, EETPU and the Joint Trade Unions in the Building Industry; small groups of specialist craftsmen mainly by specialist unions such as the Amalgamated Society of Wool-Comb, Hackle and Gill Makers in respect of pinsetters and the National Society of Brushmakers; and supervisory staff by ASTMS (Managers' and Overlookers' Section) and the Yorkshire Association of Power Loom Overlookers.

IRC agreements with NAUTT mainly set minimum rates of pay, minimum earnings levels, overtime rates, hours of work, shift allowances, holidays, and sick pay. The IRC negotiates with the GMWU for employees in woolcombing, and this agreement covers a similar range of matters. IRC agreements with the AUEW cover rates of pay and grading, but agreements with the EETPU and the Joint Trade Unions in the Building Industry follow the rates of pay in the respective parent industries; the other terms and conditions of employment follow the IRC/NAUTT or the IRC/GMWU agreements respectively, depending on the sector of the industry in which the maintenance workers are employed. The agreements between IRC and the individual specialist unions, and each of the two unions representing supervisory staff, cover a similar range of matters. Clerical workers follow the IRC/NAUTT settlement (except in the woolcombing sector), although there are separate discussions between APEX and IRC on how the settlement should be applied. Process workers in the dyeing and finishing sector are covered by the agreement between the BTEA and NUDBTW for workers in cotton textiles and man-made fibres (see page 148).

The minima for manual workers can be enhanced by bonus schemes and piece rates negotiated by the individual unions at company and plant level. There has been a trend towards plant-level bargaining in respect of other matters — for example, selection for redundancy, enhanced severance payments, improved sick pay, pensions; and some comprehensive procedural agreements have been concluded, although the plant-level agreements may be based on IRC guidance. There is also some company-level bargaining for white-collar workers.

2 SCOTLAND

In Scotland minimum rates of pay, hours of work, overtime and shift rates, holidays, sick pay, guidelines for productivity bargaining and apprenticeship arrangements are set for production workers by a Joint Negotiating Committee normally composed of the Scottish Woollen Trade Employers' Association, which represent the great majority of the largest companies, and a Joint Trade Union Committee of the GMWU, NUDBTW and TGWU. Rates of pay are often enhanced by bargaining at company level.

In the Harris Tweed industry, there are negotiations between the Hebridean Spinners' Advisory Committee, which represents the three main employers, and the TGWU. They result in two separate agreements: one for millworkers and warpers and the other for weavers. Basic pay and terms and conditions are agreed for millworkers. However, for warpers the agreement is concerned with rates since employment is on a piece rate basis. As the weaving of Harris Tweed is a cottage industry and the weavers are self-employed, the weavers' negotiations are also mainly concerned with rates.

There are no regional negotiations for other categories of employee. There is some company-level bargaining for maintenance workers, foremen, and clerical staff. The main unions involved are the GMWU, NUDBTW, ACTS and ASTMS.

3 WEST OF ENGLAND

In the West of England, minimum rates of pay, sick pay, overtime, holidays, a guaranteed week, other terms and conditions, and a disputes procedure are set for all manual workers and supervisors by the West of England Joint Industrial Council for the Woollen and Worsted Industry. This brings together the

West of England Wool Textile Employers' Association, which represents all the employers in the area, and the NUDBTW and the TGWU. There is some supplementary local bargaining, and also some local bargaining for clerical and managerial staff.

Jute

The jute industry is concentrated in the Tayside area. In Tayside 23 companies, employing about 7000 people, all belong to the Association of Jute Spinners and Manufacturers. Outside Dundee, six of these companies, employing about 1500, make up the Forfar and Kirriemuir Manufacturers' Association and are also members of the Association of Jute Spinners and Manufacturers.

The dominant trade union is the NUDBTW representing hourly paid textile workers. Two Joint Industrial Councils, one each for Dundee and Forfar/Kirriemuir, bring together the appropriate Association and the NUDBTW and settle the main terms and conditions of employment of textile workers. There are agreed disputes procedures. A job-evaluated grading structure known as the Jute Wages Structure has existed in Dundee since 1952; changes are negotiated within the JIC.

Company or plant bargaining is limited to the negotiation of bonus schemes and fringe benefits. Unions representing craftsmen and other small specialist groups negotiate wages separately with the employers' associations but follow the general conditions of employment set by the JICs.

Rope, twine and net

About 5000 people are employed in some 150 companies engaged in the manufacture of rope, twine and net, of natural or man-made fibres. The industry is covered by the Rope, Twine and Net Wages Council (Great Britain), on which employers are represented by the Cordage and Net Manufacturers' (Employers) Association, and employees by the TGWU, GMWU and the NUDBTW. The Council sets minimum time rates and piecework basis time rates.

Hosiery and other knitted goods

This industry, with over 800 enterprises, employs over 100 000 people, mostly in the East Midlands though a sizable minority in Scotland. The great majority of enterprises employ under 200 people. A wide range of clothing and furnishings is produced, mainly by the knitting of yarn into fabric or fashioned outerwear and the making up of garments by machinists performing 'cut and sew' operations on knitted fabric.

In England and Wales over three-quarters of the manual workers are covered by the National Joint Industrial Council (NJIC) of the Hosiery Trade. Employers are represented through the Knitting Industries Federation (KIF) which has over 300 member companies.

The sole trade union in the NJIC is the National Union of Hosiery and Knitwear Workers (NUHKW). The NJIC Agreement on Wages and Conditions of Employment covers virtually all categories of employee other than 'staff'. However, no minimum wage is agreed; increases awarded through NJIC negotiations are variously implemented in local joint settlements. Throughout almost the whole industry knitters are paid by a basic wage plus production bonus, and operatives employed in making-up operations by piecework. As stipulated in the NJIC Agreement, piece rates, contingencies, machine efficiencies, methods and workloads are negotiated domestically. Courtaulds, the largest firm in the industry, although a member of the KIF have a separate agreement with the NUHKW which is similar to the NJIC agreement. Courtaulds also negotiate centrally with the NUHKW's Clerical, Administrative, Technical and Supervisory Association (CATSA) for weekly paid staff, and with a staff association for senior grades.

Some companies carry out their own dyeing and finishing. Workers in dyeing and finishing companies connected to a manufacturer may be covered by the NJIC or by the Midland Joint Industrial Council (MJIC) of Hosiery Bleachers, Scourers, Dyers and Finishers. Employers are represented on the MJIC by the Knitted Textile Dyers' Federation, and employees by NUHKW, the Nottingham and District Dyers' and Bleachers' Association, and the Hinckley Hosiery and Textile Dyers' Association. These unions form the Midland Workers' Council of Hosiery Dyers and Finishers which represents some 5000 East Midlands employees of about 35 companies handling work from all over the country. The MJIC national agreement sets standards of pay and conditions which are adhered to by most employers, with a number of matters reserved for domestic negotiation.

At Hinckley in Leicestershire there is a district agreement covering about 8000 production workers between NUHKW and the Hinckley and District Knitting Industry Association. It sets minimum wage values for every job in the industry in the area and they are adjusted automatically in accordance with the annual NJIC awards. In practice, the minima are generally supplemented through company and plant bargaining.

In Scotland, excepting Hawick (see below), the national agreements of a Joint Negotiating Committee apply to all hourly paid production workers. The employers are represented by the Scottish Knitwear Association whose membership includes the great majority of companies having over 50 employees. Employees are represented by a Hosiery Organising Committee made up of the TGWU, NUDBTW, GMWU and NUHKW.

District bargaining arrangements, including wage negotiations, cover the Hawick (Borders) area of Scotland. The collective bargaining is done by a Joint Negotiating Committee made up of the Hawick Knitwear Manufacturers' Association and the GMWU. A union membership agreement applies to all job-graded employees — production, maintenance, clerical, supervisory and junior management.

153

Lace

The lace industry employs about 5000 people and is concentrated in Nottinghamshire and Derbyshire, and in Strathclyde. There are three main types of lace — Raschel lace, made by high-speed knitting machines, and furnishing laces and Leavers lace both of which are made by traditional methods.

Manual production workers in the Raschel industry in Nottinghamshire and Derbyshire have minimum pay, holiday pay, sick pay and other basic terms and conditions of employment set by the Lace Industry Joint Wages Council. This brings together the British Lace Federation, which represents virtually all the employers, and the NUHKW, which is organised at most of the larger firms. There is some additional bargaining at company level, involving both the NUHKW and the TGWU, which is recognised in some companies. In the furnishing and Leavers lace sectors there is some collective bargaining at company level for manual workers involving the TGWU and NUHKW.

In Strathclyde, minimum terms and conditions for production workers are set by a Joint Board made up of the Scottish Lace and Window Furnishing Association, to which all the employers belong, and the Scottish Lace and Textile Workers' Union. There is additional bargaining at company level.

Throughout the industry there is some company-level bargaining for maintenance workers, involving the appropriate craft unions. A few hundred workers, virtually all of whom are homeworkers engaged on lace finishing operations and paid on a piecework basis, are covered by the Lace Finishing Wages Council, on which the BLF and NUHKW are represented.

Carpets

The carpet manufacturing industry employs about 30 000 people and is concentrated in three areas: Kidderminister in the West Midlands, West Yorkshire, and the West of Scotland.

The British Carpet Manufacturers' Association (BCMA) consists of approximately 70 member companies representing, by turnover, over 95% of carpet production. Acting as area bodies to BCMA are the Kidderminister and District Carpet Manufacturers' and Spinners' Association, the Northern Area Carpet Manufacturers' Association and the Scottish Carpet Manufacturers' Association.

A large majority of manual workers are represented by five trade unions which form the National Affiliation of Carpet Trade Unions. They are the Kidderminister-based Power Loom Carpet Weavers' and Textile Workers' Union (PLCW&TWU), the Scottish Carpet Workers' Union (SCWU), the Northern Carpet Trade Union (NCTU), NUDBTW and GMWU. Basic terms and conditions of employment of production workers — including minimum earnings levels, hours, holidays, shift and overtime rates and conditions and guaranteed week arrangements — are set by the National Joint Committee (NJC) for the Carpet Industry, which comprises employer representatives nominated by the three District associations and employee representatives nominated by the affiliated unions. The GMWU is not directly represented. There are also three District Joint Councils (DJCs) for the Carpet Industry, which consider negotiable issues outside the scope of the NJC and conclude district agreements. There are disputes procedures at both district and national level.

At company level there is considerable bargaining over procedural matters, incentive pay, and matters such as job grading and redundancy.

Workers employed in craft and ancillary occupations are represented mainly by the AUEW, EETPU, UCATT and TGWU, and are covered by collective bargaining at company level. There is also some company-level bargaining for white-collar workers, a substantial number of whom are now unionised. They are mainly represented by ASTMS, APEX, NUDBTW and SCWU.

Narrow fabrics

This is one of the smaller textile industries, employing about 10 000 people and producing labels, ribbons, tapes, elastics and belting. There is well developed negotiating machinery. The Joint Industrial Council (JIC) for the Narrow Fabrics Industry has employer representatives from the Association of Solid Woven Belting Manufacturers, the British Federation of Narrow Elastic Manufacturers, the British Federation of Trimmings and Braids Manufacturers, and the Tape and Webbing Manufacturers' Association. The trade unions represented are the NUHKW, NUDBTW, GMWU, TGWU, ASTWKT and ATWU. The JIC negotiates the basic terms and conditions for about two-thirds of the industry's manual workers. The remaining manual workers were covered by the JIC for the Silk Industry (see page 149).

One or two of the significantly larger employers have withdrawn from federated pay negotiation machinery and negotiate with the unions at plant level. A number of firms pay wages well above the JIC minimum.

Skilled maintenance workers are usually members of an appropriate craft union which negotiates directly with the companies.

Made-up textiles

About 20 000 people are employed in this industry which is concerned with the production of household textiles, handkerchiefs, and canvas goods, sacks and other made-up goods. Minimum rates of pay for about three-quarters of the industry's workforce are set by three wages councils.

The Made-up Textiles Wages Council (Great Britain) has employer representatives from the Made-up Textiles Association Ltd and employee representatives from the National Union of Tailors and Garment Workers (NUTGW).

On the Linen and Cotton Handkerchief and Household Goods and Linen

Piece Goods Wages Council (Great Britain) employers are represented by the Employers' Association of the Linen and Cotton Handkerchief and Household Goods Wages Council and by the Hemmers' Association. Employees are represented by the NUDBTW, TGWU, GMWU, and the Amalgamated Textile Warehousemen.

On the Sack and Bag Wages Council (Great Britain) employers are represented by the United Kingdom Jute Goods Association Ltd and the National Association of Sack Merchants and Reclaimers Ltd. Employees are represented by the TGWU, GMWU and NUDBTW.

There is some collective bargaining at Association, company and plant level to enhance statutory minima or negotiate the rates for grades not in the scope of the three wages councils.

ORDER XIV   LEATHER, LEATHER GOODS AND FUR

In all about 40 000 people are employed in the industries within this Order.

Leather and leather goods

These industries cover processes from the preservation of skins to the production of finished leather goods. Total employment is about 36 000. For industrial relations purposes, the industry can be divided into six sectors — fellmongery, hide and skin markets, leather production, industrial leather, leather goods, and saddlery. The great majority of employees are in leather production, leather goods or saddlery.

In each sector minimum terms and conditions for production workers are set by national agreements, with some supplementary bargaining at local level often over piecework rates. Each sector is described separately below. The main trade union involved is the Leather Trades Group of the National Union of Footwear, Leather and Allied Trades (NUFLAT). Apart from a few agreements at company level there is little collective bargaining for either maintenance craftsmen or white-collar staff.

1 FELLMONGERY

This sector includes the removal of wool from sheepskins and lambskins and the making of sheepskin rugs. It is a small industry, to some extent seasonal. Most employers belong to the UK Fellmongers' Association (incorporating British Fellmongers and Scottish Skinners). The Transport and General Workers' Union (TGWU) has sole rights in a few Scottish firms, but elsewhere NUFLAT represents production workers. NUFLAT and the Association have a national agreement setting minimum pay rates and other conditions including hours, time rates, piecework rates, overtime rates, holidays, and time allowances for changing, washing and clocking out.

156

2 HIDE AND SKIN MARKETS

This is also a relatively small industry, but widespread geographically. Minimum terms and conditions of employment are set by a Joint Industrial Council on which the employer representatives are elected by the six areas of the National Federation of Hide and Skin Markets and the employee representatives are from the TGWU, NUFLAT, the National Union of General and Municipal Workers (GMWU), and the Union of Shop, Distributive and Allied Workers (USDAW).

3 LEATHER PRODUCTION

Firms in this industry vary widely in size, but the great majority belong to one of the constituent associations of the Leather Producers' Association (LPA). Most process workers are unionised; the majority belong to NUFLAT but the TGWU and GMWU have rights in a few firms.

All the LPA's constituent associations, and the three unions, are represented on the industry's Joint Central Conference which agrees national minimum time rates, hours, piecework rates, shift and overtime rates, holidays, periods of notice, skill classification of occupations, and safety measures.

4 INDUSTRIAL LEATHER

About 30 firms, mainly small, produce items for industry, traditionally made of leather but now incorporating other materials, such as belting. Most belong to the Industrial Leathers Federation (ILF). There are national agreements between NUFLAT and the ILF's Wages Committee which set time rates, merit rates, overtime rates, holidays, skill classification of occupations, and allowances for working in customers' premises and training.

5 LEATHER GOODS

Most firms in this industry are relatively small; most belong to the British Leathergoods Manufacturers' Association (BLMA), a constituent member of the British Jewellery and Giftware Federation. Half the production workers in the industry belong to NUFLAT. The National Joint Wages Board for the Leathergoods and Allied Trades which brings together BLMA and NUFLAT sets hours, weekly earnings (including a guaranteed minimum earnings level), piecework and incentive bonus premium, overtime rates and conditions, holidays, and provides a disputes procedure.

6 SADDLERY

There are a large number of small firms in this sector, most making and selling saddlery and often retailing other leather goods. Most firms belong to the Society of Master Saddlers, though a few of the larger firms belong to BLMA. Although few workers employed by firms in the Society belong to a union, the

Society and NUFLAT have a national minimum wage agreement covering hours, hourly rates, piecework rates, overtime and holidays, and most employers pay rates well above the minima.

Fur

The fur industry is distributed through most of Great Britain, with a main concentration in London. About 5000 people are employed in some 650 establishments in the industry; about 1000 in buying and selling raw furskins, a similar number in dressing and dyeing by chemical processing, and about 3000 in manufacturing fur garments. About half of the employers belong to the British Fur Trade Association (BFTA).

Trade union membership is low, and concentrated in chemical processing. USDAW, NUFLAT, the National Union of Tailors and Garment Workers (NUTGW), and GMWU have members in the industry. Collective bargaining is confined to chemical processing and covers a very small proportion of workers and establishments. Of the 13 chemical processing establishments one has formal establishment-level negotiating arrangements with the GMWU covering all workers, one establishment follows the national agreement for leather production and three negotiate with USDAW on a joint committee which negotiates rates for one group of workers — fleshers.

The industry is also covered by the Fur Wages Council (Great Britain) on which, at its last reconstitution, employer members were nominated by BFTA and by the Secretary of State for Employment, and worker members by USDAW and NUFLAT. The wages council sets minimum rates of pay (including holiday pay) and holiday entitlement.

Order XV   CLOTHING AND FOOTWEAR

These two industries employ about 360 000 people. The separate collective bargaining arrangements are described below.

Clothing

The clothing industry is concerned with the manufacture of garments which are normally made up by cutting and sewing together flat pieces of cloth or other material, usually woven or knitted. This includes most types of garments from overcoats and suits to corsetry and children's wear. However, it excludes fully fashioned jerseys and other products of the hosiery and knitwear industry (see page 152).

The industry is divided into a number of sectors which vary widely in size. The two largest are ready-made and wholesale bespoke tailoring, and dressmaking, which together make up over two-thirds of the industry. There are about 7000 manufacturing establishments employing nearly 300 000 people. These are now widely dispersed geographically; there has been a trend for companies to establish themselves away from the traditional centres of the industry such as Leeds and London. A high proportion of the establishments are small, nearly three-quarters of the workforce are women, and there are some homeworkers.

There are a number of employers' associations in the industry: all still operate also as trade associations and several have close links with one another. Five have plans for forming a single organisation.

The main union in the industry is the National Union of Tailors and Garment Workers (NUTGW). About two-fifths of all employees in the industry are members, and membership is higher amongst production workers, particularly in the ready-made tailoring sector. It has a number of union membership agreements with individual firms. Through its Clerical and Supervisory Staff Section it has a significant membership among supervisory, clerical, administrative and managerial grades. The Transport and General Workers' Union (TGWU), the National Union of General and Municipal Workers (GMWU), the National Union of Footwear, Leather and Allied Trades (NUFLAT) and a number of craft unions have a limited membership among operatives and ancillary workers in particular sectors of the industry, as have the Association of Scientific, Technical and Managerial Staffs (ASTMS) and the Association of Professional, Executive, Clerical and Computer Staff (APEX) among clerical, administrative and managerial grades. The TGWU has an agreement with the NUTGW providing for the NUTGW to have the sole right to organise the 'sewing grades' and the TGWU 'dispatchmen and road transport workers' employed in the industry. The Felt Hatters' and Trimmers' Union of Great Britain (FHTU) organises most of the workers, and in particular the skilled workers, in the felt hat section in the Manchester area.

For the production workers in most sectors of the industry there are national agreements covering earnings, minimum rates of pay, holidays, holiday pay, overtime premia and waiting time rates. The parts of the settlements concerned with minimum terms and conditions are then endorsed by the industry's various wages councils to be given statutory force. The NUTGW normally makes its first claim in the industry to the Clothing Manufacturers' Federation (CMF) on behalf of workers in the ready-made and wholesale bespoke tailoring sector. The CMF discusses the claim with all of the principal employers' associations, through the British Clothing Industry's Joint Council, an organisation representing all the major employers' organisations in the industry, before concluding a settlement.

This heavily influences the subsequent settlements in other sectors. In some of the smaller sectors there are different arrangements. In glove manufacture there is a national agreement but no wages council; in hat, cap and millinery there is a wages council and a regional agreement; and in ostrich and fancy feather and artificial flower there is only a wages council.

The detailed structure and coverage of the national and statutory machinery is set out below. There are ten wages councils within the industry

159

Order, but in addition two small groups of workers are covered by wages councils which are mainly for other industries — workers in the manufacturing section of the fur trade are covered by the Fur Wages Council (see page 158), and workers in cerement making by the Coffin Furniture and Cerement Making Wages Council (see page 143).

There is some collective bargaining at local level for production workers, mainly over yield levels for standard performance, fall back rates and how industry increases are to be implemented.

Other manual workers and white-collar staff in the dressmaking and overall manufacture sectors are covered by the national agreements negotiated by the NUTGW. Elsewhere there is some local bargaining for these groups of staff.

NATIONAL MACHINERY

1 READY-MADE AND WHOLESALE BESPOKE TAILORING

The agreement between the CMF and NUTGW sets the basic terms and conditions and also contains a recognition clause and a disputes procedure with stages at local, area and national level and provision for arbitration. It covers about two-thirds of the production workers employed in this sector, and also some employees who come under the scope of the wholesale mantle and costume and hat, cap and millinery wages councils.

2 DRESSMAKING AND WOMEN'S LIGHT CLOTHING

Both manual and white-collar staff employed by members of the British Apparel Manufacturers' Association (BAMA) are covered by an agreement with NUTGW which sets minimum terms and conditions and also deals with work study, work organisation, recognition and disputes.

3 WHOLESALE MANTLE AND COSTUME

Production workers employed by members of the BAMA are covered by an agreement with the NUTGW on pay, recognition and disputes.

4 OVERALL MANUFACTURE

Both manual and white-collar staff employed by members of the Overall Manufacturers' Association (OMA) are covered by an agreement with the NUTGW on pay, recognition and disputes. This sector does not have a separate wages council; employees are normally covered by the Ready-made and Wholesale Bespoke Tailoring or the Wholesale Mantle and Costume Wages Councils.

5 SHIRTMAKING

Production workers employed by members of the Shirt, Collar and Tie

Manufacturers' Federation (SCTMF) are covered by an agreement with NUTGW which is similar to the CMF/NUTGW agreement.

6 CORSETRY

Production workers employed by members of the Corsetry Manufacturers' Association (CMA) are covered by an agreement with NUTGW which closely parallels the SCTMF/NUTGW agreement.

7 HAT, CAP AND MILLINERY

The FHTU and the Northern Members of the British Headwear Industries Federation (BHIF) have an agreement for production workers which covers hours, holidays, waiting time rates, rest periods, and recognition, and includes a cost-of-living clause and a grievance procedure.

8 RETAIL BESPOKE TAILORING

The Federation of Merchant Tailors (FMT) and NUTGW have a national agreement covering minimum rates of pay and increases in earnings, and also sit on a London Joint Conciliation Board (LJCB) which sets a list of standard piecework rates which are followed by most London tailors, even those not members of FMT.

9 RUBBER PROOFED GARMENT MAKING

The CMF and NUTGW have an agreement covering production workers which closely parallels their agreement in the ready-made and wholesale bespoke tailoring sector.

10 GLOVE MANUFACTURE

In this sector, which has no wages council, terms and conditions of employment for production workers engaged in the manufacture of leather and fabric dress gloves and industrial gloves are determined by the National Joint Standing Committee for the Glove Industry. The Committee is composed of members nominated by the National Association of Glove Manufacturers (NAGM) and representatives of NUFLAT, GMWU and TGWU. The agreement, covering some 76 employers employing about 4000 operatives, deals with minimum rates of pay, payment for waiting time, overtime, annual and statutory holidays. It also contains a disputes procedure.

Wages Council	Main employers' association(s)	Union(s)
Ready-made and Wholesale Bespoke Tailoring (GB)	CMF	NUTGW
Dressmaking and Women's Light Clothing (E & W)	BAMA	NUTGW GMWU
Dressmaking and Women's Light Clothing (Scotland)	Scottish Light Clothing Manufacturers' Assocation; BAMA	NUTGW
Wholesale Mantle and Costume (GB)	BAMA, CMF	NUTGW
Shirtmaking (GB)	SCTMF	NUTGW; London Society of Tie Cutters
Corset Manufacture (GB)	CMA	NUTGW
Hat, Cap and Millinery (GB)	British Hat Guild (BHG); BHIF	NUTGW FHTU NUFLAT
Retail Bespoke Tailoring (GB)	FMT	NUTGW
Rubber Proofed Garment Making (GB)	CMF	NUTGW
Ostrich and Fancy Feather and Artificial Flower (GB)	No employers' organisation	NUTGW GMWU

Footwear

The footwear industry employs about 75 000 people. Almost all the employers in the industry belong to the British Footwear Manufacturers' Federation (BFMF) except for footwear manufacturers in Lancashire who belong to the Lancashire Footwear Manufacturers' Association (LFMA).

These organisations have their parallel on the trade union side. NUFLAT has a post-entry union membership agreement with the BFMF covering all manual workers directly engaged in the manufacture of footwear, and in Lancashire the great majority of manual workers belong to the Rossendale Union of Boot, Shoe and Slipper Operatives (RUBSSO).

At national level, BFMA and NUFLAT negotiate through a National Joint Conference which fixes substantive issues such as minimum wage rates (traditionally index-linked), hours of work and holiday entitlements. There is an agreed disputes procedure. The LFMA/RUBSSO agreement covers a similar range of issues.

At local level, manufacturers and trade unions are represented on local Boards of Conciliation and Arbitration which settle the framework for piece-work prices for the many different operations in, and styles of, footwear and deal with issues in dispute. In addition, some of the larger firms in the industry have concluded local agreements on such matters as job evaluation, shift working, productivity bargaining, sick pay and pension schemes.

There are no national negotiations for white-collar staff. There is some company-level bargaining, mainly involving ASTMS for foremen and ASTMS and APEX for clerical staff.

Order XVI BRICKS, POTTERY, GLASS, CEMENT, ETC

The industries in this Order differ widely, and are treated separately below. Together they employ about a quarter of a million people.

Bricks, fireclay and refractory goods

The brickmaking and refractory industries employ about 40 000 people. In England and Wales these industries can be divided into three sectors:
1 The manufacture of building bricks and associated products
2 The manufacture of fletton bricks
3 The manufacture of fireclay and refractory goods.
The building brick industry employs over half the total workforce.

1 THE BUILDING BRICK INDUSTRY

Standard minimum rates of pay, occupational differentials, piece workers' rates, and shift allowances for process, transport and canteen workers in England and Wales are set by the National Joint Council for the Building Brick and Allied Industries (NJC). This brings together a number of employers' federations, representing either regional groups of employers or covering specialised products, and two unions, the National Union of General and Municipal Workers (GMWU) and the Transport and General Workers' Union (TGWU). The minimum rates set cover most of the operatives in the

163

industry but there is also widespread local bargaining over productivity payments and some local agreements on differentials. Some firms have post-entry union membership agreements. There is regional bargaining machinery, but it mainly operates as part of the disputes procedure.

Terms and conditions of employment for maintenance craftsmen, where they are negotiated, are set at local level between employers and the appropriate craft unions. There is little collective bargining for white-collar workers.

2 THE FLETTON BRICK INDUSTRY

The London Brick Company (LBC) is the sole producer of fletton bricks, which are made from a shale found in the areas around Peterborough, Bedford and Bletchley.

Pay and conditions for manual workers are settled by a Joint Negotiating Committee. Process workers, drivers and catering workers are represented by the TGWU and GMWU; maintenance and engineering craftsmen by the craft unions and the TGWU. A post-entry union membership agreement covers all manual workers. Staff Foremen are represented in a joint negotiating committee of the Association of Scientific, Technical and Managerial Staffs (ASTMS), the Amalgamated Union of Engineering Workers (AUEW), and TGWU. There is considerable white-collar unionisation; the Association of Professional, Executive, Clerical and Computer Staff (APEX) has a union membership agreement for clerical staff and pay and conditions for this group are negotiated through a National Joint Staff Council.

3 THE REFRACTORIES INDUSTRY

Standard minimum rates of pay and shift allowances for process and canteen workers and for some maintenance craftsmen are set by a National Joint Wages Board for the Refractories Industry. Occupational differentials and piecework rates are for the most part negotiated locally. The Board brings together several employers' associations, of which the two largest are the Refractories Association of Great Britain and the Calcium Silicate Brick Association, and two unions, the GMWU and TGWU. The minimum rates set cover most of the operatives in the industry but in some firms there is additional local bargaining. Some firms have post-entry union membership agreements. There is some regional bargaining machinery but it mainly operates as part of the disputes procedure.

Maintenance craftsmen are mainly represented at local level by the AUEW and the Electrical, Electronic, Telecommunication and Plumbing Union (EETPU). There is little collective bargaining for white-collar workers.

In Scotland the Scottish Employers' Council for the Clay Industries (SECCI) represents companies which employ about 85% of the 3000 workers in the building brick and refractories industries. SECCI negotiates general conditions of employment with the GMWU and TGWU, which are often enhanced by local bargaining.

Ceramics

The ceramic or pottery industry employs nearly 60 000 people, the great majority in North Staffordshire. Its main products are tableware, ceramic tiles, sanitary ware and electrical porcelain.

All the main terms and conditions of employment for process workers in the industry are determined by the National Joint Council for the Ceramic Industry (NJC). This brings together the British Ceramic Manufacturers' Federation (BCMF), which represents most of the firms in the industry, and the Ceramic and Allied Trades Union (CATU). CATU represents almost all process workers in the industry, having sole bargaining rights reinforced by a nationally agreed union membership agreement. The NJC agreements cover about 70% of the industry's process workers directly, and most non-federated firms also follow the agreements. At company level there is often supplementary bargaining, mainly over piecework.

Terms and conditions for maintenance craftsmen are negotiated at national level between BCMF and two unions — the AUEW and EETPU. At plant level there is widespread supplementary bargaining, mainly over differentials, shift premia and allowances. In some firms maintenance craftsmen belong to and are represented by CATU.

For drivers, there is a national agreement setting terms and conditions between BCMF and the TGWU, which is sometimes supplemented at plant level by negotiations over bonus rates. There is also a nationally agreed post-entry union membership agreement.

The main unions involved in the white-collar sector are ASTMS — for managerial, professional and technical employees, and also clerical employees already covered by ASTMS agreements — and CATU's clerical staff section, which has a national agreement with the BCMF setting terms and conditions for clerical staff.

Glass

The industry employs about 70 000 people in three fairly discrete sectors:
1 The manufacture of glass containers and domestic glassware
2 The manufacture of flat, safety, pressed and optical glass and glass fibre
3 Glazing and the processing of flat glass.

1 GLASS CONTAINERS AND DOMESTIC GLASSWARE

Most glass container companies are members of the Association of Glass Container Manufacturers (AGCM). United Glass Ltd and Rockware Glass Ltd each command about a third of the market. The industry is concentrated primarily in St Helens, in South and West Yorkshire, in London and in Central Scotland.

Process workers, of whom over 90% are unionised, are represented by the GMWU, TGWU, and the Union of Shop, Distributive and Allied Workers

165

(USDAW). One of the three unions usually occupies an exclusive position at one plant, a position sometimes reinforced by a union membership agreement. Most maintenance craftsmen are represented by the AUEW, EETPU and the Union of Construction, Allied Trades and Technicians (UCATT) — which tend to enjoy *de facto* closed shops. The main white-collar union is ASTMS, but membership is relatively low.

Minimum rates of pay and most conditions of employment for process workers are determined by the National Joint Industrial Council for the Glass Container Industry (NJIC) on which the AGCM and the three process unions are represented. However, these are widely supplemented at company and plant level through locally determined job evaluation systems and incentive schemes. There is also an NJIC agreed disputes procedure. Maintenance workers, drivers and white-collar workers bargain at company and plant level. The main firms manufacturing fine crystal glassware are outside the NJIC and have collective bargaining arrangements of their own.

2 FLAT, SAFETY, PRESSED AND OPTICAL GLASS AND GLASS FIBRE

There is no national bargaining machinery, but Pilkington Brothers Ltd dominates this sector. Over half the company's 23 000 employees work in St Helens.

Pilkingtons have separate central negotiating committees, which cover the St Helens-based manufacturing plants (and one or two plants outside St Helens that are linked historically), for process workers, maintenance craftsmen, drivers, foremen and white-collar staff. Elsewhere there is plant bargaining and even in the plants covered by central arrangements there is some local negotiation over bonuses and job grading.

Process workers are represented in St Helens and one or two outside plants by the GMWU which has a post-entry union membership agreement. It sends both lay and full-time officials to the Central Negotiating Committee, which determines pay and conditions (including pensions) but refers its decisions to a body of elected representatives from the shop floor — the Union Industrial Committee.

ASTMS represents the majority of white-collar staff and foremen and has a post-entry union membership agreement covering staff in most of the main plants.

3 GLAZING AND THE PROCESSING OF FLAT GLASS

This sector contains a large number of firms of all sizes. The Flat Glass Council (FGC), the employers' organisation within the Glass and Glazing Federation, and the Scottish Glass Merchants' and Glaziers' Association represent most of the firms.

The three predominant unions for manual workers are the EETPU (glaziers); the Furniture, Timber and Allied Trades Union (FTAT) (indoor process workers); and the National Society of Operative Printers, Graphical and Media Personnel (NATSOPA) (workers engaged in decorative work). Union membership among white-collar workers is low though there is a procedure agreement with the FGC recognising the white-collar sections of the three manual unions.

The FGC negotiates with a joint union committee, consisting of a mixture of lay and full-time officials of EETPU, FTAT and NATSOPA, on the National Joint Council for the Flat Glass Industry. This covers about 7000 manual workers and sets minimum terms and conditions of employment. The agreement also lays down basic criteria for bonus schemes, which are settled in detail at company level, subject to the approval of Local Joint Secretaries. There is also a disputes procedure which has a provision for arbitration as its final stage.

In Scotland, glaziers are represented by the GMWU which negotiates separately with the Scottish Glass Merchants' and Glaziers' Association, but in general follows agreements in the building industry.

Cement

The manufacture of calcareous (Portland) cement is carried out by six companies together employing some 17 000 people. All six belong to the Cement Makers' Federation (CMF).

The terms and conditions of employment for process workers are regulated by the National Joint Industrial Council for the Cement Manufacturing Industry (NJIC) which brings together the CMF and two unions, the TGWU and GMWU. There is an NJIC Job Grading Scheme, under which responsibility for grading process workers' jobs rests with locally constituted job evaluation panels for the eight lowest grades and at national level for the three highest grades.

Terms and conditions of employment for craftsmen are decided by the Craftsmen's Committee for the Cement Manufacturing Industry. There is no direct connection between this committee and the NJIC but all the employers and three craft unions — the AUEW, EETPU, and the Amalgamated Society of Boilermakers, Shipwrights, Blacksmiths and Structural Workers (ABS) — have representatives on the committee.

The other two employee groups, drivers and staff, are covered by negotiations at company or local level.

Abrasives and building materials, etc not elsewhere specified

Nearly 80 000 people are employed in this sector, which contains a number of distinct industries. Six have well established national negotiating arrangements for manual workers. These are asbestos manufacturing, cast stone and cast concrete, ready mixed concrete, monumental masonry, mastic asphalt, and slag. Elsewhere in the sector collective bargaining, where is exists, is at company or plant level.

167

1 ASBESTOS MANUFACTURING

This has two sectors, asbestos cement and asbestos textile products, and employs over 10 000 people. Minimum rates of pay, hours, holidays and other important terms and conditions for manual workers in the two sectors are negotiated by separate standing committees of the National Joint Industrial Council of the Asbestos Manufacturing Industry (NJIC). The NJIC brings together the Asbestos Association Limited (AAL), which covers a substantial proportion of the employers in the industry, and three unions, the GMWU, TGWU and the Amalgamated Textile Workers' Union (ATWU), which together represent all the manual workers in the industry. The NJIC agreements also make provision for plant-level bargaining over piecework and bonus rates, and, in textiles, over job grading. There is an agreed disputes procedure.

Some white-collar staff are unionised, but no unions are recognised nationally and there is only limited collective bargaining at company level.

2 CAST STONE AND CAST CONCRETE PRODUCTS

This is one of the largest industries in the sector, employing about 30 000 people. There is separate negotiating machinery for England and Wales, and Scotland, though the range of matters determined is very similar.

In England and Wales, minimum rates of pay, hours, holidays, sick pay and other main terms and conditions for manual workers are set by the National Joint Industrial Council for the Cast Stone and Cast Concrete Products Industry. This brings together the British Precast Concrete Federation, which covers the great majority of the industry, and two unions, the TGWU and GMWU. There is a national job classification scheme with grading differentials set by seven Area Councils. These Area Councils also act as part of the national disputes procedure, which contains provision for arbitration. There is considerable supplementary bargaining at plant level over matters such as productivity, pensions and sick pay schemes. In Scotland, minimum terms and conditons for manual workers are set by the Joint Industrial Council for the Scottish Precast Concrete Products Industry, which brings together the same two unions and the Scottish Precast Concrete Manufacturers' Association. There is a similar pattern of supplementary local bargaining.

No unions for white-collar staff are recognised at national level, and there is little company-level bargaining.

3 READY MIXED CONCRETE

This industry is concerned with the blending of the raw materials and transportation to customers' construction sites. Because the product has to be delivered quickly and used immediately, the mixing depots are widely spread throughout the UK and each has a very small workforce. There are about 3000 direct employees and a similar number of owner/drivers employed on contract.

Minimum hourly rates of pay, overtime and shift premia, subsistence allowances, hours, holidays, sick pay and other main terms and conditions for plant operators, drivers and other non-craft manual workers are set by the National Joint Council for the Ready Mixed Concrete Industry. This brings together the British Ready Mixed Concrete Association (BRMCA), which represents virtually all the employers in the industry, and the TGWU and GMWU, both of which have extensive membership in the industry. There is a disputes procedure, with provision for reference to conciliation or arbitration. Plant-level bargaining is concerned mainly with productivity bonus payments.

Terms and conditions for fitters, electricians and other maintenance craftsmen are settled at company and plant level. The main unions involved are the AUEW and EETPU. There are no negotiating arrangements for white-collar workers.

4 MONUMENTAL MASONRY

This industry employs about 1000 people, in the preparation and working of stone for building and monumental purposes; it is closely connected with funeral operations. It is widespread geographically and is composed mainly of small firms employing fewer than ten people.

Standard minimum rates of pay, hours, holidays, and other terms and conditions of employment, notably sick pay, death benefits and various allowances, for manual workers are set by the National Joint Council for the Monumental Masonry Industry (NJC), after following settlements reached by the National Joint Council for the Building Industry. The NJC is composed of representatives from the one employers' association for the industry, the National Association of Master Masons, and three trade unions, UCATT, TGWU and GMWU. There is also some local bargaining, mainly over company bonus schemes. There is no significant collective bargaining for white-collar workers.

5 MASTIC ASPHALT

There are two parts to this industry — the manufacture of mastic materials and their laying.

Mastic asphalt manufacture is carried out by about a dozen small firms together employing about 150 people. Standard minimum rates of pay, hours, holidays and other terms and conditions for operatives are set by the National Joint Council for the manufacturing side of the Mastic Asphalt Industry. This brings together the Mastic Asphalt Council and Employers' Federation (MACEF), which has all but one of the employers in membership, and three unions, the Amalgamated Union of Asphalt Workers (AUAW), the GMWU and TGWU. There is plant bargaining over piecework and bonus sharing schemes, and over plus rates for various operatives. There is some local bargaining for maintenance craftsmen, but no bargaining for white-collar workers.

About 4500 people are employed in the laying side of the industry. Most of the large firms are members of MACEF which provides the employers' side of the National Joint Council (NJC) for the laying side of the Mastic Asphalt Industry. The AUAW is the only union represented on the employees' side. The NJC covers apprentices, labourers, craftsmen and chargehands and determines all major terms and conditions including productivity and job grading schemes. There is also an NJC disputes procedure. The TGWU is recognised in some companies outside the NJC.

6 SLAG

This small industry, made up of six companies employing about 400 people, processes slag aggregate from furnaces which is used for roadmaking materials, in filter beds and as railway ballast.

Minimum rates of pay, hours, holidays, shift and overtime premia, and other basic conditions of employment for process workers, are set by the Joint Industrial Council for the Slag Industry. This brings together the Slag Employers' Association, to which all six companies belong, and four unions — the Iron and Steel Trades Confederation (ISTC), the National Union of Blastfurnacemen, Coke Workers, Miners and Kindred Trades (NUB), the GMWU and TGWU. Membership of the unions is virtually 100%, but there are no union membership agreements. There is an agreed disputes procedure with provision for reference to arbitration. There is widespread local bargaining over differential rates and bonus schemes. Some local bargaining takes place for maintenance craftsmen but there is no bargaining for white-collar workers.

Order XVII TIMBER, FURNITURE, ETC

The timber and furniture industry employs about 250 000 people, mostly in relatively small firms. For industrial relations purposes it can be divided into seven main sectors which are listed below. The largest is furniture manufacturing, with timber sawmilling a close second: together these two sectors contain about three-quarters of the employees in the industry. The sectors are:

Furniture

Timber sawmilling

Veneers, plywoods and laminates

Bedding and mattresses

Fillings (for upholstery and bedding)

Cooperage

Other wooden containers.

There are three other small sectors with established national negotiating arrangements. Two — ladder manufacture and shop fitting — are covered by agreements of the National Joint Council for the Building Industry (see page 187). The third — fencing — is also covered in Construction (see page 189). There are a few other small industries in the Order, but they do not have significant collective bargaining arrangements.

In each of the main sectors basic terms and conditions of employment for production workers — normally minimum rates of pay, hours of work, overtime rates, holidays and pay, sick pay, shift premia, and a disputes procedure which often contains provision for conciliation and arbitration — are set by the national negotiating machinery tabulated below. Most firms belong to one or other of the employers' associations, and so well over half the production workers in the industry are covered by national agreements. These are often enhanced by company and plant bargaining. Payment by results schemes and pensions are solely determined at local level. Throughout the industry skilled production workers are represented mainly by the Furniture, Timber and Allied Trades Union (FTAT), and the Union of Construction, Allied Trades and Technicians (UCATT), and unskilled workers by the Transport and General Workers' Union (TGWU) and the National Union of General and Municipal Workers (GMWU). In small firms it is not unusual to find one union representing skilled and unskilled. In the fillings industry, the National Union of Dyers, Bleachers and Textile Workers (NUDBTW) also negotiates for production workers. There are some *de facto* closed shops, and some formal union membership agreements in the furniture industry.

Sector	Employers' Association(s)	Union(s)	No. of employees covered	National machinery
1 Furniture	British Furniture Manufacturers' Federated Association	FTAT UCATT GMWU TGWU	75 000	British Furniture Trade Joint Industrial Council (JIC)
2 Timber sawmilling	National Sawmilling Association (NSA)	FTAT GMWU TGWU	50 000	[a]National Joint Council (NJC) for the Imported Timber Sawmilling Industry in England and Wales
	Home Timber Merchants' Association of England and Wales (HTMA)	FTAT GMWU TGWU	10 000	[a]National Joint Industrial Council (NJIC) for the Home Grown Timber Trade

[cont. overleaf]

Sector	Employers' Association(s)	Union(s)	No of employees covered	National machinery
	Scottish Timber Merchants' and Sawmillers' Association (STMSA)	FTAT GMWU TGWU	3 500	[a]Direct negotiation
3 Veneers, plywoods and laminates	Association of British Plywood and Veneer Manufacturers	FTAT UCATT GMWU TGWU	2 000	NJIC for the Veneer Producing and Plywood Manufacturing Industry
4 Bedding and mattresses	National Bedding Federation	FTAT	12 000	Bedding and Mattress Manufacturing Trade JIC
5 Fillings	National Fillings Trades Association	FTAT GMWU TGWU NUDBTW	5 000	National Conciliation Board for Upholstery, Bedding and other Fillings Materials Manufacturing Trades
6 Cooperage	National Cooperage Federation	GMWU	1 000	[b]NJIC of the Cooperage Industry
7 Other wooden containers	Timber, Packaging and Pallet Confederation	FTAT UCATT GMWU TGWU	12 500	[c]NJIC for the Timber Container Industry
	Scottish National Federation of Packing Case Manufacturers (SNFPCM)	FTAT UCATT	1 000	[c]Direct negotiation

NOTES:
(a) The NJC and NJIC both cover England and Wales only. STMSA covers only the sawmilling of imported timber in Scotland. There is no national agreement covering the sawmilling of home grown timber in Scotland, but most firms tend to follow the STMSA agreement.
(b) Cooperage is mainly based in Scotland as a service industry to whisky distilling.
(c) The NJIC covers only England and Wales. SNFPCM negotiates in Scotland.

172

There are no national negotiations for other groups of workers. Maintenance workers, in general, belong to the Amalgamated Union of Engineering Workers (AUEW), the Electrical, Electronic, Telecommunication and Plumbing Union (EETPU) and FTAT. Terms and conditions of employment are settled at local level. For white-collar workers there is relatively little collective bargaining; where it does exist the recognised unions are mainly the Association of Scientific, Technical and Managerial Staffs (ASTMS) and FTAT. In addition the Association of Professional, Executive, Clerical and Computer Staff (APEX) is recognised by some firms in the furniture industry, and the TGWU's Association of Clerical, Technical and Supervisory Staffs (ACTS), and the GMWU's Managerial, Administrative, Technical and Supervisory Section (MATSA) in timber sawmilling.

Order XVIII   PAPER, PRINTING AND PUBLISHING

There are two main parts to this industry Order — the production of paper, and printing and publishing. Together these employ over half a million people.

Paper and board

The industry employs about 200 000 people and is divided into the following sectors:
1 The manufacture of all types of paper and board
2 The conversion of paper and board in its manufactured state.

1 PAPER AND BOARD MANUFACTURE

In this sector most firms are members of the British Paper and Board Industry Federation (BPBIF). Unionisation of manual workers is approximately 90%. The main process union is the Society of Graphical and Allied Trades (SOGAT), though the Transport and General Workers' Union (TGWU) and the National Union of General and Municipal Workers (GMWU) also have membership in this area. Maintenance craftsmen are represented by the Amalgamated Union of Engineering Workers (AUEW), the Electrical, Electronic, Telecommunication and Plumbing Union (EETPU), the TGWU and the Union of Construction, Allied Trades and Technicians (UCATT). White-collar unionisation is lower: the unions recognised are SOGAT; the GMWU's Managerial, Administrative, Technical and Supervisory Section (MATSA); the TGWU's Association of Clerical, Technical and Supervisory Staffs (ACTS); the AUEW's Technical, Administrative and Supervisory Section (TASS); and the EETPU's Electrical and Engineering Staff Association (EESA).

173

The BPBIF negotiates wages and working conditions separately with groups of unions representing process and general workers (SOGAT, TGWU, GMWU) and maintenance craftsmen (AUEW, EETPU, TGWU, UCATT). There are also separate procedure agreements for these categories. In some companies the terms of national agreements are implemented as such while in others they form the basis for further local bargaining. The national agreements cover recognition, disputes procedures, hours, rates and holidays but do not cover pensions, bonus payments or productivity schemes which are all regarded as appropriate for determination at company or establishment level. Many of the larger firms have entered into local agreements with the relevant unions. At national level there are currently no substantive agreements for white-collar staff, though there are jointly agreed recognition and disputes procedures.

2 PAPER AND BOARD CONVERSION

The main product divisions in this sector are:
  1 Bag manufacture
  2 Box manufacture
  3 Carton manufacture
  4 Multiwall sack manufacture
  5 Fibreboard packing case manufacture
  6 Wallcoverings.

There is an employers' association for each of the main product divisions listed above. The associations are, respectively, the British Bag Federation (BBF), the British Paper Box Association (BPBA), the British Carton Association (BCA), the Multiwall Sack Manufacturers Employers' Association (MSMEA), the Fibreboard Packing Case Employers' Association (FPCEA) and the Association of Independent Wallcovering Manufacturers (AIWM). The first four associations listed form the Packing Employers' Confederation, a forum for consultation on industrial relations and other matters. Most companies involved in the manufacture of paper and board are members of the relevant employers' association.

The main unions for production workers are SOGAT and the GMWU. Other unions with members are the TGWU (particularly in the Multiwall Sack and Fibreboard Packing Case sectors), the National Society of Operative Printers, Graphical and Media Personnel (NATSOPA) (particularly in the Bag and Fibreboard Packing Case sectors), and the National Graphical Association (NGA) and the AUEW (both in the Fibreboard Packing Case sector). In the Wallcovering sector the NGA is the main union but the Society of Lithographic Artists, Designers, Engravers and Process Workers (SLADE) represents workers engaged in the production of cylinders for printing and embossing. The level of unionisation among production workers varies according to the size of firm. It is lowest in the Box sector, where small firms predominate, and highest in the Multiwall Sack sector, where a few large firms dominate production. Union membership agreements are fairly common among larger firms.

Among white-collar employees unionisation is much lower though there is some membership of SOGAT and of the Association of Scientific, Technical and Managerial Staffs (ASTMS). SLADE represents designers and artists in some plants.

Minimum rates of pay and conditions of employment for process workers are determined under separate national agreements between the various employers' associations and the relevant union, as follows:

The BBF — SOGAT, NATSOPA

The BPBA — SOGAT, GMWU

The BCA — SOGAT, GMWU

The MSMEA — SOGAT, GMWU, TGWU

The FPCEA — SOGAT, GMWU

The AIWM — NGA.

In some companies the terms of national agreements are implemented as such while in others they are a basis for local bargaining. The national agreements do not cover pensions, bonus payments, or productivity schemes, which are all regarded as appropriate for local determination. Many of the larger firms have entered into local agreements with the relevant production unions. Some firms negotiate locally the terms and conditions of white-collar employees but there are no national agreements.

Printing and publishing

The printing and publishing industry employs about 335 000 people. Of these about 75 000 work in the production of newspapers, 60 000 in the production of periodicals and 200 000 in general printing and book publishing. Except in provincial newspapers the size of the workforce has declined steadily in recent years. In most parts of the industry the introduction of new technology based on phototypesetting has had, and will continue to have, considerable implications for employment and industrial relations.

Because some firms engage in both printing and publishing activities, for example the production of newspapers, there is some overlap between the different sectors examined below:

1 Newspapers
2 Periodicals
3 General printing
4 Book publishing
5 Printing ink manufacture.

1 NEWSPAPERS

This sector comprises the printing and publishing of all kinds of national and provincial newspapers. For the most part the national press is based in London, but some national newspapers are also produced in Manchester. Provincial newspapers are produced in most centres of population.

The Newspaper Publishers' Association (NPA) is the employers' association for national newspapers, the Newspaper Society (NS) that for provincial newspapers in England, Wales [and Northern Ireland]. The Scottish Daily Newspaper Society (SDNS) covers morning, evening and Sunday newspapers produced in Scotland, and the Scottish Newspaper Proprietors' Association (SNPA), which is affiliated to the Society of Master Printers of Scotland (SMPS), covers weekly and bi-weekly newspapers produced in Scotland.

The level of unionisation of manual employees is very high and in most houses *de facto* closed shops operate. The principal production unions are the NGA, NATSOPA, SOGAT and SLADE. The NGA organises all apprentice-trained employees in composing, reading, foundry and machine rooms in newspaper houses in England and Wales while NATSOPA organises photographic technicians, the only personnel actually apprenticed by NPA managements. In Scotland the NGA organises foundry and telecommunications workers, the other occupations being organised by the Scottish Graphical Division of SOGAT. Except in Scottish weekly newspaper houses NATSOPA represents the majority of non-craftsmen in the composing and machine departments. In the provincial press NATSOPA also represents the majority of non-craftsmen in the warehouse departments but in some provincial and nearly all national newspaper houses representation in this area is through SOGAT. In Scottish weekly newspaper houses SOGAT represents the majority of non-craftsmen in each of these three departments. Throughout Great Britain employees in the artist, camera and reproduction departments are represented by SLADE.

The great majority of editorial workers (principally journalists) are organised by the National Union of Journalists (NUJ) but the Institute of Journalists (IOJ) has significant support in some houses, mainly in England and Wales.

Most ancillary workers in administrative and clerical positions and in general services are organised in England and Wales by NATSOPA, which also has membership among middle and senior management in national newspapers. SOGAT is the recognised union for these groups in Scotland. SOGAT also organises clerical workers in publishing departments, and circulation representatives. Advertising executives in national and provincial newspapers are organised by NATSOPA.

In national newspapers the majority of maintenance workers are members of the AUEW's Engineering Section (mechanical maintenance engineers, linotype mechanics) or of EETPU (electricians and their assistants). Other unions with membership in national newspapers are UCATT (bricklayers, carpenters, painters); the National Union of Sheet Metal Workers, Coppersmiths and Heating and Domestic Engineers (NUSMW) (heat engineers and

176

maintenance workers); GMWU (canteen and catering staff); the Confederation of Health Service Employees (COHSE) (industrial nursing staff); and the TGWU, the Association of Professional, Executive, Clerical and Computer Staff (APEX), and ASTMS.

Negotiating machinery

In the national press there are some 30 national agreements between the NPA and individual unions, and some 70 basic rates, but in practice actual rates are normally settled at house level. A number of other matters, for example pension and sick pay arrangements, are currently left for negotiation solely at house level. Also there are nationally agreed disputes procedures with individual unions. These procedures are similar but their final stages differ. The most common final stage is for an NPA committee of union and management representatives to appoint an arbitrator. All the national procedures allow issues to be dealt with first by domestic procedures which are agreed at house level.

The bargaining process between houses and individual unions is characterised by the absence of formal procedures and the wide range of matters which are negotiable. House-level bargaining takes place between managements and individual chapels. The number of chapels with which management negotiates may range from 20 or more in single-title houses to 50 or more in dual and multi-title houses. The Morning Star, the Mirror Group Newspapers, and Times Newspapers are the only national papers not covered by NPA agreements, although the Morning Star applies them where appropriate.

In the provincial press the NS has separate agreements with NATSOPA (including the union's clerical branch), SLADE, NUJ, and IOJ. The NS also negotiates with the NGA but generally does this jointly with the British Printing Industries Federation (BPIF). Although the NS has no agreement with SOGAT, in practice SOGAT members are usually covered by the NS agreement with NATSOPA for production workers. The NS has no arrangements for national negotiations with AUEW or EETPU. NS agreements cover a wide range of terms and conditions, but those with NUJ, IOJ and the clerical branch of NATSOPA are somewhat more restricted in scope and do not cover such things as working in meal breaks and productivity. In most instances house-level negotiations are restricted to matters not covered in national agreements, but some larger houses do have comprehensive agreements designed to supplement national agreements.

In Scotland the SDNS conducts negotiations on behalf of most daily newspaper companies with NGA, NATSOPA, SLADE, the Scottish Graphical Division of SOGAT, AUEW, EETPU, and TGWU.

Scottish weekly newspaper houses are covered by agreements negotiated jointly by the SMPS and the SNPA with the NGA, SLADE and the Scottish Graphical Division of SOGAT, but by the SNPA only with the NUJ. No agreements exist between the SMPS/SNPA and the AUEW, EETPU, NATSOPA (production or clerical), and IOJ. The IOJ is generally consulted by the SNPA when negotiations have been concluded with the NUJ, and terms identical to the NUJ agreement are then agreed between the SNPA and IOJ.

The range of topics covered by the SMPS/SNPA agreement with the production unions and the SNPA with the NUJ are similar to those negotiated in England and Wales by the NS.

2 PERIODICALS

Unlike newspaper companies, periodical companies usually confine themselves to either printing or publishing. In England and Wales the employers' association for the printing side is the BPIF; in Scotland, the SMPS. There is no equivalent body for the publishing side, the Periodical Publishers' Association being solely a trade association. Where companies combine periodical and book publishing they are usually members of the Publishers' Association (PA).

All the unions which represent employees in newspaper production are recognised in periodical production.

The periodical printing side is largely covered by agreements between the BPIF/SMPS and most of the printing unions. On the publishing side there are some house-level agreements and, in appropriate cases, the agreement between the PA and SOGAT for warehouse staff is applied where firms are PA members, and may be used as a point of reference where the firms are not. The majority of houses have comprehensive agreements with the unions organising editorial, administrative and distribution staffs. Conditions of employment for clerical and advertising personnel are the subject of house agreements with NATSOPA.

3 GENERAL PRINTING

This sector, which includes manufactured stationery, is dominated by small firms although in recent years larger firms have developed and some multinational companies have become involved. The main employers' associations are, for England and Wales, the BPIF and, for Scotland, the SMPS. Between them these bodies cover more than 90% of production, though there are several other small specialist employers' associations.

There is a very high level of unionisation among production workes in printing. There are no formal union membership agreements but *de facto* closed shops are widespread. In England and Wales the NGA is the dominant union representing workers engaged in stereotyping, lithoprinting, letterpress, gravure printing, flexography composing, and litho-plate making. SLADE represents workers engaged in camera retouching, preparation of visual display work, process engraving and preparation of gravure cylinders. SOGAT represents workers engaged in bindery, warehouse and finishing. SOGAT also represents some machine operatives in smaller firms but in larger firms machine operatives are represented by NATSOPA. In Scotland SOGAT is the dominant union, representing all machine operatives, and, in addition, workers engaged in composing and gravure printing.

Most maintenance workers are represented by the AUEW and the EETPU. Some NGA members are engaged in electrical maintenance. Unionisation among white-collar staff is much lower and is concentrated in the larger firms, with NGA, SOGAT and NATSOPA most involved.

For production workers the BPIF and SMPS each have separate national agreements with NGA and SOGAT. The BPIF also has a national agreement with NATSOPA as does the SMPS with SLADE. These agreements set minimum terms and conditions of employment but in practice these minimum terms and conditions are enhanced by negotiations at house level. The various specialised employers' associations also have agreements with the appropriate process unions. The Tin Box Federation has an agreement with NGA to cover workers engaged in printing on to tin surfaces.

There are no national agreements for maintenance workers or white-collar staff.

Two organisations not covered by the national agreements for process workers are Her Majesty's Stationery Office (HMSO), with some 8000 employees, and the Bank of England (about 7000). Both have separate house agreements with each of the process and maintenance unions. Non-industrial employees in HMSO have civil service status and are covered by relevant national agreements; in the Bank they are covered by separate machinery (see page 231).

4 BOOK PUBLISHING

Many book publishing houses are small with highly varied structures and publishing activities. The employers' association for this sector is the PA, of which most companies are members. The Scottish Publishers' Industrial Relations Group (SPIRG), of which the Scottish General Publishers' Association is a member, serves the special needs of publishing firms in Scotland. SPIRG has not entered into collective agreements but does act for individual member firms on specific issues.

Throughout Great Britain the main union for workers in distribution warehouses is SOGAT; a formal post-entry union membership agreement operates in England and Wales. The NUJ is the main union for editorial staff. The main unions for clerical staff are SOGAT, particularly so in Scotland, and ASTMS, although NGA and SLADE have some membership.

The Warehouse Employers Group of the PA negotiates with SOGAT on behalf of publishers with distribution warehouses. Their agreement covers basic rates and other conditions of employment which are applied by PA member companies in England and Wales, but not to any significant extent in Scotland. Some companies negotiate supplementary house agreements for warehouse staff, principally covering productivity and bonus incentive schemes. In larger houses agreements covering editorial and allied staff and other office staff may be negotiated with the appropriate unions.

5 PRINTING INK MANUFACTURE

The principal products are printing ink and printers' rollers. About 6000 workers are employed. The employers' association is the Society of British Printing Ink Manufacturers (SBPIM).

The only union which is a party to agreements covering printing ink is NATSOPA. Unionisation of the production workers is at a high level — in many large firms there are *de facto* closed shops, although these are not formally provided for in the national agreement. NATSOPA is also the main union for clerical and technical workers, though unionisation here is much lower.

Wages and working conditions of production workers are negotiated nationally between the SBPIM and NATSOPA, and are normally enhanced by local negotiations. There are no national agreements covering white-collar staff but the SBPIM acknowledges NATSOPA as the appropriate union for clerical and technical employees.

Order XIX   OTHER MANUFACTURING INDUSTRIES

Well over 300 000 people are employed in the diverse manufacturing industries which comprise this Order. They are distributed as follows:

	Approx
1 Rubber	110 000
2 Linoleum, plastics floor covering, leathercloth, etc	14 000
3 Brushes and brooms	9000
4 Toys, games, children's carriages and sports equipment	40 000
5 Miscellaneous stationers' goods	8000
6 Plastics products not specified in other Orders	120 000
7 Musical instruments; all other manufacturing industries not specified in other Orders	24 000

A number of firms operating here are also engaged in other industries, notably the engineering industry, and are covered by the negotiating arrangements in those other industries. Overall, about two-thirds of the manual workers, and about one-third of the white-collar employees in the Order, are covered by collective bargaining arrangements. Most of the bargaining is at company or plant level, though there is some national bargaining for production workers that is specific to industries in this Order. The descriptions below concentrate mainly on this national machinery.

Rubber

Seven major tyre manufacturing companies account for about half the output of the rubber industry. In addition, around 350 companies, many quite small, are involved in the manufacture of general rubber goods such as hose, belting, seals, and cellular products.

Until 1977, terms and conditions of employment for process workers were determined by the National Joint Industrial Council for the Rubber Manufacturing Industry (NJIC) on which the employers were represented by the British Rubber Manufacturers' Association and the employees by the Transport and General Workers' Union (TGWU), the National Union of General and Municipal Workers (GMWU) and the Union of Shop, Distributive and Allied Workers (USDAW). In the years before 1977, agreements reached by the NJIC had been increasingly regarded as minima on which to build local agreements, except for items such as working hours, the length of annual holidays, and payment for annual and statutory holidays which remained unaltered. In 1977 the unions withdrew from the NJIC and collective bargaining is now conducted solely at company or plant level.

Particularly in the larger companies, the level of unionisation among manual workers is high. Process workers are represented by the TGWU, GMWU and USDAW. Craftsmen are represented by the Amalgamated Union of Engineering Workers (AUEW), the Electrical, Electronic, Telecommunication and Plumbing Union (EETPU), the National Union of Sheet Metal Workers, Coppersmiths and Heating and Domestic Engineers (NUSMW), the Union of Construction, Allied Trades and Technicians (UCATT) and other craft unions. There are some union membership agreements and *de facto* closed shops.

White-collar workers are represented by the AUEW's Technical, Administrative and Supervisory Section (TASS), the Association of Scientific, Technical and Managerial Staffs (ASTMS), the Association of Professional, Executive and Computer Staff (APEX), the TGWU's Association of Clerical, Technical and Supervisory Staffs (ACTS) and the GMWU's Administrative, Technical and Supervisory Section (MATSA). Levels of membership are generally lower here than in the manual workers' unions.

The matters negotiated at company and plant level cover all aspects of pay and conditions of employment.

Linoleum, plastics floor covering, leathercloth, etc

There are no national negotiations in this industry. Many of the larger

181

manufacturing companies combine the manufacture of floorings with the manufacture of other products, and workers in scope of this sector are covered by negotiated agreements within these other industries.

Brushes and brooms

The great majority of the workers in this industry are employed by members of the British Brush Manufacturers' Association (BBMA) which has about 150 firms in membership. Most firms recognise trade unions; the principal unions in the industry are the National Society of Brushmakers and General Workers (NSBGW), the Furniture, Timber and Allied Trades Union (FTAT), TGWU, GMWU, AUEW and ASTMS.

Minimum rates of pay and other basic terms and conditions for workers throughout the industry are set by a National Joint Committee (NJC) on which BBMA and NSBGW are represented. These are supplemented through negotiations at local level in many firms.

Toys, games, children's carriages and sports equipment

These light manufacturing industries together employ some 40 000 people. The employers range from large companies to small firms specialising in a single product.

1 TOYS AND GAMES

Most people in the sector work in this industry, which has a significant proportion of part-time workers and homeworkers. The terms of employment for the great majority of manual workers in the industry are set by the Toy Manufacturing Wages Council (Great Britain) which fixes statutory minimum rates of pay for normal time work, piecework and overtime, and holiday entitlements for production workers. In the larger firms these minimum rates are often enhanced by company-level bargaining.

The employers' representatives on the council are nominated by the British Toy and Hobby Manufacturers' Association (BTHA) which represents about 90% of manufacturers. The unions represented are the TGWU, GMWU, FTAT and UCATT. The AUEW also has members in the industry, and some companies belong to the Engineering Employers' Federation (EEF). Levels of union membership are generally low and rise above 50% only in the larger establishments. There is no significant collective bargaining for white-collar employees.

2 CHILDREN'S CARRIAGES

This is the smallest section of the group. Statutory minimum rates of pay, for normal time work, piecework and overtime, and holiday entitlements for skilled, semi-skilled and unskilled manual workers are set by the Perambulator and Invalid Carriage Wages Council (Great Britain), and are enhanced by collective bargaining in the larger firms. The employers' representatives on the council come from the British Baby Products Association (BBPA) which represents the principal firms. The unions represented are the TGWU and FTAT. Some companies belong to the EEF and negotiate locally with the AUEW. There is no significant collective bargaining for white-collar employees.

3 SPORTS EQUIPMENT

The industry is dominated by the International Sports Company (a division of Dunlop Ltd) which has about 3500 employees. The main manual unions in the industry are the TGWU, GMWU, FTAT and the National Union of Footwear, Leather and Allied Trades (NUFLAT). The main white-collar unions are ACTS, MATSA, TASS, APEX and ASTMS.

There is no national negotiating machinery and all collective bargaining is at company or plant level. The International Sports Company negotiates on a local plant basis for production workers, but across the company for maintenance engineers and white-collar staff. A number of the other firms belong to the EEF.

Through the British Sports and Allied Industries Federation (BSAIF) there are negotiations between two unions — FTAT and the Teston Independent Society of Cricket Ball Makers (TISCBM) — and the employers of workers producing hand-finished cricket balls.

Miscellaneous stationers' goods

This industry is concerned with the manufacture of fountain pens, ballpoint pens, felt tip pens, pencils, rubber stamps, etc. It has close links with the engineering industry; many employers are members of the EEF and are thus covered by collective bargaining machinery in the engineering industry. Where unions are recognised they are members of the Confederation of Shipbuilding and Engineering Unions. There is some collective bargaining at company level mainly in the larger companies.

Plastics products not specified in other Orders

This sector covers a variety of different industries. There are no national negotiating arrangements which cover this sector in particular, though there is considerable bargaining at company or plant level for manual workers, and some bargaining for white-collar workers. Some manufacturers are members of the EEF and thus are covered by collective bargaining machinery in the engineering industry. In particular the EEF has an agreement with the TGWU and the GMWU linking rates of pay of plastics workers with the general engineering agreement. In addition one of the large companies in the sector also manufactures concrete tiles and applies the agreements of the National Joint Industrial Council for the Cast Stone and Cast Concrete Industry to its manual employees (see page 168).

Musical instruments; all other manufacturing industries not specified in other Orders

Only two industries in this sector have any national negotiating machinery for manual workers — pianoforte manufacture and button manufacture. Other manual workers where unionised bargain at local level; there is little collective bargaining for white-collar employees.

1 PIANOFORTE MANUFACTURE

There are about 1500 workers in this industry. The Joint Industrial Council for the Pianoforte Manufacturing Trade comprises representatives of the Pianoforte Industries and Export Group Committee, to which most of the employers belong, and FTAT.

It sets minimum time rates of pay, hours, payment by results rates, and shift and night allowances for both skilled and unskilled workers.

The industry closely follows the agreements of the British Furniture Trade Joint Industrial Council (see page 171). There is some local bargaining, mainly over payment by results schemes.

2 BUTTON MANUFACTURE

About 1000 people in some 50 firms are employed in the manufacture of buttons. The Button Manufacturing Wages Council (Great Britain) sets minimum rates of pay and some other terms and conditions for manual workers in the industry — both full-time employees and homeworkers — and also for manual workers involved in covering buttons and fixing them on to cards. Employers are represented on the council by the British Button Manufacturers' Association and employees by the GMWU, TGWU and NUFLAT. Formal negotiating arrangements exist in some of the larger companies where button manufacture is only one of several activities. The trade unions involved are the AUEW, GMWU, TGWU and, for some button coverers, the National Union of Tailors and Garment Workers (NUTGW).

Order XX CONSTRUCTION

The construction industry, in which 1·2 million people are employed, can be divided into three sectors: building, which is mainly concerned with the erection and repair of buildings of all types; civil engineering, which covers construction work on roads, bridges, tunnels, docks, sea defences, reservoirs, and on heavy steel and reinforced concrete structures such as power stations, the laying of sewers, gas and water mains and electricity cables and the extraction of coal from opencast workings; and specialist trades of which there is a wide variety (see page 188). Mechanical construction is dealt with under Engineering. The construction operations of central and local government are dealt with under Public Administration. Construction work carried out by employees of gas, electricity and water undertakings is covered by collective bargaining machinery in those undertakings. Some glazing is carried out by firms involved in glass processing and is in scope of the Flat Glass Council (see page 166).

Collective bargaining for manual employees is well developed. National agreements affect the pay and conditions of employment of over three-quarters of the manual employees in the industry. Many firms simply apply the nationally agreed terms; there is only a limited amount of supplementary bargaining at company or site level. The national-level collective bargaining bodies in building and civil engineering also have arrangements for common negotiation of some terms and conditions which apply in both sectors. In the specialist trades, however, collective bargaining is fragmented, with many employers' associations negotiating separately with trade unions. Throughout the industry union recognition tends to be confined to the larger companies. For white-collar employees there is little collective bargaining at any level except in three of the specialist trades — electrical contracting, heating and ventilating, and plumbing, where there is national negotiating machinery.

Building

In the building industry the majority of employees covered by collective bargaining machinery are employed by firms in membership of one or more of the three employers' associations:

National Federation of Building Trades Employers

Scottish Building Employers' Federation

Federation of Master Builders.

The National Federation of Building Trades Employers (NFBTE) covers England and Wales and has about 12 000 firms of all sizes in membership; some in direct membership and some in 11 affiliated specialist associations. These specialist associations cover plastering, house building, scaffolding, shopfitting, window manufacture, painting and decorating, stonework, woodworking, formwork, suspended ceiling contracting and building sub-contracting.

The NFBTE engages in collective bargaining on behalf of its members; it also provides advice on industrial relations matters and gives assistance to

185

members on claims before industrial tribunals. Member firms, including those of the specialist associations, are grouped into some 240 local associations organised into ten regions.

The Scottish Building Employers' Federation (SBEF) is independent of the NFBTE but affiliated to it and has about 1800 firms in membership. These are organised in 28 associations and three affiliated bodies. As well as general builders the membership includes specialists in joinery, glazing, plastering, scaffolding, shopfitting and house building. The SBEF gives advice on industrial relations and represents members at industrial tribunals.

The Federation of Master Builders (FMB), which has in membership about 20 000 mainly smaller and medium-sized firms, has until recently confined its activities to those of a trade association. However, the Federation and the Transport and General Workers' Union (TGWU) have now established a joint negotiating body called the Building and Allied Trades Joint Industrial Council.

The main trade unions in the building industry are the Union of Construction, Allied Trades and Technicians (UCATT), the TGWU, the National Union of General and Municipal Workers (GMWU) and the Furniture, Timber and Allied Trades Union (FTAT). In general, UCATT represents bricklayers, joiners, stonemasons, painters; TGWU represents plasterers, scaffolders, mechanical plant operators and roof slaters and tilers; and FTAT represents woodcutting machinists, french polishers and cabinet makers employed in woodworking factories. Labourers, depending on which trade they are working in, may be in any one of these unions or in the GMWU. White-collar unionism is limited although the white-collar sections of the manual unions all have some members.

Civil engineering

The Federation of Civil Engineering Contractors (FCEC) has about 600 firms in membership and a relatively high proportion of these are large or medium-sized. The members are grouped in eight area sections, but the Federation's work is largely centralised. It engages in collective bargaining on behalf of its membership, provides advice on industrial relations and acts as a trade association.

The main trade unions in civil engineering are TGWU, UCATT and GMWU. TGWU has substantial membership throughout the industry, including opencast coal mining; craftsmen such as carpenters are mainly in UCATT; GMWU has strong representation in gas distribution. White-collar union membership is not large.

COLLECTIVE BARGAINING ARRANGEMENTS IN BUILDING AND CIVIL ENGINEERING

Terms and conditions of employment for most manual employees — both craftsmen and operatives — are formulated partly by the Building and Civil

Engineering Joint Board (BCEJB) and partly by the National Joint Council for the Building Industry (NJCBI) and the Civil Engineering Construction Conciliation Board (CECCB). The procedure is that the BCEJB reaches agreement on certain terms and conditions of employment and puts them to the NJCBI and the CECCB which, if they so wish, promulgate them in the Working Rules for the building and civil engineering industries respectively. These Working Rules also contain subjects dealt with by the NJCBI and the CECCB independently. For one particular group of workers — road transport workers in the building industry in England and Wales — the NFBTE has a separate agreement with the TGWU. In Scotland there is no national-level agreement covering such workers and their rates are determined at company and plant level. For electricians in civil engineering the FCEC agrees basic rates of pay with the Electrical, Electronic, Telecommunication and Plumbing Union (EETPU).

The Building and Civil Engineering Joint Board (BCEJB) draws its representatives from the employers' and employees' sides of the NJCBI and the CECCB. The terms and conditions negotiated by the BECJB include basic wage rates, a guaranteed minimum supplement over the basic wage, a guaranteed minimum bonus, hours, holidays, death benefit and sick pay. Two basic rates are determined, one for London and Liverpool and the other for the rest of Great Britain. Joint Board negotiations cover some 700 000 employees.

The National Joint Council for the Building Industry (NJCBI) covers about 600 000 operatives and has representatives from the NFBTE, the SBEF and the National Federation of Roofing Contractors (NFRC) on the employers' side and UCATT, TGWU, GMWU and FTAT on the employees' side. The NJCBI has eleven Regional Joint Committees and a large number of Local Joint Committees. The Working Rules promulgated by the NJCBI cover, in addition to those matters subject to discussion by the BCEJB, a guaranteed weekly wage, extra payments for such things as risk and extra responsibility, conditions of service and termination of employment, travelling and lodging allowances, trade union recognition procedures, and grievance and disputes procedures. Agreements also cover such matters as safety, health and welfare, racial discrimination, apprenticeship and training.

There is some limited scope for the Regional Joint Committees to make variations to the Working Rules, for instance on rules for travelling payments where geographical considerations make 'straight line' calculations unrealistic. There are more substantial variations in Scotland, however, where the Scottish Regional Committee makes variations to the Rules on travel, overtime premia and certain tool allowances; and there are also special arrangements for determining the wages and conditions of employment of apprentices, which are independent of those for England and Wales. Local and Regional Committees also play a part in the stages of the disputes procedures.

The Civil Engineering Construction Conciliation Board (CECCB) has representatives from the FCEC, UCATT, TGWU and GMWU. The Conciliation Board promulgates a Working Rule Agreement which, in addition to those matters dealt with by the Joint Board, includes clauses on a minimum earnings guarantee, payment for time lost because of bad weather or lay off, night and shift work premia, 'plus rates' for additional skills or particular working conditions, travel and subsistence allowances, transfer, termination of employment, and disputes and discipline procedures. The CECCB has no regional or local machinery and disputes are referred from site level directly to the Board. There is no regional variation to the Agreement which covers over 100 000 operatives.

SPECIALIST TRADES

There are two main employers' organisations in this sector, the Federation of Specialists and Subcontractors (FASS) and the Committee of Associations of Specialist Engineering Contractors (CASEC). Both, however, are only trade associations and unlike some of their member associations do not engage in collective bargaining. There are a large number of specialist trades in or serving the construction industry; the joint machinery for collective bargaining is detailed below.

Joint Machinery	Employers' Association(s)	Union(s)
Joint Conciliation Committee of the Heating, Ventilating & Domestic Engineering Industry	Heating & Ventilating Contractors' Association (HVCA)	National Union of Sheet Metal Workers, Coppersmiths & Heating & Domestic Engineers (NUSMW)
Joint Industrial Board for the Electrical Contracting Industry (covers England & Wales)	Electrical Contractors' Association (ECA) (covers England & Wales)	EETPU
Scottish Joint Industrial Board for the Electrical Contracting Industry	Electrical Contractors' Association of Scotland (ECA of S)	EETPU
National Joint Council for Environmental Engineers & Allied Staffs	HVCA, ECA, ECA of S, National Association of Plumbing, Heating	EETPU's Electrical and Engineering Staff Association (EESA)

Joint Machinery	Employers' Association(s)	Union(s)
	and Mechanical Services Contractors (NAPHMSC)	
Joint Industrial Board for Plumbing Mechanical Engineering Services in England & Wales	NAPHMSC, NFBTE	EETPU
Scottish & Northern Ireland Joint Industrial Board for the Plumbing Industry	Scottish & Northern Ireland Plumbing Employers' Federation	EETPU
Demolition Industry Conciliation Board	National Federation of Demolition Contractors Limited	GMWU, TGWU, UCATT
National Joint Council for the Steeplejack Industry	National Federation of Master Steeplejacks & Lightning Conductor Engineers	UCATT
National Joint Council for the Felt Roofing Contracting Industry	Felt Roofing Contractors Employers' Association	EETPU
National Joint Council for the Fencing Industry	Fencing Contractors' Association, Chestnut Fencing Manufacturers' Society	GMWU, TGWU, UCATT
National Joint Council for the Exhibition Industry	British Exhibition Contractors' Association (BECA)	UCATT, TGWU, National Society of Operative Printers, Graphical and Media Personnel (NATSOPA)

[cont. overleaf]

189

Joint Machinery	Employers' Association(s)	Union(s)
National Exhibition Electrical Joint Industrial Council	BECA	EETPU
National Joint Council for the Thermal Insulation Contracting Industry	Thermal Insulation Contractors' Association	GMWU, TGWU
Scottish Painting Council	Scottish Decorators' Federation	UCATT
Joint Industrial Council for the Floor Covering Trade in Scotland	Association of Floor Covering Contractors (Scotland)	FTAT
No specific title for machinery; agreement known as the 'Plant Hire Working Rule Agreement'	Contractors' Plant Association (CPA)	TGWU, UCATT, GMWU
No specific title for machinery; agreement known as the 'Consolidated Crane Agreement'	CPA	AUEW
No specific title for machinery	National Master Tile Fixers' Association	National Tile, Faience and Mosaic Fixers' Society
No specific title for machinery	Refractory Users' Federation.	UCATT, TGWU, GMWU

Most of these agreements cover relatively small numbers of employees though a few deal with more substantial numbers. The agreement for white-collar staff in environmental engineering, which spans three trades within the sector — heating and ventilating, electrical contracting, and plumbing — covers about 30 000 employees and those for manual workers in these trades are similarly substantial: heating and ventilating — 35 000, electrical contracting (England and Wales) — 44 000, and plumbing (England and Wales) — 30 000. The Plant Hire Working Rule Agreement covers the great majority of the 35 000 people employed by CPA member firms.

Most of the agreements clearly specify the various categories of operatives affected, and cover a range of terms and conditions similar to those contained in the building and civil engineering agreements. Some of the agreements expressly follow NJCBI rates — for example those concerned with steeplejack and lightning conductor engineering, refractory users, felt roofing and fencing. The Plant Hire Working Rule Agreement generally closely follows the CECCB agreement, and the Consolidated Crane Agreement is linked in some respects to the Mechanical Construction Engineering Agreement (see page 136).

Order XXI GAS, ELECTRICITY AND WATER

The three industries contained in this Order are treated separately below. In addition to a description of collective bargaining arrangements in the nationalised gas industry there is also an account of arrangements in the petroleum and natural gas extraction industry which is formally part of Order II.

Gas

The gas industry employs about 103 000 people. It was nationalised in 1948 and the Gas Act 1972 set up the British Gas Corporation (BGC). The Corporation has overall responsibilities for the manufacture (or acquisition) and bulk transmission of gas; and its 12 regions, each of which is a complete management unit, are responsible for the supply of a large proportion of the gas to customers and the sale, installation and servicing of appliances. Its employees, however, are not directly involved in the gas extraction industry, and the arrangements within this industry are described separately below.

There is separate national collective bargaining machinery for manual workers; maintenance craftsmen; administrative, professional, technical and clerical staff; and higher management. National agreements set pay and principal terms and conditions of employment. All but the higher management group are covered by post-entry union membership agreements. Over 90% of manual workers and maintenance craftsmen, and over 80% of administrative, professional, technical and clerical staff are union members.

For all employees other than maintenance craftsmen (who have their own agreement) there are staged procedures to handle disputes, grievances and grading appeals. If a dispute is unresolved at domestic level it goes to the appropriate Regional Manager, then to a joint Regional Appeals Committee, and finally to a joint National Appeals Panel. There is also provision for arbitration at the request of either party.

191

MANUAL WORKERS (OTHER THAN MAINTENANCE CRAFTSMEN)

Most manual workers, of whom there are about 40 000, are represented by the National Union of General and Municipal Workers (GMWU) and some by the Transport and General Workers' Union (TGWU). There is in a few regions a significant number of gas fitters in membership of the Electrical, Electronic, Telecommunication and Plumbing Union (EETPU). There are thirteen representatives from the GMWU and two from the TGWU on the employees' side of the National Joint Industrial Council for the Gas Industry (NJIC).

The NJIC determines principal terms and conditions for all manual workers in scope and outlines job requirements and rates of pay for two-thirds of these workers. Rates of pay for the remainder are determined within upper and lower limits of the national framework by Regional Joint Industrial Councils (RJICs). The RJICs cover the regions of the BGC.

About three-quarters of the industry's manual workers are covered by work study based incentive payment schemes. These schemes have been negotiated and introduced at RJIC level.

Local Joint Industrial Committees (LJICs) are in the process of being set up to determine details of local working arrangements within NJIC and RJIC agreements. The GMWU and TGWU are represented on each RJIC and LJIC.

MAINTENANCE CRAFTSMEN

There are about 1200 maintenance craftsmen and they are represented by unions in membership of the Confederation of Shipbuilding and Engineering Unions (CSEU) (see page 132). Representatives from the CSEU meet the Craftsmen's Committee of the British Gas Corporation. There is a national agreement which establishes national categories of maintenance jobs, basic rates of pay and outlines job requirements.

ADMINISTRATIVE, PROFESSIONAL, TECHNICAL AND CLERICAL STAFFS

White-collar workers are represented by the National and Local Government Officers' Association (NALGO), the Managerial, Administrative, Technical and Supervisory Section of the GMWU (MATSA), the TGWU's Association of Clerical, Technical and Supervisory Staffs (ACTS), the Association of Scientific, Technical and Managerial Staffs (ASTMS) and the Technical, Administrative and Supervisory Section of the Amalgamated Union of Engineering Workers (TASS). All these unions sit on the National Joint Council (NJC) for Gas Staffs and Senior Officers. The NJC covers 58 000 administrative, professional, technical and clerical staffs up to a cut-off point determined by grade. The NJC establishes national grading and salary structures. The Regional Joint Councils (RJCs) for Gas Staffs and Senior Officers determine the grading of particular posts. The RJCs are mainly concerned with the implementation of agreements entered into by the NJC and issues particular to their Region. Local Joint Committees are in the process of being set up.

HIGHER MANAGEMENT

There is a Higher Management National Joint Council which covers about 2500 staff employed in grades above those in scope of the NJC, but not the most senior management. The trade union side is composed of NALGO representatives. In each BGC region there is a Regional Joint Council for Higher Management.

CONSULTATIVE MACHINERY

The negotiating machinery at national, regional and local level also acts as consultative machinery. In addition, there are two joint BGC/Trade Union committees. The Trade Union Advisory Committee brings together the Corporation's top management and the most senior trade union officials to exchange and develop views on broad policy matters. A slightly less senior group, the Trade Union Planning Liason Committee, was formed in 1977; it meets bi-monthly to discuss major issues of joint concern such as the BGC's five-year corporate plan, the marketing of gas, and the development of employee participation.

Petroleum and natural gas

This is a comparatively new industry in Great Britain which in a short time has increased its labour force from a few hundred employees to tens of thousands. It is an industry that involves the participation at one time or another of many other major industries, either directly or in the supply of goods and services.

There are three main geographical areas of activity: the oil and gas fields in the Scottish area of the North Sea, the gas fields off the East Anglian coast and a limited, but developing, land-based section in Nottingham, Lincolnshire and Dorset.

There are a number of stages in the extraction of oil and gas from a field: surveying, exploration, development and production. Surveying produces a picture of the underlying strata and from it areas are selected for exploration in which specialist drilling contractors are involved, though some drilling is done by the very largest operators with their own equipment. This is the first stage in which significant numbers of people are involved, in that each drilling rig requires a staff of about one hundred with a similar number in support services at sea, at the airports and in supply bases and elsewhere.

Development of a field is essentially a large-scale civil engineering process. It involves the construction and siting of rigs, pipelines and land terminals with associated treatment plant. Once again the majority of the labour force at this stage is employed by contractors in a wide variety of industries. Production employs comparatively few people: about 200 per location, who are mainly directly employed by the operators themselves. Specialist services such as maintenance, catering, supply of ships and helicopters, tend to be provided by sub-contractors.

As one might expect, there are no overall collective bargaining arrangements covering this wide range of activities. Such arrangements as there are tend to have arisen from the imposition or adaptation of existing agreements in those industries with long-established bargaining traditions; for example for seamen through the British Seafarers' Joint Council; in constructional engineering through agreements negotiated by the Oil and Chemical Plant Constructors' Association and in electrical contracting by the Joint Industry Board for the Electrical Contracting Industry. For operations exclusively or primarily part of the oil and gas exploration and production industry proper, union membership is at a very low level and there is little collective bargaining.

There is, however, an Inter Union Offshore Oil Committee (IUOOC) in Aberdeen. Its representatives come from the EETPU, TGWU, TASS, ACTS, ASTMS, the Amalgamated Union of Engineering Workers (AUEW), the Amalgamated Society of Boilermakers, Shipwrights, Blacksmiths and Structural Workers (ASB), the National Union of Seamen (NUS), the Merchant Navy and Airline Officers' Association (MNAOA), and the Radio and Electronic Officers' Union (REOU).

The IUOOC and the employers' association, the United Kingdom Offshore Operators' Association (UKOOA) have agreed a procedure for union recognition in respect of workers on platforms and other fixed installations.

Electricity

The industry employs about 178 000 people. Employment has contracted in recent years because of technological change, massive capital investment, and the introduction of work study based measures of workload and productivity.

Electricity supply was nationalised by the Electricity Act 1947. The structure was modified by the Electricity Reorganisation (Scotland) Act 1954 and by the Electricity Act 1957 and now is as follows:

England and Wales
The Electricity Council (EC) — which formulates general policy and gives advice on the industry to the Secretary of State for Energy;

The Central Electricity Generating Board (CEGB) — which owns and operates power stations and main transmission lines; 12 Area Electricity Boards (AEBs) — which distribute electricity to consumers and sell electrical appliances;

Scotland
Two Scottish Boards (SBs) — the North of Scotland Hydro Electric Board, and the South of Scotland Electricity Board — which generate,

transmit and distribute electricity, and are accountable to the Secretary of State for Scotland.

The industry is extensively unionised. For negotiating purposes employees are divided into five different groups, below, each of which is also known within the industry by the title of its joint negotiating body.

Industrial (Manual) Staff up to and including foremen (NJIC staff) (93 500) who are represented by the EETPU, GMWU, TGWU and AUEW.

Industrial (Manual) Staff — Building and Civil Engineering (NJ(B&CE)C Staff) (2800) who are mainly represented by the Union of Construction, Allied Trades and Technicians (UCATT), though some belong to the EETPU, GMWU and TGWU.

Professional, Administrative, Clerical and Sales Staff (NJC staff) (50 000) who are mainly represented by NALGO, and also by the Association of Professional, Executive, Clerical and Computer Staff (APEX), MATSA and ACTS.

Technical, Engineering and Scientific Staff (NJB staff) (29 500) who are represented by the Electrical Power Engineers' Association (EPEA), a constituent group of the Engineers' and Managers' Association (EMA).

Managerial and Higher Executive Grades (NJMC staff) (1700) who are mainly represented by the EPEA, and also by NALGO and the EETPU's Electrical and Engineering Staff Association (EESA).

All NJIC and NJC staff are covered by post-entry union membership agreements.

NEGOTIATING MACHINERY

The 1947 and 1957 Electricity Acts require the Electricity Council to establish and maintain, in conjunction with the Electricity Boards in Scotland and 'by agreement with any organisation appearing to the Council to be appropriate' (in effect, with trade unions recognised by the industry), negotiating machinery for settling terms and conditions of employment throughout the industry.

A single system has been established for Great Britain. For each of the main employee groups there is a separate national negotiating body, made up of senior members of the Electricity Boards in Great Britain, together with senior officials of the trade unions, which determines pay and conditions of employment. Then, for NJIC, NJC and NJB staff, there are in addition subsidiary district bodies for each Area to ensure that the agreements negotiated nationally are properly applied and to resolve any difficulties. Beneath the district bodies are local committees usually covering an operating unit such as a power station which within the terms of the national agreement deal with such matters as the timing of working hours, shift rotas, schedules, and internal grievances. For NJ(B&CE)C staff there are no formal district or local bodies, but there are arrangements in each Area for dealing with local problems. NJMC staff have joint managerial committees in each Area which

195

handle local matters. There are agreed disputes procedures with stages at local, district and national level. The details of each of the negotiating structures are tabulated below:

Employee group	National Body Title	Employers' representatives	Union representatives	District Bodies	Local Committees
Industrial Staff including Foremen (NJIC staff)	National Joint Industrial Council (NJIC)	EC CEGB AEBs SBs	EETPU GMWU TGWU AUEW	14 District Joint Industrial Councils	Works and Foremen's Committees
Building and Civil Engineering Industrial Staff (NJ (B&CE) C Staff)	National Joint (Building and Civil Engineering) Committee (NJ(B&CE)C)	EC CEGB AEBs SBs	UCATT EETPU GMWU TGWU	Arrangements for Local discussions in each Area	
Professional, Adminis- trative, Clerical and Sales Staff (NJC staff)	National Joint Council (NJC)	EC CEGB AEBs SBs	NALGO APEX MATSA ACTS	14 District Joint Councils	Staff Committees
Technical, Engineering & Scientific Staff (NJB staff)	National Joint Board (NJB)	EC CEGB AEBs SBs	EPEA	16 District Joint Boards (including 1 for Headquarters Staff and 1 for Development and Construction Staff)	Technical Staff Committees
Managerial and Higher Executive Grades (NJMC staff)	National Joint Managerial & Higher Executive Grades Committee (NJMC)	EC CEGB AEBs SBs	EPEA NALGO EESA	Joint Managerial Committees in each Area	

Matters of common concern to some or all of the negotiating bodies were formerly considered by the appointment of national multipartite committees which had employee representatives from each of the groups concerned. However, a National Joint Negotiating Committee is being formed which will cover all five employee groups and consider matters of common interest referred to it by mutual agreement of the separate negotiating bodies.

CONSULTATIVE (CO-ORDINATING) MACHINERY

Consultative machinery is also required by the 1947 Electricity Act. At national level there is a National Joint Co-ordinating Council (NJCC) for Great Britain, which was created to replace two earlier national joint advisory councils in 1977. It considers such matters of common interest as corporate plans, policy on the building or closure of power stations, technological change and fuel policy. There are subsidiary joint co-ordinating committees for England and Wales, and for Scotland, and specialist committees on health and safety, and on education and training. There are also 12 district joint advisory councils and nearly 400 local advisory committees.

Water supply

The water supply industry, which employs over 74 000 people, has in recent years been restructured by legislation and reorganised and developed with substantial capital expenditure.

The Water Act 1973, which specifically excluded Scotland, set up nine publicly owned regional Water Authorities in England, a Welsh National Water Development Authority, and provided for continued supply from some 30 'statutory' water companies. Under the Act, a National Water Council (NWC) was given responsibilities which included the establishment and maintenance of the industry's negotiating machinery. Four national negotiating bodies resulted.

Nearly half the workforce are manual workers covered by the National Joint Industrial Council for the Water Service (NJIC). There, representatives of the Authorities and the companies negotiate wage rates, productivity payments and detailed conditions of employment with the GMWU, TGWU, the National Union of Public Employees (NUPE) and the National Union of Agricultural and Allied Workers (NUAAW). There is a national-level disputes procedure. Craftsmen are covered by a separate agreement (a supplement to the main NJIC agreement) negotiated for them by the CSEU and the operatives' representatives of the National Joint Council for the Building Industries. A post-entry union membership agreement for manual workers was implemented nationally in 1976, and one for craftsmen in 1977.

Negotiations for white-collar workers are conducted in the National Joint Council for Water Service Staffs (NJC), by NALGO, NUPE, GMWU, the Thames Water Staff Association, the Greater London Council Staff

197

Association and representatives of professional staffs. There is very extensive membership of staff unions.

The third and fourth bodies are the Joint National Council for Water Service Senior Staffs (NJC) (concerned with some 500 senior staff), on which NALGO and a number of small professional bodies are mainly represented, and the National Joint Committee for Chief Officers of the Water Services.

For manual staff, Regional Joint Industrial Councils (RJICs) were set up, with NJIC agreement, 'for the purpose of maintaining harmonious local relationships and for the implementation of agreements and decisions' made nationally. The establishment of RJICs for craft trades has been agreed. Regional Joint Councils (RJCs) operate for white-collar staff.

For Scotland, the Local Government (Scotland) Act 1973 provided for the setting up of nine regional and three islands councils whose responsibilities include water supply and services. Collective bargaining for the industry is undertaken within the negotiating machinery for local government in Scotland, the National Joint Councils for Local Authorities' Services (Scottish Councils).

Order XXII   TRANSPORT AND COMMUNICATION

Nearly one and a half million people are employed in the transport and communication industries which are described below in nine sectors:

Railways

Road passenger transport

Road haulage for hire or reward

Other road haulage

Sea transport

Port and inland water transport

Air transport

Postal services and telecommunications

Miscellaneous transport services and storage.

Railways

Almost all railways in Great Britain are operated by the British Railways

Board or the London Transport Executive. The collective bargaining machinery of each of these organisations is described in turn below.

1 BRITISH RAILWAYS BOARD

The railways were nationalised by the Transport Act 1947. The British Railways Board (BRB) was set up by the Transport Act 1962, and it employs about 240 000 people in operations divided among its businesses:

British Rail

Freightliners Limited

British Rail Engineering Limited

Sealink UK Limited

British Rail Hovercraft Limited

British Transport Hotels Limited

British Rail Property Board

Transportation Systems and Market Research Limited

British Transport Advertising Limited

British Transport Police.

Three principal trade unions operate in the railway industry:
(i) The National Union of Railwaymen (NUR) is an industrial union with membership in nearly all grades in the railways and in other transport and ancillary undertakings. Its main membership is in the operating grades.
(ii) The Transport Salaried Staffs' Association (TSSA) takes into membership all grades of salaried staff employed in the transport industry.
(iii) The Associated Society of Locomotive Engineers and Firemen (ASLEF) represents train drivers, other footplate staff and some motive power supervisors.
Union membership agreements operate for all grades except management.

NEGOTIATING MACHINERY

Throughout BRB, pay and conditions of employment are almost entirely settled at national level. For the purpose of collective bargaining, BRB staff fall into five main categories. There is a 'machinery of negotiation' for each category, covering all staff in the category, whatever business they work in. In addition, there are separate arrangements for some of the staff of Freightliners

199

Limited, Sealink UK Limited, British Transport Hotels Limited, British Rail Hovercraft Limited, and British Transport Police. The five main categories of staff are:

(i) Salaried and Conciliation Staff. These make up about three-quarters of BRB staff, and are covered by the 'Machinery of Negotiation for Railway Staff 1956', known as the 'main machinery'. The grades covered by the agreement are 'classified' salaried staff within specified salary ranges (ie clerical, railway supervisory and traffic control staff), and 'conciliation' staff. Conciliation staff are a wide range of manual workers engaged in day-to-day operation of the railways at stations, marshalling yards and signal boxes; also included are train crews, staff engaged in the construction and maintenance of permanent way and signal and telecommunications installations, and certain workers in railway-owned docks and on ferries and in other activities of Sealink UK Limited. Staff within the main machinery are represented by NUR, TSSA and ASLEF.

(ii) Workshop Staff. Known also as 'railway shopmen', these grades are employed in the building and maintenance of locomotives and rolling stock, and of stations, tunnels, bridges, and in the maintenance of ships. They are represented by the NUR and the Confederation of Shipbuilding and Engineering Unions (CSEU). The CSEU Railway Sub-Committee comprises representatives of the Amalgamated Union of Engineering Workers (AUEW) (Foundry and Engineering Sections); the Amalgamated Society of Boiler-makers, Shipwrights, Blacksmiths and Structural Workers (ASB); the Electrical, Electronic, Telecommunication and Plumbing Union (EETPU); the National Union of Sheet Metal Workers, Coppersmiths and Heating and Domestic Engineers (NUSMW); and the Transport and General Workers' Union (TGWU) (Vehicle Building and Automotive Group).

(iii) Workshop Supervisory staff. This category covers inspectors and foremen who supervise workshop staff. Workshop supervisors are represented by TSSA, NUR, CSEU, AUEW and the Association of Scientific, Technical and Managerial Staffs (ASTMS).

(iv) Professional, Technical and Research Staff. This group is engaged in such activities as design, drawing office work and technical investigation. Employees in this category are represented by TSSA.

(v) Management Staff. All BRB management staff within specified management staff salary ranges are represented by TSSA and the British Transport Officers' Guild (BTOG). Senior officers are not covered by collective bargaining arrangements.

There is separate machinery for the following staffs:

(i) Freightliners Limited has its own negotiating arrangements for all grades. Wages staff are represented by NUR and salaried staff by NUR and TSSA.

(ii) Sealink UK Limited staff on cross-Channel services are covered by the National Maritime Board negotiating machinery (see page 210). Officers are represented by the Mercantile Marine Service Association (MMSA), the Merchant Navy and Airline Officers' Association (MNAOA), the Radio and Electronic Officers' Union (REOU) and the AUEW. Ratings are represented by the National Union of Seamen (NUS).

(iii) British Transport Hotels Limited has its own negotiating arrangements for all grades except management. Salaried staff other than management are represented by TSSA and NUR. Train catering staff are represented by NUR. Hotels, station catering and laundry staff (wages grade) are represented by NUR, with CSEU and NUR representing craftsmen.

(iv) British Rail Hovercraft Limited also has its own negotiating arrangements for staff other than management. Flight deck officers are represented by MNAOA. Other staff are represented by TSSA, NUR, NUS, MNAOA, REOU and CSEU.

(v) British Transport Police has its own negotiating arrangements for all grades except civilian staff who are covered by the main machinery of negotiation. Police ranks below that of superintendent are represented by the British Transport Police Force Federation.

The 'main machinery' for salaried and conciliation staff has three levels — national, regional and local. At national level, there are three separate bodies — the Railway Staff Joint Council (RSJC), the Railway Staff National Council (RSNC), and the Railway Staff National Tribunal (RSNT).

The RSJC is the first stage of negotiation at national level. It meets in four sections: salaried, locomotive, traffic, and general (ie matters common to the sections). The Council considers all proposals to vary a national agreement, questions of general principle involving recruitment and conditions of service, and matters on which there has been a failure to agree at Regional Headquarters level, other than those originating at the local level of the machinery. Each section consists of representatives of the relevant trade union(s) and management representatives from BRB HQ and the regions.

The Railway Staff National Council consists of eight representatives of the three main trade unions and eight management representatives, including both BRB members and officers. It deals with major issues on which the Railway Staff Joint Council has failed to agree, including pay claims.

The Railway Staff National Tribunal (RSNT) is an arbitration body consisting of three members not associated with the railways or railway trade unions, one selected by the BRB, one by the unions and a Chairman appointed by agreement between the Board and the unions. Its function is to decide on 'issues of major importance' on which the Railway Staff National Council cannot agree. An award of the Tribunal is binding on the parties only if there is an agreed reference. There is also provision for binding arbitration by the Chairman of the RSNT on interpretative and certain other issues on which the Railway Staff Joint Council cannot agree.

At regional level — the railways are divided into 5 regions — there are 4 Sectional Councils representing sections of staff. The Councils consider such matters as the application of national agreements and the agreed promotion and redundancy arrangements, claims for reclassification or regrading of posts, and matters on which there has been failure to agree at local level. If there is failure to agree at Sectional Council level the matter may be referred to the appropriate Regional Headquarters by the headquarters of the trade union(s) concerned. Local Departmental Committees (LDCs) exist at stations

201

or depots when the number of staff in a department or group of grades is 35 or over. They discuss local working conditions and arrangements. Where there are fewer than 35 staff, one or two local representatives are appointed by the staff to discuss these local issues with management.

Consultative procedures in parallel with each Machinery of Negotiation exist at local, regional and national levels.

The other machineries of negotiation broadly resemble the main machinery. The following bodies are analogous to the Railway Staff National Council in the respective machineries of negotiation:

Railway Shopmen's National Council

Railway Workshop Supervisory Staff National Council

Railway Professional and Technical Staff National Council

Management Staff National Joint Committee

Freightliners Limited Joint Negotiating Committee

BTH Ltd Staff National Council (Salaried and Wages Staff other than train catering)

Staff National Council (BTH train catering staff)

Hovercraft Staff National Council

British Transport Police Force Conference.

In each case provision is made for reference to independent arbitration in the event of failure to agree at the appropriate national body.

2 LONDON TRANSPORT EXECUTIVE

The London Transport Executive (LTE) operates railway and bus services in Greater London under the Transport (London) Act 1969. (For bus services see page 204.) About 23 000 staff are employed in the railway operating and associated departments.

As with BRB the three main trade unions for LTE railway operating and maintenance staff are NUR, TSSA and ASLEF. In LTE, ASLEF represents some guards and station staff as well as motormen. Workshop staff belong to the AUEW, EETPU, NUSMW and NUR. Union membership agreements cover most staff except management.

Pay and conditions of employment are settled at company level, with separate machinery for different groups of staff. The arrangements are as follows:

(1) Clerical, Technical and Railway Operating and Maintenance Staff. About 5000 clerical and technical staff and 15 000 railway operating and maintenance staff are covered by a single scheme of Negotiating and Consultative Machinery established in 1957 by an agreement between LTE, NUR, ASLEF and TSSA.

(2) Railway Workshop Staff. Approximately 3800 staff are covered by negotiations with a Joint Committee of Unions comprising equal representation of the NUR and the craft unions (AUEW, EETPU, NUSMW, and the Vehicle Building and Automotive Group of the TGWU). Separate machinery covers some 450 road and rail workshop and building trade supervisors, with ASTMS and TSSA also represented.

(3) Executive and Control Grades. 1900 staff are covered by two separate machineries: for the 1500 Executive grades (excluding senior management) the unions are TSSA and BTOG, for the 400 Control grades TSSA, NUR and ASTMS.

(4) Electricity Generation and Distribution Staff who number about 800. Separate agreements exist for Wages and Supervisory staff as well as Control grades associated with these staff.

Supervisory staff are represented by AUEW, EETPU, NUR and TSSA. These unions plus the TGWU and the National Union of General and Municipal Workers (GMWU) represent Wages Grades. There are additional separate agreements covering building trades wages staff (AUEW, NUR, EETPU, Union of Construction, Allied Trades and Technicians (UCATT), National Society of Operative Printers, Graphical and Media Personnel (NATSOPA) and the Furniture, Timber and Allied Trades Union (FTAT)); canteen staff (NUR, TGWU); food production staff (TGWU) and miscellaneous staff (rail: NUR, road: TGWU). There are also four national-level consultative committees broadly covering road, rail, engineering and electricity generation staff.

The main negotiating body on terms and conditions for Clerical, Technical and Railway Operating and Maintenance Staff is the Railway Negotiating Committee, composed of 6 LTE representatives and 2 from each of the 3 unions. In the event of a major disagreement matters can be referred either jointly or unilaterally to a Wages Board with an independent chairman, whose decision may be binding by prior agreement. Other consultative and local negotiating arrangements extend down to depot level where local interpretation and administration of agreements is dealt with.

A similar pattern of consultative, negotiating and arbitration machinery applies to the three other groups of staff mentioned above, but in the case of Railway Workshop staff no formal machinery exists.

Road passenger transport

The industry employs about 200 000 people. It has two main parts:
Bus and coach services
Taxis and car-hire services.

1 BUS AND COACH SERVICES

These can be divided into two parts. Bus services, known as stage carriage services, have fixed routes, time-tables and fares, and are mainly operated by large publicly owned undertakings. Coaching — tours, private hire and contract work — is undertaken by some publicly owned bodies, but is mostly carried out by very small private firms.

There is a statutory background influencing terms and conditions of employment. Drivers' hours are limited by the Transport Act 1968 and by EEC Regulation 543/69 which the UK is now implementing; section 152 of the 1960 Road Traffic Act, as amended by the Transport Act 1968, requires operators to observe the terms of the Fair Wages Resolution (see page 86) for their employees.

The employers

There are five main employers or groups of employers:

(i) London Transport Executive. The LTE operates bus services, and rail services (see page 202), in Greater London under the Transport (London) Act, 1969. About 36 000 staff are employed in the Road Operating and associated Departments.

(ii) The seven Passenger Transport Executives (PTEs) (Greater Manchester, Merseyside, West Midlands, South Yorkshire, West Yorkshire, Tyne and Wear, and Greater Glasgow) set up for the large conurbations by the 1972 Local Government Act. They mainly run bus services.

(iii) Some 50 other local authorities, which also run bus services.

(iv) The publicly owned undertakings — principally the National Bus Company (NBC) and the Scottish Bus Group Limited (SBG). Both the NBC and the Scottish Transport Group of which the SBG is a part were established by the Transport Act 1968 and operate through subsidiaries, many of which have retained their original company names.

(v) Private firms. Most are small — in 1976 almost three-quarters had under six vehicles — many are family businesses or partnerships also running road haulage, vehicle repair or car-hire services, and they rely heavily on part-time, seasonal or casual drivers.

There are in total about 6000 operators in the industry. The overwhelming majority of these are private operators, yet it is the large public sector employers who employ most of the employees.

There are two main national employers' organisations, one for local authorities — the Federation of Public Passenger Transport Employers (FPPTE) — and one, predating nationalisation, covering both the NBC and SBG subsidiaries and a few of the larger private operators — the Conference of Omnibus Companies (COC). There are also two regional associations of private operators — the Coach Operators' Federation (COF) which is concentrated in the south and west, and the Midlands Area Coach and Transport Association (MACTA).

The unions

Almost all public sector employers operate union membership agreements for manual workers, but unionisation in the private sector is much lower. Most drivers and conductors belong to the TGWU though some belong, for historical reasons, to the NUR or to GMWU. Maintenance craftsmen and other manual workers belong to the AUEW, EETPU, NUSMW, TGWU, and FTAT.

For white-collar staff in the publicly owned undertakings the National and Local Government Officers' Association (NALGO) and the TGWU's Association of Clerical, Technical and Supervisory Staffs (ACTS) are recognised throughout Great Britain and the NUR is recognised in England and Wales. The TSSA is recognised in London Country Bus Services (LCBS) (an NBC subsidiary), and ASTMS in the SBG. NALGO and ACTS are the main unions for staff in the local authorities and PTEs; TSSA and ACTS are the staff unions in London Transport, and both have union membership agreements. In the private sector there is little staff unionisation.

NEGOTIATING MACHINERY

London Transport has its own negotiating machinery. For the other employers there are two national negotiating structures, one for local authorities (which also influences, to some extent, the PTEs), the other for the nationalised sector and some of the private companies. In addition there are a few regional negotiating structures for private operators.

A) London Transport

Pay and conditions of employment are determined at company level, with separate machinery for different groups of staff. The arrangements are as follows:

(i) Road Operating Wages Staff. About 20 000 drivers, conductors and driver/operators are covered by machinery agreed in 1971 between LTE and TGWU.

(ii) Road Operating Supervisors. About 2500 staff are covered by discussions between LTE and ACTS. (No formal procedure exists.)

(iii) Garage Maintenance Wages Staff. About 3000 unskilled and semi-skilled staff are covered by an agreement of 1963 between LTE and TGWU.

(iv) Road Workshop Wages Staff. About 3500 staff are covered by negotiations between LTE and a Joint Trades Committee comprising AUEW, EETPU, NUSMW and TGWU (Vehicle Building and Automotive Group).

Negotiating arrangements for clerical and technical staff, workshop supervisors, catering staff and executive and control grades are conducted through separate procedures which cover staff employed on bus or rail work.

For Road Operating Wages Staff, the principal negotiating body is a meeting between senior managers of LTE, led by an Executive Member, and the Central Bus Negotiating Committee, composed of the TGWU's London District Secretary and eight elected TGWU representatives, led by the TGWU's National Secretary (Passenger Services Group). Failing agreement, the parties consult over the appropriate course of action. Other consultative and local negotiating arrangements extend down to garage level.

Similar patterns of consultative and negotiating machinery apply to the other groups mentioned. For Garage Maintenance Wages Staff, an agreement provides for unresolved matters to be referred to a Board of Referees with an independent chairman.

B) Local authorities and PTEs

The National Joint Industrial Council (NJIC) for the Road Passenger Transport Industry is composed of 18 employers' representatives from the FPPTE, 17 members from the TGWU and one from the GMWU. Its agreements cover about 20 000 platform, semi-skilled and unskilled staff. A separate National Joint Council (NJC) for Craftsmen employed in Municipal Passenger Transport Undertakings covers about 3000 skilled workers.

Until 1967 both Councils set standard national rates of pay, and employers who exceeded them could be expelled from the FPPTE. This, together with the competition for labour in the main industrial areas, put considerable strain on the national machinery, and following the 1967 Report by the National Board for Prices and Incomes (NBPI) ('Productivity Agreements in the Bus Industry': Report No 50) the Councils now set minimum terms and conditions which are extensively enhanced through local productivity bargaining conducted within a framework laid down by the NJIC and NJC. The agreements cover mainly pay, hours, rates for overtime, shift and rest-day working, holidays and sick pay. They also set out disputes procedures which have local and national stages and include a provision for emergency committees to be appointed to visit and investigate local disputes.

The NJIC and NJC now loosely influence the PTEs. As each PTE has had to integrate a number of undertakings previously run by its area's local authorities, often with different local agreements, all have developed their own bargaining structures for manual employees. The Merseyside PTE, for example, has a Joint Negotiating Committee which meets every six weeks, negotiates substantive agreements on pay and conditions and has union representatives (TGWU and GMWU) from each garage. PTEs do not, however, negotiate terms and conditions that are inferior to those agreed by the NJIC and NJC.

Terms and conditions for white-collar staff are generally settled differently. In local authority transport undertakings they are covered by the normal local authority negotiating machinery. Four of the PTEs (Merseyside, Greater Manchester, West Midlands, and Tyne and Wear) have established a Joint Negotiating Committee for Non-manual Staff, with 11 union representatives — nine from NALGO, two from ACTS. The other PTEs bargain independently.

C) The publicly owned undertakings and some private companies

The National Council for the Omnibus Industry (NCOI) covers about 60 000 employees. There are 20 employer representatives from the COC, and union representatives from the TGWU (15), NUR (3), GMWU (1) and the craft unions (1). It took a long time for the multitude of company rates to be replaced by national recommended rates and even now the main agreement — the Council's National Conditions Agreement — covers drivers and conductors only for bus services and semi-skilled and unskilled garage staff. Skilled maintenance workers are covered by the NCOI Model Agreement, except in SBG where they have a separate negotiating body. The agreements are similar — both in coverage, and in the actual terms and conditions of employment laid down — to those set for local authorities by the NJIC and NJC.

Rates for excursions, tours and private hire — predominantly coaching work — are normally negotiated at operating company level. Only SBG — where there was one dominant private operator with such an agreement at nationalisation — has a group-wide agreement for coaching work.

LCBS has its own negotiating machinery, similar in structure to that operated by London Transport, for all its employees. NBC and SBG have their own separate negotiating machinery for white-collar staff.

D) The remainder of the private sector

The remainder of the industry is very fragmented and national bargaining has not developed, though there is regional negotiating machinery in three regions. The Southern and Western Joint Industrial Council (SWJIC) brings together the COF and the TGWU, and its agreements cover drivers on private hire, contract, excursion and tours work. In the Midlands, MACTA and the TGWU have an agreement covering drivers, conductors and garage staff. Both agreements set minimum rates, hours of work, overtime, shift and rest-day payments and holidays. In the North West, a group of employers and the TGWU have an agreement covering principally minimum rates and holidays for drivers and ancillary manual staff.

With the very high proportion of small firms there is minimal collective bargaining at company level, apart from in the London area where about one-third of the larger operators (more than 5 vehicles) have agreements, often containing union membership agreements.

2 TAXIS AND CAR-HIRE SERVICES

Taxis operate under legislation, with set fares, and licences for cabs and drivers. There are different types of driver — owner-drivers, employees, and 'journeymen' who rent cars from proprietors and pay them a commission. Earnings are effectively determined by fare levels, commission rates and the hours drivers individually devote to work. The TGWU is the main union for drivers, representing mainly journeymen and some owner-drivers; in London within its cab section, elsewhere through its passenger services trade group. In London there is also a Licensed Taxi-Drivers' Association (LTDA) formed by owner-drivers in 1967 in opposition to mini-cabs.

Only London has any multi-firm negotiating machinery — a Joint Cab Trades Committee. This brings together the London Motor Cab Proprietors' Association (LMCPA), to which most of the larger proprietors belong, and the TGWU. Its agreements cover about 3000 drivers. They set minimum commission rates and minimum conditions of employment, but indicate that better terms may be negotiated at garage level. Both sides also make regular representations to the appropriate authorities about fare levels and licensing, and this is in fact the main preoccupation of local proprietors' associations and the TGWU outside London.

Mini-cabs and other hire cars are prohibited from plying for hire in London. Elsewhere there is little licensing and fares are not controlled. There is minimal unionisation or collective bargaining—most drivers are self-employed and often work part-time.

Road haulage contracting for general hire or reward

This industry, which has private and public sectors, employs about 190 000 people, mostly in the private sector. Until September 1978 a Wages Council existed to determine minimum levels of remuneration and set minimum standards for a number of conditions of employment.

1 THE PRIVATE SECTOR

The Road Haulage Association Limited (RHA) has the majority of the employers in the industry in membership. It represents private sector employers for industrial relations purposes. While it speaks for employers nationally its eighteen constituent groupings negotiate separately. Three unions operate in the industry: the TGWU, GMWU, and the United Road Transport Union (URTU).

In the latter years of the Wages Council period, collective bargaining with the unions over pay for manual workers developed through small local groups of haulage firms, who were termed 'Assenting Hauliers' because they accepted the terms of negotiated pay settlements. In some areas these developed into Joint Industrial Councils (JICs). In Scotland, for example, the JIC for the Road Haulage Industry, composed of RHA and TGWU representatives, is the sole body involved in collective bargaining. The abolition of the Wages Council hastened the creation of formally constituted collective bargaining machinery and the industry has established a number of Regional or Area JICs. The terms of reference of the JICs include rates of remuneration, subsistence allowances, holidays, redundancy procedures and payments, procedures for dealing with disputes, grievances and disciplinary matters, and in the majority of cases sickness and personal accident schemes.

There is some supplementary bargaining at company level, and a small number of very large companies are outside the RHA machinery and negotiate on a national basis with one or other of the three unions. There is very little collective bargaining for white-collar employees.

2 THE PUBLIC SECTOR

The public sector operates under the aegis of the National Freight Corporation (NFC), created by the Transport Act 1968. Its operating companies include National Carriers Limited (NCL) and British Road Services (BRS). NCL has its own collective bargaining machinery. The 'BRS Machinery' covers not only BRS but the remaining operating companies which include Roadline UK Ltd, Pickfords Removals Ltd, Tank Freight Ltd, Containerway and Road Ferry Ltd. Other specialised companies in car transportation, waste management and cold storage tend to negotiate directly with the unions — mainly TGWU, URTU, AUEW and EETPU — for their manual staff, but their white-collar staff are covered by the BRS machinery.

A) The 'BRS Machinery'

The companies covered by the BRS Machinery employ about 20 000 people. All staff except senior management are covered, and the collective bargaining machinery operates at national, company and establishment level.

Pay and other terms and conditions of employment are negotiated at national level by national joint negotiating committees (NJNCs). There are separate NJNCs for each of the three main categories of staff: operating and other wages grades, who are represented by the TGWU and URTU; engineering, maintenance and repair grades, who are represented by the AUEW, EETPU and TGWU; and administrative, professional, technical, supervisory and clerical grades, who are represented by ACTS and TSSA. If an NJNC fails to agree, the matter goes to the National Staff Council (NSC) which has representatives from NFC management and all the trade unions, or to arbitration. The NSC also considers any matters of national importance covering more than one category of staff.

At BRS operating company and establishment level, there are separate Company Joint Committees and Local Joint Committees for the three categories of staff. The main functions of these committees are to implement the national agreements and to act as stages in the disputes procedure.

B) National Carriers Limited

NCL employs about 8000 people, all of whom, except senior management, are covered by collective bargaining machinery which, as in the BRS Machinery, operates at national, company and establishment level. As with the BRS Machinery, pay and other standard conditions of service are settled at national level, with separate machinery for each of the three categories of staff. In NCL these are joint negotiating committees (JNCs). Operating and other wages grades are represented by NUR; engineering, maintenance and repair grades by NUR and CSEU; and administrative, professional, technical, supervisory and clerical grades by NUR and TSSA. If a JNC fails to agree, there is provision for the matter to be dealt with at a special meeting of the JNC at which an independent chairman, appointed by the JNC (or, if there is failure to agree, nominated by ACAS) presides.

At NCL operating company and establishment level there are separate Company Councils and Local Joint Committees for the three categories of staff. As in BRS these mainly implement the national agreements, and act as stages in the disputes procedure.

Other road haulage

This branch of the road haulage industry covers any operation of road haulage where transportation is not the prime business of the company concerned. About 20 000 workers are employed in such activities which have the term 'own account' road haulage applied to them.

The Freight Transport Association represents the collective interests of its member employers in the 'own account' sector and offers advice on a variety of matters, including industrial relations. However, it does not negotiate on behalf of its members with trade unions.

The main union in the industry is the TGWU, though many firms do not recognise trade unions, particularly those with a small fleet of vehicles or small vans whose drivers also act as salesmen and warehousemen. Where a union is recognised for drivers, the white-collar section of that union is often recognised for the clerical workers connected with the road haulage activities. Managers are not usually unionised.

About three-quarters of manual employees are covered by collective bargaining, and terms and conditions of employment are normally settled at company level. In some industries, however, such as textiles the national machinery also covers road transport workers. Even where national agreements do not cover road transport workers directly, firms may apply to their drivers the terms and conditions set for other manual workers.

Sea transport

Sea transport employs nearly 100 000 people. There are three main categories of staff:
  (i) seafaring personnel employed by shipping companies
 (ii) shore-based personnel of shipping companies
(iii) pilots.

The collective bargaining arrangements described below cover only seafaring personnel. There is little collective bargaining for shore-based personnel, and pilots are dealt with under Port Transport (see page 211).

Most shipping companies (except owners of fishing vessels) belong to the General Council of British Shipping (GCBS) which has a membership of some 45 trade associations and about 160 individual companies. Wages and conditions of employment of most seafarers are negotiated by the National Maritime Board (NMB) which is composed of representatives from the GCBS and the seafarers' trade unions which are the NUS, AUEW, ASB, MNAOA, MMSA and REOU. There is a union membership agreement for all officers and ratings.

Negotiations in the NMB are undertaken in six panels, each dealing with different groups of employees:

	Panel	Union(s) represented
(A)	Officers panels:	
	Shipmasters	MMSA, MNAOA
	Navigating Officers (including cadets)	MNAOA
	Engineer Officers (including cadets)	MNAOA, AUEW
	Radio Officers	REOU
(B)	Ratings panels:	
	Sailors and firemen	NUS, ASB
	Catering department	NUS

In practice, rates of pay and conditions of employment affecting officers generally are dealt with simultaneously by all the officers' panels. Matters concerning the ratings are usually considered jointly by the two ratings' panels. Matters of common interest such as disciplinary procedures or repatriation in special circumstances are settled by all the panels together. There is considerable supplementary negotiation at company level.

By NMB Agreement, the GCBS operates the Merchant Navy Established Service Scheme, which functions like an employment agency and supplies ratings for employment in the ships of those companies which are party to the scheme.

Port and inland water transport

There is separate collective bargaining machinery for the ports and inland waterways. In addition ferries operated by British Rail are dealt with under Railways (page 199); and the Clyde ferry services are covered by negotiations between the Scottish Transport Group and the TGWU, NUR, NUS and the AUEW's Technical, Administrative and Supervisory Section (TASS).

1 PORT TRANSPORT

This industry is concerned with the loading and unloading of cargo bound for or discharged from sea transport, and with associated work such as storage and warehousing. It employs about 56 000 people of whom just under half are dock workers (the great majority registered dock workers). About a quarter of the total are skilled tradesmen, and the rest are managerial, supervisory and clerical workers.

A statutory framework, which covers most major ports, is laid down by the Dock Work Regulation of Employment Act 1946 and its accompanying Dock Labour Scheme. New provisions were included in the Dock Work Regulation Act 1976 which has not been fully implemented.

The Scheme established a system of registration of employers and dock workers. It does not apply to other classes of employee. The overall responsibility for registration lies with the National Dock Labour Board (NDLB) on which equal numbers of representatives of employers and unions in the industry sit together with independent members. It operates through 22 Local Dock Labour Boards (LDLBs) which have independent members and which are responsible for the detailed administration of the Scheme within their areas. The most important non-Scheme ports are Felixstowe, Dover, Shoreham, Portsmouth and those run by British Rail.

THE EMPLOYERS

There are about 200 port authorities and companies employing registered dock workers in the port transport industry. The port authorities are responsible for managing, maintaining and improving docks and harbours. Some ports are run by the nationalised sector, British Transport Docks Board (BTDB), Sealink UK Ltd, and the British Waterways Board (BWB). Some ports, for example London, are owned by port trusts; some, notably Bristol, are municipally owned; others, such as Manchester and Felixstowe are owned by public companies. The companies operating within ports are wharfingers, warehouse and cold storage firms, stevedores, and lighterage firms.

Almost all employers in Scheme ports and some in non-Scheme ports are members of the National Association of Port Employers (NAPE) which has eight regional groupings.

UNIONS

Unionisation is high amongst manual, supervisory, clerical and administrative staff, and quite high amongst management staff. The great majority of dockers belong to the TGWU. The National Amalgamated Stevedores' and Dockers' Union (NASDU) has some membership in London and Hull; it is formally recognised only in London. The GMWU and NUR also have members in some ports.

Most maintenance and craft workers are represented by unions belonging to the CSEU (see page 132). Most other specialist port workers who are not registered dockers are generally represented by the TGWU or, in BTDB ports and a few others, the NUR. Some marine staff are represented by the MNAOA.

Supervisory staff belong to different unions in different ports; the main

212

unions are the TGWU, NUR, TSSA and NALGO. One of the craft unions generally represents craft supervisors.

Clerical and administrative staff are also represented by various unions, predominantly NALGO, ACTS, TSSA and NUR. Management grades are represented by NALGO, TSSA and BTOG.

River pilots are self-employed but are generally members of the United Kingdom Pilots' Association (UKPA) or the TGWU. Port police are members of their own port police federations or of the British Transport Police Federation.

COLLECTIVE BARGAINING MACHINERY

a) Dock workers

For registered dock workers, the national negotiating machinery is the National Joint Council (NJC) for the Port Transport Industry. The negotiations are carried out by an Executive Committee which has representatives drawn from NAPE, TGWU and GMWU. The NJC agreements cover guaranteed minimum daily payments, minimum holiday and sick pay, standard holiday entitlements, a 40 hour week for normal day work, pensions and severance arrangements. The NJC also nominates employers' and union representatives on the NDLB.

A sub-committee of the NJC is the National Conciliation Committee which handles disputes arising from interpretations of national agreements and also disputes arising from individual ports.

Port-level collective bargaining is now the most significant level of negotiations in respect of pay rates for registered dock work. This is conducted by Port Joint Committees (PJCs) which have different titles in different ports. Port agreements cover such matters as rates of pay, overtime, and bonus or piecework rates. They also establish machinery for settling disputes. This machinery often includes a board or panel to arbitrate over particular disputed cargoes and usually has a final stage involving the PJC or its executive body, with reference to the NJC as a last resort.

In addition to the port-level agreements, some ports or employers have special agreements covering shift work and pay on terminals handling containerised cargo or employing other modern methods of mechanised cargo handling. Disputes which are not settled at individual port or employer level may be referred to the relevant wider port machinery. Registered dock workers who work on fishing vessels are covered by arrangements in the fishing industry (see page 102).

For dock workers in non-scheme ports, there is no national machinery. The TGWU has some company-level agreements with the larger port authorities and employers.

b) Other employees

For employees other than dock workers there are no industry-wide agreements. The BTDB does have national agreements for such staff in most of its ports although in the port where it employs most staff, Southampton, it also

213

has separate port agreements with the CSEU and the TGWU for, respectively, maintenance and supervisory workers.

In most ports, maintenance staff are covered by negotiations between the port authority and the CSEU or individual unions. The TGWU most commonly represents other non-registered manual grades. The MNAOA is a party to negotiations for marine staff.

The BTDB has a national agreement for its non-docker manual grades (other than maintenance workers at Southampton) with the unions representing these grades — the NUR, TGWU, CSEU, EETPU, and UCATT. This particular agreement provides a national grading structure and rates of pay. It also provides for maintenance and operational councils in the port groups and beneath these, and in the small ports, local port committees for each section or department. These negotiate and consult on matters not in conflict with the national agreement.

Most port authorities have comprehensive agreements with the different unions which represent clerical and administrative workers. The BTDB has national agreements with TSSA and NUR. In the municipal ports such as Bristol where NALGO represents these grades local authority terms and conditions apply; the NJC for Local Authorities' APT & C Staff (see page 284) has a Ports Committee which considers separate matters relating to ports staff. Some of the larger private employers have agreements with the relevant unions, though collective bargaining for white-collar staff among private employers in the industry is limited.

Technical and managerial staff may be covered by the collective bargaining arrangements for clerical and administrative staff. The BTDB has a separate national agreement for technical staff though not yet for management staff.

HM Customs Officers at British ports are civil servants and are covered by the civil service arrangements.

Pilots are represented by the UKPA or the TGWU. What are termed 'Letch' agreements are made with the local area of the General Council of British Shipping. These agreements set the number of pilots needed for ships using the port, which provides the basis for levying pilotage charges.

Port Police normally follow the terms and conditions established for their relevant civilian police force or, in the case of BTDB police, settle them by negotiation with the BTPF.

2 INLAND WATER TRANSPORT

This industry, employing about 4500 people, covers three sectors: the maintenance of waterways; freight transport; and pleasure boat hire.

Maintenance of waterways

While water authorities and local authorities control some stretches of navigable water, the maintenance of rivers and canals is largely the responsibility of the nationalised British Waterways Board (BWB) which has over 3000 employees. BWB is also involved in freight transport.

Manual staff (termed Wages Grades) are represented by the TGWU and the NUR, and salaried staff by NALGO and TSSA.

Collective bargaining arrangements for manual staff are conducted through a National Joint Council (NJC) and five Local Joint Councils (LJCs). The NJC determines the wage and grade structures for manual staff, and other terms and conditions, and deals with problems referred to it by any LJC. For salaried staff there is a similar structure with an NJC and four District Joint Councils (DCs).

Freight transport

The majority of inland waterway transport firms belong to the National Association of Inland Waterway Carriers.

Only the TGWU organises workers in the industry. It has a majority of the relevant staff of Association firms in membership. The Association and the union meet on a Joint Negotiating Committee (JNC). The JNC agreements set guaranteed fall back rates, holidays and sick pay. There is also collective bargaining at company level. Company agreements normally cover basic and supplementary pay, overtime, tonnage or trip bonuses, sick pay, holidays and holiday pay. There is no significant collective bargaining for white-collar staff.

Pleasure-boat hire

There are no national bargaining arrangements for these businesses. Some individual pleasure-craft operators have agreements with the TGWU for manual workers. There is no significant collective bargaining for white-collar staff.

Air transport

For collective bargaining purposes air transport can be divided into two parts: Airlines and Airports. In total the industry has some 85 000 employees.

1 AIRLINES

By far the biggest employer is British Airways (BA), a nationalised corporation with 57 000 employees. Private domestic airlines and a large number of foreign-based airlines employ a further 18 000. BA has a statutory duty under the British Airways Board Act 1977 to negotiate the terms and conditions of all its employees through collective bargaining and is the main participant on the employers' side of the National Joint Council for Civil Air Transport (NJCCAT).

There are statutory provisions influencing terms and conditions of employees in the industry. The Civil Aviation Act 1949 requires that terms and conditions of employees of British companies engaged in passenger air transport should be no less favourable than those applying to equivalent staff on comparable work in British Airways, except where a collective agreement is in operation between the employees and their employer.

The NJCCAT

The employers' side of the NJCCAT is composed of thirteen representatives from BA, two each from British Caledonian Airways Ltd (BCAL), Dan Air Services Ltd, and International Aeradio Ltd and one from British Island Airways Ltd (BIA). There are eleven sub-committees called National Sectional Panels (NSPs) which cover different groups of occupations such as air cabin crew, engineering, maintenance and administrative staff. A General Purposes Committee deals with matters of concern to more than one NSP. Not all the employers are represented on every panel. The union representatives come from:

TGWU	NUSMW	ACTS
GMWU	TASS	ASTMS
AUEW	FTAT	MNAOA
EETPU	UCATT	

Association of Professional, Executive, Clerical and Computer Staff (APEX)

GMWU's Managerial, Administrative, Technical and Supervisory Section (MATSA)

British Airways Stewards' and Stewardesses' Association (BASSA) (part of TGWU)

British Airline Pilots' Association (BALPA).

The level of unionisation in the NJCCAT companies is high and there are some union membership agreements.

NJCCAT agreements cover such things as statutory holidays, payment during sickness and absence, and introduction of productivity schemes. For each NSP there are separate agreements reached for each airline represented on that panel. Each of these separate agreements tends to follow the same pattern and show a broad similarity of pay levels. The substantive matters covered by NSP agreements vary. The manual staff panels cover such items as pay, hours, overtime premia, shift allowances, and manning levels while the pilot officers panel covers pay, health care, flying times, licence loss compensation, seniority and transfer arrangements.

Two forms of local committee have been established. These committees are known as Local Panel Committees (LPCs) and Local Joint Panel Committees (LJPCs). The LPCs deal with matters concerning the local application of NSP agreements, local health and safety, and are also concerned with the settlement of local grievances and disputes. The LJPCs deal with matters covering more than one LPC in a geographical area. Both are also involved as one of the stages in the NJCCAT agreed disputes procedure, the final stage of which allows for joint requests to ACAS for conciliation and arbitration, or to the NJC's own Conciliation Committee.

Airlines outside the NJCCAT
Among the airlines outside the NJCCAT the British-based companies are highly unionised. They tend to follow NJCCAT and NSP agreements. There are over 40 foreign airlines operating in Great Britain. Some of those with passenger handling facilities engage in collective bargaining in respect of clerical staff, the main unions for these staff being ASTMS and APEX. Airlines which have, in addition, cargo handling facilities employ manual staff who are sometimes the subject of agreements with the TGWU, the AUEW and the EETPU.

2 AIRPORTS
The majority of airports in Great Britain are controlled either by the British Airports Authority (BAA) or by local authorities.

British Airports Authority
The BAA is responsible for Heathrow, Gatwick, Stansted, Prestwick, Glasgow, Edinburgh and Aberdeen airports, and almost all its 7500 employees are covered by collective bargaining arrangements. It is required under the Airports Authority Act 1975 to set up, as appropriate, negotiating arrangements to settle terms and conditions of employment for its employees.

BAA recognises the AUEW, EETPU, UCATT and NUSMW as representing craftsmen and craft related employees and the GMWU and TGWU as representing operative grades, firemen and leading firemen. Four unions represent clerical, administrative and professional staffs and fire service officers: the Civil and Public Services Association (CPSA), Society of Civil and Public Servants (Executive, Directing and Analagous Grades) (SCPS), Civil Service Union (CSU) and the Institution of Professional Civil Servants (IPCS).

The BAA and all these unions are represented on a Central Joint Council (CJC) and a Joint Negotiating and Consultative Committee (JNCC). The CJC provides a forum for consultation on major issues. The JNCC and its four standing committees provide a forum within which actual terms and conditions of employment are negotiated. Three of its standing committees cover non-industrial staff, industrial staff and fire service personnel respectively and there is also a standing committee for matters which affect more than one group of employees. Agreements are subsequently ratified by the JNCC.

At each airport there is a Local Joint Committee (LJC) in which matters of local interest are negotiated. The four Scottish airports have a Scottish Airports Joint Committee between LJC level and the JNCC, reflecting a different organisational structure in Scotland. These committees are also

217

stages in the disputes and individual grievance procedures, in which there is a provision for joint reference to ACAS for arbitration.

Municipal airports

There are more than 20 municipal airports of which the largest is Manchester Airport. Pay and conditions of service are determined by the collective bargaining machinery for local authorities. The main manual grades are covered by the National Joint Council (NJC) for Local Authorities' Services (Manual Workers); craftsmen by the Joint Negotiating Committee for Local Authorities' Services (Engineering Craftsmen); and air traffic control staff as a separate group by the NJC for Local Authorities' APT & C Staff (see page 284).

There is some bargaining at airport level over such matters as charge-hand allowances and productivity bonuses, but productivity agreements have to follow the framework laid down by the NJC.

Postal services and telecommunications

This sector is dominated by the Post Office, but there are also a few private companies in operation.

1 POST OFFICE

The Post Office is by far the largest organisation providing postal, telephone and telegraph services. It was set up as a public authority by the Post Office Act 1969 and is divided into three separate businesses: Telecommunications and Data Processing, Posts, and National Girobank. Together these employ over 425 000 people. In common with the other nationalised industries the Post Office is under a statutory duty to establish negotiating and consultative machinery with its unions to settle the terms and conditions of employment, and promote the efficiency, safety, health and welfare of its staff.

The Post Office recognises nine unions, and over 90% of staff are in membership of the union appropriate to their grade. All the unions but one — MNAOA, which has recognition for a very small and specialised group of cable ship officers — are constituent or associate members of the Council of Post Office Unions (COPOU). The COPOU unions, the main grades each represents and the approximate numbers of employees in these grades are listed in the table on page 219.

Negotiating machinery

All major terms and conditions of employment are settled at national level. Negotiations take place separately with each union or, on matters of common concern, with COPOU. Most of the unions have members in Posts, Telecommunications and National Girobank and negotiate on issues affecting their members in each of the businesses. The NFSP is exceptional as it covers self-employed sub-postmasters and sub-postmistresses and deals with such

Unions	Grades	Number of employees
Full COPOU members		
Union of Communication Workers (UCW)*	Postmen, Postal Officers, Telephonists and related grades	200 000
Post Office Engineering Union (POEU)	Engineering and Technical grades	126 000
Civil and Public Services Association (CPSA)*	Clerical grades	38 000
Society of Post Office Executives (SPOE)	Management and certain supervisors in telecommunications, engineering and technical grades	22 000
National Federation of Sub-Postmasters (NFSP)	Sub-postmasters and sub-postmistresses	20 000
Post Office Management Staffs' Association (POMSA)	Middle management in Posts; certain supervisors in Telecommunications	20 000
Associate COPOU members		
SCPS	General management grades	7000
Telephone Contract Officers' Association (TCOA)	Telephone sales representatives	1000

The Associate COPOU members are unable to vote on COPOU committees or to hold officerships on these committees.

* Indicates union membership agreement in operation.

things as remuneration and responsibility for cash and stock. The Post Office and all of the unions except for the MNAOA and the NFSP are parties to the Post Office Arbitration Tribunal (POAT).

Consultative machinery

As required by the 1969 Act the Post Office and COPOU have established a procedure for consultation through national and regional joint councils and local joint committees.

219

A National Joint Council on which the Post Office and all the unions are represented oversees the machinery. Each of the three separate businesses has its own Business Joint Council. The Posts and Telecommunications businesses also have Regional Joint Councils, and in all three businesses there is an extensive system of Local Joint Committees.

This system combines consultation and negotiation on such matters as efficiency, health, safety and welfare and the implementation of national agreements at the Business or local levels.

Industrial democracy

At the beginning of 1978 the Post Office began a two-year experiment in industrial democracy, authorised by the Post Office Act 1977. The Post Office Board was reconstituted to allow the appointment of up to seven management and seven union members and five independent members two of whom are particularly qualified to represent the interests of consumers. A parallel experiment is taking place at regional and local level.

This experiment is not part of the existing negotiating and consultative machinery and union members of the Post Office Board are required to relinquish any negotiating responsibilities during their term of office.

2 PRIVATE COMPANIES

There are a small number of companies outside the Post Office engaged in telephone, telex and telegraph services. Collective bargaining takes place at company level. Unions recognised include ASTMS and the Union of Shop, Distributive and Allied Workers (USDAW).

Miscellaneous transport services and storage

This sector of the transport industry covers a wide variety of services. Firms vary widely in size, and employ in total about 180 000 people. There is no industry-wide collective bargaining machinery, but some manual employees are covered by the national agreements of other industries, and there is considerable local-level bargaining. The TGWU is recognised in a number of companies involved in warehousing and storage. Collective bargaining for white-collar employees is much less common, but ASTMS and APEX are recognised in one of the motorists' organisations, and TSSA in some of the large travel agencies and tour operators.

Order XXIII   DISTRIBUTIVE TRADES

The distributive trades employ nearly $2\frac{3}{4}$ million people and can be divided into wholesaling, retailing and other dealing. About 40% of the employees are in scope of four wages councils. Collective bargaining in the industry is not highly developed, but there is some company bargaining, and several areas where there are negotiating arrangements above company level.

Wholesale distribution

Over half a million people people are employed in wholesaling. The areas where there is industry-wide collective bargaining are the wholesaling of food and drink, and newspapers. The wholesale of petroleum products is related, for collective bargaining purposes, to the refining and distribution activities of the oil companies and is thus dealt with elsewhere (see page 120).

1 FOOD AND DRINK

The wholesale grocery and provision trade covers both cash-and-carry warehouses and warehouses from which delivery is made. The wholesale distribution of fresh foods tends to be based on the large London markets — New Covent Garden, Smithfield and Billingsgate. The Co-operative Wholesale Society (CWS) serves the needs of the retail co-operative societies. For collective bargaining purposes the distribution of milk is related to milk processing and is thus covered elsewhere (see page 115). The main unions in the industry are the Union of Shop, Distributive and Allied Workers (USDAW) and the Transport and General Workers' Union (TGWU), though the National Union of General and Municipal Workers (GMWU) also has some members. Unionisation is highest in CWS and in the fresh food markets.

There are three national negotiating bodies in the industry, which deal with such matters as basic rates, hours, overtime, holidays and disputes procedures, for manual employees only. The National Federation of Wholesale Grocers and Provision Merchants (covering England and Wales), the United Kingdom Provision Trade Federation and the National Council of the Wholesale Provision Trade, along with regional wholesale provisions employers' associations from Liverpool, Manchester and Bristol and the West of England, form the employers' side of the Joint Industrial Council (JIC) for the Wholesale Grocery and Provision Trade. USDAW, TGWU and GMWU represent employees. The JIC covers some 40 000 employees. In Scotland there is separate machinery, a Joint Committee for the Wholesale Grocery Trade in Scotland which covers about 3000 employees and brings together the Wholesale Grocers' Association of Scotland, USDAW and the TGWU.

The Joint Industrial Council (JIC) Representative of Employers and Workpeople Connected with Slaughterhouses in the Meat Trade covers some 20 000 employees engaged in the slaughtering and dressing of carcasses. The employers' representatives on the JIC come from the Federation of Fresh Meat Wholesalers, the National Federation of Meat Traders, the Association of British Abbatoir Owners, the Co-operative Employers' Association and FMC (Meat) Limited, and the employees' representatives from USDAW and the TGWU.

There are no national negotiating bodies covering employees engaged in the

221

wholesale distribution of fresh food, but there are a number of local agreements which apply to manual employees in the wholesale markets. These agreements tend to be between local tenants' associations and the TGWU though in Liverpool in the fresh meat trade there is an agreement with USDAW. Subjects covered by agreements include rates of pay, hours, holidays, sick pay and disputes procedures.

There is some supplementary company-level collective bargaining for manual employees mainly in the larger firms. The CWS, which is one of the largest, is not covered by the wholesale grocery national agreement and negotiates directly with USDAW. There is little collective bargaining for white-collar employees.

2 NEWSPAPERS

There are four employers' associations in newspaper distribution and most companies belong to one or more.

Employers' Association	Geographical coverage	Daily or Sunday newspapers
Federation of London Wholesale Newspaper Distributors	London	Daily
Sunday Newspaper Distributing Association	London	Sunday
National Society of Provincial Wholesale Sunday Newspaper Distributors	England (other than London), Scotland and Wales	Sunday
Provincial Wholesale Newspaper Distributors' Association (PWNDA)	England (other than London) and Wales	Daily

All these associations have agreements in respect of manual employees with the Society of Graphical and Allied Trades (SOGAT) covering basic pay, holidays, overtime and disputes procedures. In the daily newspaper trade in Scotland there is no industry-wide collective bargaining but the larger firms tend to apply the PWNDA/SOGAT agreement.

Throughout the industry unionisation among manual employees is high and company-level bargaining is well developed. There is little collective bargaining for white-collar employees.

3 OTHER WHOLESALING

Some wholesalers belong to employers' associations where the other member firms are mainly concerned with some other aspect of the trade, and apply the relevant national agreements to their employees. Thus some wholesale dealers in millinery are members of the British Hat Guild (see page 162); some wholesalers in made-up textiles belong to the United Kingdom Jute Goods Association; and the British Stationery and Office Products Federation also has some members in wholesaling. There is some bargaining at company level — USDAW, the TGWU and the United Road Transport Union (URTU) are the main unions recognised, though the Tobacco Workers' Union (TWU) is recognised by some wholesalers in tobacco, cigarettes and cigars.

Retail distribution

Retail organisations, including department stores, are generally categorised as multiples, co-operatives or independents, this last category covering firms with fewer than 10 shops. Although there is a continuing trend to multiple retailing and the average size of shops is increasing, with large stores having several hundred employees, over 80% of retail outlets (which total about ½ million) have fewer than 10 employees. Nearly 2 million people are employed in retailing of whom over a million are covered by two wages councils. These two wages councils came into operation in September 1979, on the amalgamation of nine earlier councils.

Union membership is generally low, though growing, and is concentrated in the larger stores and the co-operative retail societies. The main union is USDAW, though the TGWU is also recognised, chiefly for warehousemen and drivers, and some drivers belong to URTU. White-collar employees, where unionised, are mainly represented by USDAW's Supervisory, Administrative and Technical Association (SATA) while the Association of Professional, Executive, Clerical and Computer Staff (APEX) and the Association of Scientific, Technical and Managerial Staffs (ASTMS) also have some membership. There are also unions specific to certain trades. A high proportion of the workforce of W H Smith and Son Ltd belongs to the Retail Book, Stationery and Allied Trade Employees' Association which is a union specific to that company. The Bakers', Food and Allied Workers' Union (BFAWU) has members engaged in the distribution of bread and flour confectionery.

NEGOTIATING MACHINERY

In retailing there are two wages councils, for food and allied trades and for non-food trades, and within these sectors there is supplementary national-level collective bargaining machinery in the co-operative societies, the retailing of groceries and provisions, and in footwear retailing. In addition there is separate voluntary negotiating machinery in meat and pharmacy. There is some bargaining at company level, mainly in the larger stores and the co-operative retail societies; USDAW has about 100 company agreements.

223

Most of this machinery covers sales assistants, though the agreements in the co-operative societies, grocery and provisions and pharmacy also cover managerial staff. For floristry and garden plants, pets and petfoods, jewellery, watches and clocks, photographic and optical goods and musical instruments, there is, at present, virtually no negotiating machinery although some are covered by arrangements at company level, mainly in enterprises retailing a range of other goods.

1 FOOD AND ALLIED TRADES

The Retail Food and Allied Trades Wages Council (Great Britain) covers over 500 000 employees in food shops, bread shops, newsagents, tobacconists and confectioners. The retailing of meat (other than bacon and some other meat products) and fresh milk are not included, as employees in these trades are covered by other bargaining arrangements. The following organisations nominate representatives to the employers' side:

British Multiple Retailers' Association

Co-operative Employers' Association

Association of Retail Distributors

National Union of Small Shopkeepers of Great Britain and Northern Ireland

National Association of Master Bakers, Confectioners and Caterers

Scottish Association of Master Bakers

Federation of Bakers

National Food and Drink Federation

Scottish Grocers' Federation

National Federation of Fish Friers

Retail Fruit Trade Federation

National Federation of Fishmongers

National Federation of Meat Traders

Dairy Trade Federation

Retail Confectioners' and Tobacconists' Association

224

National Federation of Retail Newsagents

National Chamber of Trade.

The workers' side representatives are nominated by

USDAW, TGWU, BFAWU, URTU, APEX and the Retail Book, Stationery and Allied Trades Employees' Association.

2 NON-FOOD TRADES

The Retail Trades (Non-Food) Wages Council (Great Britain) covers over 600 000 employees in bookselling and stationery; drapery, outfitting (including alterations to women's clothing) and footwear; furnishing and allied trades which include sales of furniture and household equipment (except clocks, pianos or gramophones), hardware and hand tools, saddlery, leather and travel goods, pedal cycles, perambulators and invalid carriages, toys, games and most sports equipment, wallpaper, paint and household chemicals. The following organisations nominate representatives to the employers' side; some of the smallest organisations have shared places.

British Multiple Retailers' Association

Co-operative Union

Association of Retail Distributors

National Union of Small Shopkeepers of Great Britain and Northern Ireland

National Chamber of Trade

British Stationery and Office Products Federation

Booksellers' Association of Great Britain and Ireland

Menswear Association of Great Britain

Consumer Credit Association of the United Kingdom (including Scottish Retail Credit Association)

Mail Order Traders' Association

Drapers' Chamber of Trade

National Shoe Retailers' Council

225

National Association of Retail Furnishers

Scottish House Furnishers' Association

British Hardware Federation (including National Association of Tool Dealers)

Scottish Hardware Association

Radio, Electrical and Television Retailers' Association

Federation of Sports Goods Distributors

National Association of Toy Retailers

National Association of Cycle and Motor Cycle Traders

China and Glass Retailers' Association.

The workers' side representatives are nominated by USDAW, TGWU, APEX and the Retail Book, Stationery and Allied Trades Employees' Association.

3 RETAIL CO-OPERATIVE SOCIETIES

There are some 240 retail co-operative societies in Great Britain with approximately 184 000 employees; the number of societies is tending to diminish through amalgamations. All societies are members of the Co-operative Employers' Association which through its National Wages Board negotiates pay and conditions of employment with a Joint Trade Union Negotiating Committee consisting of representatives of USDAW, TGWU, APEX and URTU. Separate agreements have been negotiated for different categories of employees, the six main agreements being for supermarket, food hall and combination store personnel; clerical workers; branch managers and manageresses; transport workers; café and restaurant workers; and general distributive workers.

4 GROCERY AND PROVISIONS

There is a Joint Committee for the Retail Multiple Grocery and Provisions Trade in Great Britain made up of representatives from the Multiple Food Retailers Employers' Association and USDAW. The Committee negotiates pay and conditions of employment which supplement the statutory minimum rates fixed by the wages council, for some 150 000 employees including managerial and clerical staff as well as shop workers.

226

5 FOOTWEAR

There is a collective agreement between the Multiple Shoe Retailers' Association and USDAW. The Committee's agreements cover minimum rates, Saturday premium payments, holidays, and a sickness absence scheme.

6 MEAT

There are two Joint Industrial Councils (JICs) for the meat trade — the JIC for the Retail Meat Trade (covering England and Wales) and the JIC for the Scottish Retail Meat Trade. The JIC for England and Wales has representatives from the Co-operative Employers' Association, the Multiple Food Retailers Employers' Association, the National Federation of Meat Traders, USDAW and TGWU. The Scottish JIC's representatives are nominated by the Scottish Federation of Meat Traders' Associations Inc and USDAW. JIC agreements cover such matters as minimum rates of pay, hours, overtime, holidays and sickness payments.

7 PHARMACY

There is a National Joint Industrial Council for Retail Pharmacy (England and Wales) made up of representatives of USDAW and the National Pharmaceutical Association, the Company Chemists' Association, the Co-operative Employers' Association and the Pharmaceutical Services Negotiating Committee, which is a committee of proprietors which negotiates with the Government on payment for chemists prescribing National Health Service medicines. About 35 000 employees are covered including pharmacists and pharmacy managers, dispensing and shop assistants. Agreements cover annual salaries for dispensing and shop assistants, and hours, overtime and rota payments, holidays and sick pay.

OTHER DEALING

There are about a quarter of a million employees in this sector. Two areas — cotton waste and general waste reclamation — are covered by wages councils, and five other areas have collective bargaining machinery above company level — dealing in scrap metal, coal and agricultural machinery, agricultural merchanting and jute importing. These arrangements cover only manual workers. Dealing in oil is covered under petroleum products (see page 120) and grain milling (see page 111) respectively. Collective bargaining in dealing in timber, and hides and skins is related to manufacture and is covered under Timber, Furniture, etc (page 170) and Leather, Leather Goods and Fur (see page 156) respectively. Some firms in reclaimed textile processing are members of the Wool Textile Manufacturers' Federation and are covered by collective bargaining machinery in the textile industry (see page 149). The remaining parts of the sector have no industry-wide collective bargaining machinery. There is some bargaining at company level. The main unions in the sector are the TGWU and GMWU, though several other unions are recognised in specific areas. There is very little collective bargaining for white-collar employees.

1 Cotton waste reclamation

The British Textile By-Products Association nominates the employers' representatives to the Cotton Waste Reclamation Wages Council (Great Britain) which covers some 40 firms and about 750 workers. The workers' representatives are nominated by the GMWU, the Amalgamated Textile Workers' Union (ATWU) and the National Association of Unions in the Textile Trade (NAUTT). The council's Wages Order lays down minimum time and overtime rates and holiday pay. There is some supplementary company-level bargaining involving, in addition to the unions represented on the wages council, unions which include the TGWU.

2 General waste reclamation

There are six employers' associations which nominate representatives to sit on the General Waste Materials Reclamation Wages Council (Great Britain):

British Scrap Federation

British Waste Paper Association

Federation of Reclamation Industries

Reclamation Association

Wiping Cloth Manufacturers' Association

British Secondary Metals Association.

Employee representatives on the council come from the GMWU and the TGWU. The council's Wages Order lays down minimum time and overtime rates and holiday pay and covers approximately 2200 firms and 20 000 employees.

3 Iron, steel and non-ferrous scrap

There are two employers' associations concerned with scrap metal, the British Scrap Federation (BSF) and the British Shipbreakers' Association. The BSF is represented on the General Waste Materials Reclamation Wages Council. These two associations nominate representatives to the Joint Conciliation Committee (JCC) for the Iron, Steel and Non-Ferrous Scrap Industry including Demolition, Dismantlement and Shipbreaking. Employee representatives come from the TGWU, the GMWU and the Iron and Steel Trades Confederation (ISTC). The JCC agreements set minimum rates of pay, hours of work, overtime, shift pay, holidays, and some other terms and conditions for about 12 500 employees, mainly process workers and drivers employed in scrap yards. The agreements generally exceed the minimum terms and conditions laid down by the wages council. There is considerable supplementary bargaining at company level.

4 Coal merchants

There are some 7000 coal merchants in Great Britain, ranging from one-man firms to companies dealing nationally. Almost all coal merchants belong to the Coal Merchants' Federation (CMF) which has twelve regional associations. The level of unionisation is low. The main unions are the TGWU, URTU, USDAW and GMWU, though the National Union of Mineworkers (NUM) also has some members.

Only two regional associations of the CMF engage in collective bargaining. The Eastern region of the CMF appoints the employers' representatives on the Eastern Regional Joint Industrial Council (JIC) for the Distributive Coal Trade. The union representatives come from the TGWU, USDAW, the GMWU and URTU. The Society of Coal Merchants (SCM), which is effectively the London and South East region of the CMF, negotiates directly with the TGWU. Both the JIC and the SCM/TGWU agreements cover minimum basic rates, hours, holidays and overtime. There is some company-level bargaining in the larger firms.

5 Agricultural and garden machinery

The British Agricultural and Garden Machinery Association (BAGMA) negotiates with the GMWU, TGWU, Amalgamated Union of Engineering Workers (AUEW), and the National Union of Domestic Appliance and General Metal Workers (NUDAGMW). The agreement covers hours, minimum weekly wage, overtime, travelling time, holidays and shiftwork for 35 000 manual employees employed in firms engaged mainly in the repair and maintenance of agricultural and garden machinery. Some of BAGMA's member firms engaged in manufacturing are also members of the Engineering Employers' Federation and are covered by collective bargaining machinery in the engineering industry (see page 130).

6 Agricultural merchanting

In this sector undertakings tend to be small, and often they are either subsidiaries of large companies or agricultural co-operatives. Several of the firms also undertake grain milling (see page 111), or limited scale animal feed manufacture (see page 117). The United Kingdom Agricultural Supply Trade Association Ltd (UKASTA) represents employers engaged in these activities which are covered by the National Joint Industrial Council (NJIC) for the Corn Trade. About 60 000 people are employed in the industry.

Throughout the sector unionisation tends to be at a relatively low level. Where mill and manual workers, and drivers, are unionised they belong mainly to the TGWU which provides all the employee representatives on the NJIC. However, in some firms GMWU and USDAW have membership among these grades. The main unions with membership among maintenance workers are AUEW and EETPU; and among white-collar workers ACTS, APEX and ASTMS have membership.

The NJIC negotiates separate agreements for mill and manual, transport, and clerical workers, which set basic rates, hours of work, job rates, overtime allowances, shift premia, holidays and holiday pay, and provide a disputes procedure. The transport workers' agreement also covers travelling and subsistence allowances and night work premia. Maintenance workers are covered by the mill workers agreement with the exception that rates are negotiated locally. In the undertakings which are subsidiaries of large companies, pensions and sickness benefit schemes are often negotiated at company level while productivity bonuses and shift allowances are negotiated at plant level.

7 Jute importing

The Jute Importers' Association negotiates with the TGWU in respect of a very small number of jute stowers in the Dundee area. Agreements cover rates of pay and other terms and conditions.

Order XXIV INSURANCE, BANKING, FINANCE AND BUSINESS SERVICES

About 1·1 million people are employed in the business activities which comprise this Order. For collective bargaining purposes it can be divided into the following sectors:

Insurance

Banking

Finance Houses

Building Societies

Advertising Agencies

Security Services

Other business services.

Insurance and banking account for over half the total employed in the predominantly white-collar industries of the Order.

Insurance

About 270 000 people are employed in this sector, the great majority of them in the 800 or so companies providing life assurance, or non-life insurance covering personal, property and business risks.

There is no employers' association co-ordinating industrial relations in the sector, and collective bargaining, which is mainly restricted to the larger companies and covers about a third of all white-collar staff, is not conducted above company level.

The Association of Scientific, Technical and Managerial Staffs (ASTMS) is the predominant trade union in insurance, with sole recognition for mainly head office staff at some 30 companies (including four of the ten largest). The Banking, Insurance and Finance Union (BIFU) — formerly the National Union of Bank Employees (NUBE) — is recognised at five companies, and the Association of Professional, Executive, Clerical and Computer Staff (APEX) has recognition at one company. There are many employee organisations whose recruitment is limited to one company. For example, the National Union of Co-operative Insurance Society Employees (NUCISE), an autonomous section within the Transport and General Workers' Union (TGWU), negotiates with the Co-operative Insurance Society on behalf of employees in district offices. Three of the ten largest companies recognise staff associations.

A minority of insurance companies employ agents who sell policies and collect premiums, usually by home visits. Agents and local office staff are represented by several unions, including ASTMS, the National Union of Insurance Workers (NUIW), and the Union of Shop, Distributive and Allied Workers (USDAW), and by staff associations.

Negotiations normally take place on a company-wide basis and agreements as well as setting salary scales and the normal conditions of service may also cover such matters as staff loans, house purchase facilities, profit sharing and flexible working hours.

Banking

About 320 000 people are employed in banking. For collective bargaining purposes they can be divided into four sectors:

The Bank of England

London Clearing Banks and other 'High Street' banks

Scottish banks

Foreign and overseas banks.

There is little collective bargaining in merchant banks.

1 THE BANK OF ENGLAND

The Bank employs about 7000 people, of whom 1500 or so are engaged in the

231

printing of banknotes. The Bank of England Staff Organisation (BESO) has sole bargaining rights for all staff other than print workers (see page 179) and senior managers, and has an agreement covering all terms and conditions of employment, including provision for conciliation and binding arbitration.

2 LONDON CLEARING BANKS AND OTHER 'HIGH STREET' BANKS

The five members of the Federation of London Clearing Bank Employers (FLCBE) employ over 200 000 people in about 11 000 branches: Barclays (55 000 employees), Lloyds (41 000 employees), Midland (44 000 employees), National Westminster (54 000 employees) and Williams and Glyn's (6000 employees).

For collective bargaining purposes employees are divided into managerial and clerical staff — that is, appointed staff (branch accountants and above) and unappointed staff (clerical grades below the level of branch accountant, and computer staff); and technical and service staff — electrical and maintenance workers, and messengers. About 97% of employees are managerial or clerical staff.

BIFU has members at all five clearing banks. ASTMS has members in the Midland Bank only and there are staff associations within Barclays, National Westminster and Lloyds. These associations, which formed the Clearing Bank Union in August 1980, have more members than BIFU both throughout the clearing banks and within each of their respective banks. There is a technical and service staff association at Barclays, and at National Westminster there is a Technical and Services Union which is part of the National Westminster Staff Association.

Collective bargaining arrangements altered substantially in 1978, when BIFU withdrew from all joint negotiating machinery for managerial and clerical staff at both national and domestic level. An inquiry followed which recommended the end of joint representation, and the merger of BIFU and the staff associations. The BIFU withdrawal was followed by the winding up of the Joint Negotiating Council which negotiated terms and conditions for clerical staff and set minima for managerial grades in the London clearing banks. At present there are no formal collective bargaining arrangements for managerial and clerical staff at Barclays and National Westminster, nor for clerical staff at Lloyds. Managers at Lloyds are covered by a separate agreement with the Lloyds Group Staff Association, and at Midland ASTMS and BIFU have signed identical agreements covering all staff. The arrangements at Williams and Glyn's, where BIFU have sole negotiating rights, have continued.

For technical and service staff at Barclays, Midland, Lloyds, and Williams and Glyn's the joint national machinery continues to operate. The national negotiations generally cover pay, hours, location allowances, overtime, holidays and employee safety, with other matters settled domestically. At National Westminster all matters are negotiated domestically.

Of the other High Street banks, the most important are the Trustee Savings

Bank (TSB) and the Co-operative Bank. The TSB (which incorporates 19 regional banks) employs about 15 000 staff. BIFU negotiates with the TSB Central Board, which represents all the regional banks. 'Agency shop' agreements signed during the period of the Industrial Relations Act (see page 21) are in operation in the TSB.

The Co-operative Bank employs about 3000 staff and negotiates on a company-wide basis with BIFU. A union membership agreement is in operation.

3 SCOTTISH BANKS

The major employers in the Scottish banking industry are the three Scottish Banks of Issue — the Bank of Scotland, the Royal Bank of Scotland, and the Clydesdale Bank, which between them employ almost 24 000 people in Head Offices and some 1500 branches. The TSB and the Co-operative Bank operate in Scotland, but have no separate bargaining machinery for their Scottish branches. The remaining 60 or so other banking organisations in Scotland employ relatively few people and have no significant collective bargaining. Several years ago the staff associations in the Bank of Scotland and the Royal Bank of Scotland merged with BIFU which is the major union in Scottish banking. The Clydesdale Bank staff association merged with ASTMS and that bank recognises both BIFU and ASTMS. Collective bargaining in respect of Scottish Banks of Issue staff is conducted at national and company level.

National-level collective bargaining of basic terms and conditions for clerical staff and of some managerial staff terms and conditions is conducted in the Joint Negotiating Council (JNC) of the Scottish Banking Industry. The employers are represented on the JNC by the Federation of Scottish Bank Employers to which all three Scottish Banks of Issue belong, and BIFU is the sole staff side representative body.

The JNC negotiates the graded salary structure of 'unappointed' staff, minimum salaries for Branch Managers and Branch Accountants on first appointment, London allowances, employee safety, hours of work, overtime, and annual holiday entitlements of 'unappointed' staff. If a matter is not resolved by the JNC the parties are committed to binding private arbitration at the request of either side.

Company-level collective bargaining for managerial and clerical staff is conducted in Joint Management-Staff Committees (JMSCs). BIFU is the sole staff side representative body in the Bank of Scotland and Royal Bank of Scotland JMSCs. In the Clydesdale Bank there are separate JMSCs for BIFU and ASTMS covering the same categories of staff. The JMSC terms of reference exclude conditions of service matters negotiable by the JNC, but in the Clydesdale Bank/ASTMS JMSC the union reserves the right to make representations on matters appropriate to the JNC on which it has no voice. The constitution of each JMSC provides for failures to agree on any negotiable matter to proceed to mediation, and in the event of continued failure to agree for either side to take the issue to binding private arbitration.

Similar collective bargaining arrangements exist at national and company levels in respect of Scottish Banks of Issue non-clerical staff (eg messengers, drivers, commissionaires).

4 FOREIGN AND OVERSEAS BANKS

About 40 000 staff are employed in this area of banking. 30 000 are in foreign banks, which are incorporated overseas and have branches in Great Britain, and 10 000 are in overseas banks which are incorporated in this country with head offices here and which operate branches outside Great Britain. The majority of London clearing banks conduct overseas operations through overseas divisions.

BIFU is the predominant union, with sole bargaining rights at 20 foreign banks and four overseas banks. ASTMS is recognised at two foreign banks and there are a number of staff associations in individual banks.

There are no national negotiating arrangements. Domestic negotiations for white-collar staff (and in some banks manual employees) generally cover rates of pay, hours, overtime and holidays, and may include such matters as uniforms, working conditions, sick leave, pensions, luncheon vouchers, and redundancy.

Finance houses

These are mainly involved in the financing of personal and commercial credit transactions. About 20 000 staff are employed in some 1700 firms. There is no national employers' association with industrial relations functions, and collective bargaining where it exists in the sector is confined to individual finance houses. The major union is BIFU, which has sole recognition in five finance houses. ASTMS is recognised in one finance house, APEX has members in another, and there are a number of individual staff associations.

Building societies

Approximately 45 000 staff are employed in over 300 building societies. The Building Societies' Association which represents the building society movement offers industrial relations advice to its employer members but has no negotiating function. Most building society staff associations (see below) are affiliated to the Federation of Building Society Staff Associations. However, all negotiations in the sector are conducted domestically.

Forty-six societies employing about 35 000 staff formally recognise TUC-affiliated trade unions or staff associations. Membership of staff associations is much greater than that of trade unions: eg six of the 10 largest building societies recognise staff associations. BIFU is recognised at 15 (mostly small) societies, ASTMS is recognised at two small building societies and APEX has some membership in the sector.

Negotiations are usually company-wide, cover all terms and conditions of employment and are conducted in joint consultative and negotiating committees (JCNCs).

Advertising agencies

About 16 000 staff are employed in approximately 750 agencies. The largest agency employs about 700 people. However, about 650 agencies employ fewer than 50 people while some employ as few as five people.

There is no national employers' association. The industry has a professional body, the Institute of Practitioners in Advertising, which represents over 300 (mostly London) agencies which employ about 90% of all agency staff. The IPA was concerned in the creation of three regional employers' associations — in Scotland, the North of England and the Midlands.

The National Graphical Association (NGA) and the Art Union Section (AUS) of the Society of Lithographic Artists, Designers, Engravers and Process Workers (SLADE) have membership concentrated in the agencies' studios. The majority of NGA members are typographers or layout artists and most SLADE members produce finished artwork. There is little trade union membership among other categories of staff.

The NGA and the AUS of SLADE negotiate jointly with the three employers' associations on behalf of artists and typographers. About 150 agencies are covered by these agreements. These negotiations set minimum terms and conditions only; the agreement states that actual rates will depend on the particular talents, experience and qualifications of each employee, though making provision for individual representation on salary questions at company level. Other matters covered include hours, overtime, holidays, sick pay, and notice, and there is a union membership agreement.

Security services

The security service industry comprises, for collective bargaining purposes within this Order, those firms which undertake the manned guarding of premises and the transport of cash and valuables. There are about 25 000 uniformed personnel in some 600 firms, and three-quarters of these employees are in the three largest firms. Some firms in this section are also involved in the manufacture of security equipment — alarms, safes and locks. Where this is the predominant activity they are dealt with as part of the engineering industry.

Collective bargaining tends to be concentrated in the larger companies. The Managerial, Administrative, Technical and Supervisory Section (MATSA) of the National Union of General and Municipal Workers (GMWU) is recognised for security staff at about 10 security service firms and has union membership agreements at the two largest. The TGWU's Association of Clerical, Technical and Supervisory Staffs (ACTS) has a union membership agreement at the third largest firm.

Negotiatons usually take place on a company-wide basis and agreements, as well as setting salary scales and normal conditions of service, normally have strict disciplinary procedures in such areas as probationary employment and dismisal, which reflects security considerations.

Other business services

There are over 400 000 employees in the remaining business services in the Order, but in only two areas — the New Towns, and Industrial Training Boards — is there any significant collective bargaining.

1 THE NEW TOWNS

There are 28 New Towns. Of these, 23 are run by development corporations, which were created to deal with the acquisition of land and the planning and establishment of New Towns, and five, which are no longer in the developmental stage, are managed either by the Commission for the New Towns or by the Development Board for Rural Wales.

Terms and conditions of employment for about 8200 administrative, professional, technical and clerical staff employed by the development corporations, the Commission and the Development Board for Rural Wales are negotiated in the Whitley Council for New Towns Staff (see page 286).

Terms and conditions for manual workers in new towns follow those set by the National Joint Council for Local Authorities' Services (Manual Workers) (see page 284).

2 INDUSTRIAL TRAINING BOARDS (ITBs)

Industrial Training Boards were set up by the Industrial Training Act 1964 to encourage training in the industries covered. There are 24 Boards employing about 5000 staff. There are no national collective bargaining arrangements. Negotiations are conducted within individual ITBs. The majority of boards negotiate with ASTMS and APEX; generally ASTMS represents training staff and APEX represents clerical staff. However, the funding of ITBs was altered by the Employment and Training Act 1973 so that any agreements changing staff terms and conditions require the approval of Government Ministers.

Order XXV PROFESSIONAL AND SCIENTIFIC SERVICES

Over 3·5 million people are employed in the services comprising this Order. The sectors, which are treated separately below, are:

Accountancy services

236

Educational services

Legal services

Medical and dental services

Religious organisations

Research and development services

Other professional and scientific services.

Accountancy services

About 90 000 people are employed in private firms of accountants or auditors. These persons normally are members of an appropriate professional institution the activities of which are confined to the protection of professional interests and standards, in particular through their roles as examining bodies. There is little or no trade union activity in the sector, and salaries, fees and conditions of employment are determined independently within each firm.

Educational services

In all about 1·8 million people are employed in educational services, the vast majority of them in the public sector. The collective bargaining arrangements in the public sector for England and Wales, and for Scotland, are described in turn below. The private sector is then treated.

PUBLIC SECTOR: ENGLAND AND WALES

The Education Act 1944 requires local education authorities to make provision for primary and secondary education. In England and Wales these authorities are the Non-Metropolitan County Councils, Metropolitan District Councils, the Inner London Education Authority, The Outer London Borough Councils and the Isles of Scilly. They are empowered to establish and maintain schools and to maintain and aid schools which have been established otherwise than by the local education authority. Normally, local authorities are the employers of non-university teachers, while university teachers, as well as non-teaching staff, are employed by the respective university authority.

The collective bargaining machinery in England and Wales can be divided into two main components – for teaching staff and for non-teaching staff. Teaching staff are employed in four main types of establishment — primary and secondary schools and further education establishments; universities; community homes; and prisons. In each case there is separate machinery for

237

pay and for conditions of employment. Non-teaching staff can be considered under five headings—staff in non-university teaching establishments; education advisers; youth and community workers; university staff; education administration.

TEACHING STAFF

1 Teachers in primary and secondary schools and further education establishments

The current machinery for the negotiation of teachers' salaries was set up under the provisions of the Remuneration of Teachers Act 1965. The Act empowered the Secretary of State for Education and Science to establish committees for the purpose of considering the remuneration payable to teachers by local education authorities (LEAs). There are two such 'Burnham' Committees; one committee covers primary and secondary teachers, the other further education teachers. The Secretary of State determines the constitution and scope of each Burnham Committee by:

appointing an independent chairman;

nominating one or more representatives of the Department of Education and Science (DES) — an important feature which was not present in the pre-1965 machinery;

determining the organisations and the numbers of their representatives who shall represent LEAs and teachers on the Management and Teachers' Panels respectively; and

giving directions specifying descriptions of the teachers who shall fall within the purview of the committee.

A Burnham Committee, when it thinks fit or when directed by the Secretary of State, reviews remuneration and makes recommendations. These set the rates payable for each grade of teacher and the rules determining the distribution of staff among various grades in any one institution. The Secretary of State is then obliged to arrange for the publication of the pay scales and other provisions which the committee has recommended, and to make an Order in Council directing that they be put into effect. It is then the responsibility of the LEAs, acting as the employers, to implement any new rates and to exercise such discretion as they possess in allocating posts within their educational establishments.

Although the Act does not give the Secretary of State effective control over Burnham Committee recommendations, a concordat with the local authority associations provides that:

the management panel's discussions are held in confidence and that the panel speaks with one voice in the full Burnham Committees;

238

the DES representatives may limit by veto the global amount which the management panel proposes to offer the teachers; and

on matters other than the global amount, the DES representatives have a weighted vote, though this does not give them an overall majority over the local authorities representatives.

When a committee is unable to reach an agreement it is open to either the Management Panel or the Teachers' Panel to ask the Secretary of State to refer the matter to arbitration. In the event of such a reference the Secretary of State gives effect to any subsequent award by a statutory instrument unless both Houses of Parliament resolve otherwise.

The terms of reference of the Burnham Primary and Secondary Committee cover about 500 000 full-time and full-time equivalents of part-time teachers in nursery, primary and secondary schools, and in remedial schools or schools for the handicapped known as Special Schools. They encompass not only teachers in schools maintained by LEAs but also teachers in voluntary schools — for example, church-owned but LEA-funded establishments. The current composition of the committee, apart from the independent chairman and supporting secretariat, includes representatives of the following:

Management Panel	Teachers' Panel
Association of County Councils (ACC)	National Union of Teachers (NUT)
Association of Metropolitan Authorities (AMA)	National Association of Teachers in Further and Higher Education (NATFHE)
Welsh Joint Education Committee (WJEC)	National Association of Schoolmasters and the Union of Women Teachers (NAS/UWT)
DES	
	Assistant Masters' and Mistresses' Association (AMMA)
	Secondary Heads' Association (SHA)
	National Association of Head Teachers (NAHT)

The terms of reference of the Burnham Further Education Committee cover about 78 000 full-time teachers, lecturers, readers, department heads, principals and vice-principals who are employed by LEAs in sixth-form colleges, polytechnics, colleges of further education, and agricultural institutes together with a number of part-time lecturers employed on an hourly basis. The current composition of the committee, apart from the independent

239

chairman and supporting secretariat, includes representatives of the following:

Management Panel	Teachers' Panel
ACC	NATFHE
AMA	Association of Principals of Colleges (APC)
WJEC	National Society for Art Education
DES	Association of Agricultural Education Staffs (AAES)

The role of the Secretary of State in determining conditions of service is a limited one. There are specific powers which enable the Secretary of State to specifiy acceptable qualifications for entry into the teaching profession and the criteria for judging fitness to teach, which are used in probation and discipline procedures. There is also a more indirect influence on teachers' conditions through the Schools and Further Education regulations. Although the basic purpose of these is to specify minimum conditions for students and pupils, they inevitably influence the working environment of teaching staff.

Otherwise, the main terms and conditions of service other than pay are negotiated in two joint negotiating bodies; one for primary and secondary school teachers, the other for further education teachers. Until the formation in 1980 of a National Joint Council, negotiations took place between the Council of Local Education Authorities (CLEA) and all those trade unions which are recognised for the purposes of their appropriate Burnham Committee. These negotiations led to a framework agreement recommended as a basis for implementation by the individual employing authorities. This framework is promulgated by the Local Authorities' Conditions of Service Advisory Board (LACSAB) which acts as the local authorities' employers' association, and produces the 'LACSAB Employee Relations Handbook'. LACSAB, whilst recognising that the composition of local staff sides is a matter for teachers and their trade unions to decide, recommends that employers should negotiate about the local implementation of national recommendations only with local representatives of those unions which are recognised for the purposes of the national negotiating machinery. However, local authorities are not obliged to follow this advice, and not all do.

2 University teachers

There are approximately 39 500 university teachers, of whom 2500 are clinical teachers. The salaries of non-clinical teachers are determined by national two-stage negotiations. The first stage, within Committee A, consists of negotiations between the Association of University Teachers (AUT) and the

University Authorities' Panel (UAP). Draft proposals are agreed by Committee A under an independent chairman and then submitted for negotiation in Committee B. Committee B consists of, on the one side the same chairman and representatives of AUT and UAP who sit on Committee A, and on the other side representatives of the Government, the two sides meeting under a chairman appointed by the Secretary of State. In the event of no settlement being reached the case may be submitted for arbitration.

Clinical teachers are wholly employed by University Medical Schools but nevertheless undertake some treatment of patients. Their pay follows that of their NHS counterparts. Decisions as to how the pay agreements for hospital doctors and dentists should be reflected in salary arrangements for clinical academic staff in universities are made by a committee consisting of representatives of a Committee of Vice-Chancellors and Principals, and the British Medical Association (BMA), British Dental Association (BDA) and AUT, with representatives of the University Grants Committee (UGC) present as observers and advisers. The Committee of Vice-Chancellors and Principals consults with the DES, DHSS and UGC before meeting the Associations.

Conditions of service for university teachers are determined entirely within each university. Consequently there is some degree of variation both in local machinery and in the conditions applied.

3 Teachers in community homes

Certain community homes, that is, those which were formerly approved schools or remand homes, provide education on the premises. Teaching staff in such homes are employed by the Social Services Departments of local authorities and do not come within scope of a Burnham Committee. Their pay and conditions of service are determined by a separate negotiating body, the Joint Negotiating Committee (JNC) for Former Approved Schools and Remand Homes in England and Wales. Heads, deputy heads and instructors are paid on special JNC scales; other teachers are paid on Burnham scales with special additional allowances negotiated in the JNC.

4 Teachers in prisons

Teachers assigned to prisons are employed by LEAs and are covered by the Joint Negotiating Committee (JNC) for Further Education Teachers assigned to Prison Department Establishments. The JNC adopts the basic pay scales fixed by the Burnham Further Education Committee and concerns itself mostly with the fixing of establishment levels as well as all other conditions of service.

Non-teaching staff

Non-teaching staff in educational institutions fall into the categories shown below.

1 *Administrative, technical and manual staff in primary and secondary schools and further education establishments*
All in this category are local authority employees, with pay and conditions of employment determined by local government collective bargaining machinery.

2 *Advisers*

The Soulbury Committee, a non-statutory body, negotiates the pay and conditions of employment of about 3000 LEA-based advisers. There are four types of adviser:

> School or Further Education Advisers to the LEA, dealing mainly with matters of curriculum advice and teacher evaluation, but not to be confused with Her Majesty's Inspectors who are employed by DES.

> Educational Psychologists

> Youth Service Officers employed to advise and supervise field staff in the Youth Service and Community Centres. (Field staff have their own JNC.)

> School Meals Organisers providing both financial and nutritional advice to schools.

Although Soulbury has the power to negotiate its own pay scales, in practice it merely validates the pay scales fixed within other collective bargaining machinery. In the case of School Advisers and Educational Psychologists, Burnham Primary and Secondary Committee rates apply. In the case of Youth Service Officers and School Meals Organisers, Soulbury prescribes rates linked to those for Local Authority Administrative, Professional, Technical and Clerical (APT & C) grades. The Soulbury Committee therefore restricts itself largely to the determination of special allowances and other national conditions of service. The committee does not preclude local negotiations but states that LEAs must apply local conditions of service to all four types of adviser which are not less favourable than APT & C conditions. In practice there is little local variation.

The composition of Soulbury includes representatives of the following under independent chairmanship:

Management Side	Staff Side
ACC	NUT
AMA	National Association of Inspectors and Educational Advisers
WJEC	British Association of Organisers and Lecturers in Physical Education
	Association of Educational Psychologists
	National Association of Youth and Community Education Officers
	National Association of School Meals Organisers of the Hotel, Catering and Institutional Management Association

3 Youth workers and community centre wardens

The non-statutory JNC for Youth Workers and Community Centre Wardens cover these persons, qualified or otherwise, when employed full-time by local authorities, together with the same types of persons (for example, Youth Club Leaders) in voluntary organisations which receive either local authority or DES grants. The JNC agrees both pay and conditions of service on a national basis, tending to use Burnham pay rates as a broad guideline, and sets the qualification standards of staff. On the JNC are included representatives of the following bodies, under the chairmanship of an alternating management side/staff side nominee:

Management Side	Staff Side
ACC	Community and Youth Service Association
AMA	
	NUT
WJEC	
	National and Local
National Council for Voluntary Youth Services	Government Officers' Association (NALGO)
	NATFHE
National Federation of Community Associations	

4 Universities — Administrative, technical and manual staff

There are some 7000 senior administrators, librarians and researchers whose pay is linked to the scales for university teachers, and a number of maintenance craftsmen whose pay is determined locally. Apart from these the machinery for the 60 000 university non-teaching staff has three levels. At the top the Central Council for Non-Teaching Staffs in Universities acts as an umbrella organisation for four functional committees — Clerical, Technical, Manual and Computer Staffs — which in turn determine the pay and conditions of service which are implemented by JNCs at some, though not all, universities.

The Central Council for Non-Teaching Staffs in Universities comprises, for the management side, the Universities Committee for Non-Teaching Staffs and, for the staff side, representatives of all the trade unions which take part in the four functional committees. Although these committees formally report to the Central Council, the main negotiations on pay and conditions are usually concluded at functional committee level, with the Central Council concerning itself with broad policy matters such as pensions. There is a general tendency for pay and conditions to parallel those of appropriate local authority groups, and in 1979 the Technical and Manual Staffs' committees asked the Standing Commission on Pay Comparability (see page 61) to make recommendations on the pay of their respective staff in the light of the pay and conditions of

243

service of other comparable groups. The four functional committees are constituted as shown below, the Management Side in each case being provided by the Universities Committee for Non-Teaching Staffs.

The Joint Committee for Clerical and Certain Related Administrative Staffs covers all junior administrative and clerical and secretarial staff employed in a consortium of 41 universities.

The Staff Side is provided by NALGO, the National Union of Public Employees (NUPE), and the Association of Scientific, Technical and Managerial Staffs (ASTMS). (Staff at other institutions are either on Local Authority scales or on locally negotiated salary scales.)

The Joint Committee for Technical Staffs, which covers all laboratory and workshop technicians employed by universities, has a Staff Side drawn from ASTMS, NUPE, and the Amalgamated Union of Engineering Workers (AUEW).

The Joint Committee for Manual and Ancillary Staffs covers all manual staff, including maintenance craftsmen, at 33 university institutions. The Staff Side representatives are from NUPE, AUEW (representing CSEU), the Transport and General Workers' Union (TGWU), the National Union of General and Municipal Workers (GMWU), and the Union of Construction, Allied Trades and Technicians (UCATT). (Staff at the remaining institutions are on either local authoritiy pay rates or locally negotiated pay rates.)

In addition to the three major groups there is a special Joint Committee for Computer Operating Staffs. The Staff Side comprises ASTMS and NALGO.

5 Education administration
This category contains DES staff, who are subject to civil service pay and conditions of employment.

PUBLIC SECTOR: SCOTLAND

The collective bargaining machinery for staff in Scottish educational establishments differs from that in England and Wales in a number of important respects. This is mainly due to the fact that there is often separate legislation for Scotland, and as a result the structure of Scottish education and Scottish local government has developed independently.

As with England and Wales, there is a broad distinction between teaching and non-teaching staff. For teaching staff there is separate machinery for teachers in each of the four main types of establishment: primary, secondary and further education establishments; central institutions; colleges of education; and universities. For non-teaching staff there is separate machinery for three groups of employees — local authority employees in non-university establishments; university employees; and civil service employees.

Teaching staff

1 Primary, secondary and further education college teachers

Here the main distinctive feature is that — in contrast with England and Wales — the pay of teachers in further education is not dealt with separately by an equivalent of the Burnham Further Education Committee.

Following the Remuneration of Teachers (Scotland) Act 1967 the Scottish Teachers' Salaries Committee (STSC) was constituted in order to consider the remuneration of the 64 000 full-time teachers employed by LEAs. (Part-time teachers are paid at rates recommended by the Scottish Teachers Service Conditions Committee.) This encompasses teachers in all those categories of establishment covered by Burnham Committees, that is, nursery, primary, secondary, remedial, special schools (for the handicapped), most technical colleges, colleges of technology, and colleges of further education, with the addition of penal institutions. Colleges providing degree courses (known as Central Institutions), and colleges of education are excluded, as are Agricultural Institutes. (In Scotland, Agricultural Institutes are known as Agricultural Colleges and run by the Scottish Department of Agriculture and Fisheries.)

The Secretary of State for Scotland is represented on the STSC, as are the twelve Scottish education authorities. The Committee includes representatives of:

Management Side	Staff Side
Secretary of State for Scotland	NAS/UWT
	Educational Institute of Scotland
	Scottish Secondary Teachers' Association
Convention of Scottish Local Authorities (COSLA)	Scottish Further Education Association

In the event of a breakdown in negotiations the Secretary of State for Scotland is required to make arrangements for arbitration and has empowered ACAS to appoint an arbiter whose recommendations may be overturned only by a resolution of each House of Parliament. Agreements in the committee take the form of recommendations which the Secretary of State for Scotland is bound to accept. There is an agreement between the constituent bodies of the management side that the side speaks with one voice. The Secretary of State for Scotland retains the power of veto on the 'global amount' of any pay award. When salary scale and other provisions are agreed, the Secretary of State makes an Order securing implementation.

Conditions of service are determined by the Scottish Teachers' Service Conditions Committee. The committee comprises the same management and staff side bodies represented on the salaries body. The one difference is that the Secretary of State is not represented directly, although he does nominate two assessors. Agreements are notified to education authorities. There is no specific

245

provision for arbitration, other than those provided under the Employment Protection Act 1975.

2 Central Institutions
The Central Institutions Academic Staffs Salaries Committee was established by the Secretary of State for Scotland in 1972 to negotiate the salaries applicable to 1200 full-time and part-time academic staff — other than Principals but including graduate and chartered librarians — at the Central Institutions. Central Institutions are those establishments which provide degree courses outside the university sector, that is, polytechnics and some technical colleges. These are establishments funded by the Scottish Education Department rather than by LEAs or DES. The composition of the committee includes representatives of the following under the alternating chairmanship of a management side/staff side nominee:

Management Side	Staff Side
Central Institutions' governing bodies	Association of Lecturers in Central Institutions
Secretary of State for Scotland	ASTMS

As with the LEA teachers' machinery, the Secretary of State retains the power of veto on the global sum of any award. Subject to this provision, agreements reached in the committee are transmitted as recommendations to the Secretary of State, who gives them effect by notifying them to the Institutions. In the event of no settlement being reached there is provision for arbitration similar to that for LEA teachers, with the exception that the Secretary of State has the power to reject an arbitration award, if he considers this is in the national interest, and substitute an alternative award. The salaries of Principals are determined by the Secretary of State.

There are no negotiating arrangements for conditions of service.

3 Colleges of Education
The National Joint Committee for Salaries of Academic Staff in Colleges of Education in Scotland was constituted by the Secretary of State in 1973 to negotiate the salaries of 1100 full-time and part-time academic staff. The composition of the committee includes representatives of the following under the alternating chairmanship of a management side/staff side nominee:

Management Side	Staff Side
Colleges of Education governing bodies	Association of Lecturers in Colleges of Education in Scotland
Secretary of State for Scotland	Association of Higher Academic Staff in Colleges of Education in Scotland

246

The arrangements for arbitration and implementation of awards are similar to those for academic staff in Central Institutions.

Conditions of service are determined by the National Joint Committee for Conditions of Service for Academic Staff in Colleges of Education. Membership of the Committee is similar to that in the salaries committee except that the Secretary of State is represented only in an advisory capacity. There is no provision for arbitration.

4 Universities
Scottish universities are funded directly by the DES and the pay and conditions of service of their teaching staff are determined by the same machinery that applies to universities in England and Wales.

Reorganisation of joint machinery
In 1974 the Report of the Committee of Inquiry into the Pay of Non-University Teachers (the Houghton report) made a number of recommendations with particular reference to the bargaining machinery in Scotland. As a result, in 1976 the Secretary of State for Scotland proposed legislative reform to repeal the Remuneration of Teachers (Scotland) Act 1967 and restructure the joint machinery to create one negotiating body for school teachers and one for teachers and academic staff in all non-university post-school education. Legislation has not yet been introduced.

Non-teaching staff
There are about 42 000 non-teaching staff in Scotland.

1 Non-university establishments
All non-teaching staff in these establishments excepting Central Institutions and Colleges of Education are local authority employees, with pay and conditions of employment determined by local government collective bargaining machinery. However, the pay and conditions of those employed by Central Institutions and Colleges of Education are linked to local authority scales.

2 Universities
All non-teaching staff are employed by their respective University Authorities. Like university academic staff, their pay and conditions of service are determined by the same machinery that applies to England and Wales.

3 Education administration
With the addition of the Scottish Education Department which is part of the Scottish Office and therefore part of a Government Department, the same machinery applies to Scotland as to England and Wales.

PRIVATE SECTOR: GREAT BRITAIN

In England, Wales and Scotland there are a number of Independent Schools,

247

so defined because they receive no public funds. This category includes the major public schools and preparatory schools as well as small local schools providing education to five or more pupils on a full-time basis. They may be registered charities or run by their proprietors for profit. All such schools are required to register with the Registrar of Independent Schools. (Similar but separate arrangements apply in Scotland.) In contrast with the public sector, there is no requirement that teachers in the private sector shall hold any formal educational qualification.

There is no formal collective bargaining machinery which determines the pay and conditions of employment of teachers in independent schools. However, most independent schools tend to apply the minimum rates fixed by the public sector machinery.

Legal services

This sector covers about 110 000 staff in two broad categories — professional staff in private practice (solicitors, legal executives, and barristers — in Scotland, advocates); and support staff (barristers' or advocates' clerks, and administrative and clerical staff). Barristers, advocates, solicitors and other legal staff employed full-time by Government, local authorities, or in other industries are part of the appropriate Orders for those activities. The arrangements in Scotland are different from those in England and Wales.

ENGLAND AND WALES

1 Professional staff

Almost all barristers (those who act as advocates in court) and solicitors (those who advise and act for clients and prepare cases for barristers) in private practice are self-employed. Both are prohibited by law from forming limited liability companies and partnerships. Many solicitors form unlimited liability partnerships, but barristers are forbidden by rules of professional conduct to act similarly. Some solicitors are employed by firms on a salaried basis (assistant solicitors) but these are in the minority. The income of most solicitors, barristers and legal executives is purely dependent upon the fees charged to each client. There is no standard scale of fees, although the Government makes Remuneration Orders which give guidance as how fees are to be arrived at. Fees in litigation are 'taxed', that is, settled by the court.

The main functions of the representative bodies within the legal profession — the Law Society and the Institute of Legal Executives — are to protect their members' professional interests and maintain professional standards. These bodies are prevented by their constitutions from acting as trade unions. No collective bargaining machinery exists at national or local level.

Parliamentary Agents are, however, a special case. The function of Parliamentary Agents is to promote and oppose private and other legislation in the Houses of Parliament. There are some six firms in which about twenty agents practise. Their charges must, under statute, accord with the list of charges approved by the Speaker. The Society of Parliamentary Agents seeks revision of the list of charges with the Speaker, as occasion requires.

2 Support staff

Most legal firms are small organisations (80% have less than five professional staff) with the number of support staff usually in single figures. However, there are a few larger firms employing as many as 60 as legal executives, articled clerks, and clerical staff. It is mainly in these larger firms that the Transport and General Workers' Union's Association of Clerical, Technical and Supervisory Staffs (ACTS) has recruited members, and in a few cases secured collective bargaining agreements.

The position of clerks to barristers' chambers is a unique one. Technically it is not the barristers themselves who employ support staff, but the clerk to chambers. The clerk takes a percentage of the fee received for each brief out of which he finances the employment of other staff in chambers. The interests of barristers' clerks are represented by the Barristers' Clerks' Association of Great Britain which is primarily a professional association.

SCOTLAND

1 Professional staff

Almost all advocates and solicitors in private practice are self-employed. Both are prohibited in law from forming limited liability companies, though solicitors may form unlimited liability companies and may form partnerships. Some solicitors are employed by firms or companies on a salaried basis. The income of most advocates and solicitors is purely dependent on the fees charged to their clients. There is a recommended scale of fees for conveyancing transactions, and some fees for court work are laid down by statutory tables. There is also a recommended minimum scale of remuneration for Law Apprentices.

The main functions of the representative bodies within the legal profession — the Law Society of Scotland and the Faculty of Advocates — are similar to those in England and Wales. Neither acts as a trade union and there is no collective bargaining machinery at national or local level.

2 Support staff

Most legal firms are relatively small organisations and employ, on average, about fifteen support staff, though a few of the largest firms employ over 100 clerical and unqualified staff. There is no collective bargaining for support staff.

Medical and dental services

About 95% of the million or so people employed in the provision of health services work within the National Health Service (NHS). The remainder are employed in private health-care establishments or within industry.

NATIONAL HEALTH SERVICE

NHS structure

The NHS was set up by the National Health Service Act 1948, but the present structure in England and Wales was created by the National Health Service Reorganisation Act 1973. The main effect of the reorganisation was to bring local authority health services within the same management structure as hospital services and to relate the administration of family practitioner services very closely to the new Area and Regional Authorities. The current structure of the NHS in England is a complex network of relationships within what is essentially a five-tier structure, as follows:

i At the top the Secretary of State is responsible for the overall direction of national policies and priorities through the Regional Health Authorities via his Department of Health and Social Security (DHSS).

ii The 14 Regional Health Authorities (RHAs) are comprised of lay members appointed by the Secretary of State from the nominees of interested bodies. RHAs are corporately responsible to the DHSS for the provision of health services in their Region, and their main role, in conjunction with DHSS, is to plan overall strategy. Each RHA delegates much of its executive responsibility to a full-time professional Regional Team of Officers (RTO) and also to the RHA's constitutent Area Health Authorities.

iii The 98 Area Health Authorities (AHAs) have lay members appointed in a similar way to RHAs and are corporately responsible to their respective RHAs for the provision of health services in their Area. The AHA is the lowest level of statutory authority and has considerable planning responsibilities together with full operational responsibilities. Consequently it is the AHA which employs the majority of NHS staff. (The exceptions are consultants and registrars employed by RHAs; independent contractors (general practitioners and dentists) employed through Area Family Practitioner Committees; and staff employed at RHA headquarters.) The AHA delegates its executive responsibilities to a full-time, professional Area Team of Officers (ATO), and also the AHA's constituent District Management Teams. The AHA is obliged to constitute a Family Practitioner Committee in order to service the independent contractors employed within its Area. In addition, as the boundaries are now coterminous the two sectors liaise closely on the inter-relationship of medical services and personal social services.

iv The 222 Districts have no statutory standing but nevertheless have a District Management Team (DMT) appointed by the AHA and directly accountable to it. The District has been deemed the smallest possible unit whereby substantially the full range of health and social services can be provided. It is also the largest unit which can realistically facilitate the active participation of professional staff in the management process through representative systems. These involve the DMT: District Medical Committee (DMC); Health Care Planning Teams (HCPTs); and Community Health Council (CHC).

v Within each District the health services are further split into sectors or

250

Divisions each of which has functional heads under the co-ordination of an Administrator.

In Scotland responsibility for the health services lies with the Secretary of State for Scotland. In Wales this responsibility lies with the Welsh Office. In both Scotland and Wales the regional tier is absent so that AHAs in Wales, and the 15 Health Boards in Scotland, are responsible directly to these ministers through their respective government departments.

The Royal Commission on the NHS, which published its report in 1979, recommended that there should be only one operational management tier below RHA. The Health Departments have since published consultative papers which include proposals for revising the structure and management of the NHS. If implemented these proposals would result in the almost universal creation of 'single-District Areas' of which there are already a number of examples throughout Great Britain. In England this would be achieved by the removal of the Area tier in most of the country and the establishment of District Health Authorities.

Whitley machinery

The pay and conditions of service of virtually all NHS staff employed by health authorities are determined by its Whitley machinery. There is one General Council, and eight operational functional councils covering the following groups:

	Total staff (approx) (whole-time equivalents, Great Britain)
Administrative and Clerical Staffs	117 000
Ambulancemen	17 000
Ancillary staffs	175 000
Nurses and Midwives	404 000
Optical (hospital opticians)	10 000
Pharmaceutical (hospital pharmacists)	3000
Professional and Technical 'A' (where there is patient contact)	30 000
Professional and Technical 'B' (minimal patient contact)	35 000

Three categories of staff are outside the Whitley system — doctors and dentists, maintenance craftsmen, and *ad hoc* grades. Although doctors and dentists are represented on the General Whitley Council they, like maintenance craftsmen, have separate bargaining arrangements which are described later. *Ad hoc* grades are grades which have not yet been allocated to a Whitley Council and have their salaries fixed by the Health Departments.

The Whitley Councils are all autonomous bodies and the functional Councils are co-equal, each covering discrete sub-groups of NHS staff. The General Council, which comprises representatives of those bodies represented on the functional councils, is not superior in status to the functional councils, but deals with issues of general application. Virtually all decisions affecting pay and conditions of employment are taken by full consensus at national level without any formal provision for bargaining at local level. The main constitution provides that each of the functional councils shall determine remuneration and all conditions of service requiring national decisions affecting directly only those persons comprised within its group. Where conditions of service other than remuneration affect two or three functional councils those conditions of service may be determined by the functional councils concerned acting together. Where conditions of service and remuneration are of general application they are determined by the General Council. The agreements reached by the Whitley Councils normally take account of the terms and conditions of employment of comparable groups where these exist. However, on a number of occasions various *ad hoc* independent review bodies have been constituted to consider specific issues. The most recent example has been the Standing Commission on Pay Comparability (see page 61) which was asked to make specific recommendations on the pay and conditions of ambulancemen, ancillary staffs, nurses and midwives, and the professions supplementary to medicine (part of Professional and Technical 'A').

The cost of any agreements reached in the Whitley Councils is wholly borne by Exchequer funds which are voted by Parliament to the Health Departments for use in the NHS. The Secretaries of State for Social Services, Scotland, and Wales are all charged with a duty to provide a national health service and are also accountable to Parliament for expenditure of Exchequer funds. The National Health Service (Remuneration and Conditions of Service) Regulations 1951 and 1974, and the equivalent regulations in Scotland, provide that Whitley Council agreements must be approved by the appropriate Secretary of State before they become binding upon Health Authorities. For this reason the three Health Departments are represented in a minority capacity in relation to the Health Authority representatives.

All organisations represented on Whitley staff sides are by definition 'nationally recognised bodies' not only for the purposes of Whitley but also for local representation — for example, on consultative committees and within grievance and discipline procedures. These nationally recognised bodies include not only professional associations with responsibilities outside the industrial relations field but also trade unions most of which are affiliated to the TUC. Whilst the characteristics of the two are quite distinct (many NHS staff join the appropriate professional association for professional reasons and also join a trade union for collective bargaining purposes) there has been a convergence of interests in recent years.

Representation on the General Council and on the functional councils is set out opposite.

Management Side	Staff Side
General Council	
Chairmen of management sides of each functional council	Staff side representatives from each functional council
Representatives from:	
RHAs	
AHAs	
Scottish Health Authorities (SHAs)	
Welsh Health Authorities (WHAs)	
DHSS	
Scottish Home and Health Department (SHHD)	
Welsh Office (WO)	

Administrative and Clerical Council

RHAs	NALGO
AHAs	NUPE
SHAs	TGWU
WHAs	Association of Hospital and Residential Care Officers (AHRCO)
DHSS	
SHHD	Association of NHS Officers
WO	Confederation of Health Service Employees (COHSE)
Dental Estimates Board Prescription Pricing Authority	
	GMWU's Managerial, Administrative, Technical and Supervisory Section (MATSA)
	Society of Administrators of Family Practitioner Committees

[*cont. overleaf*]

Ambulancemen's Council (excludes Ambulance officers who are covered by the Administrative and Clerical Staffs Council)

Management Side	*Staff Side*
RHAs responsible for Metropolitan Ambulance Services in England excluding area served by London Ambulance Services	NUPE
	GMWU
Other RHAs	TGWU
	COHSE
AHAs	
DHSS	
SHHD	
WO	
Common Services Agency (Scotland)	

Ancillary Staffs Council

RHAs	NUPE
AHAs	GMWU
SHAs	TGWU
WHAs	COHSE
DHSS	
SHHD	
WO	

Nurses' and Midwives' Council

RHAs	AHRCO
AHAs	COHSE
SHAs	MATSA
WHAs	NALGO
DHSS	NUPE
SHHD	Association of Nurse Administrators

254

Management Side	Staff Side
WO	Association of Supervisors of Midwives
	Health Visitors' Association
	Royal College of Midwives
	Royal College of Nursing of the United Kingdom
	Scottish Association of Nurse Administrators
	Scottish Health Visitors' Association

Optical Council

RHAs	ASTMS
AHAs	Association of Dispensing Opticians
SHAs	Joint Commitee of Ophthalmic Opticians
WHAs	
DHSS	
SHHD	Association of Ophthalmic Practitioners
WO	
Boards of Governors (BG)	
	Parliamentary Committee of the Co-operative Union
	Socialist Medical Association (Ophthalmic Group)
	Society of Opticians
	Scottish National Committee of Ophthalmic Opticians

Pharmaceutical Council

RHAs	ASTMS
AHAs	COHSE
SHAs	Pharmaceutical Standing Committee (Scotland)

[cont. overleaf]

Management Side	Staff Side
WHAs	
	Company Chemists' Association Ltd
DHSS	
SHHD	Co-operative Union Limited
WO	
BG	

Professional and Technical Council 'A'

RHAs	ASTMS
AHAs	COHSE
SHAs	NALGO
WHAs	NUPE
DHSS	
	Association of Clinical Biochemists
SHHD	
WO	British Association of Occupational Therapists
	British Dietetic Association
	British Orthoptic Society
	Chartered Society of Physiotherapy
	Hospital Physicists' Association
	Society of Chiropodists
	Society of Radiographers
	Society of Remedial Gymnasts

Professional and Technical Council 'B'

RHAs	ASTMS
BGs	COHSE
SHAs	NALGO
WHAs	NUPE

Management Side	Staff Side
DHSS	Supervisory, Technical, Administrative, Managerial and Professional Section
SHHD	of UCATT (STAMP)
WO	
	National Union of Gold, Silver and Allied Trades
	Union of Shop, Distributive and Allied Workers (USDAW)

Doctors and Dentists

Doctors and dentists used to be covered by the Whitley machinery but the various councils and sub-committees, though still formally constituted, have ceased to function. For remuneration, an overall review of pay levels is carried out by the Doctors' and Dentists' Review Body (DDRB), the members of which are appointed by the Prime Minister.

The Review Body makes recommendations to the Prime Minister on the remuneration of doctors and dentists taking any part in the NHS. Its reports deal separately with hospital doctors and dentists, general medical practitioners, general dental practitioners, and community doctors and dentists. The Government's decisions on these recommendations are normally announced to Parliament, and successive Governments have undertaken to accept them unless there are clear and compelling reasons for not doing so. Other conditions of service, including the format of their contracts, are negotiated directly with the three Health Departments, who act as agents of the employing Authorities. The structure is tabulated below.

Group	Representative body	Special features of negotiations
Hospital doctors and dentists (36 000)		
a) Staff in 'Training' grades (House officers, registrars et al)	BMA's Hospital Junior Staffs Committee (HJSC)	All agreements have to be approved by the Joint Negotiating Committee (JNC) for Hospital
b) Staff in 'Career' grades (Consultants et al)	BMA's Central Committee for Hospital Medical Services (CCHMS)	Medical and Dental Staff. The JNC staff side is drawn equally from HJSC and CCHMS.

[cont. overleaf]

Group	Representative body	Special features of negotiations
General medical practitioners (GPs) (27 000)	General Medical Services Committee (GMSC), composed of BMA and the Medical Practioners' Union (MPU) which is part of ASTMS	GPs are independent contractors, are not employees. Negotiations are limited to a few minor items on which specific recommendations are not made by the DDRB.
General dental practitioners (14 000)	BDA	Arrangements are similar to those for GPs. Fees, etc are worked out by a Joint BDA/Health Departments' body — the Dental Rates Study Group — to produce an income equivalent to the net income recommended by DDRB.
Community doctors (3000)	Central Committee for Community Medicine (CCCM)	CCCM and the Health Depts form a Joint Negotiating Body.
Community dentists (school dentists) (2000)	BDA	Negotiations are conducted in a Joint Negotiating Forum.

Maintenance craftsmen

There are about 30 000 maintenance staff, in three groups, whose pay and conditions of service were originally covered by the Ancillary Staffs Whitley Council but who now have separate pay negotiations direct with the three Health Departments outside the Whitley machinery. In all three cases the machinery has no formal constitution. Electricians and plumbers are represented by the Electrical, Electronic, Telecommunication and Plumbing Union (EETPU); building craftsmen by UCATT, TGWU, GMWU and the Furniture, Timber and Allied Trades Union (FTAT). Engineering grades fall into two groups — craftsmen and semi-skilled. Craftsmen are represented by the Confederation of Shipbuilding and Engineering Unions (CSEU), semi-skilled workers by NUPE, TGWU, GMWU and COHSE. There is an informal agreement with all these unions that the conditions of service negotiated in the Ancillary Staffs Whitley shall apply to their members.

Procedures

Disciplinary and redundancy payments procedures are covered by General

258

Whitley Council agreements and supported by DHSS guidance to employing Authorities. However, Authorities are expected to consult staff side representatives locally in order to develop the initial stages to fit local circumstances.

Grievance procedures are regarded as a matter for local negotiation, though there is an agreed procedure for handling individual grievances on conditions of service other than dismissal or disciplinary action. A Disputes Procedure Agreement has now been negotiated by the General Whitley Council. It provides a framework for local procedures designed to settle collective disputes which are outside the scope of the Whitley appeals machinery.

Joint consultation

In 1950 the General Whitley Council negotiated an agreement that Joint Consultative Committees (JCCs) should be established at hospital level, but by 1970 many of these original JCCs no longer functioned. However, in recent years the growth of trade unionism in the NHS, and the lack of formal negotiating machinery at local level, has led to a revival of the JCCs and to their use for negotiation. The General Whitley Council has since concluded a revised agreement on Joint Consultation Machinery reaffirming its commitment to the process as essential to the smooth working of the NHS.

PRIVATE SECTOR

Private health care establishments — nursing homes, acute hospitals (that is, surgical and medical short-stay) and non-residential clinics — employ over 60 000 staff. There are no collective bargaining arrangements at national level, although some of the larger independent hospitals have local arrangements. Advice on industrial relations matters is provided to member employers by each of the three national associations (Registered Nursing Homes Association; Association of Independent Hospitals; and the Independent Hospital Group); or alternatively via the Joint Liaison Committee for Independent Health Care — of which the three Associations are the founder members. Pay and conditions tend to reflect Whitley agreements.

Private professional services are also available in NHS establishments, and are provided by medical, dental and ophthalmic practitioners and some GPs. Fees for private medical work are fixed independently and not determined by collective bargaining machinery. Where employment agency nurses are used in NHS establishments the agencies are technically the employers, but nevertheless pay and conditions of service are set by specific Whitley agreements.

Industrial Medical Officers are not strictly part of the private sector: they are employed in industry and are therefore outside the NHS. Their interests are represented by the BMA. The Royal College of Nursing represents occupational health nursing officers. The pay and conditions of both groups tend to reflect those of their counterparts in the NHS.

Religious organisations

About 30 000 people are employed in this sector — in church administration;

as clergy; or in other religious bodies and fringe organisations. There is no significant collective bargaining except for three groups. The pay and conditions of employment of the 400 or so employees of the Church Commissioners are based upon those of civil servants having equivalent responsibility and are therefore determined indirectly by civil service Whitley machinery. The Commissioners have their own type Whitley Council, on which five civil service unions — the Civil Service Union (CSU), the Civil and Public Services Association (CPSA), the Society of Civil and Public Servants (Executive, Directing and Analagous Grades) (SCPS), the Institution of Professional Civil Servants (IPCS), and the Association of First Division Civil Servants (FDA) — are represented. It deals with local issues.

Prison chaplains (about 1000) are employed by the Home Office Prison Service and their terms and conditions are set by the normal civil service Whitley machinery. Hospital chaplains (about 1000) have their pay and conditions of service set by the NHS Professional and Technical 'A' Whitley Council (see page 251).

Research and development services

In this sector about 110 000 people are employed in three broad types of organisations: central government bodies; trade research associations; and private firms. The collective bargaining arrangements in each of the first two areas are described below: research staff in private firms are normally covered by the arrangements for other white-collar staff.

1 GOVERNMENT RESEARCH

Central government sponsors research in two ways: directly through government departments, and through fringe bodies over which a Minister has only indirect control. When the sponsorship is direct, for example within the Department of Industry itself or in research establishments such as the National Physical Laboratory, the employees are civil servants and are covered by the normal collective bargaining machinery. However, fringe bodies' staff are employees of their respective governing bodies and therefore not civil servants.

There are 20 fringe bodies with research as their primary function, employing over 30 000 people. Almost all are in the seven organisations which in addition to promoting research actually undertake it:

Agricultural Research Service (ARS) (which includes the Agricultural Research Council)

Medical Research Council (MRC)

Natural Environment Research Council (NERC)

Science Research Council (SRC)

Social Science Research Council (SSRC)

Pay Research Unit (PRU)

United Kingdom Atomic Energy Authority (UKAEA).

ARS and the four other research councils follow the pay and gradings negotiated for the civil service, and most negotiate separately other terms and conditions of employment. The general pattern is that for non-industrial staff there are Whitley Councils with appropriate union representation drawn from the CSU, CPSA, SCPS, IPCS and FDA. For industrial staff there are Joint Industrial Councils with union representatives from the CSU, NUAAW, AUEW, TGWU, GMWU, UCATT, EETPU, Association of Government Supervisors and Radio Officers (AGSRO), and the National Union of Sheet Metal Workers, Coppersmiths and Heating and Domestic Engineers (NUSMW). In NERC the pay and conditions of about 200 maritime staff are aligned to agreements reached between the General Council of British Shipping, the National Union of Seamen (NUS) and the Merchant Navy and Airline Officers' Association (MNAOA) (see page 210).

PRU staff are seconded Civil Servants. All terms and conditions for UKAEA staff are negotiated either by its Whitley Council or its Joint Industrial Council. The remaining 13 promotional fringe bodies employ less than 500 staff in total and tend to apply Civil Service terms and conditions. Staff are usually represented by one or other of the Civil Service unions, though the Association of Professional, Executive, Clerical and Computer Staff (APEX) has members in the National Research Development Corporation.

2 TRADE RESEARCH ASSOCIATIONS

There are about 40 associations, employing some 5000 people, which, on an industry basis, provide research facilities for member firms. Collective bargaining, where it exists, is at association level; rather less than a quarter of all staff are covered by agreements with either ASTMS or the Association of Management and Professional Staffs (AMPS).

Other professional and scientific services

There are about 135 000 staff in this sector, most of whom are self-employed or in private practice. Only three groups — veterinary surgeons, commercial artists, and writers — have significant collective bargaining arrangements; each is described separately below. In addition, some architects belong to ASTMS, or to the AUEW's Technical, Administrative and Supervisory Section (TASS); some consulting engineers to the EETPU's United Kingdom Association of Professional Engineers (UKAPE); and public analysts who work under contract to local authorities are represented by the Society of Public Analysts and Other Official Analysts, which negotiates fees through a technical panel established by LACSAB.

1 VETERINARY SURGEONS

There are about 6500 veterinary surgeons practising in Great Britain. Of these, approximately 5000 are either self-employed or employed in private practice. The fees for this work are not determined by collective bargaining. However, the fees for part-time work carried out for various other bodies are negotiated on the practitioners' behalf by the British Veterinary Association (BVA). Of the remainder about 750 are employed full-time by the Ministry of Agriculture, Fisheries and Food, and are covered by the normal Civil Service machinery on which they are represented by IPCS. Another 300 or so are employed by universities, are represented by the AUT, and are covered by the machinery for university teachers. The remaining 450 or so are employed in various private sector research establishments.

2 COMMERCIAL ARTISTS

About 4000 commercial artists working in art studios and photographic laboratories, advertising agencies or publishing houses are represented by the Society of Lithographic Artists, Designers, Engravers and Process Workers (SLADE). Most collective bargaining is at house level, though there are some regional and national agreements. Agreements cover the full range of terms and conditions and in most cases this includes a post-entry union membership agreement.

Artists employed in art studios and photographic laboratories are covered by agreements between SLADE and the Art Studios and Photographic Laboratories Association (ASPLA). ASPLA is an association of London-based employers, but where an employer has provincial branches these are covered by the same agreements. Some artists in advertising agencies are covered by agreements between SLADE, the National Graphical Association (NGA), and regional advertising agency associations. Artists in publishing houses are normally covered by the agreements in the publishing industry.

3 WRITERS

About 1500 authors and playwrights are represented by the Writers' Guild of Great Britain (WG) which has negotiated a standard contract in theatre, film, television and radio covering minimum royalty rates, subsidiary rights, and the degree of influence which an author may exert upon the production of his or her work. The Guild now has similar collective agreements covering the publication of books and plays with various publishing houses.

About 4500 freelance journalists are covered by the collective agreements in the printing and publishing industry, normally by specific clauses on freelance rates and conditions. Most are members of the National Union of Journalists (NUJ); the remainder belong to the Institute of Journalists (IOJ).

Order XXVI MISCELLANEOUS SERVICES

This Order encompasses a wide range of service industries employing, in total, over 2¼ million people. For collective bargaining purposes they can be divided into nine sectors each of which is described separately below:

Entertainment

Sport and other recreations

Betting and gambling

Hotels and catering

Hairdressing and manicure

Laundries and dry cleaning

Motor repairers, distributors, garages and filling stations

Boot and shoe repairing

Other services.

Entertainment

For the purposes of collective bargaining this industry can be divided into six main sectors — cinemas, theatres, orchestral music, opera and ballet, variety and other entertainment, and television and radio broadcasting. It employs approximately 100 000 people, though numbers fluctuate since a considerable proportion are employed on short-term contracts or on a casual basis. Unionisation is extensive and collective bargaining is generally well developed. Most employers belong to one of the employers' associations.

1 CINEMAS

This sector employs about 30 000 people, mostly in cinema film processing, distribution and exhibition. The remainder are involved in film production where continuity of employment does not exist for the majority. In each part of the industry there are a few large firms and a considerable number of smaller companies.

2 THEATRES

There are 500 or so theatres in Great Brtiain. Most of the people employed in them are on short-term contract or in casual employment. In a given week there may be anywhere between 8000 and 15 000 people at work in theatres.

3 ORCHESTRAL MUSIC

Outside of opera and ballet and excluding the BBC, three groups of professional orchestras operate in Great Britain — four London orchestras, seven permanent regional orchestras and a number of other orchestras with permanent managements but with players engaged on a casual basis. The London and regional orchestras employ about 1000 musicians; 2000 more work on a contract basis. The London orchestras are co-operative bodies and do not take part in the industry's collective bargaining machinery, though they do observe the minimum rates negotiated.

4 OPERA AND BALLET

In this sector there are a few permanent establishments and a number of touring and seasonal companies. At any one time no more than about 2000 people are working. The artistes tend to work on short-term contracts and the technicians more often in longer term employment.

5 VARIETY AND OTHER ENTERTAINMENT

In this sector there are a few large employers with a chain of establishments, and many smaller employers. The artistes tend to be employed on short-term contracts.

6 TELEVISION AND RADIO BROADCASTING

Television and radio broadcasting employs in total nearly 40 000 people and is controlled by two bodies — the British Broadcasting Corporation (BBC) which employs 27 000, and the Independent Broadcasting Authority (IBA). The IBA, unlike the BBC, does not produce services but licenses contracting companies to provide television or radio services for specified areas of the country during specified periods.

UNIONS

The main unions involved in the entertainment industry are:

Union	Employees represented
British Actors' Equity Association (Equity)	Actors, dancers, singers, variety artistes.
Musicians' Union (MU)	Musicians, arrangers, copyists.
Film Artistes' Association (FAA)	Film extras.
Electrical, Electronic, Telecommunication and Plumbing Union (EETPU)	Electronic, lighting and maintenance staff.

264

Union	Employees represented
Association of Broadcasting and Allied Staffs (ABS)	Broadcasting staff in BBC, IBA and Independent local radio.
Association of Cinematograph, Television and Allied Technicians (ACTT)	Camera crews, directors and technicians.
Writers' Guild of Great Britain (WG) Theatre Writers' Union (TWU)	Writers.
National Association of Theatrical, Television and Kine Employees (NATTKE)	Film production, bingo, video, cinema, make-up and hairdressing, and TV craft employees.
National Association of Executives, Managers and Staffs (NAEMS)	Managers and assistant managers in cinemas.
National Union of Journalists (NUJ)	Journalists.

There are formal union membership agreements, or *de facto* closed shops, covering studio film production, employees in the large cinema chains, theatres, orchestral music, opera and ballet, and independent television companies.

NEGOTIATING MACHINERY

The employers' associations, trade unions, and joint bodies involved in collective bargaining in each sector are set out below.

Sector	Employers' Association(s)	Trade union(s)	Negotiating arrangements
Cinemas			
Studio production	British Film Producers' Association (BFPA)	Equity, MU, EETPU, ACTT, NATTKE, WG	Separate negotiation with each union
	BFPA	FAA	A Joint Council for Crowd Artistes in films, with an independent chairman.

[cont. overleaf]

Sector	Employers' Association(s)	Trade union(s)	Negotiating arrangements
Film processing	Association of Film Laboratory Employers	ACTT	Direct negotiation.
Film distribution	Kinematograph Renters' Society	NATTKE	Direct negotiation.
Exhibition	Cinema Exhibitors' Association	NATTKE, NAEMS	Separate negotiation with each union.
Theatres			
	Society of West End Theatre Managers (SWET)	Equity MU, NATTKE, WG	Separate negotiation with each union. There is a joint conciliation committee called the London Theatre Council.
	Theatre Managers' Association (TMA) (regional and provincial theatres)	Equity, MU NATTKE	Separate negotiation with each union. There is a joint conciliation committee called the Provincial Theatre Council.
Orchestral music			
	Association of British Orchestras (ABO)	MU	Direct negotiation.
Opera and ballet			
	None	Equity, MU, NATTKE	Standard Contracts are negotiated with Equity by the Theatres National Committee (TNC).
			As regards touring orchestras a Standard Contract is negotiated with the MU by the TMA. Many individual companies negotiate house agreement variations to these contracts.

266

Sector	Employers' Association(s)	Trade union(s)	Negotiating arrangements
Variety, etc	SWET, TMA, Entertainment Agents' Association (EAA), British Resorts Association (BRA)	Equity, MU	Negotiations with Equity are conducted through the Variety and Allied Entertainments Council (VAEC), on which SWET, TMA and EAA are represented. The MU negotiates with the BRA.
Radio and television BBC		Musicians, orchestras: MU.	Direct negotiations between MU and BBC.
		Performers, freelances *et al*: ABS, Equity, MU, WG, NUJ.	Unions negotiate jointly with BBC.
		Other staff: ABS, NUJ, EETPU, NATTKE, Society of Graphical and Allied Trades (SOGAT).	Unions negotiate separately with BBC.
Independent Broadcasting	Independent Television Companies Association	ACTT, EETPU, NATTKE, NUJ, Equity, MU, WG.	Separate negotiations with each union, except that EETPU and NATTKE negotiate jointly on craftsmen's terms and conditions.
	Association of Independent Radio Contractors (AIRC)	NUJ, Equity, MU, WG, Society of Authors.	Separate negotiations with each union.
		ABS, ACTT.	These unions negotiate jointly with AIRC. The IBA itself negotiates only with ABS.

The agreements between the employers' associations and unions in the entertainment industry normally set minimum terms and conditions, though sometimes in considerable detail. These are often enhanced at company level and by individual performers negotiating their own contracts directly. Many of the agreements contain disputes procedures.

Sport and other recreations

About 100 000 people are employed in services connected with the provision of sport and other recreations.

Most sporting and recreational facilities are provided in small units and the general level of union membership is low. However, in services provided by local authorities, for example in swimming baths, tennis courts and golf courses, employees are mainly represented by the National Union of General and Municipal Workers (GMWU). Professional footballers and stable staff employed by racehorse trainers each have their own Association and there is some representation by the Transport and General Workers' Union (TGWU) in other areas.

Wages and working conditions of about 4000 stable staff employed by racehorse trainers are negotiated through the National Joint Council for Stable Staff, comprising representatives from the National Trainers' Federation, the TGWU and the Stable Lads' Association (SLA).

Minimum terms and conditions of employment of about 2500 professional footballers are determined through the Professional Footballers' Negotiating Committee jointly representing the Football League and the Professional Footballers' Association (PFA). There is also a jointly agreed disputes procedure. The Football Association (FA) is responsible for promoting international football and controlling discipline within the game. Negotiating procedures exist between the FA and the PFA and provision is also made in the constitution of the Professional Footballers' Negotiating Committee for the FA to participate in negotiations when necessary.

Collective bargaining for local authority employees connected with the provision of sport and recreational facilities is through the established local authority negotiating machinery.

Betting and gambling

This industry covers bookmaking, football and racing pools, amusement arcades, casinos and bingo halls. It employs just under 100 000 people.

The industry has grown considerably in recent years and is dominated by a handful of very large companies whose operations often cover several of the areas mentioned above as well as other parts of the leisure industry. Unionisation is generally low; there is no collective bargaining in amusement arcades and casinos. Arrangements in bookmaking, pools and bingo halls are described separately below.

268

1 BOOKMAKING

There are about a dozen companies operating on a significant national or regional scale, and hundreds of smaller companies, some operating only one betting shop. There are some agreements giving individual representational rights in respect of small groups of workers in national companies. The only concern to recognise unions for collective bargaining is the government owned Totalisator or Tote Board which employs about 1500 permanent staff supplemented by a similar number of casual staff mainly engaged for on-course work. Terms and conditions of employment for permanent staff up to senior level are negotiated with the TGWU's Association of Clerical, Technical and Supervisory Staffs (ACTS).

2 POOLS

Littlewoods dominates this sector. It has about 5000 employees, half of whom are employed part-time. Clerical staff are represented by the Union of Shop, Distributive and Allied Workers (USDAW); the craft trades are represented by their appropriate unions, and supervisors are represented by USDAW's Supervisory, Administrative and Technical Association (SATA). There are some union membership agreements in operation.

3 BINGO HALLS

As with betting shops, a large number of bingo halls are operated by the large leisure groups, together with a number of smaller chains, often based in one region or area. Unionisation among employees is patchy, with a number of unions involved. The main union is NATTKE, reflecting the fact that many bingo halls were originally cinemas. There is no national industry agreement between NATTKE and the National Association of Licensed Social and Bingo Clubs, but NATTKE is recognised as being the appropriate union for the industry and it does engage in collective bargaining with some of the biggest bingo hall operators.

Hotels and catering

The hotel and catering industry includes hotels and other residential establishments, restaurants, cafés and snack bars, public houses, clubs, and catering contractors. There is a high degree of part-time and seasonal employment; throughout most of the year nearly 900 000 people are employed in the industry but this number can nearly double during the summer months. Most people work in small establishments.

The industry is most easily divided into the following five sectors, defined mainly by whether or not the establishment is residential, and whether or not it is licensed to serve alcohol. The first three sectors are covered by wages councils. The largest parts of the industry are the two licensed sectors, each of which has over a third of the employees in the industry.

1 Licensed hotels, holiday camps, residential clubs, and restaurants
2 Unlicensed restaurants, cafés and snack bars
3 Licensed public houses and non-residential clubs
4 Unlicensed guest houses and hotels
5 Industrial and staff canteens.

Trade union membership in the industry is generally low although it has increased in recent years. Union activity is co-ordinated at national level by the TUC Hotel and Catering Industry Committee which was established in 1973 and nominates employee representatives to the three wages councils. It brings together the TGWU, GMWU, USDAW, NATTKE, MU, National Union of Railwaymen (NUR), Transport Salaried Staffs' Association (TSSA), National Union of Public Employees (NUPE), National Association of Licensed House Managers (NALHM), Civil Service Union (CSU), and the Association of Scientific, Technical and Managerial Staffs (ASTMS).

A section of GMWU, the Hotel and Catering Workers' Union (HCWU) was formed in 1980.

1 LICENSED HOTELS, HOLIDAY CAMPS, RESIDENTIAL CLUBS, AND RESTAURANTS

There are over 20 000 firms in this part of the industry, still mostly small independently owned businesses, though since the mid-1960s there has been a trend towards employment in larger, often conglomerate companies. There is considerable seasonal employment. For manual workers, minimum rates of pay and conditions are set by the Licensed Residential Establishment and Licensed Restaurant Wages Council with some supplementary bargaining at local level. There is virtually no collective bargaining for white-collar staff.

There are two main employers' organisations. The British Hotels, Restaurants and Caterers' Association (BHRCA) represents over 9000 establishments directly and nearly 6000 other establishments through the affiliation of local associations. It dominated the employers' side of the wages council, with about two-thirds of the seats. The Brewers' Society (BS) is the trade association for brewers and has in membership virtually all the brewery firms in the UK. There are, in addition, four specialist or regional trade associations which are represented on the wages council: the National Association of Holiday Centres Limited (NAHC), the National Union of Licensed Victuallers (NULV), the Scottish Licensed Trade Association (SLTA) and the Association of London Clubs (ALC).

Trade union membership is generally low, but has grown in recent years, aided by the trend towards larger companies. The main union is the GMWU, though the TGWU also has members, mainly in hotels and restaurants in London, and USDAW has members in restaurants run by Co-operative Societies and department stores. All three unions are represented on the wages council, but the GMWU dominates, with about three-quarters of the employee seats. The GMWU and the TGWU have a spheres of influence agreement relating to the various hotel groups. The NALHM, whose main

270

membership is amongst managers in public houses, also has members amongst managers in this sector.

Collective bargaining for manual workers at company level is still limited but has grown in recent years, particularly in the larger companies. For example, the GMWU and TGWU have a national agreement with one of the biggest holiday camp organisations which makes union membership a condition of employment and covers hours, holidays, sickness and accident benefits, pensions, redundancy, health and safety, manpower problems, training, and equal opportunities. It also contains a disciplinary and disputes procedure.

2 UNLICENSED RESTAURANTS, CAFÉS AND SNACK BARS

This sector is predominantly made up of about 20 000 very small family-operated businesses. Once again the BHRCA dominates the employers' side of the wages council, but six other organisations are also represented:

The Parliamentary Committee and Co-operative Union Limited

The Cinematograph Exhibitors' Association of Great Britain and Ireland

The Council of Voluntary Welfare Work

The National Association of Master Bakers

The National Federation of Fish Friers

The Association of Metropolitan Associations.

There is a high proportion of part-time women workers, and considerable seasonal employment. Trade union membership is very low. The main unions involved are USDAW and the GMWU, but the TGWU, NUPE and the Bakers', Food and Allied Workers' Union (BFAWU) are also represented on the wages council.

Minimum rates of pay and conditions for manual workers are set by the Unlicensed Place of Refreshment Wages Council. In addition, USDAW and the GMWU negotiate with one or two of the larger companies, particularly some of those who hold franchises for motorway stations. There is virtually no collective bargaining for white-collar staff.

3 LICENSED PUBLIC HOUSES AND NON-RESIDENTIAL CLUBS

There are some 60 000 public houses in Great Britain, with the majority of employees working part-time. Public houses fall into the following categories:
(i) managed houses — those owned by a brewery, catering company or an individual proprietor and run by a manager or manageress

(ii) tenanted houses — those owned by a brewery or catering company and let or leased to a tenant who is under a commercial contract to the company to operate a tied trade

(iii) privately owned houses — able to operate a free trade.

There are about 14 000 non-residential clubs.

BS is the employers' organisation in the public house sector and its membership consists of practically all brewery companies or groups operating a tied trade. Its Management and Hotels Committee is if necessary advised on industrial relations policy by the Society's Employment Committee.

NULV represents tenants of public houses and the free house proprietors. SLTA has a membership of about 5000 private owners who are organised into 70 local associations representing various types of clubs, the main one of which is the Working Men's Club and Institute Union Limited (CIU).

Union membership among bar staff in public houses is generally low, although in recent years the TGWU in particular has recruited in this sector and its membership has grown. USDAW also has a few members among bar staff in public houses, but its main strength in this sector comes from its membership among stewards and bar staff in clubs, particularly in South Wales but also in Lancashire and Yorkshire. The GMWU has membership among stewards and bar staff in clubs in the North East and Humberside. The National Union of Club Stewards (NUCS) also has about 2000 members in clubs.

By far the most strongly organised group in this sector, however, is public house managers, the great majority of whom belong to NALHM which was formed in 1969 from the managers' section of the National Federation of Licensed Victuallers. NALHM has post-entry closed shop agreements covering about one-third of its membership, mainly those employed by the major breweries. ACTS also has members among public house managers in the Midlands and Scotland. The GMWU has an agreement for managers and bar staff employed by a major brewery.

Minimum rates of pay and conditions of employment for club stewards and bar staff of both public houses and clubs are set for all establishments by the Licensed Non-residential Establishment Wages Council. Public house managers do not come within the scope of the council. The employers are represented by BS, NULV, SLTA, CIU and by other organisations representing various types of clubs. Employees are represented by USDAW, GMWU, TGWU and NUCS. In addition terms and conditions for bar staff in public houses owned by three Scottish-based breweries are negotiated directly by the TGWU.

NALHM negotiates directly on behalf of managers with all the major brewery companies and with most of the smaller companies employing managers. Agreements between brewery companies and NALHM (or ACTS in the three companies in the Midlands where that union is also recognised for house managers) typically cover pay, bonuses, holidays and redundancies, together with features unique to the licensed trade such as allowances for catering, spillage and living out. Salary scales are generally related to bar takings or average staff hours required, and annual bonuses tend to be geared to the profit of houses. Managers' wives usually receive an honorarium, but there is growing pressure for rates of pay to be negotiated for wives in their own right.

4 UNLICENSED GUEST HOUSES AND HOTELS

Like the unlicensed place of refreshment sector, this sector is characterised by very small establishments which are generally family-operated. A high proportion of women and part-time workers are employed, and the establishments and numbers employed are liable to considerable seasonal fluctuations. Trade union membership is minimal: the TGWU and GMWU have a few members, but there is no significant collective bargaining.

5 INDUSTRIAL AND STAFF CANTEENS

In this sector the most important distinction from the point of view of organisation and collective bargaining practice is between those units which are run directly by employers and those which are run by catering contractors. The latter account for just over a quarter of the sector's labour force, which is predominantly female. About one-third of all employees are part-timers. The great majority of workers are employed in small units. In the contract sector about half of the employees are concentrated in five companies.

The three unions with the largest membership among canteen workers are the TGWU, USDAW and the GMWU. A number of other unions also have catering workers in membership, generally in establishments in which the unions represent the main body of workers.

In the public sector the majority of industrial catering units are run directly by employers and most workers are covered, along with other categories of workers, by Whitley Councils or National Joint Industrial Councils (NJICs) whose agreements either lay down specific terms and conditions for catering workers or link them to appropriate grades in the structure. The other wage-negotiating and procedural arrangements also cover catering workers. Some public sector organisations — the National Coal Board for example — have separate national-level negotiations for catering workers.

In the directly-run private sector units the most common arrangement is for the collective agreements covering other groups of workers to include appropriate rates for catering workers. But other arrangements also exist: for example, there may be separate negotiations for catering employees after negotiations for other manual workers have been completed.

Collective bargaining for catering employees in predominantly white-collar establishments is less well developed, but the indications are that its scope is extending as collective bargaining develops among white-collar workers generally.

In contractor-run units, the contractors frequently follow the terms and conditions negotiated by the client company and the unions in respect of its own employees, or some appropriate nationally agreed rate in the industry served by the catering unit. In a few cases contractors have agreements with trade unions for catering staff either locally or nationally.

Hairdressing and manicure

About 100 000 people are employed in this sector, almost all in small establishments. There is virtually no collective bargaining but minimum time and overtime rates, holidays and holiday pay for hairdressers and manicurists employed in hairdressing undertakings are set by the Hairdressing Undertakings (Great Britain) Wages Council. Four employers' organisations — the National Hairdressers' Federation, the Incorporated Guild of Hairdressers, Wigmakers and Perfumers, the National Chamber of Trade and the Co-operative Employers' Association (CEA) — nominate employers' representatives on the Council; the workers' side members are unorganised members, that is, not nominated by a trade union. USDAW has some members in the industry and is recognised in a few of the larger establishments.

Laundries and dry cleaning

These industries employ about 80 000 people, distributed as follows:
1. Laundries — about 53 000
2. Dry cleaning — about 25 000
3. Launderettes — about 7000 (including some self-employed owners).
Some firms are engaged in more than one of the industries.
1. Laundries. There are several large laundry businesses and a large but declining number of small and medium-sized firms. Many laundries have diversified into the commercial 'rental' business, hiring out and cleaning linen, towels and workwear, as the domestic laundering market has contracted. Most firms are members of the Association of British Launderers and Cleaners (ABLC), and, where appropriate, of the British Textile Rental Association (BTRA). Co-operative Societies are members of the Co-operative Union Limited.

With a few exceptions, levels of union membership are low. The principal unions for manual workers are the GMWU, TGWU, USDAW, and, for some transport workers, the United Road Transport Union (URTU). For white-collar staff, the main unions are USDAW, the National Association of Co-operative Officials (NACO) and the Association of Professional, Executive, Clerical and Computer Staff (APEX), but their membership tends to be restricted to the Co-operative Societies.

Minimum rates of pay and conditions of employment for process workers, transport workers and operating supervisors in laundries (other than those operated by non-commercial bodies such as hospitals, and by British Transport Hotels) are determined by the Laundry Wages Council (Great Britain) (LWC). The employers' side of the LWC is made up of representatives from the ABLC and the Co-operative Union Limited. Representatives of the GMWU, TGWU, USDAW and URTU make up the workers' side.

A number of firms conduct local negotiations which supplement the LWC rates, but the only national machinery to do this is in Co-operative Society laundries, where the CEA has agreements with USDAW, GMWU, TGWU, and URTU for manual staff, and with NACO and APEX for white-collar staff.

2. Dry cleaning. The market is shared by a multitude of small firms, with one or a handful of outlets, and two large groups. The typical firm consists of 'unit shops' where cleaning is done on the premises, although some work is processed in bulk at factories. Some dry cleaning firms are also engaged in 'rental' (see Laundries above). Most firms are members of ABLC, some additionally of BTRA.

Two unions, the TGWU and the National Union of Dyers, Bleachers and Textile Workers (NUDBTW), have some membership concentrated in distribution work and in a few large processing units. USDAW also has membership engaged in distribution. Shop staff are rarely unionised.

There is no national machinery, but a few of the largest firms bargain at local level with the TGWU and NUDBTW.

3. Launderettes. The typical launderette business comprises one or two outlets with very few employees or none. There are some groups with more than 20 outlets. Many firms are members of the National Association for the Launderette Industry (NALI). There is no significant union membership and no collective bargaining.

Motor repairers, distributors, garages and filling stations

Motor repairers, distributors, garages and filling stations make up a sector of industry characterised by an extremely large number of firms and outlets most of which have a small number of employees. There are two combined trade and employers' associations concerned with collective bargaining: the Motor Agents' Association (MAA), which covers England, Wales, Northern Ireland and the Isle of Man, and the Scottish Motor Trade Association (SMTA). Together they have in membership some 15 500 firms and cover most of the 450 000 employees in the industry. Distributors tend to be under licence to a particular motor manufacturer, and filling stations to a particular oil company, but these commercial relations do not affect collective bargaining. There is little collective bargaining in respect of filling stations whether oil company owned or licensed.

Union membership in the industry is modest. Five unions are recognised nationally for manual workers — the TGWU, GMWU, EETPU, the Engineering Section of the Amalgamated Union of Engineering Workers (AUEW), and the National Union of Sheet Metal Workers, Coppersmiths and Heating and Domestic Engineers (NUSMW). Of these, the TGWU has the largest membership. Where white-collar staff are represented by a union they tend to be members of the white-collar sections of the manual unions.

National-level collective bargaining takes place under the auspices of the National Joint Council (NJC) for the Motor Vehicle Retail and Repair Industry. The employers' representatives are provided by the MAA and the SMTA. All five unions are represented on the NJC, though the TGWU has half the employees' seats.

The agreements reached by the NJC cover manual workers including leading hands, chargehands and certain non-manual employees such as reception engineers, estimators and testers. They deal with such matters as minimum rates, hours, premium rates for shift and night work and overtime, holidays, outworking and subsistence allowances, and a disputes procedure with a final stage providing for discretionary conciliation or arbitration. A particular feature of the agreement on minimum rates is the classification of adult employees into job-evaluated groups. There are separate rates for apprentices and unindentured junior employees.

The NJC agreements specifically exclude managerial, supervisory, security and office staffs; sales staff; and cleaners. There are as yet no national agreements covering white-collar staff. The NJC has issued a policy statement which directs the attention of those non-manual employees who may be seeking union membership to the white-collar affiliates of the manual unions on the NJC.

The MAA has six regional offices which give guidance on the implementation of national agreements, and are also involved in one of the stages of the nationally agreed disputes procedure. There is no separate regional collective bargaining and only limited company and establishment level bargaining, although many managements pay employees, in particular, skilled employees, above national minimum rates.

Boot and shoe repairing

There are many small firms in this sector, which employs about 5000 people. Manual workers are covered by the Boot and Shoe Repairing Wages Council (Great Britain). The employers' representatives on the council come from the National Association of Shoe Repair Factories, the St Crispin's Boot Trades Association Limited, the Co-operative Employers' Association and the British Surgical Trades Association, whose interest in the trade is in the repair of surgical footwear. Employee representatives come from USDAW and the National Union of Footwear, Leather and Allied Trades (NUFLAT). The Wages Council sets minimum time, piece and overtime rates; guaranteed weekly pay, and guaranteed daily pay for casual workers; and holidays and holiday remuneration. There is also some collective bargaining in the larger companies, involving NUFLAT and USDAW.

Other services

This sector employs over half a million people in a great diversity of services. In the public sector collective bargaining is well developed. National and local government-run museums, art galleries, botanical gardens, cemeteries, crematoria, orphanages and homes for handicapped children, disabled or aged persons are covered by collective bargaining in the Civil Service or local government. The probation service is also covered by collective bargaining in local government.

Funeral services is the only area in the private sector where collective bargaining above company level exists. The Furniture, Timber and Allied

Trades Union (FTAT) has agreements with the Proprietary Crematoria Association, whose member firms run privately owned crematoria and cemeteries, and with the London Association of Funeral Directors covering funeral firms in London and the South East of England. There is also some company bargaining in the larger funeral firms; in particular, FTAT has an agreement covering retail Co-operative Societies in the South of England, and FTAT, USDAW, and the TGWU have an agreement with the Co-operative Wholesale Society Limited covering funeral depots in Great Britain. These agreements cover about 3000 funeral operatives and set pay, staffing, holidays, sickness, health and safety and disputes procedures.

Other areas where there is some collective bargaining at company level include some of the larger photographic processing firms where the TGWU and ASTMS are recognised; the trade unions, where the main union recognised is APEX, though some employees of trade unions are members of their employing union; and contract cleaning where the TGWU and GMWU are recognised in a few large firms.

Order XXVII PUBLIC ADMINISTRATION AND DEFENCE

For collective bargaining purposes, or the determination of pay and conditions otherwise, this Order can be divided into five sectors:

> National Government Service
>> The Armed Forces
>> Government Departments

> Local Government Service
>> Local Government, with separate treatment of
>> Police
>> Fire Service.

National Government Service

THE ARMED FORCES

These comprise the Royal Navy and Royal Marines, the Army and the Royal Air Force, the three Women's Services, and the three Women's Nursing Services. Armed Forces personnel number about 300 000.

This is the only sector in which there is no collective bargaining. The pay and allowances of all but the most senior officers, and charges for food and accommodation levied on all members of the armed forces, are the concern of the Review Body on Armed Forces Pay. The Review Body is appointed by, and reports to, the Prime Minister, and its recommendations on pay are largely based on earnings in civilian jobs of comparable skill and responsibility. The Government's decisions on these recommendations are normally announced to Parliament. Successive governments have undertaken to accept them unless there are clear and compelling reasons for not doing so.

The pay of the most senior officers is covered by the Review Body on Top Salaries (see page 282). Ministry of Defence civilian staff are covered by the arrangements for Government Departments.

GOVERNMENT DEPARTMENTS

This sector, in which over 700 000 people are employed, also includes a number of national Commissions, Agencies and bodies outside central government but related to it.

Government Departments are staffed by civil servants — servants of the Crown paid from funds voted by Parliament. Under the Prime Minister as Minister for the Civil Service, the Civil Service Department (CSD) is responsible for pay, pensions and conditions of employment in the civil service and its Permanent Secretary is the official head of the Home Civil Service. The arrangements for industrial civil servants (manual employees), non-industrial civil servants (white-collar employees), and senior civil servants are described separately below.

1 Industrial civil servants

There are approximately 170 000 industrial civil servants, all manual workers. They are employed mainly in government industrial establishments, though substantial numbers of them provide support services of various kinds elsewhere — for example, heating, lighting and maintenance services in government offices and in prisons, domestic services in staff restaurants and military messes, security services for government offices and chauffeurs in the government car service. About three-quarters of all industrial civil servants are employed by the Ministry of Defence (MOD). Other major employers are the Property Services Agency of the Department of the Environment (DOE), the Home Office (HO) (mainly in the Prison Service) and Her Majesty's Stationery Office (HMSO) where they undertake manual work in establishments dealing with government printing and the storage and distribution of government publications and stationery for government offices.

The trade unions representing industrial civil servants, and recognised for purposes of negotiation and consultation over pay and conditions of service, are the national manual unions which represent comparable workers in outside industry. These are listed below. The extent of unionisation can vary considerably between one kind of government establishment and another and indeed from one part of the country to another. Industrial civil servants are encouraged to join the appropriate union and, overall, union membership is around 75 per cent. The unions are:

Amalgamated Society of Boilermakers, Shipwrights, Blacksmiths and Structural Workers (ASB)

Amalgamated Union of Engineering Workers (AUEW)

278

Association of Patternmakers and Allied Craftsmen (APAC)

Electrical, Electronic, Telecommunication and Plumbing Union (EETPU)

Furniture, Timber and Allied Trades Union (FTAT)

National Society of Metal Mechanics (NSMM)

National Union of Agricultural and Allied Workers (NUAAW)

National Union of General and Municipal Workers (GMWU)

National Union of Sheet Metal Workers, Coppersmiths and Heating and Domestic Engineers (NUSMW)

National Union of Tailors and Garment Workers (NUTGW)

Transport and General Workers' Union (TGWU)

Union of Construction, Allied Trades and Technicians (UCATT).

All but about 8000 industrial civil servants are employed under a common structure of basic pay and conditions of service the main features of which, such as basic pay, hours, holidays, sick pay and sick leave, are negotiated nationally. The national negotiating body for this purpose is the Joint Co-ordinating Committee for Government Industrial Establishments (JCC).

In addition, there are four Trades Joint Councils (TJCs) which deal with grading and allowance matters where the primary consideration is the industrial working environment. The TJCs and the main areas which they cover are:

Shipbuilding Trades Joint Council (STJC)	Royal Dockyards
Engineering Trades Joint Council (ETJC)	Royal Ordnance Factories, REME Workshops, other engineering establishments.
Works Services Trades Joint Council (WSTJC)	Property Services Agency of DOE, Prison Service.
Miscellaneous Trades Joint Council (MTJC)	All other industrial environments including naval, military and Air Force stores, depots and operational, administrative and training establishments.

The Official Sides of the JCC and the TJCs consist of representatives of the Civil Service Department and the main employing departments. The Chairman and Secretary of the JCC are CSD officials. The Chairmen and Secretaries of the STJC, the ETJC and the MTJC are MOD officials. The Chairman and Secretary of the WSTJC are DOE officials.

Membership of the Union Sides of the JCC and TJCs is determined by the trade unions themselves and, generally, reflects the extent of each union's interests and membership in the field of activity concerned. Representatives are normally full-time officials. There is a good deal of common membership between the JCC and the four TJCs, on both the official and trade union sides.

The remaining 8000 or so industrial civil servants comprise a number of specialist groups such as printers and warehousemen in the publications field (in HMSO), agricultural workers (at government experimental farms and agricultural research stations), firemen in the Army and Air Force fire brigades, and cinematic and television technicians (in the Central Office of Information) (COI). For these groups, known as 'trade-raters', the pay and conditions of service are related more narrowly to those of their main industry. In some instances, the outside trade and industry rates are applied automatically: in others, such as HMSO, some 'in-house' negotiations take place in the light of the trade or industry rates.

For the purposes of consultation and negotiation on non-pay matters, such as day-to-day operating practices, discipline, etc and for the purpose of negotiating productivity and incentive schemes, each of the main employing departments has appropriate departmental joint Whitley machinery. The body concerned is usually called the Departmental Joint Industrial Council — but there are other titles.

2 Non-industrial civil servants
There are around 550 000 non-industrial civil servants.

All the main conditions of employment which affect grades in general are negotiated centrally, either formally or informally, under the aegis of the Civil Service National Whitley Council. Pay determination principles are also agreed by the Council but each of the recognised unions negotiates separately on actual rates of pay for the grades it represents.

On the National Whitley Council the Official Side takes the permanent role of employer on behalf of the government of the day and is made up of serving civil servants: the Head of the Home Civil Service (Chairman of the Council), other senior representatives of CSD, and the Permanent Secretaries of the main employing departments. The Council of Civil Service Unions (CCSU), into which the National Staff Side restructured itself in 1980, has a full-time secretariat led by a Secretary General, who is chief negotiator, and is composed of the nine recognised Civil Service Unions. These unions, and the grades each represents, are set out in the table on page 281.

All grades of staff are encouraged to belong to an appropriate union and membership levels are high — about 75% overall and nearly 90% in some grades.

The full National Whitley Council rarely meets; in practice, national

Unions and grades represented

Organisation	Number of seats	Grades represented
Civil and Public Services Association (CPSA)	20	Clerical, Typing and Data Processing Grades
Society of Civil and Public Servants (Executive, Directing and Analagous Grades) (SCPS)	11	General and Departmental Executive Grades
Institution of Professional Civil Servants (IPCS)	11	Professional, Scientific and Technical Grades
Inland Revenue Staff Federation (IRSF)	8	Departmental Grades in the Inland Revenue
Civil Service Union (CSU)	6	Basic Grades (eg Messengers) and Specialist Grades (eg Instructional Officers)
Prison Officers' Association (POA)	3	Prison Grades
Association of Government Supervisors and Radio Officers (AGSRO)	2	Radio and Stores, etc Grades
Association of First Division Civil Servants (FDA)	Associated Unions } 2	Administrative Legal Grades
Association of Her Majesty's Inspectors of Taxes (AIT)		Tax Inspectorate Grades in Inland Revenue.

negotiations are conducted through a network of standing and *ad hoc* joint committees, by informal meetings of CCSU Officers and members of the Official Side, and by correspondence. There are Joint Standing Committees, on pay research, personnel management, dispersal, management services, computers, welfare, accommodation, training, and superannuation. Where a matter affects only the grades represented by a single union the union normally negotiates directly with CSD and the relevant employing departments.

Negotiations on pay are normally based on reports on the pay and conditions in comparable jobs outside the civil service, prepared by the Civil Service Pay Research Unit (PRU). PRU has a director appointed by the Prime Minister and operates under the general control and direction of a Pay Research Unit Board and the National Whitley Council.

In addition to the national machinery there are over 80 Departmental

Whitley Councils operating in government departments and related bodies. Official Sides are composed of senior civil servants of the Department. The unions appoint the members of the Union Sides which normally include serving civil servants, and full-time union officials with special responsibilities within the appropriate section of the unions. The Councils are concerned with aspects of conditions of employment which are domestic to the individual department — for example, staffing levels, deployment of staff, duties relative to grading, departmental promotion, staff training, staff welfare, general standards of premises and accommodation — with any problems over the implementation of national agreements, and any matters referred to them by other Whitley committees within the Department. The large departments also have regional, local or office Whitley Committees which are primarily concerned with matters generated locally — for example, arrangement of working hours; premises and accommodation; training facilities — or referred from the Departmental Whitley Council.

Disagreements between the two sides of a Whitley Council, or between government departments and recognised trade unions over pay, hours or leave of civil service grades (though not disputes over individual cases) may be referred for arbitration to the Civil Service Arbitration Tribunal. The tribunal has an independent chairman and two other members drawn from Official and Union Side panels respectively.

3 Senior civil servants

Although all the other conditions of service of senior grades are dealt with through the Civil Service National Whitley Council the pay of civil servants at Under Secretary level and above is the responsibility of the Review Body on Top Salaries. The Review Body is appointed by, and reports to, the Prime Minister. Its recommendations take account of levels of remuneration for jobs of equivalent weight outside the civil service as well as other factors such as stability of employment, individual job security, promotion prospects and job satisfaction. The Government's decisions on these recommendations are normally anounced to Parliament. Successive governments have undertaken to accept them unless there are clear and compelling reasons for not doing so. The Review Body also advises on the pay of senior officers of the armed forces (Major General or equivalent and above), senior members of the judiciary and the Chairmen and members of nationalised industry Boards. It has undertaken three reviews of Parliamentary remuneration.

Local Government Service

Local authorities employ about 2·8 million people. Those who work in schools and other educational establishments are covered by the collective bargaining machinery for educational services (see page 237). There is separate machinery for the police and fire services, which is described in the sectors following. The remaining local authority employees are covered by the collective bargaining arrangements described below.

The present structure of local government was established by the London Government Act 1963, the Local Government Act 1972 and the Local Government (Scotland) Act 1973. There are four main associations of local authority employers to which almost all local authorities belong:

The Association of County Councils (ACC)

The Association of Metropolitan Authorities (AMA)

The Association of District Councils (ADC)

The Convention of Scottish Local Authorities (COSLA).

An industrial relations and manpower advisory service is provided to local authorities and their associations by the Local Authorities' Conditions of Service Advisory Board (LACSAB), which acts as the employers' side secretariat on national negotiating committees.

Union membership levels are high and some 60 trade unions and professional associations are recognised, with representation on the appropriate national joint negotiating bodies.

NEGOTIATING MACHINERY

There is negotiating machinery (and disputes and grievance procedures) at national, provincial and local level. At national level there are two main National Joint Councils (NJCs) — one for white-collar and one for manual employees — and a number of other negotiating bodies, some of which act as sub-committees to the main Councils, covering specialised groups of staff, including five covering specialised groups in Scotland. These national bodies agree general terms and conditions for all employees in the appropriate categories (except for white-collar staff in London — see below) and although local authorities tend to follow the terms of the national agreements there is some scope for provincial and local level negotiation.

The various national negotiating bodies are set out below, together with their employee representatives. The two main negotiating bodies have employer representatives from the Provincial Councils (see below), the Scottish Councils, ACC, AMA and ADC. The other national bodies in England and Wales have employers' sides drawn, according to the character of the committee, from the same organisations plus the Greater London Council, government departments and voluntary organisations. [Representatives from Northern Ireland also sit on some bodies.] COSLA provides the employers' representatives on all the Scottish bodies (see table on page 284).

At provincial level there are, in England and Wales, 27 separately constituted Provincial Councils, joint bodies with representatives from the appropriate local authorities and the main trade unions, which consider matters referred by the main NJCs, interpret and implement NJC agreements, and make recommendations to the NJCs in respect of issues arising within the

283

Negotiating body	Employee representation
Main bodies and their sub-committees:	
National Joint Council for Local Authorities' Administrative, Professional, Technical and Clerical Staff (NJC–APT & C) (covering over ½ million employees)	Provincial Council Staff Sides, Scottish Council Staff Sides, National and Local Government Officers' Association (NALGO), National Union of Public Employees (NUPE), Confederation of Health Service Employees (COHSE), GMWU's Managerial, Administrative, Technical and Supervisory Section (MATSA), TGWU
Residential Establishments Officer Committee and Standing Joint Advisory Committee for Staffs of Children's Homes	COHSE, NALGO, NUPE, MATSA, Association of Community Home Schools, Association of Hospital and Residential Care Officers, Association of Heads and Matrons of Assessment Centres, TGWU's Association of Clerical, Technical and Supervisory Staffs (ACTS)
Ports Committee	NJC–APT & C Staff Side, ACTS
National Joint Council for Local Authorities' Services (Manual Workers) — (NJC–MW) (covering over 1 million employees)	GMWU NUPE TGWU
Committee for Employees in Residential Establishments	GMWU NUPE TGWU COHSE NJC–MW Scottish Council (Trade Union Side)
County Roadmen's Committee	TGWU GMWU NUPE NUAAW
Municipal Airports Panel	TGWU GMWU NUPE
School Caretakers' Committee	TGWU GMWU NUPE
NJC–APT & C (Scottish Council) (covering 65 000 employees)	NALGO NUPE MATSA TGWU

Negotiating body	*Employee representation*
NJC–MW (Scottish Council) (covering 120 000 employees)	GMWU NUPE TGWU

Other bodies:

Joint Negotiating Committee (JNC) for Chief Executives of Local Authorities	Association of Local Government Chief Executives
JNC for Chief Officers of Local Authorities	NALGO, Society of Education Officers, Association of Public Service Professional Engineers (APSPE), Association of Public Service Finance Officers (APSFO), Association of Passenger Transport Executives and Managers, Association of Planning Officers, Association of Local Authority Chief Architects, Union of County and District Surveyors, Guild of Directors of Social Services
JNC for Chief Officials of Local Authorities (Scotland)	NALGO, APSFO, APSPE, Association of Local Authorities' Chief Executives, Association of Directors of Administration, Association of Directors of Education in Scotland, Scottish Assessors' Association, Association of Directors of Social Work, Association of Directors of Water & Sewerage Services, Scottish Society of Directors of Planning, Association of Scottish Passenger Transport Executives and Transport Managers, Association of Local Government Engineers and Surveyors, Association of Chief Architects of Scottish Local Authorities
JNC for Coroners	Coroners' Society of England and Wales
JNC for the Fees of Doctors assisting Local Authorities	British Medical Association
JNC for Justices' Clerks	Justices' Clerks' Society
JNC for Justices' Clerks' Assistants	Association of Magisterial Officers

[cont. overleaf]

Negotiating body	Employee representation
JNC for Local Authorities' Services (Building and Civil Engineering)	EETPU UCATT TGWU GMWU
Scottish JNC for Local Authorities' Services (Building and Civil Engineering)	UCATT TGWU GMWU FTAT
JNC for Local Authorities' Services (Engineering Craftsmen)	Confederation of Shipbuilding and Engineering Unions (CSEU)
Scottish JNC for Local Authorities' Services (Engineering Craftsmen)	CSEU
JNC for the Probation Service	National Association of Probation Officers, Standing Conference of Chief Probation Officers
NJC for Workshops for the Blind	National League of the Blind and Disabled
Scottish JNC for Local Authorities' Services (Craftsmen — Electricians and Plumbers)	EETPU
Scottish JNC for Local Authorities' Water Supply Services (Manual Workers)	NUPE TGWU GMWU
Standing Conference for Engineers	EETPU
Standing Conference for Heating, Ventilating and Domestic Engineers	NUSMW
Whitley Council for New Towns Staff	NALGO, New Towns' Chief Officers' Association
Whitley Council for the Staffs of the Industrial Estates Corporations and Development Agencies	NALGO

provincial area. The Provincial Councils also negotiate agreements on matters such as local working practices, standby arrangements, plus rates, and training, as well as on matters upon which there is no national agreement.

At local level there are, in most local authorities, Joint Consultative Committees (JCCs) which deal with such matters as productivity and bonus schemes, job evaluation, demarcation, special leave facilities, redundancy procedures, health and safety, and welfare.

In London the Greater London Council (GLC), and the Inner London Education Authority (ILEA) which is responsible for education in the inner London Boroughs, together operate an autonomous Whitley Council in which salaries and conditions of service for APT & C staff are negotiated outside the NJC — APT & C. The Staff Side has representatives from the Greater London Council Staff Association (GLCSA), NALGO, and the Senior Officers' Guild. GLC/ILEA manual workers, including craftsmen, are covered by the various national negotiating bodies, but act together on the GLC domestic Trade Union Joint Committee (TUJC) to negotiate such matters as productivity and bonus schemes, gradings, allowances and holidays.

Police

There are 51 police forces in Great Britain, with a combined strength of about 130 000. Each force is maintained by a police authority. For the Metropolitan Police that authority is the Home Secretary; for the City of London Police it is a standing committee of the Court of Common Council; for the 33 County Forces and 8 Combined Forces (each covering two or more local authority areas) in England and Wales, it is a Police Committee comprising two-thirds elected councillors and one-third magistrates from the area or areas covered; and for the 8 forces in Scotland, it is a committee of the Regional Council composed entirely of elected councillors, or in one case a separate Police Board covering the area of two Regional Councils.

Trade union membership and industrial action are prohibited. There are, however, six associations, each restricted to particular ranks, which can negotiate pay and other terms and conditions of employment of their members through the Police Negotiating Board. These are:

All ranks above Chief Superintendent
>   The Association of Chief Police Officers of England, Wales and Northern Ireland
>   The Association of Chief Police Officers (Scotland)

Superintendents and Chief Superintendents
>   The Police Superintendents' Association of England and Wales
>   The Association of Scottish Police Superintendents

All ranks below Superintendent
>   The Police Federation of England and Wales
>   The Scottish Police Federation.

All police officers are automatically members of the appropriate association. The associations are not independent trade unions and do not have the right of free association with other bodies. The Police Federations have statutory recognition and prescribed constitutions which give equal representation at both local and national levels to all grades (Inspectors, Sergeants and Constables) regardless of their numerical strength.

Pay and almost all terms and conditions of employment are negotiated at national level in the Police Negotiating Board, which was inaugurated in 1979 following recommendations made by a Committee of Inquiry chaired by Lord Edmund-Davies. The Board has an independent Chairman appointed by the Prime Minister and an independent secretariat provided by the Office of Manpower Economics.

The composition of the Official Side reflects the interests of both central and local government and includes representatives of the Home Office, Scottish Home and Health Department, County Councils, Metropolitan Authorities, and Scottish Local Authorities, with one-third of the representatives of County Councils and Metropolitan Authorities being magistrates rather than elected councillors. The Staff Side includes representatives of all the staff associations together with the Commissioner of Police of the Metropolis and two women police officers nominated respectively by the Superintendents' Associations and the Federations. The work of the Board is conducted by five autonomous Standing Committees which consider matters peculiarly affecting, in turn, Chief Officers; Superintendents; Inspectors, Sergeants, Constables and Cadets; issues common to all ranks; and pensions. Any disagreement may be referred to an independent panel of three arbitrators — the Police Arbitration Panel — appointed by the Prime Minister.

Most agreements of the Board and its Committees are implemented through Police Regulations. Since these are Statutory Instruments any dispute about their interpretation or application can be pursued through the courts. To avoid this, Dispute and Conciliation Panels for each Standing Committee consider any differences that arise from the implementation of Agreements. Their recommendations are regarded as binding in honour on the parties though without prejudice to the individual officer's legal right to resort to the courts.

A few matters are negotiated at local level, including the rent allowances paid to officers for whom accommodation is not provided by the police authority.

There is also national consultative machinery in the form of Police Advisory Boards for England and Wales, and for Scotland, which are made up of representatives of the Home Departments, police authorities and staff associations and which cover any non-negotiable issue.

Fire Service

There are 63 fire brigades in Great Britain employing about 35 000 whole-time uniformed staff in England and Wales and about 4000 in Scotland. In addition all brigades but the London Fire Brigade employ part-time retained or volunteer staff numbering about 17 000 in England and Wales and 3000 in Scotland.

There are three nationally recognised unions in the fire services: the Fire Brigades Union (FBU), the National Association of Fire Officers (NAFO), and the Chief and Assistant Chief Fire Officers' Association (CACFOA).

Collective bargaining in the fire service is conducted by specialised machinery within the wider framework of the system of Whitley Councils for local authority staffs. Under the Fire Services Act 1959 the pay and conditions of service (other than pensions) of members of all fire brigades below the rank of Chief Officer are set by the National Joint Council for Local Authorities' Fire Brigades (NJC). The employer representatives on the NJC are drawn from the ACC, AMA, GLC, COSLA [and the Fire Authority for Northern Ireland]. The employees are represented by the FBU and NAFO. Under the NJC an autonomous Officers Committee with representatives drawn from the same bodies negotiates the ranks, pay and allowances, hours of duty and leave and welfare arrangements for officers. The pay and conditions of Chief Officers (Firemasters in Scotland) are set by the NJC for Local Authorities' Fire Brigades' Chief Officers which has employer representatives from the same bodies and employee representatives from CACFOA. London is excluded from scope as Senior Officers' salaries are negotiated locally. Administrative staff are covered by the NJC for Local Authorities' APT & C Staff (see page 284), with separate arrangements in London.

The pensions of uniformed operational members of fire brigades are set by the Secretary of State through the provisions of the Firemen's Pension Scheme. Collective consultation on pension matters is co-ordinated through the Joint Pensions Committee of the Central Fire Brigades' Advisory Council which is made up of representatives from the Home Office, the local authority employers' organisations and the three nationally recognised unions.

At local level, both FBU and NAFO conduct negotiations with or are consulted by Chief Fire Officers and Fire Authorities over a wide range of matters including duty arrangements, equipment, and training and welfare facilities.

Appendices

Appendix 1 Industrial analysis of collective agreements

(A) Males Percentages of full-time adult men reported to be affected by various types of collective agreements, by industry, April 1978

FULL-TIME MEN aged 21 and over, including those who received no pay for the Survey Pay-period APRIL 1978

Industry (see note)	SIC ORDER (1968)	FULL-TIME MANUAL MEN Percentage affected by					FULL-TIME NON-MANUAL MEN Percentage affected by				
		Number in sample	National and Supplementary/ Company, etc agreements	National agreement only	Company, district or local agreement only	No collective agreement	Number in sample	National and Supplementary/ Company, etc agreements	National agreement only	Company, district or local agreement only	No collective agreement
All industries and services		57 268	29·3	36·4	12·6	21·7	36 775	11·7	38·5	9·4	40·5
All Index of Production industries		38 333	34·9	32·0	14·4	18·6	13 124	14·3	19·5	15·5	50·7
All manufacturing industries		28 328	41·0	19·4	18·8	20·9	10 071	15·8	10·6	19·0	54·7
All non-manufacturing industries		28 940	17·8	53·0	6·6	22·5	26 704	10·1	49·0	5·8	35·2
Agriculture, forestry, fishing	I	1281	9	27	3	61	185	7	11	4	78
Mining and quarrying	II	2207	8	85	3	4	378	4	76	4	16

Industry		Total					Total				
Food, drink and tobacco	III	2220	18	21	37	24	843	5	10	23	62
Coal and petroleum products	IV	230	24	24	39	13	118	11	0	14	75
Chemicals and allied industries	V	1563	27	17	34	22	954	4	7	22	67
Metal manufacture	VI	2774	63	17	8	12	608	25	29	11	35
Mechanical engineering	VII	4212	49	17	10	24	1572	19	8	15	58
Instrument engineering	VIII	428	26	18	17	39	357	10	7	19	64
Electrical engineering	IX	2096	47	14	15	24	1397	17	6	27	50
Shipbuilding and marine engineering	X	1112	67	15	10	8	157	24	26	13	37
Vehicles	XI	4317	43	16	27	14	1155	29	18	30	23
Metal goods not elsewhere specified	XII	2067	37	18	16	29	542	10	5	15	70
Textiles	XIII	1588	29	29	23	19	373	6	7	18	69
Leather, leather goods and fur	XIV	101	35	27	3	35	35				
Clothing and footwear	XV	435	19	39	5	37	131	6	14	5	75
Bricks, pottery, glass, cement, etc	XVI	1158	37	25	20	18	295	11	6	18	65
Timber, furniture, etc	XVII	1018	28	35	9	28	271	4	8	11	77
Paper, printing and publishing	XVIII	1867	47	32	5	16	926	25	15	7	53
Other manufacturing industries	XIX	1142	23	5	39	33	337	12	3	17	68
Construction	XX	6506	21	60	2	17	1754	8	24	6	62
Gas, electricity and water	XXI	1292	18	81	0	1	921	15	84	0	1
Transport and communication	XXII	7132	19	58	12	11	2984	10	61	6	23
Distributive trades	XXIII	3293	15	21	14	50	3827	6	10	8	76
Insurance, banking, finance and business services	XXIV	507	13	14	10	63	3353	14	14	16	56
Professional and scientific services	XXV	1819	14	73	2	11	6172	11	64	1	24
Miscellaneous services	XXVI	2948	15	26	9	50	2057	11	21	13	55
Public administration	XXVII	1955	36	62	0	2	5073	10	89	0	1

Appendix 1 continued

(B) Females   Percentages of full-time adult women reported to be affected by various types of collective agreements, by industry, April 1978

FULL-TIME WOMEN aged 18 and over, including those who received no pay for the Survey Pay-period APRIL 1978

Industry (see note)	SIC ORDER (1968)	FULL-TIME MANUAL WOMEN Percentage affected by					FULL-TIME NON-MANUAL WOMEN Percentage affected by				
		Number in sample	National and Supplementary/ Company, etc agreements	National agreement only	Company, district or local agreement only	No collective agreement	Number in sample	National and Supplementary/ Company, etc agreements	National agreement only	Company, district or local agreement only	No collective agreement
All industries and services		12 563	25·6	32·9	12·4	29·1	28 606	11·2	48·4	7·1	33·3
All Index of Production industries		7673	32·0	24·2	16·1	27·7	5283	16·2	17·8	17·0	49·0
All manufacturing industries		7587	32·2	24·0	16·2	27·6	4329	17·0	10·9	20·1	52·0
All non-manufacturing industries		4976	15·5	46·4	6·8	31·4	24 277	10·2	55·1	4·7	30·0
Food, drink and tobacco	III	926	23	23	31	23	470	5	12	28	55
Chemicals and allied industries	V	353	14	9	36	41	394	5	5	27	63
Metal manufacture	VI	149	62	9	10	19	201	23	27	19	31
Mechanical engineering	VII	326	44	22	11	23	592	23	10	15	52
Instrument engineering	VIII	179	24	19	17	40	144	14	3	18	65
Electrical engineering	IX	1102	47	15	14	24	536	23	7	26	44

Vehicles	XI	342	55	14	17	14	323	34	18	19	29
Metal goods not elsewhere specified	XII	510	37	22	17	24	287	13	9	19	59
Textiles	XIII	982	33	29	17	21	215	13	13	21	53
Clothing and footwear	XV	1275	22	35	5	38	159	8	16	12	64
Bricks, pottery, glass, cement, etc	XVI	271	29	41	13	17	136	16	7	25	52
Timber, furniture, etc	XVII	137	26	32	10	32	104	5	5	16	74
Paper, printing and publishing	XVIII	512	33	38	7	22	483	19	16	11	54
Other manufacturing industries	XIX	424	20	8	25	47	165	19	1	22	58
Construction	XX	40					407	4	12	7	77
Gas, electricity and water	XXI	27					464	22	77	0	1
Transport and communication	XXII	386	22	49	16	13	1374	6	62	5	27
Distributive trades	XXIII	591	8	16	20	56	4476	8	20	9	63
Insurance, banking, finance and business services	XXIV	66					3040	16	20	11	53
Professional and scientific services	XXV	1764	16	73	1	10	8816	10	75	1	14
Miscellaneous services	XXVI	1667	14	27	7	52	1898	13	31	11	45
Public administration	XXVII	322	34	64	1	1	3668	9	90	0	1

(iv) no collective agreement.

Notes

1 The statistics of collective agreements are from the 1978 *New Earnings Survey*, which was based on information provided by a large sample of employers relating to the pay-period April 12, 1978.

2 Employers were asked to report whether the employees' pay and conditions were affected, directly or indirectly, by:

(i) both a nationally negotiated collective agreement and a supplementary company/district/local agreement

(ii) a national agreement only

(iii) a company/district/local agreement only

3 The results of this analysis are shown for 27 SIC Orders for full-time males and females respectively (manual and non-manual for each sex).

4 In both tables, percentages are omitted for some industries where the responding sample was considered inadequate to provide reliable estimates. If the number of responding employers was less than 100 for any of the four employee categories (manual men, non-manual men, manual women and non-manual women) no estimates are given.

295

Appendix 2 Incidence of industrial disputes in the UK 1970–79

(A) Number of stoppages

Industry (1968 Standard Industrial Classification)	Number of stoppages per 100 000 employees										Average for		
	1970	1971	1972	1973	1974	1975	1976	1977	1978	1979	5 years 70–74	5 years 75–79	10 years 70–79
Agriculture, forestry, fishing	0·9	0·5	0·2	1·4	1·2	0·5	—	0·8	0·3	—	0·8	0·3	0·6
Mining and quarrying (see note 10)	40·3	35·1	60·4	84·0	56·1	61·6	81·3	77·7	102·2	91·6	55·2	82·9	69·0
Food, drink and tobacco	18·7	9·7	11·0	12·9	20·1	12·8	10·1	20·8	17·1	14·0	14·5	15·0	14·7
Coal and petroleum products	26·9	15·8	7·1	22·2	15·2	15·2	2·7	16·4	11·0	14·1	17·4	11·9	14·7
Chemicals and allied industries	19·2	9·4	9·9	12·2	14·7	12·8	6·6	16·1	12·1	12·7	13·1	12·1	12·6
Metal manufacture	54·9	26·6	40·3	40·3	45·2	30·3	30·9	36·8	32·7	30·7	41·5	32·3	36·9
Mechanical engineering	47·4	31·8	38·0	34·0	34·6	35·6	18·3	29·9	27·2	24·3	37·2	27·1	32·1
Instrument engineering	23·3	13·3	11·4	10·6	14·3	12·2	6·0	12·7	6·1	12·8	14·6	10·0	12·3
Electrical engineering	34·7	16·5	21·7	22·8	24·4	21·0	12·7	20·3	19·8	15·1	24·0	17·8	20·9
Shipbuilding and marine engineering	63·7	43·0	35·4	35·8	46·9	34·7	21·6	23·6	24·0	24·4	45·0	25·7	35·3
Vehicles	53·6	37·3	36·6	47·9	35·3	26·7	30·8	39·2	31·9	28·2	42·1	31·4	36·8
Metal goods not elsewhere specified	29·7	14·9	24·6	26·8	28·0	23·5	23·0	31·2	24·6	23·6	24·8	25·2	25·0
Textiles	14·2	11·3	11·4	15·7	16·1	16·6	9·7	15·0	13·7	9·0	13·7	12·8	13·3
Leather, leather goods and fur	4·1	2·1	6·6	11·2	2·3	2·4	7·4	4·9	14·9	5·2	5·3	7·0	6·1
Clothing and footwear	5·9	5·9	6·9	6·8	7·3	13·4	8·1	9·8	9·4	7·1	6·6	9·6	8·1
Bricks, pottery, glass, cement, etc.	25·2	12·7	18·6	18·7	25·3	22·9	12·1	27·7	21·2	18·1	20·1	20·4	20·3

Timber, furniture, etc.	19·6	9·3	12·7	11·0	11·3	5·7	7·2	8·5	11·4	8·9	12·8	8·3	10·6
Paper, printing and publishing	12·0	4·9	7·6	9·6	12·6	11·5	6·6	10·8	15·7	8·7	9·3	10·7	10·0
Other manufacturing industries	26·1	13·0	18·0	24·1	24·6	15·7	11·8	28·4	21·5	18·7	21·2	19·2	20·2
Construction	25·2	18·7	19·0	15·9	15·3	16·1	18·7	19·5	14·5	13·1	18·8	16·4	17·6
Gas, electricity and water	5·1	2·1	3·4	3·5	6·6	4·5	7·4	7·5	4·6	5·7	4·1	5·9	5·0
Transport and communication	37·1	17·3	15·4	19·6	20·4	14·6	13·2	16·9	14·5	12·1	22·0	14·3	18·1
Distributive trades	3·1	2·1	1·3	1·9	2·7	2·2	1·6	3·2	2·2	1·6	2·2	2·2	2·2
Insurance, banking, finance and business services	0·8	0·4	0·3	0·1	0·3	0·4	0·7	0·2	0·3	0·7	0·4	0·5	0·4
Professional and scientific services	0·9	0·4	0·5	1·2	1·3	1·2	0·7	0·9	1·0	0·8	0·9	0·9	0·9
Miscellaneous services	1·5	1·0	1·1	1·7	2·3	2·4	1·2	0·9	1·4	1·4	1·5	1·5	1·5
Public administration and defence	4·5	1·5	2·5	3·3	5·3	3·9	3·7	4·0	4·8	4·3	3·4	4·1	3·8
TOTAL: All manufacturing industries	31·0	18·2	21·4	23·7	24·6	18·6	15·4	23·6	20·8	17·8	23·8	19·2	21·5
TOTAL: All industries and services	17·4	10·1	11·3	12·7	12·8	10·1	8·9	12·0	10·9	9·1	12·9	10·2	11·5

Appendix 2 *continued*
(B) Working days lost

Industry (1968 Standard Industrial Classification)	Working days lost per 1000 employees										Average for		
	1970	1971	1972	1973	1974	1975	1976	1977	1978	1979	5 years 70–74	5 years 75–79	10 years 70–79
Agriculture, forestry, fishing	70	0	2	2	53	1	—	2	0	—	25·4	0·6	13·0
Mining and quarrying (see note 10)	2657	164	28 474	249	16 122	158	224	278	585	379	9533·2	324·8	4929·0
Food, drink and tobacco	606	189	309	153	754	220	135	1139	966	1153	402·2	722·6	562·4
Coal and petroleum products	231	449	450	374	1884	1034	44	213	214	1272	677·6	555·4	616·5
Chemicals and allied industries	393	100	120	167	202	509	56	638	296	337	196·4	367·2	281·8
Metal manufacture	1014	607	1351	912	1758	745	693	1416	784	2134	1128·4	1154·4	1141·4
Mechanical engineering	797	567	1367	802	643	773	324	962	747	8125	835·2	2186·2	1510·7
Instrument engineering	496	199	680	252	745	137	124	552	56	3401	474·4	854·0	664·2
Electrical engineering	834	890	1707	638	1478	1249	302	1252	650	7321	1109·4	2154·8	1632·1
Shipbuilding and marine engineering	2156	2890	4272	1524	3923	2491	335	894	873	1760	2953·0	1270·6	2111·8
Vehicles	1762	4582	2628	3094	2564	1268	1204	3620	5231	6440	2926·0	3552·6	3239·3
Metal goods not elsewhere specified	494	162	561	369	373	374	292	515	417	1810	391·8	681·6	536·7
Textiles	292	94	400	235	414	482	76	407	266	150	287·0	276·2	281·6
Leather, leather goods and fur	3	11	77	22	11	7	17	24	28	46	24·8	24·4	24·6
Clothing and footwear	423	28	84	116	46	231	69	144	124	100	139·4	133·6	136·5
Bricks, pottery, glass, cement, etc.	1319	53	406	315	357	174	95	532	485	430	490·0	343·2	416·6
Timber, furniture, etc.	126	47	93	228	89	79	42	92	76	91	116·6	76·0	96·3
Paper, printing and publishing	250	81	145	141	465	185	73	326	554	1318	216·4	491·2	353·8
Other manufacturing industries	934	491	1202	750	755	377	207	577	695	625	826·4	496·2	661·3
Construction	183	213	3234	112	196	185	436	234	327	645	787·6	365·4	576·5
Gas, electricity and water	53	13	48	912	162	26	148	239	187	107	237·6	141·4	189·5
Transport and communication	835	4170	563	217	470	277	90	205	249	958	1251·0	355·8	803·4
Distributive trades	15	12	3	7	51	14	5	34	23	27	17·6	20·6	19·1

Insurance, banking, finance and business services	283	5									58·4	5·2	30·8
Professional and scientific services	123	15	33	104	69	8	7	13	6	381	68·8	83·0	75·9
Miscellaneous services	12	13	8	12	19	23	16	11	33	259	12·8	68·4	40·6
Public administration and defence	739	3	18	128	122	77	39	702	316	1447	202·0	516·2	359·1
TOTAL: All manufacturing industries	780	816	1013	724	953	634	319	1053	1052	3151	857·2	1241·8	1049·5
TOTAL: All industries and services	489	613	1081	318	647	265	146	448	414	1291	629·6	512·8	571·2

Notes

(a) General

1 The official statistics of stoppages of work due to industrial disputes in the United Kingdom on which the incidence rates of Appendix 2 are based relate to disputes about terms and conditions of employment.

2 Stoppages involving fewer than 10 workers or lasting less than one day are excluded except where the total of working days lost exceeds 100. There is no differentiation between 'strikes' and 'lockouts'.

3 Numbers of workers are those both directly and indirectly involved (the latter are those thrown out of work although not parties to the disputes) at the establishments where the disputes occurred. The number of working days lost is the total of days lost by the workers involved, as defined above.

4 It follows that the statistics do not reflect repercussions elsewhere, ie at establishments other than those at which the disputes occurred. For example, the statistics exclude persons laid off and working days lost at establishments not in dispute through shortages of materials caused by stoppages in other plants and industries.

5 There are difficulties in ensuring complete recording of stoppages, in particular those near the margins of the definitions: for example, short disputes lasting only a day or so. Any under-recording would of course particularly bear on those industries most affected by this type of stoppage, and would have much more effect on the total of stoppages than on the total of working days lost.

6 More information about definitions and qualifications affecting the statistics is given in the annual article on industrial stoppages, published in the August 1980 issue of the *Department of Employment Gazette*. The 1979 figures are included.

(b) Incidence rates in Tables A and B

7 The incidence rates in Table A are based on the numbers of stoppages *beginning* in each year and the mid-year estimates of employees in employment for the industries in question.

8 The estimates in Table B are based on the total numbers of working days lost in each year as a result of stoppages *in progress* in that year and the corresponding mid-year estimates of employees in employment for the industries shown.

9 The mid-year estimates of employees in employment were based on the count of national insurance cards in 1970, census of employment estimates for 1971 to 1977 and on quarterly estimates in 1978 and 1979.

10 Figures for stoppages in coal mining for the period December 1973–March 1974 are not available other than for the national stoppage of 10 February–8 March 1974.

Appendix 3   Industrial disputes—international comparisons 1969–78

Working days lost through industrial disputes per 1000 employees in selected industries (mining, manufacturing, construction and transport)

	1969	1970	1971	1972	1973	1974	1975	1976	1977	1978[a]	Average for 10 years 1969–78
United Kingdom	520	740	1190	2160	570	1270	540	300	840	840	897
Australia[b]	860	1040	1300	880	1080	2670	1390	1490	700	1010	1242
Belgium	100	830	720	190	520	340	340	560	420	650	467
Canada	2550	2190	800	1420	1660	2550	2810	2550	830	1930	1929
Denmark[c]	80	170	30	40	4440	330	110	220	240	90	575
Finland	200	270	3300	520	2530	470	310	1310	2360	160	1143
France	200	180	440	300	330	250	390	420	260	200	297
Germany (FR)	20	10	340	10	40	60	10	40	—	370	90
India	1270	1440	1100	1300	1330	2480	1450	830	1310	1280	1379
Irish Republic	2170	490	670	600	410	1240	810	840	1050	1630	991
Italy	4160	1730	1060	1670	2470	1800	1730	2310	1560	890	1938
Japan	200	200	310	270	210	450	390	150	70	60	231
Netherlands	10	140	50	70	330	—	—	10	140	—	75
New Zealand	300	470	350	300	530	360	390	950	810	790	525
Norway	—	70	10	—	10	490	10	70	40	90	79
Spain	130	240	190	120	210	310	370	2540	3350	1820	928
Sweden[d]	30	40	240	10	10	30	20	10	20	10	42
Switzerland	—	—	10	—	—	—	—	20	—	—	—
United States[e]	1390	2210	1600	860	750	1480	990	1190	1070	na	1282

Source: International Labour Office

Notes

(a) Provisional figures.
(b) Including electricity and gas; excluding communication.
(c) For Denmark, figures up to 1974 relate only to manufacturing, and are therefore not fully comparable with later figures which include construction and transport.
(d) For Sweden, figures up to 1971 relate to all sectors and are therefore not fully comparable with those for later years.
(e) Including gas, electricity and water.
na Not available.
— Negligible/less than five.

Appendix 3 continued
The international comparison of working days lost through industrial disputes per 1000 employees needs to be made with caution, partly owing to differences in the statistical definitions and recording methods used in the different countries and partly because of different national patterns of industrial employment combined with the varying incidence of strikes in the different industries.

In order to reduce the effects of the different industrial patterns and strike frequencies, the International Labour Office publishes the statistics given in Appendix 3 which limits the overall incidence rates to a broad economic sector consisting of the mining, manufacturing, construction and transport industries. The estimates for the UK in Appendix 3 do not therefore agree with those shown in the last two rows of statistics in Appendix 2 Table B.

The incidence rates vary considerably from year to year for most countries shown in Appendix 3. Comparisons between countries are accordingly best made by means of averages over a period of years. Over the decade 1969–1978 it may be seen from Appendix 3 that the UK was close to the middle of the range of estimates for the nineteen countries.

Appendix 4

Trade union membership 1900–1978

Trade union membership
1900–1978
United Kingdom

Year	Trade union membership as a percentage of civil workforce
1900	11·7
1910	13·4
1920	34·9
1930	26·4
1940	31·6
1950	44·3
1960	40·5
1970	44·9
1971	45·0
1972	45·8
1973	45·5
1974	46·6
1975	47·9
	(see note 3)
1975	47·2
1976	48·1
1977	49·4
1978	50·3

Notes

1 The percentages shown in Appendix 4 are based on end-year statistics of trade union membership and mid-year estimates of the UK civil workforce. These are the forms in which the relevant statistics are more readily available in the historical record, but the six months' disparity is not too serious on the evidence of alternative estimates in recent years.

2 The statistics of trade union membership relate in recent years to those organisations of workers which fall within the definition of a trade union as laid down in section 28(1) of the Trade Union and Labour Relations Act 1974.

3   There were 31 organisations previously regarded as trade unions which ceased to be so when that Act came into effect. In Appendix 4, there are accordingly two estimates for 1975, the first including membership of the 31 organisations in question, and the second excluding them.

4   The UK civil workforce, as used to derive the estimates in Appendix 4, consists of the working population, including the unemployed but excluding HM Forces.

5   The estimates of the civil workforce covering the period 1900 to 1960 are from the London and Cambridge Economic Service, *The British Economy Key Statistics 1900–1970*, Times Newspapers (1974). Data covering the years 1970 to 1978 are from the *Department of Employment Gazette*.

6   The percentages of Appendix 4 need to be considered with some caution, especially those in the earlier years. It should be borne in mind that the figures change because of the general growth in trade union membership and the long-term increase — but cyclical nature — of the labour force.

Appendix 5

Trade union abbreviations used in Part B

AAES	Association of Agricultural Education Staffs
ABS	Association of Broadcasting and Allied Staffs
ACTS	(TGWU's) Association of Clerical, Technical and Supervisory Staffs
ACTT	Association of Cinematograph, Television and Allied Technicians
AGSRO	Association of Government Supervisors and Radio Officers
AHRCO	Association of Hospital and Residential Care Officers
AIT	Association of Her Majesty's Inspectors of Taxes
AMMA	Assistant Masters' and Mistresses' Association
AMPS	Association of Management and Professional Staffs
AMU	Associated Metalworkers' Union
APAC	Association of Patternmakers and Allied Craftsmen
APC	Association of Principals of Colleges
APEX	Association of Professional, Executive, Clerical and Computer Staff
APSFO	Association of Public Service Finance Officers
APSPE	Association of Public Service Professional Engineers
ASB	Amalgamated Society of Boilermakers, Shipwrights, Blacksmiths and Structural Workers
ASLEF	Associated Society of Locomotive Engineers and Firemen
ASTMS	Association of Scientific, Technical and Managerial Staffs
ASTWKT	Amalgamated Society of Textile Workers and Kindred Trades
ASWDKW	Amalgamated Society of Wire Drawers and Kindred Workers
ATWU	Amalgamated Textile Workers' Union
AUAW	Amalgamated Union of Asphalt Workers
AUEW	Amalgamated Union of Engineering Workers
AUS	(SLADE's) Art Union Section
AUT	Association of University Teachers
BACM	British Association of Colliery Management
BALPA	British Airline Pilots' Association
BASSA	(TGWU's) British Airways Stewards' and Stewardesses' Association
BDA	British Dental Association

BESO	Bank of England Staff Organisation
BFAWU	Bakers', Food and Allied Workers' Union
BIFU	Banking, Insurance and Finance Union
BMA	British Medical Association
BRTTS	British Roll Turners' Trade Society
BTOG	British Transport Officers' Guild
CACFOA	Chief and Assistant Chief Fire Officers' Association
CATSA	(NUHKW's) Clerical, Administrative, Technical and Supervisory Association
CATU	Ceramic and Allied Trades Union
COHSE	Confederation of Health Service Employees
COSA	Colliery Officials and Staffs Area (of NUM)
CPSA	Civil and Public Services Association
CSEU	Confederation of Shipbuilding and Engineering Unions [not one trade union]
CSU	Civil Service Union
EESA	(EETPU's) Electrical and Engineering Staff Association
EETPU	Electrical, Electronic, Telecommunication and Plumbing Union
EMA	Engineers' and Managers' Association
EPEA	Electrical Power Engineers' Association [Constituent group of EMA]
Equity	British Actors' Equity Association Incorporating The Variety Artistes' Federation
FAA	Film Artistes' Association
FBU	Fire Brigades Union
FDA	Association of First Division Civil Servants
FHTU	Felt Hatters' and Trimmers' Union of Great Britain
FTAT	Furniture, Timber and Allied Trades Union
GLCSA	Greater London Council Staff Association
GMWU	National Union of General and Municipal Workers
GTS	Guild of Textile Supervisors
GULO	General Union of Associations of Loom Overlookers
HCWU	(GMWU's) Hotel and Catering Workers' Union
IOJ	Institute of Journalists
IPCS	Institution of Professional Civil Servants
IRSF	Inland Revenue Staff Federation
ISTC	Iron and Steel Trades Confederation

MATSA	(GMWU's) Managerial, Administrative, Technical and Supervisory Section
MMSA	Mercantile Marine Service Association
MNAOA	Merchant Navy and Airline Officers' Association
MPU	(ASTMS') Medical Practitioners' Union
MU	Musicians' Union
NACO	National Association of Co-operative Officials
NACODS	National Association of Colliery Overmen, Deputies and Shotfirers
NAEMS	National Association of Executives, Managers and Staffs
NAFO	National Association of Fire Officers
NAHT	National Association of Head Teachers
NALGO	National and Local Government Officers' Association
NALHM	National Association of Licensed House Managers
NASDU	National Amalgamated Stevedores' and Dockers' Union
NAS/UWT	National Association of Schoolmasters and the Union of Women Teachers
NATFHE	National Association of Teachers in Further and Higher Education
NATSOPA	National Society of Operative Printers, Graphical and Media Personnel
NATTKE	National Association of Theatrical, Television and Kine Employees
NAUTT	National Association of Unions in the Textile Trade
NCTU	Northern Carpet Trade Union
NFSP	National Federation of Sub-Postmasters
NGA	National Graphical Association
NSBGW	National Society of Brushmakers and General Workers
NSMM	National Society of Metal Mechanics
NUAAW	National Union of Agricultural and Allied Workers
NUB	National Union of Blastfurnacemen, Ore Miners, Coke Workers and Kindred Trades
NUCISE	National Union of Co-operative Insurance Society Employees [Within TGWU]
NUCS	National Union of Club Stewards
NUDAGMW	National Union of Domestic Appliance and General Metal Workers
NUDBTW	National Union of Dyers, Bleachers and Textile Workers
NUFLAT	National Union of Footwear, Leather and Allied Trades
NUGSAT	National Union of Gold, Silver and Allied Trades
NUHKW	National Union of Hosiery and Knitwear Workers
NUIW	National Union of Insurance Workers
NUJ	National Union of Journalists
NUM	National Union of Mineworkers
NUPE	National Union of Public Employees

NUR	National Union of Railwaymen
NUS	National Union of Scalemakers.
	National Union of Seamen
NUSMW	National Union of Sheet Metal Workers, Coppersmiths and Heating and Domestic Engineers
NUT	National Union of Teachers
NUTGW	National Union of Tailors and Garment Workers
PFA	Professional Footballers' Association
PLCW & TWU	Power Loom Carpet Weavers' and Textile Workers' Union
POA	Prison Officers' Association
POEU	Post Office Engineering Union
POMSA	Post Office Management Staffs' Association
REOU	Radio and Electronic Officers' Union
RUBSSO	Rossendale Union of Boot, Shoe and Slipper Operatives
SAIMA	Shipbuilding and Allied Industries Management Association
SATA	(USDAW's) Supervisory, Administrative and Technical Association
SCPS	Society of Civil and Public Servants (Executive, Directing and Analagous Grades)
SCWU	Scottish Carpet Workers' Union
SHA	Secondary Heads' Association
SIMA	Steel Industry Management Association
SLA	Stable Lads' Association
SLADE	Society of Lithographic Artists, Designers, Engravers and Process Workers
SNBRTU	Screw, Nut, Bolt and Rivet Trade Union
SOGAT	Society of Graphical and Allied Trades
SPOE	Society of Post Office Executives
STAMP	(UCATT's) Supervisory, Technical, Administrative, Managerial and Professional Section
TASS	(AUEW's) Technical, Administrative and Supervisory Section
TCOA	Telephone Contract Officers' Association
TGWU	Transport and General Workers' Union
TISCBM	Teston Independent Society of Cricket Ball Makers
TMA	Tobacco Mechanics' Association
TOG	Trawl(er) Officers' Guild
TSSA	Transport Salaried Staffs' Association

TWU	Theatre Writers' Union. Tobacco Workers' Union
UCATT	Union of Construction, Allied Trades and Technicians
UCW	Union of Communication Workers
UKAPE	(EETPU's) United Kingdom Association of Professional Engineers
URTU	United Road Transport Union
USDAW	Union of Shop, Distributive and Allied Workers
WG	Writers' Guild of Great Britain

Appendix 6

Trade unions at 31 December 1979

The list of trade unions is that maintained by the Certification Officer for Trade Unions and Employers' Associations. Membership figures are the latest available; this is normally 31 December 1978. Some figures include classes of members who may not pay contributions but who are members under the rules.

* — denotes a trade union holding a certificate of independence at 31 December 1979

† — denotes a trade union directly affiliated to the Trades Union Congress (branches areas and districts of these unions are not so indicated)

n.a. — membership figures not available or not applicable.

Name	Membership
England and Wales	
*Abbey National Staff Association	4463
Accrington and District Power Loom Overlookers Association	17
Alumasc Employees Association	137
†*Amalgamated Assocation of Beamers Twisters and Drawers (Hand and Machine)	1123
Amalgamated Association of Beamers Twisters and Drawers (Hand and Machine) Preston and District Branch	204
†*Amalgamated Felt Hat Trimmers Wool Formers and Allied Workers Association	623
†*Amalgamated Society of Boilermakers Shipwrights Blacksmiths and Structural Workers	131 099
†*Amalgamated Society of Journeymen Felt Hatters and Allied Workers	563
†*Amalgamated Society of Textile Workers and Kindred Trades	5959
†*Amalgamated Society of Wire Drawers and Kindred Workers	10 784
*Amalgamated Society of Woolcomb Hackle and Gill Makers	76
Amalgamated Tape Sizers Friendly Protection Society	35
Amalgamated Textile Trades Union Wigan Chorley and Skelmersdale District	1200
*Amalgamated Textile Warehousemen	2800

*Amalgamated Textile Warehousemen (Bolton and District Branch)	1251
†*Amalgamated Textile Workers Union	39 864
*Amalgamated Textile Workers Union — Oldham AWA Division	1900
*Amalgamated Textile Workers Union Rochdale Todmorden Heywood Bury	3620
*Amalgamated Textile Workers Union (Southern Area)	1858
*Amalgamated Textile Workers Union — Staff Section	1298
†*Amalgamated Union of Asphalt Workers	2492
Amalgamated Union of Block Printers of Great Britain and Ireland	14
†Amalgamated Union of Engineering Workers	n.a.
†*Amalgamated Union of Engineering Workers (Constructional Section)	35 235
†*Amalgamated Union of Engineering Workers — Engineering Section	1 199 465
†*Amalgamated Union of Engineering Workers Foundry Section	58 728
†*Amalgamated Union of Engineering Workers Technical Administrative and Supervisory Section	200 954
A Monk and Company Staff Association	793
*Anglia Hastings and Thanet Building Society Staff Association	877
Arts Council of Great Britain Staff Association	172
*Assistant Masters and Mistresses Association	n.a.
†*Associated Metalworkers Union	5262
†*Associated Society of Locomotive Engineers and Firemen	27 738
Association for Adult and Continuing Education	3541
Association of Agricultural Education Staffs	940
Association of British Dental Surgery Assistants	n.a.
†*Association of Broadcasting and Allied Staffs	14 247
*Association of Cambridge University Assistants	1192
Association of Career Teachers	211
†*Association of Cinematograph Television and Allied Technicians	20 540
*Association of Clinical Biochemists Limited	1863
*Association of Community Home Schools	337
*Association of Education Officers	524
†*Association of First Division Civil Servants	5663
Association of Football League Referees and Linesmen	n.a.
†*Association of Government Supervisors and Radio Officers	12 259
*Association of Her Majestys Inspectors of Taxes	2486
Association of HSDE (Hatfield) Employees	530
Association of Local Authority Chief Architects	173

310

*Association of Local Authority Chief Executives	464
Association of Local Government Lawyers	n.a.
Association of London Transport Officers	104
*Association of Magisterial Officers	3100
*Association of Management and Professional Staffs	7862
*Association of Managerial Staff of the National Bus Company and Subsidiary Companies	1114
*Association of National Health Service Officers	5179
*Association of Nurse Administrators	1053
*Association of Official Architects	535
Association of Operative Cotton Spinners of Haslingden and Surrounding Neighbourhood	109
*Association of Optical Practitioners Limited	4444
*Association of Passenger Transport Executives and Managers	151
†*Association of Patternmakers and Allied Craftsmen	9706
*Association of Planning Officers	424
Association of Plastic Operatives and Engineers	198
*Association of Polytechnic Teachers	2972
*Association of Principals of Colleges	649
†*Association of Professional Executive Clerical and Computer Staff (APEX)	152 543
*Association of Public Service Finance Officers	2997
*Association of Public Service Professional Engineers	2017
†*Association of Scientific Technical and Managerial Staffs	471 000
Association of Somerset Inseminators	32
Association of Staff of Probation Hostels	n.a.
†*Association of University Teachers	29 248
Association of Vice Principals of Colleges	124
Australian Mutual Provident Society Staff Association	157
†*Bakers Food and Allied Workers Union	54 912
Balfour Beatty Group Staff Association	1790
†*Banking Insurance and Finance Union	126 343
*Bank of England Staff Organisation	4715
Bank of New Zealand (London) Staff Association	172
*Barclays Group Staff Association	35 517
Beamers Twisters and Drawers Hand and Machine of Blackburn and Bolton Districts	270
Birmingham and District Association of Club Stewards and Hotel Managers	74
*Blackburn and District Amalgamated Power Loom Overlookers Association	400
Blackburn and District Tape-Sizers Society	49
*Blackburn and District Weavers Winders and Warpers Association	1750

*Bolton and District Powerloom Overlookers Trade Sick and Burial Association	269
*Bolton and District Power Loom Weavers Winders Warpers Loom Sweepers and Ancillary Workers Association	2005
*Bolton and District Union of Textile and Allied Workers	5045
*Bradford and Bingley Building Society Staff Association	893
Bradford and District Power Loom Overlookers Society	649
Britannia Airways Staff Association	n.a.
Britannic Assurance Chief Office Staff Association	587
*Britannic Field Staff Association	3305
†*British Actors Equity Association Incorporating the Variety Artistes Federation	27 152
*British Aerospace (Dynamics Group) Employees Association	530
*British Aircraft Corporation Limited Senior Staff Association	929
†*British Airline Pilots Association	6026
†*British Association of Colliery Management	16 872
*British Association of Occupational Therapists Limited	6190
*British Cement Staffs Association	2965
British Ceramic Research Association Staff Association	211
*British Dental Association	11 748
*British Federation of Textile Technicians	n.a.
*British Fire Service Federation	1006
British Hospital Doctors Federation	8674
*British Medical Association	64 966
*British Orthoptic Society	844
†*British Roll Turners Trade Society	673
*British Transport Officers Guild	2293
Burmah Engineering Senior Staff Union	98
Burnley and District Branch of the Amalgamated Associaton of Twisters and Drawers (Hand and Machine)	74
Burnley and District Tape Sizers Protective Society	37
*Burnley Building Society Staff Association	589
Burnley Nelson Rossendale and District Textile Workers Union	6069
Cadbury Limited Representatives Association	382
*Cadbury Schweppes Senior Managers Association	1300
Cadbury Typhoo Representatives Association	256
Cantonian High School Staff Association	93
Card Dressers Society	25
†*Card Setting Machine Tenters Society	132
Carlsberg Brewery Staff Association	40

Central Trustee Savings Bank Staff Association	n.a.
†*Ceramic and Allied Trades Union	51 219
*Chartered Society of Physiotheraphy	35 104
*Chelsea Building Society Staff Association	237
Chemistry Societies Staff Association	246
*Chief and Assistant Chief Fire Officers Association	165
Church and Oswaldtwistle Power-Loom Overlookers Society	36
†*Civil and Public Services Association	224 780
Civil Service National Whitley Council — Staff Side	n.a.
†*Civil Service Union	46 928
*Clerical and Secretarial Staffs Association of the University of Liverpool	448
Clerical Medical and General Staff Association	733
†*Cloth Pressers Society	40
Colman Association of Staff	401
*Colne and Craven Textile Workers Association	1560
*Colne and District Power Loom Overlookers Association	213
*Colne and District Textile Warehouse Association	480
*Colne District of the Amalgamated Association of Twisters and Drawers	278
Commercial Bank of Australia (London) Staff Association	166
*Commercial Union Group Staff Association	7320
*Community and Youth Service Association	1340
*Confederation of Bank Staff Associations	n.a.
Confederation of Employee Organisations	n.a.
†*Confederation of Health Service Employees	215 246
Construction Industry Training Board Staff Association	111
Corporation of London Staff Association	1403
*COSESA	3977
*Coventry Economic Building Society Staff Association	229
Cumberland Colliery Officials Association	114
Dean Clough Staff Association	298
Derbyshire Building Society Staff Association	266
Design Council Staff Association	61
Dexion (Hourly Paid Staff) Union	533
Diplomatic Service Association	827
*Eagle Star Staff Association	5681
Economist Bookshop Staff Association	n.a.
Electrical and Mechanical Instrument Makers Association	105

313

†*Electrical Electronic Telecommunication and Plumbing
    Union 438 269
*EMI Electronics Limited Junior and Middle Management
    Staff Association 136
Engineering Inspectors Association 50
Engineering Officers Technical Association n.a.
†*Engineers and Managers Association 47 000
English China Clays Staff Association 1700
English Chiropodists Association 283

Federation of Cadbury Schweppes Representatives
    Associations n.a.
*Federation of Nursing Personnel 1293
Federation of Professional Officers Associations 4865
†*Film Artistes Association 2203
†*Fire Brigades Union 40 097
Football League Secretaries Managers and Coaches
    Association 500
Football Pools Collectors Union 579
*Foremens Association of the British Aircraft Corporation 373
Limited Military Aircraft Division
†*Furniture Timber and Allied Trades Union 84 944

General Dental Practitioners Association 2096
General Federation of Trade Unions n.a.
General Telephone Systems Ltd and Associated
    Companies Staff Association n.a.
†*General Union of Associations of Loom Overlookers 2548
*Greater London Council Staff Association 17 186
*Grindlays Staff Association 304
Guild of County Land Agents and Valuers 33
Guild of Directors of Social Services 101
*Guild of Local Authority Valuers and Estate Surveyors 90
*Guild of Medical Secretaries 420
*Guild of Professional Teachers of Dancing 310
*Guild of Senior Officers of the Greater London Council
    and the Inner London Education Authority 705
*Guild of Textile Supervisors 307
*Guild of Water Service Senior Officers 432
*Guinness Brewing Staff Association (UK) 1034
*Guinness (Park Royal) Supervisory Association 67

Halcrow Staff Association 350
Halifax Building Society Staff Association n.a.

*Lancashire Box Packing Case and General Woodworkers Friendly Relief Sick Superannuation and Burial Society	642
Leeds and District Power Loom Overlookers Society	145
*Leek and Westbourne Staff Association	981
*Legal and General Staff Association	430
*Leicester Building Society Staff Association	1000
Leicestershire Overmen Deputies and Shotfirers Association	414
Leisure and General Holdings Staff Association	75
*Liverpool Victoria Section of the National Union of Insurance Workers	3114
*Lloyds Bank Group Staff Association	21 247
Lloyds Register (UK) Staff Association	1192
Lloyds Staff Association	23
London Jewel Case and Jewellery Display Makers Union	17
*London Society of Tie Cutters	59
*Lufthansa Staff Association United Kingdom	177
Managerial Staff Association of the Provincial Insurance Group of Companies	104
Manchester Pilots Association	73
Manchester Salford and District Society of Brewers and General Coopers	55
†*Merchant Navy and Airline Officers Association	43 750
†*Military and Orchestral Musical Instrument Makers Trade Society	220
National Amalgamated Stevedores and Dockers	3722
†*National and Local Government Officers Association	729 405
National Association of Chief Housing Officers	95
†*National Association of Colliery Overmen Deputies and Shotfirers	19 571
National Association of Colliery Overmen Deputies and Shotfirers Cannock Chase Area	499
National Association of Colliery Overmen Deputies and Shotfirers Durham Area	1810
National Association of Colliery Overmen Deputies and Shotfirers Midland Area	4122
National Association of Colliery Overmen Deputies and Shotfirers (North Staffordshire Area)	840
National Association of Colliery Overmen Deputies and Shotfirers (Northumberland Area)	830
National Association of Colliery Overmen Deputies and Shotfirers North Western Area	947
National Association of Colliery Overmen Deputies and Shotfirers (South Wales Area)	2026

National Association of Colliery Overmen Deputies and Shotfirers (Yorkshire Area)	8187
†*National Association of Co-operative Officials	5920
*National Association of Executives Managers and Staffs	1317
*National Association of Fire Officers	3924
National Association of Grooms	n.a.
*National Association of Head Teachers	22 330
National Association of Heads and Matrons of Assessment Centres	108
*National Association of Inspectors and Educational Advisers	1262
†*National Association of Licensed House Managers	15 486
*National Association of NFU Group Secretaries	437
National Association of Power-Loom Overlookers	410
*National Association of Probation Officers	4763
†*National Association of Schoolmasters and the Union of Women Teachers	140 701
†*National Association of Teachers in Further and Higher Education	69 450
†*National Association of Theatrical Television and Kine Employees	17.000
*National Association of Unions in the Textile Trade	n.a.
National Federation of Sub-Postmasters	19 649
†*National Graphical Association	109 904
†*National League of the Blind and Disabled	4250
*National Owner Drivers Association UK	1119
†*National Society of Brushmakers and General Workers	1637
†*National Society of Metal Mechanics	50 494
†*National Society of Operative Printers Graphical and Media Personnel	54 786
*National Tile Faience and Mosaic Fixers Society	247
National Unilever Managers Association	3656
†*National Union of Agricultural and Allied Workers	73 574
†*National Union of Blastfurnacemen Ore Miners Coke Workers and Kindred Trades	14 366
*National Union of Club Stewards	2800
National Union of Co-operative Insurance Agents	24
*National Union of Co-operative Insurance Society Employees	2863
†*National Union of Domestic Appliance and General Metal Workers	5155
†*National Union of Dyers Bleachers and Textile Workers	58 803
*National Union of Flint Glassworkers	2208
†*National Union of General and Municipal Workers	964 836
†*National Union of Gold Silver and Allied Trades	3094
National Union of Hebrew Teachers of Great Britain and Ireland	173

†*National Union of Hosiery and Knitwear Workers	72 858
†*National Union of Insurance Workers	20 131
*National Union of Insurance Workers Prudential Section	13 212
*National Union of Insurance Workers Royal Liver and Composite Section	1355
*National Union of Insurance Workers Royal London Section	2422
†*National Union of Journalists	30 978
†*National Union of Lock and Metal Workers	6508
†*National Union of Mineworkers	371 470
National Union of Mineworkers (Cannock Chase and Pelsall District Midland Area)	4427
National Union of Mineworkers (Cokemens Area)	7214
*National Union of Mineworkers (Colliery Officials and Staffs Area)	20 978
National Union of Mineworkers (Colliery Officials and Staffs Area) Region No. 2	4617
National Union of Mineworkers (Colliery Officials and Staffs Area) Region No. 3	2230
National Union of Mineworkers (Colliery Officials and Staffs Area) Region No. 4	4943
National Union of Mineworkers (Cumberland Area)	2212
National Union of Mineworkers (Derbyshire Area)	11 590
National Union of Mineworkers (Durham Area)	42 965
National Union of Mineworkers (Durham Enginemen Group No. 1 Area)	826
National Union of Mineworkers (Durham Mechanics Group No. 1 Area)	6503
National Union of Mineworkers (Kent Area)	4107
*National Union of Mineworkers (Leicester Area)	6179
National Union of Mineworkers (Midland Area)	14 735
National Union of Mineworkers (North Stafford Federation Midland Area)	5954
National Union of Mineworkers (Northumberland Area)	17 695
*National Union of Mineworkers (Northumberland Mechanics Group No. 1 Area)	2800
National Union of Mineworkers (North Wales Area)	1077
*National Union of Mineworkers (North Western Area)	8991
National Union of Mineworkers (North Western Area) Pendlebury Branch	750
*National Union of Mineworkers (Nottingham Area)	33 580
*National Union of Mineworkers (Power Group Area)	5000
*National Union of Mineworkers (South Derbyshire Area)	5080
National Union of Mineworkers (South Wales Area)	32 086
National Union of Mineworkers (Warwickshire District Midlands Area)	5041
*National Union of Mineworkers (Yorkshire Area)	127 233

†*National Union of Public Employees	712 392
†*National Union of Railwaymen	171 411
National Union of Recreation and Sports Employees	37
†*National Union of Scalemakers	1960
†*National Union of Seamen	39 000
†*National Union of Sheet Metal Workers Coppersmiths and Heating and Domestic Engineers	74 116
*National Union of Social Workers	431
†*National Union of Tailors and Garment Workers	116 095
†*National Union of Teachers	293 798
*National Union of Textile and Allied Workers (Rochdale Districts)	1730
†*National Union of the Footwear Leather and Allied Trades	61 789
*National Westminster Staff Association	33 906
†*National Woolsorters Society	757
*Nationwide Building Society Staff Association	2200
*Nelson and District Association of Preparatory Workers	189
Nelson and District Branch of the Amalgamated Association of Beamers Twisters and Drawers (Hand and Machine)	196
*Nelson and District Clothlookers and Warehouse Association	432
Nelson and District Powerloom Overlookers Society	520
Nelson Colne and District Tape Sizers Protective Society	111
New Towns Chief Officers Association	120
NFER Staff Association	70
*North-East Coast Tug-Boatmens Association	121
†*Northern Carpet Trades Union	2057
*Northern Colliery Officials and Staffs Association	4704
*Northern Counties Textile Trades Federation	n.a.
Northern Rock Staff Association (NORSA)	400
*Northern Textile and Allied Workers Union	2468
*Northern Lancashire and Cumbria Textile Workers Association	2286
Nottingham and District Federation of Club Stewards	93
Nottingham Dyers and Bleachers Association	466
Oldham Association of Loom Overlookers	68
*Oldham Provincial Union of Textile and Allied Workers	3880
Organisation of CPL Technicians	182
†*Pattern Weavers Society	137
Playboy Staff Association	112
*PMB Staff Association	373

Portman Staff Association	186
†*Post Office Engineering Union	121 404
†*Post Office Management Staffs Association	18 500
†*Power Loom Carpet Weavers and Textile Workers Union	6287
Pressed Glass Makers Society of Great Britain	52
*Preston and Districts Powerloom Overlookers Association	332
Preston and District Tape Sizers Association	130
Pride of Golborne Miners Lodge Trade Union and Checkweigh Fund	671
*Printing Trades Alliance	909
†*Prison Officers Association	22 189
*Professional Association of Teachers	11 226
Professional Flight Instructors Association	69
Professional Footballers Association	2593
Prosecuting Solicitors Society of England and Wales	n.a.
Provincial Building Society Staff Association	n.a.
†*Radio and Electronic Officers Union	4584
Rank Hotels Staff Association	n.a.
Redifon Flight Simulation Monthly Staff Association	168
*Retail Book Stationery and Allied Trades Employees Association	8929
*Retained Firefighters Union	7620
*Retired Officers Association	1528
Robert Hirst Staff Association	160
*Rolls-Royce Management Association	600
†*Rossendale Union of Boot Shoe and Slipper Operatives	6529
*Rowntree Mackintosh Sales Staff Association	436
*Royal College of Midwives	20 622
*Royal College of Nursing of the United Kingdom	134 389
Royal Insurance Branch Managers Association	81
RSPB Staff Association	n.a.
Rumbelows Branch Managers Association	n.a.
Schering Chemicals Representatives Association	37
Schweppes Limited Representatives Association	263
†*Screw Nut Bolt and Rivet Trade Union	2524
*Secondary Heads Association	4251
†*Sheffield Sawmakers Protection Society	241
† Sheffield Wool Shear Workers Trade Union	32
*Skipton and District Power-Loom Overlookers Association	152
Société Générale Staff Association	130
*Society of Authors Limited	2996
*Society of Chiropodists	4535

†*Society of Civil and Public Servants (Executive Directing
    and Analogous Grades) — 106 903
†*Society of Graphical and Allied Trades 1975 — 201 665
†*Society of Lithographic Artists Designers Engravers and
    Process-Workers — 25 561
*Society of Metropolitan and County Chief Librarians — 238
†*Society of Post Office Executives — 22 567
*Society of Public Analysts and Other Official Analysts — 57
*Society of Radiographers — 7786
Society of Registration Officers (Births Deaths and
    Marriages) — 1109
Society of Remedial Gymnasts — 553
†*Society of Shuttlemakers — 103
*Society of Union Employees (NUPE) — 149
*Squibb UK Staff Association — 233
Stable Lads Association — 498
Staff Association of the S W Farmer Group of Companies — 174
Staff Association of the Printing and Publishing Industry
    Training Board — 77
Staffordshire Building Society Staff Association — 233
*Star Aluminium Managerial Staff Association — 76
*Steel Industry Management Association — 11 702
*Sun Alliance and London Staff Association — 6004
*Sun Life Staff Association — 1533

*Telecommunications Staff Association — 612
*Telephone Contract Officers Association — 982
Tempered Group (Spring Division) Staff Association — 97
*Teston Independent Society of Cricket Ball Makers — 33
*Textile Manufacturing Trades Federation of Bolton and
    Surrounding Districts — n.a.
*Thames Water Staff Association — 2148
†*Tobacco Mechanics Association — 351
†*Tobacco Workers Union — 20 107
Trade Society of Machine Calico Printers — 223
†*Transport and General Workers Union — 2 072 818
†*Transport Salaried Staffs Association — 72 070
Trebor Sharps Limited Salesmens Association — 77

*Undeb Cenedlaethol Athrawon Cymru (National
    Association of the Teachers of Wales) — 2825
†*Union of Construction Allied Trades and Technicians — 325 245
*Union of County and District Secretaries — 414
†*Union of Post Office Workers — 197 157
†*Union of Shop Distributive and Allied Workers — 462 178

*United Association of Power Loom Overlookers	451
*United Friendly Agents Association	3746
*United Friendly Divisional and District Managers Association	243
United Friendly Head Office Management Association	83
United Friendly Insurance Co Ltd Assistant Managers Association	372
*United Kingdom Association of Professional Engineers	4883
†*United Road Transport Union	28 371
*Walsall Lock and Keysmiths Male and Female Trade Society	144
Whatman Reeve Angel Staff Association	131
Willerby Staff Association	244
Woolwich Independent Staff Association	n.a.
†*Writers Guild of Great Britain	1562
†*Yorkshire Association of Power Loom Overlookers	1252
*Yorkshire Society of Textile Craftsmen	913

Scotland

Aberdeen Trawl Officers Guild	161
Association of Directors of Administration in Scotland	81
*Association of Lecturers in Colleges of Education in Scotland	1193
Association of Lecturers in Scottish Central Institutions	588
District Nursing Association	n.a.
†*Educational Institute of Scotland	47 056
Glasgow and West of Scotland Power Loom Tenters Society	34
Honours Graduate Teachers Association	169
National Association of Colliery Overmen Deputies and Shotfirers (Scottish Area)	2076
National Union of Mineworkers Group 2 Scottish	

Colliery Enginemen Boilermen and Tradesmens Association	4850
Professional Staff Association of Scottish Woodland Owners Association (Commercial) Ltd	28
Scottish Approved Schools Staff Association	309
Scottish Association of Amenity Supervisory Staffs	119
Scottish Association of Local Government and Educational Psychologists	175
Scottish Association of Nurse Administrators	351
*Scottish Carpet Workers Union	5039
Scottish Equitable Staff Association	490
*Scottish Further Education Association	1732
*Scottish Health Visitors Association	850
Scottish Joint Industry Board for the Electrical Contracting Industry	823
†*Scottish Union of Power Loom Overlookers	250
*Scottish Prison Officers Association	2553
*Scottish Secondary Teachers Association	8493

Appendix 7

Employers' associations at 31 December 1979

This list of employers' associations has been compiled from information available at the Certification Office for Trade Unions and Employers' Associations. Those names entered in the statutory list of employers' associations under section 8 of the Trade Union and Labour Relations Act 1974 are marked with an asterisk.

England and Wales
*Advertising Film and Videotape Producers Association
  Amalgamated Master Dairymen Limited
*Apparel and Fashion Industrys Association
*Art Studios Photographic Laboratories Association
  Asbestos Association Limited
  Association of British Launderers and Cleaners Limited
*Association of British Orchestras
  Association of British Plywood and Veneer Manufacturers
  Association of British Roofing Felt Manufacturers Limited
*Association of Circus Proprietors of Great Britain
*Association of Clothing Contractors
*Association of Glass Container Manufacturers
  Association of Master Lightermen and Barge Owners (Port of London)
*Association of Midland Advertising Agencies
*Association of Northern Advertising Agencies
*Association of Northern Master Electrotypers and Stereotypers
  Association of Port Employers for the Medway & Adjacent Ports & Harbours
  Association of Reclaimed Textile Processors
*Association of Specialised Film Producers
  Association of Street Lighting Erection Contractors
  Association of Touring and Producing Managers

  Bacon and Meat Manufacturers Industrial Group
  Birmingham and West Midland Furniture Manufacturers
*Birmingham Horse and Motor Vehicle Owners Association
*Birmingham Wholesale Fruit Flower and Potato Merchants Association
*Blackburn District Textile Manufacturers Association
*Bolton and District Textile Employers Association
  Borough Market Tenants Association Limited

Boston Port Employers Association
Bradford and Leeds Textile Manufacturers Federation
Bristol and West of England Provision Trade Association
Bristol West of England and South Wales Clothing Manufacturers
    Association
*British Amusement Catering Trades Association
*British Association of Lithographic Plate Manufacturers
 British Ball Clay Producers Federation Limited
*British Brush Manufacturers Association
*British Carton Association
*British Ceramic Manufacturers Federation
*British Decorators Association
 British Electro-Ceramic Manufacturers Association
*British Exhibition Contractors Association
*British Film Producers Association Limited
 British Furniture Manufacturers Federated Association
 British Headwear Industries Federation
 British Jewellery and Giftwear Federation Limited
*British Lace Federation
 British Leather Goods Manufacturers Association
*British Leavers Lace Manufacturers Association
*British Lock Manufacturers Association
*British Paper and Board Industry Federation Limited
*British Paper Bag Federation
*British Paper Box Association
*British Precast Concrete Federation Limited
*British Printing Industries Federation
*British Ready Mixed Concrete Association
 British Rubber Manufacturers Association Limited
*British Scrap Federation
 British Secondary Metal Association
*British Shipping Federation
 British Surgical Trades Association (Incorporated)
 British Textile By-Products Association
*British Textile Employers Association (Cotton Man-made and Allied
    Fibres)
 British Wool Confederation
 Builders Merchants Federation
 Bury and District Federation of Cotton Spinners and Manufacturers

Cardiff and Penarth Port Employers Association
Cement Makers Federation
*Central Lancashire Engineering Employers Association
Chemical Industries Association Limited
Chestnut Fencing Manufacturers Society
*China Clay Association

*Cinematograph Exhibitors Association of Great Britain and Ireland
*Clothing Manufacturers Federation of Great Britain
 Coach Operators Federation (Southern and Western Counties)
 Coal Merchants Federation of Great Britain
 Cocoa Chocolate and Confectionery Manufacturers Industrial Group
 Conference of Omnibus Companies
*Contractors Plant Association
*Co-operative Employers Association
 Cordage and Net Manufacturers (Employers) Association
 Corsetry Manufacturers Association
 Covent Garden Tenants Association Limited
*Coventry and District Engineering Employers Association
 Cutlery and Silverwear Manufacturers Association of the United Kingdom

 Dairy Trade Federation
 Display Producers and Screen Printers Association Limited
 Durham and Northumberland Furniture Manufacturers Association
 Dyers and Finishers Association

*East Anglian Printing Industries Alliance
 East Anglian Sawmill Owners Association
*East Anglian Ship and Boat Building Employers Association
 East Cornwall Port Employers Association
*Eastern Representative Provincial Organisation of Local Authority
    Employers for Administrative Professional Technical and Clerical
    Services and Manual Worker Services
 East Midlands Brick Association
*East Midlands Engineering Employers Association
*East Midlands Local Authorities Employers Organisation
 East Midland Timber Trade Association
*Electrical Contractors Association
 Employers Association of the Port of Liverpool
*Employers Federation of Card Clothing Manufacturers
*Engineering and Shipbuilding Employers Association — Yorkshire and
    Humberside
*Engineering Employers Association of South Lancashire Cheshire and
    North Wales
*Engineering Employers East Anglian Association
*Engineering Employers Federation
*Engineering Employers London Association
*Engineering Employers Association of South Wales
*Engineering Employers Sheffield Association
*Engineering Employers West of England Association
*Essex and Hertfordshire Representative Provincial Organisation of Local
    Authority Employers (for Administrative Professional Technical and
    Clerical Services and Manual Worker Services)

*Federation of Bakers
*Federation of Civil Engineering Contractors
*Federation of Design and Engineering Contractors
*Federation of Dredging Contractors
*Federation of London Clearing Bank Employers
*Federation of London Wholesale Newspaper Distributors
*Federation of Master Builders
*Federation of Master Organ Builders
*Federation of Medium and Small Employers
 Federation of Merchant Tailors
 Federation of Paper Tube Manufacturers
 Federation of Public Passenger Transport Employers
 Federation of Reclaimed Industries
 Federation of Specialised Film Associations
 Felt Roofing Contractors Employers Association
 Fencing Contractors Association
*Fibre Reclaimers Federation
 Fibreboard Packing Case Manufacturers Association
 Food Manufacturers Industrial Group
 Freight Transport Association

 General Council of British Shipping
 Glass and Glazing Federation
*Graphic Reproduction Federation
 Grimsby and Immingham Docks Association of Port Employers
*Grimsby Fishing Vessel Owners Association

*Hampshire Yacht and Boat Builders Association
*Heating and Ventilating Contractors Association
 Hebden Bridge and District Wholesale Clothiers Association
 Heywood and District Cotton Employers Association Limited
 High Wycombe Furniture Manufacturers Society
*Hinckley and District Knitting Industry Association
 Home Counties Printing Industries Alliance
 Home Timber Merchants Association of England and Wales
*Hull Association of Port Labour Employers
*Hull Fishing Industry Association
*Hull Master Stevedores Association
 Hull Ship Labour Contractors Association

 Incorporated Guild of Hairdressers Wigmakers and Perfumers
 Incorporated National Association of British and Irish Millers Limited
*Independent Steel Employers Association
 Industrial Leathers Federation
*Institute of Iron and Steel Wire Manufacturers

*Kent Ship and Boat Building Employers Association
Kentish Ragstone Association
Kidderminster District Carpet Manufacturers and Spinners Association
Kingswood and District Boot Manufacturers Association
*Knitted Textile Dyers Federation
Knitting Industries Federation Limited

Lace and Warp Knit Dyers Association Limited
*Lancashire and Cheshire Printing Industries Alliance
Lancashire Footwear Manufacturers Association
*Leather Producers Association
Leeds and District Boot and Shoe Manufacturers Association Limited
Leeds and Northern Clothing Manufacturers Association
*Leek and District Manufacturers and Dyers Association
Leicester and County Footwear Manufacturers Association
Leicester and District Hosiery Manufacturers Association Limited
Liverpool and District Millers Association
Liverpool Meat Importers Association
Liverpool United Warehouse-Keepers Conference
London and District Sawmill Owners Association
*London and District Scaling Employers Association
*London and South Eastern Furniture Manufacturers Association
London Association of Funeral Directors
*London Association of Shore Gang Contractors
*London Dress Makers and Allied Contractors Association
*London Enclosed Docks Employers Association
London Fish Merchants (Billingsgate) Limited
London Footwear Manufacturers Association
*London Printing Industries Association
London Wharfingers Association Limited
Loughborough and District Hosiery Manufacturers Association
*Lowestoft Fishing Industry Association

Macclesfield Textile Manufacturers Association
Manchester Packing Case Employers Federation
Manchester Provision Exchange Limited
Manchester Wholesale Meat Salesmens Association
Master Carvers Association
Master Tanners Association
*Mastic Asphalt Council and Employers Federation Limited
Meat Carriers Association (Southern) Limited
Medway Public Wharfingers Association
*Medway Shiprepairers Association
*Merseyside Master Boatmen and Dock Pilots Association
Metal Packaging Manufacturers Association

328

*Mid-Anglian Engineering Employers Association
*Mid-Southern Representative Provincial Organisation of Employers Local
    Authorities Services
 Midland Bacon Curers Association
 Midland Federation of Brick and Tile Manufacturers
*Midland Printing Industries Alliance
 Midlands Area Coach and Transport Association
*Multiple Food Retailers Employers Association
*Multiple Shoe Retailers Association
*Multiwall Sack Manufacturers Employers Association
*Music Trades Association Limited

 Narrow Fabrics Federation
 National Association of Cycle and Motor Cycle Traders
*National Association of Glove Manufacturers
 National Association of Inland Waterway Carriers
*National Association of Master Bakers Confectioners and Caterers
*National Association of Plumbing Heating and Mechanical Services
    Contractors
 National Association of Port Employers
 National Association of Port Employers (South Wales Group)
 National Association of Port Employers (South West Group)
*National Association of Restaurant Engineers
 National Association of Shoe Repair Factories
 National Association of Soft Drinks Manufacturers Limited
 National Bedding Federation Limited
*National Building and Allied Hardware Manufacturers Federation
 National Childrens Wear Association of Great Britain and Northern Ireland
 National Farmers Union
*National Federation of Building Trades Employers
 National Federation of Clay Industries
*National Federation of Master Window Cleaners
*National Federation of Retail Newsagents
 National Federation of Roofing Contractors
 National Federation of Wholesale Grocers and Provision Merchants
*National Fillings Trades Association
 National Food and Drink Federation
*National Hairdressers Federation
*National Master Farriers Blacksmiths and Agricultural Engineers
    Association
 National Master Tile Fixers Association
*National Pharmaceutical Association Limited
*National Sawmilling Association
 National Small Bacon Curers Association
*National Society of Provincial Wholesale Sunday Newspaper Distributors
*National Trainers Federation

*National Union of Small Shopkeepers of Great Britain and Northern
   Ireland
 Newport (Mon) Port Employers Association
*Newspaper Publishers Association Limited
*Newspaper Society
 Northamptonshire Footwear Manufacturers Association
*North East Association of Small Mines
 North East Brewers Association
 North East Coast Fishing Vessel Owners Association Limited
 North East Coast Timber Trade Association
 North Eastern Lime and Limestone Association
*North Eastern Printing Industries Alliance
 North East Lancashire Furnishing Trades Employers Association
*North East Lancashire Textile Manufacturers Association
 Northern Brick Federation
 Northern Furniture Manufacturers Association
*North Lancashire Textile Employers Association
 North Midlands Lime and Limestone Association
*North of England Engineering Employers Association
*North Wales Slate Quarries Association
*North Western Master Printers Alliance
 North West Furniture Trades Federation
*North West Lancashire Engineering Employers Association
 North West Timber Trade Association
 Norwich Footwear Manufacturers Association
 Nottingham and East Midlands Furniture Manufacturers Association

*Office Machines and Equipment Federation
 Oil and Chemical Plant Constructors Association
 Oldham and District Textile Employers Association Limited
*Overall Manufacturers Association of Great Britain

 Paint Makers Association of Great Britain Limited
 Piano Manufacturers Association Limited
 Port Employers Association (North East Coast Group)
 Port Employers Association (Tyne and Wear Area)
 Port of Bristol Employers Association
 Port of Plymouth Employers Association
*Printing Industries Alliance of Wales
*Provincial Wholesale Newspaper Distributors Association
 Publishers Association

 Radio Electrical and Television Retailers Association (RETRA) Limited
 Reclamation Association

Refractory Contractors Association
Refractory Users Federation
*Representative National Organisation of Employers of Local Authorities
    Administrative Professional Technical and Clerical Services
*Representative National Organisation of Employers of Local Authorities
    Services (Manual Workers)
*Representative National Organisation of Employers of New Towns Staffs
*Representative Organisation of Local Authorities Services (Building and
    Civil Engineering)
*Representative Organisation of the North Eastern Provincial Employers of
    Local Authorities Administrative Professional Technical and Clerical
    Services
*Representative Organisation of the Northern Provincial Employers of Local
    Authorities Services (Manual Workers)
*Representative Organisation of the South Western Provincial Employers of
    Local Authorities Services (Administrative Professional Technical and
    Clerical)
*Representative Organisation of the South Western Provincial Employers of
    Local Authorities Services (Manual Workers)
*Representative Organisation of the Western Provincial Employers of Local
    Authorities Services (Manual Workers)
River Tees Port Employers Association
Road Haulage Association Limited
*Rochdale and Yorkshire Textile Employers Association
*Rochdale Engineering Employers Association

Sand and Gravel Association Limited
Sheerness Port Employers Association
Sheffield Cabinet Case Manufacturers Association
Sheffield Lighter Trades Industrial Section
Sheffield Spoon and Fork Blank Manufacturers Association
*Shirt Collar and Tie Manufacturers Federation
Ship and Boat Builders National Federation
Silica and Moulding Sands Association
Silsden and District Manufacturers Association
*Showmens Guild of Great Britain
*Slag Employers Association
*Smithfield Market Tenants Association London
Soap Candle and Edible Fat Trades Employers Federation
*Society of British Printing Ink Manufacturers
Society of Master Saddlers Limited
Society of West End Theatre Managers
*South Eastern Local Authorities Employers Organisation
South East Timber Association
*Southern Representative Provincial Organisation of Employers Local
    Authorities Professional Technical and Clerical Services

South Staffordshire Coal Merchants Association
South Staffordshire Iron and Steel Association
South Wales Footwear Manufacturers Association
*South Western Master Printers Alliance
South Western Roadstone Employers Federation
Southampton Port Employers Association
Spitalfields Market Tenants Association Limited
St Crispins Boot Trades Association Limited
*Stourbridge Crystal Glass Manufacturers Association
Stratford Market Tenants Association Limited
Street Association of Boot and Shoe Manufacturers
Surgical Textiles Conference
Swansea Port Employers Association

Tees Wharf Operators Association
*Test and County Cricket Board
Textile Comb Making Employers Federation
*Thames Ship and Boat Builders Association
Theatres National Committee
Theatrical Management Association
Thermal Insulation Contractors Association
*Timber Packaging and Pallet Confederation
Tobacco Industry Employers Association
Tyne Tug Owners Association

United Kingdom Fellmongers Association
United Kingdom Jute Goods Association Limited

*Vehicle Builders and Repairers Association

Wall Covering Manufacturers Association of Great Britain Limited
*Welsh Engineers and Founders Association
Western International Market Tenants Association Limited
West Mercia and Mid Wales Area Joint Industrial Council Employers Side
*West Midlands Engineering Employers Association
West of England and South Wales Furniture Manufacturers Association
West of England Wool Textiles Employers Association
*West Yorkshire and Lancashire Wool (and Allied) Textile Federation
*Wool (and Allied) Textile Employers Council
*Wollen and Worsted Trades Federation
*Woollen Yarn Spinners Federation
Worsted Spinners Federation Limited

332

Yeovil and District Association of Glove Manufacturers

Yorkshire and Humberside Representative Provincial Organisation of Employers Local Authorities Administrative Professional Technical and Clerical Services

Yorkshire and Humberside Representative Provincial Organisation of Employers Local Authorities Services (Manual Workers)

*Yorkshire Glass Manufacturers Association

*Yorkshire Printing Industries Alliance

Scotland

Aberdeen and District Building Trades Employers Association

Aberdeen Banff Moray and Kincardine Master Butchers Association

Aberdeen Fish Curers and Merchants Association Limited

*Aberdeen Granite Association

Angus and Kincardine Master Plumbers Association

Argyll Building Trades Employers Association

*Association of Floor Covering Contractors (Scotland)

*Association of Jute Spinners and Manufacturers

*Association of Scottish Advertising Agencies

Association of Scottish Bacon Curers

Ayrshire Master Builders and Joiners Association

Brewers Association of Scotland

British Fellmongers Association (Foreign Skins)

British Herring Trade Association Limited

Central Counties Plumbing and Mechanical Services

Central Scotland Whinstone Association

Clydesdale Wrights and Builders Association

Clyde Ship Riggers and Scalers Employers Association

Dumbarton and District Master Wrights Builders Association

Dundee and District Master Plumbers Association

East Scotland Quarrymasters Association

Edinburgh Leith and District Plumbing Employers Association

*Electrical Contractors Association of Scotland

*Federation of Scottish Bank Employers

Fife and Kinross Master Plumbers Association

*Flaxspinners and Manufacturers Association of Great Britain
Forth Valley Building Trades Employers Association

Glasgow and District Fishmongers and Poulterers Association
*Glasgow and District Retail Fleshers Association
Glasgow and West of Scotland Master Slaters Association
Glasgow and West of Scotland Plumbing Employers Association
*Glasgow Area Federation of Community Based Housing Associations
Glasgow Port Employers Association
Glasgow Wholesale Fruit and Vegetables Trades Employers Association
Grangemouth Dock Labour Employers Association
Greenock and District Building Trades (Employers Federation)
Greenock Port Employers Association

*Hawick Knitwear Manufacturers Association
*Hebridean Spinners Advisory Committee

Inverness and Northern District Master Plumbers Association

Jute Importers Association Limited

Lanarkshire Master Plumbers and Domestic Engineers (Employers)
Association
Lochaber Building Employers Association

Made-up Textiles Association Limited
*Malt Distillers Association of Scotland
Moray and Banff Master Plumbers Association

National Association of Port Employers (Scottish Group)
National Association of Wholesale Meat Salesmen of Scotland
*National Cooperage Federation
National Farmers Union of Scotland

Paisley and District Building Trades Employers Association
Perth and District Building Trades Employers Association
Perth and District Master Plumbers Association
Peterhead Master Builders Association

*Scottish and Northern Ireland Plumbing Employers Federation
*Scottish Association of Marine Electrical Contractors
  Scottish Association of Master Bakers
  Scottish Association of Master Blacksmiths
  Scottish Association of Soft Drinks Manufacturers Limited
  Scottish Bobbin and Shuttle Manufacturers Association
  Scottish Clothing Manufacturers Association
*Scottish Daily Newspaper Society
*Scottish Decorators Federation
*Scottish East Coast Association of Shiprepairers and Shipbuilders
  Scottish Employers Council for the Clay Industries
*Scottish Engineering Employers Association
  Scottish Federation of Merchant Tailors
  Scottish Flour Millers Association
  Scottish Furniture Manufacturers Association
*Scottish Glass Merchants and Glaziers Association
*Scottish Grocery Trade Employers Association
  Scottish Hardware Association
*Scottish House Furnishers Federation
  Scottish Knitwear Association
*Scottish Lace and Window Furnishing Association
  Scottish Leather Producers Association
  Scottish Licensed Trade Association
  Scottish Light Clothing Manufacturers Association
  Scottish Master Wrights and Builders Association
  Scottish National Federation of Building Trades Employers
  Scottish National Federation of Packing Case Manufacturers
*Scottish Newspaper Proprietors Association
*Scottish Pharmaceutical Federation
  Scottish Potato Trade Association
  Scottish Pre-Cast Concrete Manufacturers Association
*Scottish Timber Merchants and Sawmillers Association
  Scottish Wirework Manufacturers Association
*Scottish Woollen Trade Employers Association
  Skinners Association of Scotland
*Society of Master Printers of Scotland
  South West Scotland Building Trades (Employers) Association
  Stornaway Dock Employers Association

  Wholesale Grocers Association of Scotland

Appendix 8

Wages Councils at 31 December 1979

Great Britain, England and Wales, Scotland
Aerated Waters (England and Wales)
Aerated Waters (Scotland)
Boot and Shoe Repairing (Great Britain)
Button Manufacturing (Great Britain)
Coffin Furniture and Cerement Making (Great Britain)
Corset
Cotton Waste Reclamation (Great Britain)
Dressmaking and Women's Light Clothing (England and Wales)
Dressmaking and Women's Light Clothing (Scotland)
Flax and Hemp (Great Britain)
Fur (Great Britain)
General Waste Materials Reclamation (Great Britain)
Hairdressing Undertakings (Great Britain)
Hat, Cap and Millinery (Great Britain)
Lace Finishing (Great Britain)
Laundry (Great Britain)
Licensed Non-residential Establishment
Licensed Residential Establishment and Licensed Restaurant
Linen and Cotton Handkerchief and Household Goods and Linen Piece
    Goods (Great Britain)
Made-up Textiles (Great Britain)
Ostrich and Fancy Feather and Artificial Flower (Great Britain)
Perambulator and Invalid Carriage (Great Britain)
Pin, Hook and Eye, and Snap Fastener (Great Britain)
Ready-made and Wholesale Bespoke Tailoring (Great Britain)
Retail Bespoke Tailoring (Great Britain)
Retail Food and Allied Trades (Great Britain)
Retail Trades (Non-Food) (Great Britain)
Rope, Twine and Net (Great Britain)
Rubber Proofed Garment Making Industry
Sack and Bag (Great Britain)
Shirtmaking (Great Britain)
Toy Manufacturing (Great Britain)
Unlicensed Place of Refreshment
Wholesale Mantle and Costume (Great Britain)

Appendix 9

Institutions

Advisory, Conciliation and Arbitration Service
  Head Office, Cleland House, Page Street, London SW1P 4ND
British Institute of Management
  Management House, Parker Street, London WC2B 5PT
Central Arbitration Committee
  1 The Abbey Garden, Great College Street, London SW1P 3SE
Central Office of Industrial Tribunals for England and Wales
  93 Ebury Bridge Road, London SW1W 8RE
Central Office of Industrial Tribunals for Scotland
  St Andrew House, 141 West Nile Street, Glasgow G1 2RU
Certification Office for Trade Unions and Employers' Associations
  Vincent House Annexe, Hide Place, London SW1P 4NG
Commission of the European Communities
  Rue de la Loi 200, 1049 Brussels, Belgium
Commission for Racial Equality
  Elliot House, 10/12 Allington Street, London SW1E 5EH
Confederation of British Industry
  Centre Point, 103 New Oxford Street, London WC1A 1D4
Council of Europe
  Avenue de l'Europe, 67 Strasbourg, France
Department of Employment
  Caxton House, Tothill Street, London SW1H 9NA
Employment Appeal Tribunal
  4 St James's Square, London SW1Y 4JB
  Scottish Divisional Office
  249 West George Street, Glasgow G2 4QE
Equal Opportunities Commission
  Overseas House, Quay Street, Manchester M3 3HN
European Trade Union Confederation
  37–41 rue Montagne aux Herbes Potagères, 1000 Brussels, Belgium
Health and Safety Commission
  Regina House, 256/269 Old Marylebone Road, London NW1 5RR
Health and Safety Executive
  Baynards House, 1 Chepstow Place, London W2 4TF
Industrial Society
  48 Bryanston Square, London W1H 8AH
Institute of Directors
  116 Pall Mall, London SW1Y 5ED

Institute of Personnel Management
  Central House, Upper Woburn Place, London WC1H 0HX
International Confederation of Free Trade Unions
  37–41 rue Montagne aux Herbes Potagères, 1000 Brussels, Belgium
International Labour Organisation
  CH 1211, Geneva 22, Switzerland
Manpower Services Commission
  Selkirk House, 166 High Holborn, London WC1V 6PB
Office of Wages Councils
  12 St James's Square, London SW1Y 4LL
Organisation for Ecoomic Co-operation and Development
  2 rue André-Pascal, 75 Paris 16e, France
Scottish Trades Union Congress
  12 Woodlands Terrace, Glasgow G3 6DE
Standing Commission on Pay Comparability
  GKN House, 22 Kingsway, London WC2B 6LE
Trades Union Congress
  Congress House, Great Russell Street, London WC1B 3LS
Union des Industries de la Communauté Européenne
  4 rue Ravenstein, 1000 Brussels, Belgium
Wales Trades Union Council
  42 Charles Street, Cardiff CF1 4SN
World Confederation of Labour
  50 rue Joseph II, 1040 Brussels, Belgium
World Federation of Trade Unions
  Namesti Curieovych 1, Prague 1, Czechoslovakia

Bibliography

1 Combination Act 1825.

2 *11th Report of the Royal Commission on the Organisation and Rules of Trade Unions and Other Associations 1867* (Chairman: Sir William Erle), London, HMSO, 1869.

3 *Final Report of the Royal Commission on Labour Laws* (no single Chairman), London, HMSO, 1875 (C 1157).

4 *Final Report of the Royal Commission on Labour 1891–4* (Chairman: Duke of Devonshire), London, HMSO, 1894 (C 7421).

5 *Report of the Royal Commission on Trade Disputes and Trade Combinations* (Chairman: Lord Dunedin), London, HMSO, 1906 (Cd 2825).

6 *Reports of the Whitley Committee on the Relations between Employers and Employed*, London, HMSO. 1917 Cmd 8606; 1918 Cmd 9001, Cmd 9002, Cmd 9099 and Cmd 9153.

7 Inns of Court Conservative and Unionist Society, *A Giant's Strength: Some Thoughts on the Constitutional and Legal Position of Trade Unions in England*, London, the Society, Johnson, 1958.

8 Conservative Party, *Fair Deal at Work*, London, Conservative Political Centre, 1968.

9 *Report of the Royal Commission on Trade Unions and Employers' Associations 1965–8* (Chairman: Lord Donovan), London, HMSO, 1968 (Cmnd 3623).

10 *In Place of Strife*, London, HMSO, 1969 (Cmnd 3888).

11 Commission on Industrial Relations, *Report No 90*, London, HMSO, 1974.

12 *Report of the Committee of Inquiry on Industrial Democracy* (Chairman: Lord Bullock), London, HMSO, 1977 (Cmnd 6706).

13 *Industrial Democracy*, London, HMSO, 1978 (Cmnd 7231).

14 Munitions of War Act 1917.

15 Wages (Temporary Regulations) Acts 1918 and 1919.

16 The most important report was the *5th Report of the House of Lords Select Committee on the Sweating System*. HL No 62, 1890.

17 *First Report of the Whitley Committee*, London, HMSO, 1917 (Cmd 8606).

18 Equal Opportunities Commission, *Health and Safety Legislation: should we distinguish between men and women?*, March 1979.

19 *Report of the Committee on Safety and Health at Work* (Chairman: Lord Robens), 1972 (Cmnd 5034).

20 *Personal Incomes, Costs and Prices*, London, HMSO, 1948 (Cmd 7321).

21 *Incomes Policy: the Next Step*, London, HMSO, 1962 (Cmnd 1626).

22 National Economic Development Council, *Growth of the United Kingdom to 1966*, London, HMSO, 1963.

23 *Declaration of Intent on Prices, Productivity and Incomes*, House of Commons Debates, Fifth Series, Vol 704, Cols 385–388.

24 *Prices and Incomes Policy*, London, HMSO, 1965 (Cmnd 2639).

25 *Prices and Incomes Policy: an 'Early Warning' System*, London, HMSO, 1965 (Cmnd 2808).

26 National Board for Prices and Incomes, *Report No 170*, London, HMSO, 1971 (Cmnd 4649).

27 *Prices and Incomes Standstill: Period of Severe Restraint*, London, HMSO, 1966 (Cmnd 3150).

28 *Prices and Incomes Policy after 30 June 1967*, London, HMSO, 1967 (Cmnd 3235).

29 *Productivity, Prices and Incomes Policy in 1968 and 1969*, London, HMSO, 1968 (Cmnd 3590).

30 *The Attack on Inflation*, London, HMSO, 1975 (Cmnd 6151).

31   *The Attack on Inflation—The Second Year*, London, HMSO, 1976 (Cmnd 6507).

32   *The Attack on Inflation after 31st July 1977*, London, HMSO, 1977 (Cmnd 6882).

33   *Winning the Battle against Inflation*, London, HMSO, 1978 (Cmnd 7293).

34   *The Economy, the Government and Trade Union Responsibilities*, London, HMSO, 1979.

35   *Disputes Principles and Procedures*, London, TUC, 1979.

36   *Report of the 110th Annual Trades Union Congress: Brighton, 1978*, London, TUC, 1978.

37   *Report of the 107th Annual Trades Union Congress: Blackpool, 1975*, London, TUC, 1975.

38   *Department of Employment Gazette*, London, HMSO, 1971 onwards. This succeeded the *Ministry of Labour Gazette* 1924–1968, and the *Employment and Productivity Gazette*, 1968–70.

39   Department of Employment, *New Earnings Survey*, London, HMSO, 1968 onwards.

40   The results of the Census of Employment are published in the *Department of Employment Gazette*.

41   Department of Employment, *Time Rates of Wages and Hours of Work*, London, HMSO, April 1971 onwards. Earlier volumes in the series were published by the Ministry of Labour (as *Time Rates of Wages and Hours of Labour*, 1920–54) from 1920–67, and by the Department of Employment and Productivity, 1968–70.

42   Department of Employment, *British Labour Statistics Year Book*, London, HMSO, 1969 onwards. This series of yearbooks follows the publication of *British Labour Statistics: Historical Abstract 1886–1968*, London, HMSO, 1971.

43   Advisory, Conciliation and Arbitration Service, *Annual Report*, HMSO 1975; ACAS 1976 onwards.

44   *Annual Report of the Certification Officer*, HMSO 1976; Certification Office 1977 onwards.

45   Central Arbitration Committee, *Annual Report*, 1976 onwards.

46   Equal Opportunities Commission, *Annual Report*, 1976 onwards.

47   Commission for Racial Equality, *Annual Report*, London, HMSO, 1977 onwards.

48   Manpower Services Commission, *Annual Report*, 1974–5 onwards.

49   Health and Safety Commission, *Annual Report*, London, HMSO, 1974–6, 1976–7 onwards.

50   This is published as part of the Health and Safety Commission's Report.

51   Social Science Research Council, *Research supported by the SSRC*, London, SSRC, 1979. Issued annually.

52   Department of Employment and Manpower Services Commission, *Research 1978–79*, London, HMSO, 1979. Issued annually. *Research supported by the Nuffield Foundation*, London, The Foundation, 1979. Issued annually. *Research supported by the Trustees of the Leverhulme Trust: No 8, 1971–75*, London, The Trust, 1976. Issued every five years.

53   G S Bain and H A Clegg 'A strategy for industrial relations research in Great Britain', *British Journal of Industrial Relations*, XII, 1, March 1974, pp 91–114. G Strauss and P Feuille 'Industrial relations research: a critical analysis', *Industrial Relations*, 17, 3, October 1978, pp 259–277. G Strauss 'Can social psychology contribute to industrial relations?', in G M Stephenson and C J Brotherton (eds), *Industrial Relations: a social psychological approach*, Chichester, John Wiley, 1979.

54   75/129/EEC. Official Journal of the European Communities (OJ) L 48/29. 22.2.75.

55   77/187/EEC. OJ L 61/26. 5.2.77.

56   75/457/EEC. OJ L 199/32. 30.7.75.

57   Commission proposals R/859/78 of 14 April 1978, and 5886/79 of 21 March 1979.

58   Council Directive of 10 February 1975 on equal pay (75/117/EEC. OJ L 45/19 19.2.75) and Council Directive of 9 February 1976 on equal treatment (76/207/EEC. OJ L 39/40 14.2.76). These have been implemented in the UK by the Equal Pay Act 1970 and the Sex Discrimination Act 1975.

59 Bulletin of the European Communities, Supplement 8/75.

60 Commission proposal R/2128/72 of 9 October 1972.

61 Commission proposal R/1279/75 of 13 May 1975.

62 International Labour Office, *Yearbook of Labour Statistics*, Geneva, ILO, 1935–6 onwards.

63 Australia, Austria, Belgium, Canada, Denmark, Finland, France, West Germany, Greece, Iceland, Ireland, Italy, Japan, Luxembourg, the Netherlands, New Zealand, Norway, Portugal, Spain, Sweden, Switzerland, Turkey, United Kingdom, United States of America.

64 A catalogue of OECD publications is available from the OECD Publications Office, 2 rue André-Pascal, 75775 Paris Cedex 16.

65 There are now 20 members including, in addition to the ten founders, Austria, Cyprus, West Germany, Greece, Iceland, Malta, Portugal, Spain, Switzerland and Turkey.

66 *Industrial Relations Code of Practice*, London, HMSO, 1972.

67 *Code of Practice 2: Disclosure of information to trade unions for collective bargaining purposes*, ACAS, 1977.

68 *Code of Practice 3: Time off for trade union duties and activities*, ACAS, 1977.

69 *Code of Practice 1: Disciplinary Practice and procedures in employment*, ACAS, 1977.

70 Health and Safety Commission, *Safety Representatives and Safety Committees*, London, HMSO, 1977.

71 *Time off for the training of Safety Representatives*, Health and Safety Commission, no date.

Index

For reasons of space the names of employers' associations, trade unions and, in general, negotiating bodies are not included in this index.

glasshouse crop growing, 102
glass industries, 33, 149, 165–7
glove manufacture, 161
glue, 124
'golden formula' for legal immunities, 83
goldsmiths, 141–1
government contractors: terms and conditions of employment, 29–30, 86
government departments, 278–9
government research, 260–1
grain milling, 111–2
grocery and provisions, 226
guarantee payment, 90, 92
guest houses, 273

hairdressing, 33, 274
handicapped workers: wages and conditions, 31
hand tools, 140
hat, cap and millinery industry, 161
health and safety at work, 7, 23, 33–4, 63–4, 70, 76, 86, 88–9
Health and Safety at Work, etc. Act 1974, 34, 63, 81, 86, 88–9
Health and Safety Commission (HSC), 33–4, 56, 63–4, 86, 89
Health and Safety Executive, 34
heating, ventilating and domestic engineering, 188, 190–1
hemp, 149
hide and skin markets, 157
HMSO, 280
holiday camps, 270–1
holidays with pay, 31–2, 70, 73, 99
Holidays with Pay Act 1938, 31–2
Holidays with Pay in Agriculture (ILO Convention No 101), 73
Hornby v Close, 11–2
horticulture, 101–2
hosiery and other knitted goods, 152–3
hospital chaplains, 260
hospital services, 38, 249–59
hotels and catering, 31–3, 199–202, 269–73
hours of employment, 7, 10, 29, 31, 33, 70, 73, 99
Hours of Employment (Conventions) Act 1936, 33
hovercraft, 199–202

incomes policy, 7, 29, 35–8
Independent Broadcasting Act 1973, 59
individual rights, 7, 20–4, 34–5, 46–7, 60–2, 69–70, 81–2, 86, 89–98
Industrial Arbitration Board, 21, 29
Industrial Court, 28
Industrial Courts Act 1919, 26, 59, 83
industrial democracy, 24, 70
industrial disputes, 10–1, 14–5, 18–23, 25–7, 45–7, 80–5
incidence in UK (*table*), 296–9
international comparisons (*table*), 300–1
Industrial Disputes Order (Order 1376), 27–9
Industrial Disputes Tribunal (IDT), 27–8
industrial engines manufacture, 130–9
industrial medical officers, 259
industrial plant manufacture, 130–9
Industrial Relations Act 1971, 19, 21–3, 35, 61, 80, 85, 94
Industrial Relations Code of Practice 1972, 22, 85
Industrial Relations Journal, 67
Industrial Relations Research Unit, 66
Industrial Relations Service, 28
Industrial Society, 53–4
Industrial Society, 54
Industrial Training Act 1964, 60, 236
Industrial Training Boards (ITBs), 236
industrial tribunals, 60
Inland Revenue, 214, 280–1
inland waterways, 214–5
In Place of Strife, 20
Institute of Directors, 54
Institute of Personnel Management (IPM), 54–5, 67
institutions, list, 337–8
instrument engineering, 130–9
insurance, 230–1
International Confederation of Free Trade Unions (ICFTU), 77
International Labour Organisation (ILO), 7, 68, 70–4, 78
International Labour Review, 74
International Organisation of Employers (IOE), 77–8
IPM Digest, 55
Iron and Steel Act 1967, 126
Iron and Steel Act 1975, 128
iron and steel production, 11, 126–30

public houses, 271
publishing, 175–9
pumps, valves and compressors, 130–9

quarrying, 103–9

Race Relations Act 1968, 34
Race Relations Act 1976, 34, 60, 89, 97
racial discrimination, 34, 62, 86, 90, 97
radar equipment, 130
radio broadcasting, 264–7
radio receivers, 130
rail transport, 13, 15, 23, 36, 198–203
railway rolling stock and track manufacture, 130–9
recreational facilities, 268–9
redundancies, 69, 81, 87–8, 90, 94–6
Redundancy Fund, 96
Redundancy Payments Act 1965, 34, 89
redundancy payments rebate, 88
refractories, 164
refractory users, 191
Register of Trade Unions and Employers' Associations, 12, 21–3, 39, 49, 80–1
religious organisations, 259–60
Remuneration of Teachers Act 1965, 238
Remuneration of Teachers (Scotland) Act 1967, 245
research and development services, 260–1
research institutions, 66–7
restaurants, 270–1
restraint of trade, 9, 12, 80
restrictive practices, 12
retail co-operative societies, 226
retailing, 31–3, 223–30
Retail Price Index, 37
road haulage, 31–3, 208–10
Road Haulage Wages Act 1938, 27, 31–2
road passenger transport, 203–8
roadstone quarrying, 106–7
Road Traffic Act 1960, 204
Robens Commission, 34
roof slaters and tilers, 186–91
Rookes v Barnard, 15
rope, twine and net, 152
Royal Commission on Labour 1891, 13–4, 25

Royal Commission on Labour Laws 1875, 13
Royal Commission on Trade Unions and Employers' Associations, 19, 22, 35
Royal Dockyards, 279–80
Royal Mint, 140
Royal Ordnance Factories, 279–80
rubber, 181
rubber-proofed garment making, 161

sack manufacture, 174–5
saddlery, 157–8
safety at work *see* health and safety at work
safety representatives, 81, 88–9
Safety Representatives and Safety Committees Regulations 1977, 88–9
sand and gravel, 108
scaffolding, 185–91
scale beam and weighing machine service, 136
scalemakers, 130
scientific services, 236–62
Scottish Trades Union Congress (STUC), 48
scrap metal, 228–9
sea transport, 13, 15, 199–202, 210–1
secondary action, 17, 22, 83–4
security services, 235
Select Committee on the Sweating System, 29
'severe restraint' on wage increases, 36
sex discrimination, 34, 70, 86, 90, 96–7
Sex Discrimination Act 1975, 33, 34, 60, 61, 89, 96–7
shiftwork payments, 99
shipbuilding and marine engineering, 143–6
shipwrights, 130–43
shirtmaking, 160–1
shoes *see* footwear
shopfitting, 171, 185–91
Shops Act 1950, 33
shops, retail, 223–7
shop stewards, 16, 18–20, 100
sick leave, right to payment, 90, 92
silica and moulding sands, 108
silk, 148–9
silverware, 139–40, 140–41

Printed in England for Her Majesty's Stationery Office
by the Alden Press, Oxford
Dd 696986 K160 10/80